# The Gardener's Garden

# The Gardener's Garden

Φ

When I was first approached about becoming involved with
*The Gardener's Garden* – a global survey of gardens – I was impressed,
if not a little daunted, by the ambition of the project. It took months for an
international team of leading garden writers, designers and horticultural
experts to formulate an expanded and near-exhaustive list of favourite
gardens from across the globe, from the world-famous to the unknown,
the public to the private, the grand to the intimate, the historic to the
contemporary; climate zones from deserts to steamy rainforests; and
garden styles from Baroque formality to naturalistic wilderness.

Personally this colossal task allowed me to look back to those particular
gardens that evoked for me unique sensations of spirituality, tranquillity
and individual character – those special gardens that were created with
passion. I can recall with precise vividness thirty-five years later the damp,
fresh wetness of the terraced gardens after a spring rain at Villa Noailles in
Grasse, France; or nearly two and a half decades ago the sultry dense heat
of August afternoons spent in the deep shade of the modest village garden
created by the late English artist Teddy Millington-Drake on the remote
island of Patmos, Greece, and now greatly expanded by John Stefanidis,
the English interior designer.

For centuries humans have been captivated by the plant kingdom,
collecting, cataloguing, trading and transporting across the globe plant
specimens that even today in the twenty-first century continue to entrance
us. That primal fascination has spurred the creation of gardens worldwide,
and it explains why we remain spellbound by gardens in all their forms
and what they represent to us.

The act of creating a garden, for the amateur and the professional
alike, remains very often the same. Although it can be intimidating at times,
both faced with a blank slate or working within an existing framework,
making a garden can also be the start of an endless but satisfying quest.
The beginning is always the same. In the wise words of the great late
English garden designer Russell Page, any new garden adventure should
begin with observation, observation – and more observation. It is only by
looking, chronicling and absorbing the many variables – weather patterns,
orientation, climatic conditions, soil composition, nearby vegetation –
that the garden designer can comprehend the parameters that compose
a future site or project. Once these fundamentals are well understood
and absorbed, the excitement commences – and the passion begins!

Throughout *The Gardener's Garden*, more than 250 examples illustrate the vast wealth of human expression when it comes to the creation and definition of what makes a garden. Covering the continents from Oceania and Asia to Europe, Africa and North and South America, the range is impressive and vastly varied. Historical gardens figure, such as Villa Lante, the jewel-like Renaissance garden in Viterbo, Italy, or André Le Nôtre's world-renowned creation for Louis XIV at Versailles in France – both gardens that influenced and inspired garden-makers well into our own time.

Poetic gardens, such as Shalimar Bagh, the Mughal masterpiece on the sloped shores of Lake Dal in Kashmir, India, have equally stimulated and impacted garden designers throughout the ages. So, too, have the great plant collectors such as Jacques Majorelle, with his unequalled Jardin Majorelle in Marrakech, Morocco, and quirky gardens such as Prospect Cottage in Dungeness, Kent, created in the late 20th century by the filmmaker Derek Jarman, whose tiny shingle plot transformed contemporary definitions of what a garden can be and demonstrated the possibility of finding beauty even within the shadows of one of the world's largest nuclear power stations.

Some gardens included in *The Gardener's Garden* are examples of the great influential designers of the past, such as Capability Brown, André Le Nôtre, Thomas Jefferson, Gertrude Jekyll or Russell Page; others display the talents of more contemporary designers, such as Beth Chatto, Piet Oudolf or Dan Pearson. But just as fascinating to discover is the vast range of relatively unknown gardens from across Asia and South America, and new plant introductions from Oceania, which represent a wealth of information for the garden designer and the garden lover alike.

In today's world, in which the rapidly changing natural environment is at well-documented risk, the importance of gardens and their role has never been greater. The role of both amateur and professional gardeners is vital to understanding the delicate balance that is needed for humans to sustain ourselves in a global state of transformation. While a source of inspiration for some and a practical guide for many, *The Gardener's Garden* is also a testament to centuries of human passion for the garden. Passion is the key factor – and it is passion that has created all the examples the reader will discover within *The Gardener's Garden*.

Madison Cox

## Oceania

# Alice Springs Desert Park

Near Alice Springs,
Northern Territory, Australia

Various

20th century

52 hectares / 128 acres (central area);
1,300 hectares / 3,212 acres (park)

Dry Arid

Botanical / Dry / Ecological / Grasses /
Landscape / Naturalistic

In the red heart of Australia, the Alice Springs Desert Park can look like an undistinguished patch of semiarid land. But after rain, the whole park explodes into waves of colour, bursting with renewal.

Nothing about the park suggests a conventional botanic garden – yet that is indeed what this is. A look beyond the vivid flowers and the bright red dust reveals a richly designed structure of interlinked habitats that form a showcase for more than 400 plant species and 100 animal species. These habitats include a watercourse in which river red gums (*Eucalyptus camaldulensis*) are the key trees, while melaleucas and grasses are other defining plants. In the 'sand' country, there are more ephemeral growths – many of them perennials, such as pink everlastings (*Xerochrysum bracteatum*), which spring up after rain – although the plants are predominantly mulga (*Acacia aneura*) and spinifex (*Triodia*), which are typical of such arid land. The woodland is home to what are called re-sprouters: plants that rely on dormant buds to regrow after fires, such as ghost gums (*Eucalyptus papuana*), hakeas, ironwoods (*Ostrya virginiana*) and acacias.

Although the park seems natural and unplanned, every shrub, tree or clump of grevillea is recorded on a GPS map and corresponding database, accurate to 30 centimetres (12 inches) or 50 centimetres (20 inches). The park staff share the knowledge they gather about arid/dry-environment species with institutions around the world, and they participate in research such as the Millennium Seed Bank Project, run by the Royal Botanic Gardens, Kew at Wakehurst, for long-term conservation of plant varieties.

Since its launch in 1997, Alice Springs Desert Park has attracted about 100,000 visitors each year. The guided night tours are particularly popular – in the desert much of the animal action takes place when the sun goes down. The integration of flora and fauna, with a respectful presentation of their place in the traditional lore of the indigenous people alongside the science, is being used as a model for future botanic gardens from South Africa to Arizona.

1—Careful planting and the use of natural red sand for roads mean that the created landscape at the heart of the park still appears entirely natural.
2—Mulla mulla (*Ptilotus polystachyus*) and woolly oat grass (*Enneapogon polyphyllus*) thrive on a rocky hillside.
3—*Grevillea juncifolia* burst into a rich golden colour after rain.
4—Among the native Australian shrubs and herbs in the park is cattle bush (*Trichodesma zeylanicum*).

# Heronswood

Dromana, Victoria,
Australia

| | |
|---|---|
| Edward La Trobe Bateman, Clive Blazey | |
| 19th & 20th century | |
| 1.8 hectares / 4.5 acres | |
| Temperate Oceanic | |
| Cottage / Edible / Nursery / Rooms | |

Heronswood is the garden home of the renowned Australian mail-order company Diggers Seeds, founded in 1978 by Clive and Penny Blazey. Originally designed by Edward La Trobe Bateman in the nineteenth century, Heronswood enjoys a spectacular site on Victoria's Mornington Peninsula, facing north towards Port Phillip Bay, yet is protected from the prevailing southerly winds. Diggers Seeds specializes in hard-to-find plants, and at Heronswood the Blazeys have been instrumental in reviving interest in both cottage gardening and heirloom vegetables, reintroducing many old cultivars to home gardeners and commercial producers alike. The garden is part of the recently formed Diggers Garden and Environmental Trust, with Clive Blazey as chairman.

Until relatively recently, Heronswood was primarily a perennial garden, with a series of garden rooms featuring cottage flowers, vegetables and perennials for a dry climate. But, under the influence of Clive Blazey, the focus has changed to an emphasis on food-producing plants, particularly vegetables and subtropical fruiting trees that thrive in Australia's hot summers. Blazey's publications *The Australian Vegetable Garden* (1999) and *The Australian Flower Garden* (2001) record his thirty-years' experience using the Heronswood garden as a trial ground, based on his philosophy that freshness, diversity and taste are the most important reasons for growing food in the domestic garden.

An added attraction at Heronswood is the Gothic Revival stone house, with its picturesque roof structure, completed in 1871 to designs by La Trobe Bateman. Many of the fine specimen trees in the garden also date from the nineteenth century, including Moreton Bay figs (*Ficus macrophylla*), cypress, oaks and a superb Cook Island pine (*Araucaria columnaris*). Palms and Himalayan cedars were added in the 1930s. These now-mature trees frame the views of Port Phillip Bay in a manner that is highly reminiscent of French Riviera landscapes.

1 — Sunrise illuminates the Dry Garden in spring; close to the sea, this area is home to hardy drought- and salt-tolerant plants, such as succulents, flax and lavender.
2, 3 — The Herb Garden is arranged around a lotus pond and flanked by olive trees; it mixes clipped hedges with mounds of herbs and ornamental grasses; purple *Echium* flowers in October.
4 — One of Heronswood's renowned Moreton Bay figs, planted in the nineteenth century, provides a massive backdrop to the Subtropical Garden.
5 — Cabbage, lettuce, Swiss chard and parsley grow in the Vegetable Garden, with nasturtiums flowering in a bed behind.

# Cloudehill

Olinda, Victoria,
Australia

Jeremy Francis

20th century

2 hectares / 5 acres

Temperate Oceanic

Arts & Crafts / Borders / Foliage /
Rooms

The garden at Cloudehill is the result
of a twenty-year artistic endeavour by
Jeremy Francis, who was raised on a
farm in Western Australia but dreamed
of creating a cool-climate garden.
The Cloudehill site, in the hills outside
Melbourne, had been a working garden
– part nursery and part cut-flower farm –
but had been seriously neglected for
decades when Francis took over. The
garden still contained elements of
structure and mature plants, however,
some of which were quite rare. Its other
natural assets were its deep, rich soil,
reliable rainfall and absence of frost.

From the old nursery Francis inherited
weeping maples, rhododendrons and
enkianthus, imported from Japan in the
1920s. There were also named forms
of European beech, from England, and
bulbs from Holland. Rhododendrons
were grown as hedgerows for easy
cutting. The remnants of the garden
structure inspired Francis to create a
series of separate garden rooms linked
by paths and steps. As the visitor
walks around the hillside, the rooms
unfold in a pattern of enclosures and
exuberant planting schemes typical
of the English Arts and Crafts
movement. The long series of
colour-themed borders bursting with
flowers and foliage is Francis's homage
to Hidcote in Gloucestershire, by
Lawrence Johnston (see page 148).

The flowers, however, are secondary
to the main colour story of the garden –
its variety of foliage. Some old maples
with burgundy leaves have been resited
to create a marriage between brick path
and plant form. Dwarf spruces line up
along a flight of steps and direct the
eye to the sweep of the theatre lawn,
backed with beech. A hedge of green
box frames clipped mounds of silver
*Pittosporum tenuifolium* 'Argentea Nana';
golden hops trail over an archway; a
wall of heart-shaped ivy leaves makes
a relaxed contrast to another box hedge,
where topiary spirals mark another
change in the garden levels.

The garden framework is most clearly
seen in autumn and winter. The physical
structure of hard landscaping and the
architectural beauties of both evergreen
and deciduous plants are clear evidence
of Francis's passion and dedication.

1—A spring sunrise in The Meadows
illuminates an avenue of copper beech
behind an apple tree and bluebells.
2—The central path leads through an arch
to the Water Garden past the muted flowers
and ornamental grasses of the Cool Border
in summer.
3—A hornbeam hedge borders the gently
sloping circular Theatre Lawn.
4—Even when winter reveals more of the
physical structure of the garden, the yellows
and reds of the herbaceous perennials and
shrubs of the hot borders remain bright.

3

4

# Lambley

Ascot, Ballarat, Victoria,
Australia

| |
|---|
| David Glenn, Criss Canning |
| 20th century |
| 1.2 hectares / 3 acres |
| Temperate Oceanic |
| Dry / Edible / Nursery / Plantsman |

The garden at Lambley is a marriage of nature and art. Designed by nursery owner David Glenn and his artist wife, Criss Canning, the entire garden is a showcase for the nursery, which specializes in perennials, bulbs and grasses. Glenn uses his plant knowledge to select suitable species, while Criss uses shape, texture and colour to incorporate plants into an overall vision of how the garden should look. The result is dynamic in every area, from the stunning Dry Garden – planted as a result of a long drought in Victoria – to the nursery beds and the extensive Vegetable Garden.

The display in the Dry Garden has two spectacular peaks during the year. The first occurs when the most impressive bulbs, such as groups of magnificent *Allium* 'Globemaster', burst into flower. Their spherical heads of deep lavender are echoed by the early-blooming lavender and the foliage of *Salvia verticillata* 'Purple Rain', making a brilliant picture. The second flowering climax comes when the garden reaches its late-summer peak and slowly drifts into autumn, when the sedums, salvias and late-flowering agapanthus come into their own.

One of the key design ideas in the garden is to use plants to create a series of waves and fountains. While the ground might be covered with mounds of artemisia or euphorbia, sedum or salvia, other plants introduce fountains of flowers and foliage. In spring *Asphodelus aestivus* creates a shower-like effect of white flowers; later lilies rise up like great candelabra over the perennials. At different seasons, verbascums, yuccas and alliums add to the effect. Even a trellis of sweet peas contributes to the vertical interest.

In late autumn, the Vegetable Garden showcases its magnificence. Bursting rows of vegetables – massive pumpkins, lettuce and artichokes – and decorative sunflowers are a sight to inspire any cook and gardener. Even the entrance driveway at Lambley is sensational in different seasons, as drifts of cherry blossom in spring give way to borders of blue agapanthus mirroring the summer sky.

1 — The Dry Garden reflects the need for drought-tolerant planting in the hot, dry climate, including (left to right) lavender, *Gladiolus communis* subsp. *byzantinus*, *Echium pininana* and *Phlomis grandiflora*.
2 — Dianthus borders in the Vegetable Garden in spring; Glenn uses the flower beds to grow brightly coloured and often neglected annuals.
3 — *Sedum* 'Matrona' flowers in front of *Agapanthus* 'Guilfoyle' in the Dry Garden.
4 — In the Pear Walk in early autumn, *Pyrus calleryana* lines a path through clouds of *Salvia nemorosa*.

# Mawallok

Stockyard Hill, Victoria,
Australia

| |
|---|
| William Guilfoyle |
| 20th century |
| 2.5 hectares / 6 acres |
| Temperate Oceanic |
| English Landscape / Formal / Historic / Vistas / Water |

Mawallok was laid out in 1909 for the Russell family of Australian pastoral pioneers by the Australian landscape designer William Guilfoyle, in the year of his retirement from Melbourne's Royal Botanic Gardens. The garden is one of Guilfoyle's last works – and perhaps his grandest private design.

As with many nineteenth-century properties on the windy plains of western Victoria, the homestead and garden at Mawallok are surrounded by thickly planted belts of trees, especially conifers such as Monterey pines (*Pinus radiata*) and cypress. Within this sheltering framework of trees, Guilfoyle's garden was planned to complement the newly built homestead – a picturesque composition of gables, sweeping roofs and roughcast walls. The house's simple and boldly stated forms can be read at a great distance: its off-white walls and red roof form the focal point among the expansive lawns and great trees.

Guilfoyle's plan shows clearly that the main organizing principle was the northerly vista to the Pyrenees Ranges, and in particular Mount Cole, about 20 kilometres (12 miles) to the north. His distinctive style is evident in the open lawns flowing through the garden to the dense woodland plantings on the fringes. He added dramatic, sentinel-like palms on the sweeping lawns to frame the northern vista in a formal design with the house as centrepiece.

These views were enhanced in the 1920s when a lake – fed from a natural spring on the property – was landscaped. A ha-ha, constructed in 1937, divides the garden proper from a six-hole golf course and allows an unimpeded view from house to lake.

Extensive and sympathetic renovation and renewal have returned paths and beds to their positions on Guilfoyle's original plan. Walks weave through the perimeter shrubberies and beneath mature deciduous trees, including horse chestnut, copper beech, plane, lime and oak. Mawallok is an elegant reflection of the eighteenth-century English landscape style in an Australian context.

1 — The setting sun catches treetops and throws a band of light across the lawns looking north from the terrace beside the house towards the lake.
2 — Citrus trees grow in what was once an orchard at the back of the house. It is now being turned into a vegetable garden with raised beds.
3 — One of William Guilfoyle's signature palm trees rises above a border planted with a forest pansy tree and foxgloves.
4 — Sinuous walks lead through the densely planted shrubberies at the edges of the garden, giving carefully framed vistas across the lawns.

# Mawarra

Sherbrooke, Melbourne,
Victoria, Australia

Edna Walling

20th century

1.5 hectare / 3.5 acres

Temperate Oceanic

Arts & Crafts / Cottage / Italianate / Terraces / Woodland

In the pantheon of Australian garden designers, Edna Walling stands tall – and Mawarra, in the ranges flanking Melbourne's eastern suburbs, is proof of her talents. This garden on sloping land, developed in the early 1930s for three sisters, Mrs A W McMillan and the Misses Marshall, has a good case to be considered Walling's finest and most intact design.

Walling was active from the 1920s to the 1970s, working as both a garden designer and a journalist-author. Her work had two phases: she produced Arts and Crafts, cottage-type gardens until the late 1940s, but then underwent a dramatic reappraisal of native Australian plants.

Walling's watercolour plans on thick Whatman paper were to her clients what Humphry Repton's Red Books had been to his: enticements to future glory for owners, and a lasting legacy for their designer. In technique Walling's drawings echoed John C Shepherd and Geoffrey Jellicoe's plans in *Italian Gardens of the Renaissance* (1925), and the surviving plan for Mawarra is among her finest. Mawarra's design also drew inspiration from Italian formal gardens, with deftly controlled terracing and linked sequences of compartments.

As the visitor enters along the drive at Mawarra, mature trees and shrubs excite a sense of expectation before the cottage is revealed at the last turn. Descending steps invite exploration of parallel walks of rhododendron and azalea, cool-climate interlopers that flourish in this elevated locale. On an axis with the cottage, stone steps descend in hemispherical array, with an herbaceous border to the left, birch woodland in the middle distance, an enticing pool at the foot of the stairway and occasional distant glimpses of towering Australian mountain ash (*Eucalyptus regnans*). The sequence is tightly controlled, yet within this formal structure a beguiling intimacy is maintained by the contrast between dense shrubberies and open woodlands, and seasonal delights of deciduous plantings and bulbs. Walling regarded Mawarra highly, calling it 'not so much a garden as a symphony in steps and beautiful trees'. That opinion is echoed by all who visit.

1—Low topiary hedges interplanted with foxgloves (*Digitalis*) and alliums adorn the lawn in the centre of the Cottage Garden.
2, 3—The garden's centrepiece is the sweeping stone staircase that leads down to the octagonal Reflecting Pool.
4—The buildings of a model Tudor village (a later addition) give a unique homely feel to the Orchard and Nursery.

# Olinda

Olinda, Victoria,
Australia

Phillip Johnson

21st century

2 hectares / 5 acres

Temperate Oceanic

Naturalistic / Sustainable / Water

High in the hills in the Dandenong Ranges east of Melbourne is an outstanding showcase of the ideas of Australian garden designer Phillip Johnson. In 2013 Johnson was confirmed as a leading light of his generation when he won the Best in Show award for his stunning design for the Australian show garden at the Chelsea Flower Show in London.

Johnson's own garden bears out his reputation and adaptability. It is on an extremely steep site – at an angle of 23 degrees – with difficult access. One of the major challenges during construction was to prevent erosion, exposed tree roots and possible landslides. It took 360 truckloads of material – sand, mulch and rocks – to create the natural-looking garden that now merges seamlessly into the surrounding bushland.

As in all Johnson's gardens, water is the vital element; the entire design is animated by the movement of water over and around the hard landscaping. There is no mains water supply, so water harvesting, recycling and managing storm-water run-off are priorities. Rainfall in these hills averages just 90 millimetres (3½ inches) a year, and every drop that falls is captured on site and directed into three storage tanks that hold 150,000 litres (33,000 gallons). This is endlessly recycled and moved around the garden through a series of pools and tanks. The water also helps protect the house during the bushfire danger season (the property is in one of the most fire-prone areas of Australia). There is an elaborate computer-driven fire prevention system, which triggers the spraying of the roof, among other protective measures.

Among the rocks and pools, large tree ferns (*Dicksonia antarctica*), with their elegant green fronds, thrive in the cool glades beneath the monumental Australian mountain ash trees (*Eucalyptus regnans*). Colour in the garden comes in seasonal splashes – from wattles in spring, particularly *Acacia dealbata*, to the correas with their petite green bells tucked in among the rocks in autumn/winter. Garden and bush blend together in this remarkable composition.

1 — At the heart of the garden, an ironbark boardwalk snakes over a natural swimming pool shaded by tall Australian mountain ash trees (*Eucalyptus regnans*). Water is central: the garden's 'billabongs' also act as natural fire protection.
2 — Rocks and blue-green tussocks of the grass *Lomandra confertifolia* subsp. *rubiginosa* line a sandy pathway near the lower pool.

# Australian Garden

Royal Botanic Gardens,
Cranbourne, Melbourne,
Victoria, Australia

Taylor Cullity Lethlean Landscape
Architects with Paul Thompson

20th–21st century

15 hectares / 37 acres

Temperate Oceanic

Artistic / Botanical / Bush / Native /
Plant Collection

The Australian Garden is a botanic garden about storytelling, intended to engage and inspire rather than simply to present a collection of plants. It forms the jewel-like core of a 363-hectare (897-acre) remnant of endangered wet heathland, and complements the nineteenth-century landscaping of Melbourne's Royal Botanic Gardens. The accent is on Australian flora in all its diversity, but, rather than naturalistic or taxonomic arrangements, the garden integrates artistry and design with botany and landscape, affirming the powerful ethos with which Australian plants can imbue gardens. The temperate climate means that upwards of 3,000 species sourced from the whole continent (approximately 10 per cent of the Australian flora) can be grown here.

The central Red Sand Garden gives the garden an internal energy, with the sinuous watercourse – here dry, there gushing in torrents – seeming to spring from its depths before flowing to a serene melaleuca-fringed estuary. The striking north–south line dividing the red micro-desert suggests a rich interplay between nature and culture, with impressions of natural elements predominating to the west and cultural interpretations to the east. From the Zen-like Sand Garden the visitor is drawn almost imperceptibly along a sweeping path, past semipermanent display gardens, towards twin hills that reveal the further reaches of the site.

The radiating organization offers themed displays for the home gardener, a Weird and Wonderful Garden replete with striking forms and foliage, and ancient Gondwanan flora displaying Australian conifers such as wollemi pine (*Wollemia nobilis*). Completing the circuit, a Eucalypt Walk showcases Australia's best-known genus and the flora that live beneath. The planting design is carefully modulated, with restful voids balancing rich sequesters. The design is entertaining – exhilarating, even – yet full of purpose. At every turn something new entices.

1—The Red Sand Garden forms a spectacular centre to the garden and is the source of the water whose journey the wider garden follows.
2—Circular beds of hedge saltbush (*Rhagodia spinescens*) grow among the sand and crescent mounds of the Red Sand Garden, designed to echo the shapes and colours of the deserts of Central Australia.
3—In the Forest Garden, the 'Scribbly Path' leads visitors through collections of grasses; the twisting walk evokes the patterns on the trunks of scribbly gum (*Eucalyptus haemastoma*).
4—In the Coastal Edge Garden, near the end of the water's journey through the landscape, bands of melaleucas, reeds and abstract sand spits evoke Australia's rich estuarine topography.

18

3

4

5

5—A diversity of native flora provides varying texture, form and colour.
6—A Queensland bottle tree (*Brachychiton rupestris*) – named for its trunk – grows in the Weird and Wonderful Garden.
7—The thick vegetation, including *Doryanthes excelsa* and *Eucalyptus* var., offers glimpses of the crescent mounds of the Red Sand Garden at the garden's heart.
8—The Rockpool Waterway is framed by an Australian smooth-barked apple tree (*Angophora costata*), rising over dwarf lilly pillies and Guinea flowers. Other plants include *Bauera rubioides* and yellow-flowered goodenia along the water's edge, the Darling lily (*Crinum flaccidum*), the Gymea lily (*Doryanthes palmeri*) with its massive flower spike, and the blue-flowered tall bluebell (*Wahlenbergia stricta* 'Blue Mist').

6

# Karkalla

Sorrento, Victoria,
Australia

| | |
|---|---|
| Fiona Brockhoff | |
| 20th century | |
| 0.8 hectares / 2 acres | |
| Temperate Oceanic | |
| Coastal / Dry / Naturalistic | |

Fiona Brockhoff's coastal garden remains a showcase of exceptional design in a challenging location more than twenty years after it was created. The inspiration came from observing the forces of nature and wind-pruned plants, combined with an understanding of and respect for the physical and ecological qualities of the Mornington Peninsula site. The coast on the Bass Strait was formed 10,000 years ago, when rising seas washed billions of fragments of marine skeletons ashore to form the rolling dunes seen today.

Brockhoff's design set out to avoid modifying the natural topography, to improve the ecological fit with the dune system and to maintain existing wildlife corridors. The house sits atop a gentle rise with a view of Arthur's Seat, and its limestone walls, which were built by Brockhoff's partner, David Swann, have been used as a link between house, garden and surrounding bush. They also provide enclosure to the sunny, north-facing garden.

From the northern terrace the view sweeps around Port Phillip Bay. Mass plantings of white correa (*Correa alba*) and local sea box (*Alyxia buxifolia*) form a sculptured hedge enclosing the area. Succulents, hebe and phormium provide foliage colour and texture, which Brockhoff prefers to flowers.

On the south side of the house, sheltered when the north wind is blowing, is a quiet area complete with outdoor shower for use after swimming. The featured plants here are a mix of colour and textural contrast, from spear grass (*Austrostipa stipoides*), cushion bush (*Leucophyta brownii*) and sea box, to the native hibiscus *Alyogyne huegelii*, coastal banksia and daisies.

The transition from domestic garden to the surrounding bushland is almost imperceptible. Walkways of beams, granitic gravel and shell-grit give structure and form. Moonahs (*Melaleuca lanceolata*) and she-oaks (*Allocasuarina*) are planted progressively to replace senescent tea trees (*Leptospermum*). Nature sets the parameters in this stylish garden.

1 — Neatly clipped she-oak, moonah topiary and sea box in the dining area contrast with the surrounding wild coastal vegetation.
2 — Olive trees frame the view out from the house towards Port Phillip Bay.
3 — Quirky stone columns rise above wild trees in a view from the entertaining area.
4 — The limestone-clad walls that define the garden were built by David Swann.
5 — An olive tree grows behind orange wallflowers (*Erysimum*), *Phlomis* and drought-tolerant succulents such as coastal banksia and the evergreen perennial *Aeonium* 'Zwartkop'.
6 — Echium flower in the northern part of the garden with *Aeonium* 'Zwartkop'; in the distance, garden planting merges into local moonah and tea trees.

1

2

3

4

5

6

# Stringybark Cottage

Noosa, Sunshine Coast,
Queensland, Australia

| |
|---|
| Cheryl Boyd, Bob Boyd |
| 20th–21st century |
| 1 hectare / 2.5 acres |
| Temperate Humid Subtropical |
| Artistic / Bush / Ferns / Rainforest / Rooms / Trees |

Noosa, on Queensland's Sunshine Coast, is a picture-perfect Australian beach resort: blue sea, sand and a diamond-bright sky overhead. A short drive inland, through the hills surrounding the market town of Eumundi, and the scenery becomes entirely different. Statuesque trees of the Queensland rainforest, 35 to 40 metres (15–30 feet) tall, crown the ridges. Here the sun seems a long way above the treetops as it filters down through Queensland maples, tallowwoods and red stringybarks (*Eucalyptus resinifera*). They cast long shadows over the garden at the appropriately named Stringybark Cottage, where Cheryl Boyd has brought together horticultural knowledge, garden design and art in stunning yet subtle ways.

Boyd is a horticulturalist and garden designer, and she describes the garden as a frost-free zone where she can grow a marvellous array of plants from subtropical to cool-climate, and where her emphasis is on foliage, rather than flowers – particularly form, texture and colour. Themed garden rooms, each with its own distinct atmosphere, are entered through vine-covered arches. Groundcover makes creative use of variegated leaves; liquorice-dark foliage is used as a foil for dark green; brilliant reds and yellows shine out from heliconias, anthuriums, bromeliads and hippeastrums, grabbing the spotlight. The planting operates on various levels, with epiphytes such as stag- and bird's-nest ferns, vanda, dendrobium and many species of orchid all finding a home in the trees.

A large, uncluttered lawn area – an important void among all the verticals – is a perfect backdrop for ferns such as *Dicksonia antarctica* and the magnificent group of Bismarck palms near the swimming pool. Boyd's artworks, from hanging orbs of barbed wire suspended between the trees to a giant 'birds' nest' made of twigs and an immaculate twig tepee, only enhance this exceptional expression of gardening ideas.

1—Vivid bromeliads add colour to a border beneath a canopy of stately tree ferns, *Dicksonia antarctica*.
2—Beautiful Australian fan palms (*Licuala ramsayi*) provide a backdrop for the spiky red bracts of *Heliconia angusta*.
3—Cheryl Boyd's twig bird's nest fits perfectly among the tree trunks.
4—Stately palms, including *Bismarckia nobilis*, make a stunning backdrop to the swimming pool.
5—The garden features a wide array of planting, with an emphasis on form, texture and colour.
6—A pruned *Lagerstroemia indica* grows among bromeliads near the cottage.

4

5

6

# Garangula

South Western Slopes,
New South Wales, Australia

| Vladimir Sitta, Terragram |
| --- |
| 20th century |
| 1.6 hectares / 4 acres |
| Temperate Oceanic |
| Modern / Rooms / Sculpture / Water |

The Czech-born landscape architect Vladimir Sitta believes in curiosity, playfulness, mystery and the unexpected, and all play a part in his design for the garden at Garangula. His innovative ideas are an exciting, thought-provoking contrast to the nineteenth-century homestead in this pastoral region of New South Wales.

The garden has been created in increments, with Sitta gradually transforming the landscape around the house into a series of rooms, with a pool, tennis court and outdoor terraces. But despite these traditional features of country living, there is nothing traditional about Sitta's approach. While each area has a specific function, together they form a cohesive entity charged with mystery and surprise.

In the Pool Garden, the usual sunken rectangle is softened by the changing shapes and textures of the hard landscaping, with paving at a minimum and grass set off by clipped, rounded shrubs. A 'mist' shower has been added for further effect. In another area Sitta has constructed a 'green cathedral' made of alder trees that slope inwards to form a spire. To experience the scene fully, the visitor should descend a long flight of steps that leads well below ground level.

Water is all-important in Australia, a land renowned for its droughts and flooding rains. At Garangula Sitta uses water in many ways – from sudden showers to tranquil pools – to animate the garden, articulate a space or create a mysterious atmosphere. For example, he has created a long, straight walkway, bordered with cypress, leading from the house to a slim, rectangular trough atop a low stone wall. The pool of water reflects the sky but is far from static, and the view to the paddocks beyond is open, rather than enclosed. Sitta has even had a playful adventure with the lake, building a partially collapsed stone 'bridge' over a waterbed that dries up or fills to overflowing in different seasons.

Sitta's remarkable understanding of the bush environment is testimony to the time he has spent walking in the Blue Mountains near Sydney. He says that spending time alone in such a glorious natural space provides oxygen and inspiration for his work – and Garangula is one of the most spectacular proofs.

1—The garden at Garangula has been fashioned from and remains integrated with the surrounding bushland.
2—At the far end of a misty avenue of cypress, a low pool of water opens on to a view of the paddocks beyond.
3—Statues loom through the mist among tree trunks.
4, 5—A sculpture of tangled wire echoes the mist rising from the poolside shower, from where water flows through an apparent crack in the concrete paving to the swimming pool.

# Eryldene

Sydney, New South Wales,
Australia

| |
|---|
| Eben Waterhouse |
| 20th century |
| 0.4 hectares / 1 acre |
| Temperate Oceanic |
| Botanical / Plant Collection / Rooms |

Eryldene, on Sydney's North Shore, is a fitting memorial to Professor Eben Waterhouse's passion for camellias. A linguist and academic, Waterhouse became one of the world's foremost authorities on camellias, planting his first six at Eryldene in 1914. He raised and named many popular varieties, founded Sydney's famous Camellia Grove nursery and was president of the International Camellia Society. Waterhouse was an authority on the history and nomenclature of early camellia cultivars, and he raised hundreds of seedlings. The hybrids – Camellia x williamsii 'E.G. Waterhouse', C. x w. 'Margaret Waterhouse', C. x w. 'Lady Gowrie' – are among Waterhouse's many successes that have remained popular with Australian gardeners since their introduction in 1954. Waterhouse was an influential writer and lecturer; he wrote three books on camellias: Camellia Quest (1947), illustrated by Adrian Feint, The Magic of Camellias (1968) with Norman Sparnon, and Camellia Trail (1952) with paintings by Paul Jones. They are arguably the most beautiful books on botanical art published in Australia.

The house at Eryldene – in the early colonial style with strong Georgian influence – is recognized today as the finest unaltered example of domestic work by the architect William Hardy Wilson. The garden was planned by Waterhouse as a sympathetic extension to the house in a series of rooms, each leading to the next, filled with trees, shrubs and flowers, and of course many camellias.

Superbly proportioned buildings designed by Wilson – a secluded study, a temple and a delightful shingled pigeon house – furnish the garden. The Chinese-inspired pavilion (1927) beside the tennis court is a testament to Waterhouse's and Wilson's romance with China. It remains a joyous surprise in an Australian garden, and its exoticism only adds to Eryldene's historic atmosphere. Eryldene has remained largely unchanged since it was built in 1913, which gives it an important place in Australian architectural and horticultural history.

1, 2—The garden of Eben Waterhouse at Eryldene provided not only a fine setting for the distinguished architecture of William Hardy Wilson but also a field for horticultural experimentation by Waterhouse. The pink flowering shrub is Camellia 'Eryldene Excelsis'. 3—The beautifully proportioned temple in the front garden, surrounded by flowering shrubs such as azaleas, offers a shady place to sit and exemplifies William Hardy Wilson's architectural approach.

# Ayrlies

Whitford, Auckland,
North Island, New Zealand

Beverley McConnell, Malcolm McConnell

20th century

4.8 hectares / 12 acres

Temperate Humid Subtropical

Naturalistic / Perennials / Plantsman /
Rooms / Tropical / Water

In 1964 Beverley and Malcolm McConnell purchased a property of bare rolling pastoral land on heavy clay soil to raise their family. Over the next fifty years, the pair wrought a transformation, creating a magical garden that is among the first rank of twentieth-century gardens. Beverley McConnell has been called the Vita Sackville-West of New Zealand, and many renowned gardeners have visited Ayrlies. With her husband, whose engineering skills are behind a series of impressive water features, and with the talent and knowledge of Oliver Briers, a gardener hired from England, McConnell transformed the property into an oasis of horticultural delights and savvy garden design. Briers created the architecture of the garden with bridges, paths and walls, while McConnell used her skilled eye and taste to work in the vast array of plants.

The garden started with a fenced-off area and a shopping list of 500 native and exotic trees. Within fourteen years it had expanded to cover the site, filled with native trees like eucalyptus and four new ponds and waterfalls. The mature garden has woven together as if it were always there.

McConnell divided the large property into a series of rooms. The Rockery, the Pool Garden and the Lurid Border – named for its use of colours such as red, chocolate, orange, hot pink and gold – are all feats of garden design. Brave combinations are McConnell's signature. *Aeonium* 'Zwartkop' is paired with *Alstroemeria* 'Red Baron' and *Canna* 'Parkes' with winter-flowering *Kniphofia*. The Rose Garden is home to many types, but focuses on fragrant and old varieties. The Coral Garden, the Blue Room, the Temple House and the Meadow Garden are dense with plants.

Magnolias and roses sit comfortably with exotics such as *Thunbergia coccinea* and *Passiflora quadrangularis*, South African gems such as *Haemanthus coccineus*, the peculiar *Puya berteroana*, with its 1.8-metre-high (6-foot) stalks and iridescent, peacock-blue flowers, as well as various iris, crinum, aloe and bromeliads. Although the heavy soil and coastal climate are at times a challenge, they are also a gift, allowing gunneras, alocasia and tree ferns to flourish.

1, 2—The garden at Ayrlies is characterized by informal but detailed planting and a series of water features, including four ponds. Near the swimming pool, steps climb through a border of agave, aloe and cycad.
3—Succulents and grasses grow in June, which is winter in the garden.
4—Giant rhubarb (gunnera) grows next to a pond with a small wooden summerhouse.

# Pukeiti Gardens

New Plymouth, Taranaki,
North Island, New Zealand

William Douglas Cook

20th century

360 hectares / 890 acres

Temperate Oceanic

Botanical / Rhododendron / Woodland

At the base of Mount Egmont on New Zealand's North Island is one of the world's greatest single-species gardens. At Pukeiti around 2,000 species and hybrids of rhododendron flourish among the native temperate rainforest and in the borders that surround the lawn in front of the members' clubhouse. These gardens were among the first to organize a voluntary trust of members, who provided not only money but also labour – a method that has become far more common among gardens today.

Pukeiti Rhododendron Gardens were the creation of William Douglas Cook, owner of an arboretum near Gisborne and one of New Zealand's pioneering conservationists. Cook dreamed of having a huge natural garden of rhododendrons, which would act in part as a genetic resource to preserve endangered species and allow them to be reintroduced to the wild. In 1950 Cook bought a block of wild bush on a hill named Pukeiti, near Taranaki, with wide views over the coast and Mount Ruapehu. Taking advantage of its sheltered location, temperate climate and heavy rainfall, Cook oversaw the regeneration of the native bush and introduced naturalistic species such as camellias, magnolias, primulas, hydrangeas and old-fashioned perennials – while also creating his remarkable collection of rhododendrons from around the world.

The garden is particularly attractive after one of the area's frequent downpours, when the sunlight glints on the glossy leaves and flowers. Whatever the season, there are rhododendrons in flower in a whole range of colours. Some are standards while others are far less common, such as the vast *R. protistum* var. *giganteum* 'Pukeiti', which was originally grown from seed obtained from Burma by the renowned plant hunter Frank Kingdon-Ward in 1953. Its pink pompom flowers tend to provide some of the earliest blooms of the winter. The more tender species, such as those from the cloud forests of Southeast Asia, are sheltered in a shade house. The borders near the lawn provide what the garden calls a 'perennial paradise', with peacock flowers (*Tigridia*) from South America and Mexico, green-flowered *Galtonia viridiflora* and astilbes, which are either in bold colours or in more subtle tones.

1 — Mature rhododendrons grow amongst the lush New Zealand rainforest.
2 — An aerial view shows the lawns set amid the rhododendrons near Pukeiti's Gatehouse and Lodge.
3 — A North American hemlock tree contrasts with Pukeiti's azalea borders.
4 — The pink flowers of the large-leaf *Rhododendron* 'Pukeiti' are some of the earliest blooms to come out in the winter.

# Barewood Garden

Awatere Valley, Marlborough,
South Island, New Zealand

| |
|---|
| Carolyn Ferraby, Joe Ferraby |
| 20th–21st century |
| 1.4 hectares / 3.5 acres |
| Temperate Oceanic |
| Allées / Borders / Cottage / Potager / Roses |

Discovering Barewood in the Awatere Valley is like coming across a Southern Hemisphere version of Monet's Giverny (see page 240). The picturesque farmhouse nestles within the garden as if this has always been its setting. But it was not until Carolyn Ferraby arrived as a young bride, and water became available, that she began to weave her magic garden web around it.

As a former florist, Ferraby likens the garden to a large floral arrangement. In spring the house is swathed in flowering plants, the veranda shaded under a veil of white *Wisteria sinensis* 'Alba' and climbing *Rosa* 'Wedding Day', *R.* 'Madame Alfred Carrière' and *R. moschata*. Beside the house, a potager enclosed by a hornbeam hedge has replaced the old vegetable garden. An *allée* of crab apples (*Malus tschonoskii*) leads from the potager to the box-edged herbaceous borders.

Joe Ferraby has created hardscaping in keeping with the house. Beginning with a simple fountain at the entrance, he has constructed all the paths, walls, fences and even the summerhouse, which provides a focal point at the end of the Hawthorn Walk. Planted with *Crataegus laevigata* 'Plena', a grafted variety chosen for its white blossom, which turns to peachy pink, the Walk rises naturally from a grassy meadow, echoing the wild hawthorns dotted about the hills.

Despite the many European influences at Barewood, their treatment is unmistakably local. Native trees and shrubs mingle with exotics chosen for their flowers and foliage. Ferraby has selected plants of subtly different shades to produce a patterned, layered effect. Variegated foliage, for example, takes on a new look when blended with plants with creamy white flowers.

Wrought out of such an unpromising clay canvas, with freezing temperatures in winter and hot, dry winds in summer, Barewood is a remarkable gardening achievement, not to be missed.

1—In the Potager, double-arched apple trees are surrounded by herbs, vegetables, soft fruits and flowers.
2—White gates lead to the Hawthorn Walk, where the blossom of *Crataegus laevigata* 'Plena' turns from white to pink.
3—The summerhouse is clothed in David Austin and other old roses and flowers in apricot, cream and blue shades.
4—Clipped box edges the double tapestry borders, with buttresses of contrasting *Berberis thunbergii* f. atropurpurea 'Rose Glow'.
5—In the blue-and-yellow border, shrubs *Physocarpus opulifolius* 'Dart's Gold' and *Viburnum opulus* 'Xanthocarpum' mingle with *Iris pseudacorus* 'Variegata', *Hosta* 'Sum and Substance' and *Saxifraga stolonifera*.

# Ohinetahi

Lyttelton, Canterbury,
South Island, New Zealand

| | |
|---|---|
| Sir Miles Warren | |
| 20th–21st century | |
| 1.2 hectares / 3 acres | |
| Temperate Oceanic | |
| Borders / Formal / Rooms / Sculpture | |

Ohinetahi lies in a sheltered enclave of Governors Bay, where rolling hills and shining water provide a magnificent background to a garden where botany, history and architecture are inextricably linked. Here, in 1865, one of New Zealand's first botanists, Thomas Potts, planted a great variety of exotic trees and shrubs, many of which still stand.

After Potts died in 1888, the garden and house gradually fell into disrepair. In 1977 Sir Miles Warren, his sister Pauline and her husband, John Trengrove, bought and restored the house and began the present garden. Having been designed by two architects and an artist, the garden has a strong structural framework, with a series of separate garden 'rooms' arranged around two axes, one running east–west and the other north–south.

The most formal area of the garden, set on a series of horizontal planes, has a lawn; a rose garden enclosed by box hedges and planted with apricot and cream roses to blend with the stone of the house; a traditional double herbaceous border leading to a gazebo; a walled garden with a red-and-green colour theme; and a hedge of pleached hornbeams. The green 'architecture' of the garden is complemented by building fragments and modern sculpture.

Below the gazebo, steps lead down to the Woodland Garden, through which a stream flows to the bay. This area, shaded by many of Potts's original trees, is home to rhododendrons, camellias and New Zealand species suited to the damp environment.

The garden was extended in 2008 with the purchase of more of Potts's original site; piles of rubbish and weeds have been removed, but the great nineteenth-century oaks remain. Stone-edged paths now lead to an amphitheatre for concerts, and large sculptures are being installed in the parkland setting.

The house at Ohinetahi was severely damaged in the earthquake of September 2010, but has been rebuilt with the central block now two storeys tall rather than the original three. All the stone structures in the garden – walls, towers, follies and ornaments – have been restored. In 2012 Sir Miles Warren gifted the entire property to the people of New Zealand.

1—A path descending through novel topiary borders draws visitors down the terraces of the formal part of the garden.
2—A gazebo at the end of a herbaceous border dominated by pinks and mauves with the mountains beyond.
3—A sculpture rising from a bed of ornamental grass makes a dramatic statement in front of a sweeping view of Governors Bay.
4—Steps link terraces in the formal garden.
5—The colour scheme in the Walled Garden is based on the bright vermillion of Flanders poppies and the climbing rose 'Parkdirektor Riggers'.

# Blair Garden

Near Queenstown, South Island,
New Zealand

| |
|---|
| Janet Blair |
| 20th–21st century |
| 5.5 hectares / 14 acres |
| Temperate Oceanic |
| Borders / Edible / Picturesque / Topiary / Trees / Vistas |

When Janet Blair began creating the garden at her home in the early 1970s, she soon learned that the spectacular views of New Zealand's mountains came at a price. Harsh southerly winds stream up the valley, dictating the planting and design. Greatly influenced by the work of the renowned garden designer Russell Page, Blair heeded his dictums on how to retain 'the excitement of the distant view' and yet create a domestic-scale garden that has been recognized in New Zealand as a garden of national significance.

When Blair set about creating a beautiful haven for her family, there were no trees around the nineteenth-century stone cottage tucked away in a valley not far from Queenstown, a premier skiing location in the South Island. There was no shelter, no shade and no birdsong. Now, mature trees – from ash, oaks and horse chestnuts to fruit trees such as apricots and walnuts – frame the views and filter the effects of the wind. Ribbons of green hedging in box and yew bind the garden into a harmonious entity.

Another initial challenge to Blair's garden-making was the lack of a reliable water supply – a surprising problem when there is so much snow and rain in the area. She was therefore forced to water many of the plants by hand at first, to ensure they survived. That fact alone is hard for a visitor to comprehend when strolling through the garden today.

Blair's preference is for formal gardens, but any tendency to severity is dispelled by playfulness, as expressed in beds of topiary and serpentine hedges. Twirls, spires, cones and balls all abound – even a topiary pack of cards is dealt out in the Vegetable Garden.

Four decades on, Blair's plantings now complement the drama of the picturesque mountain landscape. Hedges and trees in seasonal beauty provide shelter from the wind and define intimate garden spaces, while a short walk to a nearby vantage point reveals the majesty of nature beyond.

1—Janet Blair's garden preserves its views of the spectacular mountains despite the many hedges and trees – both deciduous and evergreen – that provide shelter from icy winds tearing down the valley.
2—The precise clipping of lines of box hedges guides the visitor's eye from the Vegetable Garden to the borrowed landscape beyond.
3—The intimate family area near the house is especially beautiful in autumn, when golden leaves on the apricot trees in the foreground and the two standard wisteria contrast with the red leaves of the ornamental grapevine and the green of the neatly clipped box.
4—Turning leaves provide a display of seasonal beauty in the autumn.

# Larnach Castle

Dunedin, South Island,
New Zealand

| | |
|---|---|
| Margaret Barker | |
| 20th century | |
| 14 hectares / 35 acres | |
| Temperate Oceanic | |
| Coastal / English Landscape / Historic / Natives / Romantic | |

Larnach Castle, an iconic Gothic Revival castle on the spectacular Otago Peninsula, was the first garden to be awarded the title of International Garden of Significance by the New Zealand Gardens Trust. Built by William Larnach (born in Australia to Scottish parents) after he made his fortune in the Otago gold rush of the 1860s, the castle fell into disrepair in the hands of its later owners. It was essentially derelict when Margaret Barker and her late husband found it while holidaying in the area. They bought it in 1967 and began a painstaking process of restoration.

At the entrance to the garden and near the castle, Barker shows her respect for the European landscape-gardening heritage from which the building sprang. The drives are still in the same place as they were in 1870, and a simple round pond reflects the sky in the vast lawn in front of the castle. On a similar scale, an enormous laburnum walkway frames the view of hills and the sea. Carefully selected rhododendrons in the Stumpery form a brilliant spectacle in spring, while borders in front of the ballroom feature azaleas, heathers and *Thalictrum delavayi*, with its purple haze in late summer. Behind the ballroom, a temperate rainforest features native podocarps and a collection of tree ferns.

The process of unearthing a lost Rock Garden, once famous for its alpine plants, kindled in Barker a passion for travel and botanical discovery. As a result, she broadened her palette and developed innovative new gardens beyond the original property, using native plants, including Nikau palms (*Rhopalostylis sapida*) and a large collection of metrosideros, alongside exotic plants such as aloes and agaves that thrive in the dry, windswept coastal environment. Dry-stone walls echo those built by the early Scottish settlers, while ancient, strategically retained *Cupressus macrocarpa* trees serve to integrate the garden with the backdrop of the surrounding farmland. Today the Barker family continue to welcome visitors to explore the extensive gardens that now anchor Lanarch so securely to the powerful landscape.

1—The tall laburnum pergola frames the view of the hills and the sea beyond.
2—In the Temperate Rainforest Garden tree ferns grow beneath a New Zealand red beech (*Nothofagus fusca*).
3—The Tapestry Garden is densely planted to give the impression of woven colours and textures, with autumn colour from deciduous azaleas and blooming Scottish heather supported by naturally mounded grey-green *Hebe topiaria*.
4, 5—The South Seas Garden features plants native to Oceania, including agave, aloe, euphorbias and New Zealand iris (*Libertia ixioides*).

3

4

5

# This is Not a Framed Garden

Bsalim, Lebanon

| |
|---|
| Frederic Francis |
| 21st century |
| 0.6 hectares / 1.5 acres |
| Mediterranean |
| Architectural / Modern / Rooms / Vistas / Water |

The name of this garden high in the hills overlooking Beirut is somewhat ironic, as there are frames of various types everywhere, provided either by the mature pines that were growing there decades before the garden was created in 2011, or by the stark white Modernist walls and lintels that focus the eye on different aspects of the 260-degree view of the city below and the blue Mediterranean Sea beyond. This series of artificial frames not only highlight the more distant scenery but also alter the way in which the viewer sees the more immediate pine forest, which surrounds the garden, by turning it into, variously, a green wall or a dramatic, framed picture. At dusk, lights carefully positioned amid the umbrella pines and olive trees enhance the sense of theatre.

And yet in one important way This is Not a Framed Garden does, indeed, lack a frame. It blends seamlessly into the natural forests that surround it, so that the visitor can move freely between the structured, modern environment and ancient pathways worn by generations of feet. The landscape architect, French-trained Frederic Francis, chose a design that made the most of the dramatic setting but also melded with the natural vegetation. He therefore created a modern patio with a seating area and a swimming pool that doubles as an infinity pool, reflecting the surrounding planting.

Nearby is a more naturalistic pool, edged with heavy rocks and fed by a stream that tumbles down the hillside in a narrow channel. Around the house and pools Francis created a series of grassy lawns and planted stands of bamboo and rushes. From the patio an archway invites visitors through to a lower level of the garden, where Francis designed a series of individual 'rooms': a Japanese Garden, a Bamboo Garden, a Rock Garden and a Modern Garden. These areas provide a stimulating contrast with the structured world of the house and patio, and blend into the lush greenery.

1, 2—The startling white structure of the infinity pool creates a dialogue between the garden and its surroundings, reflecting and framing the sky and the natural trees beyond.
3—Below the house, in contrast to the stark modernity of the infinity pool, plantings of rushes and ornamental grasses give a natural feeling to the pond fed by a stream running down the hillside.
4—A simple cube-shaped deck is suspended over the nauralistic pond; its uprights and roof provide more frames for viewing the surrounding garden.

3

4

# Miracle Garden
## Dubai, UAE

| |
|---|
| Akar Landscaping Service and Agriculture |
| 21st century |
| 7 hectares / 18 acres |
| Dry Arid |
| Bedding / Display / Modern |

There is much about the Dubai Miracle Garden of which many gardeners would disapprove. Its floral displays are in every sense excessive: 45 million flowers massed to create floral clocks, pyramids, a falcon, a mountain, boats and cars and the world's longest floral wall. But you don't have to delight in every floral display in the Dubai Miracle Garden to appreciate the sheer achievement it represents.

Opened on Valentine's Day 2013 in Dubailand, the United Arab Emirates' massive amusement complex, this huge circular site is the largest natural flower garden in the world. Just how 'natural' a continuous blooming array of this size in a desert can be remains an open question, although its developers, Akar Landscaping, claim that its highly efficient drip-irrigation system makes sparing use of water.

In truth, the garden is more a testament to the region's economic and engineering prowess – and sheer confidence – than a lesson in ecological plant care. Occupying a cultural position somewhere between Disneyland and Tivoli, the Dubai Miracle Garden features displays in the shape of giant flowers, hundreds of hanging baskets, lily-shaped street lamps, a section dedicated to Ferrari cars, a VIP gate, mosques and even a floral Burj Khalifa – a reminder that the world's biggest flower display is close to the world's tallest building.

Despite its size, most of the garden is planted with just forty-five different varieties of familiar flower, such as chrysanthemums, petunias, dahlias and daisies. The garden will eventually include more varied beds in an aromatic and medicinal section, and in an edible garden, where visitors will be able to pick their own salads and fruits.

Akar Landscaping, which is based in the Abu Dhabi city of Al Ain, sources many of these plants locally, and has gained an international reputation for effective and impressive landscaping in a region not known for its horticulture. The firm is also planning a nine-dome Butterfly Garden at the Miracle Garden. While that might not be the sort of development likely to impress many landscape architects, it is a clever addition to a garden that has managed to turn a desert into a theme-park-style attraction.

1 — At the heart of the garden are seven 12-metre-high (40-foot) pyramids representing the seven emirates of the UAE; the pyramids' sides are studded with thousands of petunias.

1

# Bahá'í Haifa

Haifa, Israel

Fariborz Sahba

20th century

20 hectares / 50 acres

Mediterranean

Modern / Religious / Terraces / Water

The gardens that stretch down the side of Mount Carmel in Haifa are spread over nineteen terraces – a reference to the nineteen original founders of the Bahá'í faith, known as the 'Letters of the Living'. In the middle of the broad staircase that climbs from the German Templar Colony of the city is the golden-domed mausoleum of the Báb, the prophet who announced the coming of the Prophet-Founder of the Bahá'í faith, Bahá'u'lláh, and who was martyred in 1850 in Iran. His remains were brought to the Holy Land some fifty years later. This memorial was completed in 1953, and the gardens were constructed by his followers as an expression of beauty to counterbalance the ills inflicted on the Báb in life. The golden dome acts as the focal point of the garden. From here nine concentric circles – representing the world's major religions – spread out up and down the terraces like ripples on a pond.

Gardens celebrate both inclusion and diversity; they beautify this holy spot. The Báb's follower, who became known as Bahá'u'lláh, was a prisoner all of his life. When the conditions of his imprisonment were relaxed at the end of his life, he lived in a mansion in a renowned garden in the nearby city of Akko. It was he whose vision lay behind the garden in Haifa. On a visit to Haifa in 1891, he pointed to the spot where the remains of the Báb would be buried; at that time, the whole hillside was still barren scrub.

The gardens, fountains and plants have no purpose other than to beautify this holy place and to enhance the experience of visiting the shrine. The Bahá'í garden makes a feature of fountains, pools and channels that fill the terraces with the calming sound of water. The terraces are planted with formal arrangements of flowers and trees, but each terrace is deliberately different – even down to the pattern of the paving – to reflect the Bahá'í belief in unity in diversity.

Around the mausoleum itself, with views over Haifa and the Mediterranean, is the Persian Garden. It has topiary sculpted into eight-pointed stars. Next to the shrine are the Hanging Gardens, which contain secluded areas that are home to the tombs of other members of the family of Bahá'u'lláh. The offices from which the world faith is administered are nearby.

1 — The spectacular gardens rise towards the Báb's mausoleum above Haifa in a series of terraces that feature grass, paving, flower beds and trees. The garden's axis is aligned with the resting place of Bahá'u'lláh in a nearby Bahá'i garden in Akko (Acre).
2 — The upper terraces of the garden are inspired by Islamic gardens, with traditional eight-pointed stars laid out in the lawns and bright, contrasting areas of gravel.

1

2

# Chehel Sotoun

Isfahan, Iran

| | |
|---|---|
| Shah Abbas II | |
| 17th century | |
| 6.7 hectares / 17 acres | |
| Dry Semiarid | |
| Formal / Historic / Islamic / Water | |

At the end of the sixteenth century, Isfahan was a byword for beauty and elegance, a new capital laid out as a city of palaces and gardens by Shah Abbas I, the greatest leader of the Iranian Safavid dynasty. Today most of the great gardens with their elegant palaces and pavilions and evocative names have been lost. Chehel Sotoun is one of only four of the sixteen palace gardens to survive – and only as a detached garden, where it was once part of a complex of palaces and gardens. Its name means 'forty columns', and refers to the slender, elegant, wooden columns – once much more decorative than they are today – that support the *talar* (covered veranda) at the end of the long reflecting pool; the *talar*'s twenty columns are doubled by their reflection.

Chehel Sotoun was completed in 1647 during the reign of Shah Abbas II, but what is seen today is a reconstruction built following a fire in 1706. It would have been used for pleasure or to receive dignitaries and ambassadors, either on the airy, spacious *talar* or in one of the stately reception halls that feature six large, recently restored friezes depicting Safavid court life and their military exploits. (In *The Road to Oxiana* in 1937, Robert Byron described one of the reception halls as 'spread with carpets, lit with pyramids of lamps'.) As well as protecting those who sit beneath it from the light and heat of the sun, thus symbolizing divine protection, the Achaemenid-inspired *talar* served as a connection between the pavilion and the garden.

Today the imposing yet elegant structure sits facing east at the head of a long, rectangular, mirroring pool flanked by two long beds of roses; there is a shorter pool of the same width at the rear of the building. Surrounding the *talar* is an almost-square garden. This does not have the typical Islamic quadripartite division by rills into a *chahar bagh*; instead paths of various widths define a series of rectangular and square beds that are mostly given over to lawn, all of which are heavily shaded by conifers and *chenar* or plane trees (*Platanus orientalis*). According to the Islamic faith, the *chenar* is the earthly counterpart of the *tuba* tree that grows in *janna* (paradise), where it gives shade, bears all manner of fruits and yields calyces, from which are made the clothes of those who dwell in paradise.

1, 2—The slender wooden columns that support the *talar* were once decorated far more opulently than they are today, so the effect of their reflection in the long mirror pool would have been overwhelming for visitors to the Safavid court.
3—The long beds on either side of the pool are filled with roses. The rest of the garden is largely given over to lawns, shaded by plane trees and conifers.

# Abbasi Hotel

Isfahan, Iran

| |
|---|
| Unknown |
| 20th century |
| 0.6 hectares / 1.5 acres |
| Dry Semiarid |
| Courtyard / Formal / Islamic / Water |

Overlooked by the dome and minarets of the Madraseh-e-Chahar Bagh, the Abbasi Hotel has a long history of accommodating weary travellers. The structure was originally built some 300 years ago under the Safavid dynasty as a school, bazaar and *caravanserai* known as the Madar-Shah (meaning 'King's mother'). The building fell into disrepair, but in the 1950s André Godard, director of the Iranian Archeological Services, encouraged a sympathetic restoration of the derelict complex into what is arguably Iran's finest hotel.

The hotel surrounds an inner courtyard 80 metres (262.5 feet) square. Where there was once a dusty space bustling with beasts of burden and teeming courtiers, merchants and traders, there is now a tranquil garden oasis. The garden layout follows the traditional *chahar bagh* quadripartite pattern. One of the two perpendicular axes is a broad, blue-tiled rill – the Farshadi stream – flanked by elegant fountain jets that not only form a high sparkling arch of water above the rill but also create the delicious sound of rainfall pattering back into the water: a refreshing combination in this hot, arid climate. The second perpendicular axis is a wide path paved with large hexagonal tiles that crosses the rill by means of a bridge. Within each of the courtyard's four quarters (*chahar bagh* literally means 'four gardens'), and linked by paved paths, is a central geometric pool with a fountain. Four small octagonal pools, each with its own fountain, are located in the corners of each quarter, bringing the courtyard's total of pools and fountains to twenty.

The spaces defined by the paths are given over to lawns edged with flower beds. Although not authentically planted, the displays of brightly coloured bedding plants are attractive. Also set within the lawns are a number of low trees, some of which are clipped into spherical lollipops, while towering over the gardens are several palms and plane trees (*Platanus orientalis*). The garden is illuminated at night, when it looks particularly enchanting.

1 — The garden in the Inner Courtyard follows the design of a traditional Islamic *chahar bagh*, one axis of which is formed by a broad, blue-tiled rill. The rill is lined on either side with many high, slender fountain jets, angled to form a high arch of fine spray that rains down over the rill.
2 — In the cool of the evening the delightfully lit gardens continue to welcome guests in a tradition that extends back some three centuries, to when the complex was a royal *caravanserai*.

# Bagh-e Fin

Kashan, Isfahan, Iran

Shah Abbas I

16th & 19th century

2.3 hectares / 6 acres

Dry Arid

Formal / Historic / Islamic / Water

Anyone who wants to understand the importance of gardens in Islamic culture need look no further than Bagh-e Fin, the epitome of the Persian-inspired Islamic garden. The cool, shady, well-watered and verdant garden is a paradise of wonder when compared with the arid, inhospitable desert beyond its walls.

Bagh-e Fin – one of nine 'Persian gardens' collectively listed as a UNESCO World Heritage site – was built in 1590. However, what is visible today is mostly a nineteenth-century renovation attributed to Fath 'Ali Shah. This monumental royal garden – a different tradition from tomb gardens such as the Taj Mahal (see page 56) – belongs to a style that arose when Muslim conquerors blended the ancient garden tradition they encountered in Persia with their own ideal of the Islamic paradise garden as described in the Koran.

The essence of Bagh-e Fin is water. It originally arrived in the garden from a mountain spring, having been carried by a system of *qanats* or underground aqueducts. Aligned on the main axis in front of the Khan-e Sardar (Entrance Hall) is a rill that leads the eye to the Main Pool, which reflects the open-sided Kushak (Safavid Pavilion). Within the pavilion, under an ornate ceiling tiled in colourful geometric patterns, is the square pool that feeds the garden's system of rills and pools. The pools and watercourses are themselves lined with blue faience tiles whose colour makes the water even more enticing. Fountains create a delicious bubbling sound.

On the west side of the complex is now a museum; the rectangular garden occupies the remaining space. The garden design is not quadripartite in the classic Islamic style, but it does exhibit axial order, geometrical precision, repetition and symmetry in a layout that has a carpet-like quality. Shaded by plane and cypress trees – both of which have a religious symbolism in Islam – the grid of rills and cobbled paths demarcates square and rectangular beds. Being enclosed by clipped hedges and mostly given over to lawn, the modern beds are elegant – but they would be more engaging were they planted as the lush 'flowering orchard' they would have originally been.

1 — The central rill carries water from the Kushak (Safavid Pavilion) through a pool between hedged compartments lined with cypress and plane trees.
2 — All the water channels in the garden – here in the Long Pool behind the Safavid Pavilion – are lined with blue faience tiles that intensify the colour of the water.
3 — The way in which canals intersect in rectangular basins is reminiscent of the ancient Persian city of Pasargadae, the capital of Cyrus the Great, and may be a stone version of how irrigation canals met in the lost gardens of Mesopotamia.

# Bagh-e Shahzadeh

Mahan, Kerman, Iran

| |
|---|
| Naser ad-Douleh |
| 19th century |
| 3.5 hectares / 8.5 acres |
| Dry Semiarid |
| Beds / Formal / Historic / Islamic / Terraces / Water |

If there was ever an example of how a garden can be an earthly paradise, Bagh-e Shahzadeh is it. This haven in the midst of a dusty desert – to the west is the bleak Dasht-e Lut, the 'Emptiness Desert' – is cooled and enlivened by moving water, shaded by tall trees and provisioned by lower trees laden with fruits. Enriched by sweetly smelling and brightly coloured flowers, the garden within the tall enclosing walls is calm. With its elongated rectangular shape and its backdrop of distant mountains, Bagh-e Shahzadeh ('Prince's Garden') has echoes of the Islamic Mughal gardens of Kashmir (see pages 50 and 51). But here the water that flows the 270 metres (886 feet) between the large pools in front of the buildings at the top and bottom of the garden arrives from the distant mountains by means of qanats (underground canals), and the climate is much harsher. The garden was created for Mohammad Hasan Khan Qajar Sardari Iravani in the 1850s and later extended in the 1880s by the Governor of Kerman, Naser ad-Douleh, who died in 1891 before work was completed.

Leaving the desert, the visitor passes through a gate at the northern or lower end of the sloping garden into a lofty, airy two-storey pavilion, now partially in ruins. From the pavilion a vista leads straight up the long main axis to the Governor's residence at the head of the garden. The axis is composed of a wide watercourse that makes its way over a series of identical terraces between the square upper and lower pools. Where the levels change, the water drops by means of a soft waterfall.

Running along the terraces either side of the watercourse are beds filled with roses and bedding plants. The beds separate twin paved paths, the outer of which is flanked by an avenue of cypress (*Cupressus sempervirens*). In Islam these trees are symbolic of eternity, and here they also draw the eye to the pavilion and the mountains beyond. The space between the cypresses and the high walls is planted with orchards of pear and pomegranate. Shaded by large chenar or plane trees (*Platanus orientalis*), these open spaces are the perfect spot to soak up the tranquil atmosphere of this paradise in the desert.

1—An aerial view shows the garden's desert setting; a system of underground canals carries water from the distant mountains.
2, 3—A long central rill bordered by a modern variety of red and white roses carries water over a series of small waterfalls.
4—The Sardar Khaneh, the pavilion at the lower entrance to the garden, is now in a state of disrepair.
5—Fountains play among modern roses and box hedges; once it has passed through the garden, the water is used by local people for agricultural irrigation.

# Bagh-e Babur

Kabul, Afghanistan

| |
|---|
| Zahiruddin Babur |
| 16th & 21st century |
| 11.5 hectares / 28.5 acres |
| Dry Semiarid |
| Formal / Islamic / Terraces / Tomb |

For Muslims, a garden designed in the prescribed quadripartite style and planted with symbolic plants as described in the Koran truly is an earthly paradise. And Babur, the first emperor of the Islamic Mughal dynasty in India, was a great garden-maker. He initially commissioned Bagh-e Babur as a pleasure garden in around 1528, as one of ten gardens he made in his then-capital in Kabul. Once Babur had conquered India, he moved his seat of power to Agra, where he died. His body was eventually transported back to his beloved Kabul and interred in Bagh-e Babur by his wife. The tomb garden became a site of pilgrimage for subsequent emperors, but it decayed following the collapse of the Mughal Empire in the mid-nineteenth century.

Cascading down the slope of Kuh-e Sher Darwaza southwest of the old city of Kabul, Bagh-e Babur is today a rare urban green space, providing a haven from the bustle of the city. Following decades of occupation and warfare in Afghanistan, the garden was a ruin by 2003, when the Aga Khan Trust for Culture undertook a four-year restoration – having first cleared the site of unexploded ordnance.

Once again enclosed within what is by Mughal standards a plain white marble mausoleum, Babur's tomb stands on the fourth of the fifteen terraces. From there the visitor enjoys a magnificent view west down over the garden with its restored pavilion and out over the walls, across the Kabul River and towards distant peaks. As in Babur's time, water – that most essential element of any Islamic garden – is the focal point. A watercourse forms the garden's main axis, flowing its length in a marble-lined channel and series of tanks, crossed by stone and flanked on both sides by lawn. Either side of the lawns are stone pathways and steps that link the terraces, flanked by avenues of plane trees interspersed with pomegranates, apricots, apples, cherries and peaches. The grassed terraces have been re-created as authentically as possible, with flowers, roses and orchards of those most symbolic of trees as mentioned in the Koran: mulberry, apricot, fig and almond. Copses of walnut are planted along the reconstructed perimeter walls.

1 — Babur's garden spills down the hillside in a series of fifteen terraces. The emperor's white marble mausoleum stands near the top, looking west across the garden and the Kabul River.
2 — Babur's tomb is a relatively small white structure on the fourth of the garden's fifteen terraces.
3 — Trees and lawns welcome visitors on the lowest level of the garden as they pass through the main gate into this green haven in the middle of the city.

# Shalimar Bagh

Lahore, Punjab, Pakistan

Khalilullah Khan, Ali Mardan Khan, Mullah Alaul Maulk Tuni

17th century

17 hectares / 42 acres

Dry Semiarid

Islamic / Terraces / Water

Like other Islamic gardens, that constructed to the northwest of central Lahore, Punjab, by the Mogul emperor Shah Jahan in 1641 revolves around water. Its shape is dictated by the traditional Islamic *chahar bagh*, a quadripartite design repeated across three terraces that descend from south to north in steps of about 4.5 metres (15 feet). From the uppermost Zanana Terrace, which was reserved for the ladies of Shah Jahan's court, there is a spectacular view through two pavilions across the reservoir on the narrow central terrace to the lowest one, where the emperor held public audiences. A high crenellated red sandstone wall, famous for its fretwork, encloses the entire Shalimar Bagh and has a tower in each corner.

The top and bottom terraces each comprise square *chahar bagh*, divided into a four-fold pattern by a 6-metre-wide (20-foot) canal with fountains, which ends in a water tank. The canal is flanked by two parallel walkways paved with traditional Lahore bricks. The quarters are subdivided by narrow water channels and walkways, forming sixteen parts in all.

Meanwhile the *chahar bagh* on the middle terrace is more elongated, to take account of its narrow depth. This level is home to the garden's most impressive features, especially the square marble platform surrounded by water. The water flows beneath it, then over a fluted marble 'chadar' – a waterfall that breaks up the flow of the water to make an attractive sound – and under the emperor's white marble throne before it enters the Sawan Bhadun pavilion. In the sunken courtyard there are lantern niches in the wall. The pavilion also offers another spectacular view across the gardens.

Shalimar Bagh is well structured to reflect the original planting. For this, Shah Jahan is said to have ordered fruit trees from Kabul and Kandahar. These included mangoes, cherries, apricots, peaches, plums, apples, seedless almonds, mulberries and both sweet and sour oranges. Abundant shrubs and flowers now fill the garden year-round, making it one of the most impressive and delightful of surviving Mughal gardens.

1, 2—The Middle Terrace is home to many of the garden's most impressive features, including the Sawan Bahun pavilion and a square marble platform that sits in the middle of the water.

# Nishat Bagh

Srinagar, Jammu and
Kashmir, India

| Asaf Khan IV |
| --- |
| 17th century |
| 18 hectares / 44 acres |
| Humid Subtropical |
| Formal / Islamic / Terraces / Water |

Nishat Bagh means 'Garden of Delight', and the name is well justified. This Islamic-inspired garden on the eastern side of the Dal Lake commands a breathtaking view across the lake to the snow-capped peaks of the Pir Panjal.

Unusually for a Mughal garden, its creator – Asaf Khan – was a mere noble rather than a member of the royal family. He completed Nishat Bagh in 1633, in a style that is typical of an Islamic *chahar bagh* but adapted to suit the steep topography of the site down which water flows. Instead of the usual four-square design, the walled garden is rectangular and terraced on either side of the axial canal, which is 4 metres (13 feet) wide and begins at the top of the garden, emptying into the lake at the bottom. Today the lowest terrace has been destroyed, and instead the water passes under the lakeshore road that replaced it.

Originally each of the twelve terraces was associated with a sign of the zodiac, and the garden was divided into two: a public pleasure garden and a private harem garden used only by the women of Asaf Khan's household. Today visitors can enjoy views of the garden from the top terrace.

The canal creates a unifying link between the terraces, with the water descending by means of *chadar* (sloping chutes) that make it jump and catch the light. The flowing water is also enlivened by a central row of jetting fountains. Square pools and their fountains grace the terraces. Visitors exploring the garden by means of flights of steps find stone benches that straddle the water channel and provide opportunities to enjoy the vistas.

The planting was anglicized by the British in the nineteenth century and so the garden has something of the feel of a Victorian public park. Yet it remains very pleasant, with the verdant lawns providing a calm foil to the water and beds of brightly coloured bedding plants, roses, lilies and evergreens hinting at the richness of the original planting. Near the 5.5-metre-tall (18-foot) walls are stately plane trees – the remains of twin avenues that ran the length of the garden – and these provide welcome shade.

1, 2—The central canal provides a link between the different terraces, carrying water from the top of the garden to the lake at the bottom.
3—Water links the different levels of the garden, flowing down *chadar* (sloping chutes) that turn the slow-flowing water into a bubbling, frothing sheet.
4—Fountains play amid lawns and bedding plants, which contribute to the anglicized feel of the garden and reflect the influence of the British in the nineteenth century.

# Shalimar Bagh

Srinagar, Jammu and
Kashmir, India

| |
|---|
| Emperor Jahangir, Zafar Khan |
| 17th century |
| 12.4 hectares / 31 acres |
| Dry Semiarid |
| Formal / Islamic / Terraces / Water |

Kashmir is home to some of the finest gardens created by the Islamic Mughal dynasty. One of the outstanding examples is Shalimar Bagh (Sanskrit for 'abode of love'), despite being damaged by recent planting and particularly the introduction of large lawns. Its name is appropriate, for the garden was created by Emperor Jahangir for his wife, Nur Jahan, in 1619. Under Shah Jahan the garden was extended, in 1630, by Zafar Khan, who was governor of Kashmir.

Shalimar Bagh stands on Lake Dal in front of a towering backdrop of mountains. These are the source of the tumbling stream that enters the uppermost of the garden's three terraces. Not only is water central to Shalimar Bagh; it was also the way early visitors reached the garden, via an approach canal 1.6 kilometres (1 mile) long.

The uppermost terrace was reserved for the emperor and the ladies of the court. It held the Diwan-a-Am (hall of public audience), a black marble pavilion with water cascading on three sides into a large pool via waterfalls that were lit up at night by oil lamps placed in niches behind the water. This pool no longer exists, however, having been replaced by a road. The middle terrace was the emperor's garden and was the location of the Diwan-a-Khas (hall of special public audience), where the emperor held his daily court whenever he was in Kashmir.

The black marble pavilion surrounded by crystal-clear water is the most popular feature in the garden. The pavilion is entered by narrow bridges across the large water tank in which it sits. Fountains send plumes of water into the air, cooling the surrounding air. This sight lingers in the memory for a long time after the visitor leaves the garden. The view from the pavilion of illuminated cascades and the distant mountains is another highlight.

Shalimar Bagh today suffers from its altered planting. The original garden must have been carefully filled with fruit trees, shrubs and bulbs, and the current garden still has some of the larger plants, especially the oriental plane trees along the main canal. These provide an appropriate scale for the backdrop of the mountains and the broad expanse of Lake Dal.

1, 4—At the heart of the garden is water, running in rills, filling the main canal and shooting from fountains.
2—The towering mountains that form the spectacular backdrop to the garden are also the source of its water.
3—The black marble Diwan-a-Am is surrounded by water and has a view over Lake Dal.

# Rashtrapati Bhavan

New Delhi, Delhi, India

Edwin Lutyens

20th century

5.3 hectares / 13 acres

Dry Semiarid

Bedding / Formal / Islamic / Water

With 340-rooms – it is bigger than the Palace of Versailles – the Rashtrapati Bhavan was designed as the focal point of New Delhi by British architect Edwin Lutyens. Originally built for the British Viceroy, it is now the official home of India's President.

As in all his projects, Lutyens unites house and garden with a lightness of touch through the ingenious use of symmetry and geometry. The Mughal Garden to the west of and behind the house comprises three parts. Nearest the building is the square Main Garden, which clearly shows the Mughal influence of the quadripartite *chahar bagh* garden form – but with a twist. Rather than use perpendicular canals to divide the space, Lutyens placed a square lawn in the centre of the garden and used paths rather than canals to demarcate the quadripartite form. He further divided each quarter into four by means of two pairs of canals running north–south and east–west, then quartered each of these sixteenths with geometrically-patterned paths. In an acknowledgement of India's diverse religious heritage, Lutyens also introduced Hindu influence in the form of six lotus-shaped fountains at the intersections of the canals, which create a calming murmur.

Much of the garden is smooth lawns which, like the canals, create a backdrop for bright bedding plants such as salvias, dahlias, marigolds and heliotrope. Height is introduced by dome-clipped moulsari (*Mimusops elengi*) trees. Forming the northern and southern boundaries are raised terraces, each with flower beds and a fountain that falls inwards to form a well.

West of the Main Garden and bound by walls covered with climbers including *Pyrostegia venusta*, jasmine and *Campsis grandiflora* is the Long or 'Purdha' Garden. Sixteen beds of roses line a main path with a pergola smothered with *Petrea*, bougainvillea, vines and climbing roses. The path leads to the tranquil Circular Garden, with a central pool and fountain surrounded by lawn and circular raised beds of bright bedding plants.

1—Evening light illuminates the Residence behind borders planted with dahlias and annuals and topiary moulsari trees in the square Main Garden.
2—Hindu-inspired lotus-shaped fountains feed stepped rills that divide the garden in characteristically Islamic fashion.
3—A moon gate and arches of glowing stone punctuate the walls of the Sunken Garden.
4—In the Circular Garden, lawn divides curved, tiered borders of flowers such as salvias, marigolds and heliotrope.
5—A stone rill with corrugated details passes a border of violas and *Antirrhinum*.
6—Dahlias are among the many flowers used in the beds in the garden.

3

4

5

6

# Sanskriti Kendra

New Delhi, Delhi, India

| |
|---|
| Mohammad Shaheer |
| 20th century |
| 2 hectares / 5 acres |
| Dry Semiarid |
| Containers / Informal / Landscape / Sculpture / Water |

The garden at this cultural centre in the outskirts of New Delhi, some 40 kilometres (24 miles) from the city centre, surrounds a cluster of buildings – museums, amphitheatre, library and residential studios – that house the private collection of artefacts and textiles amassed by its founder, O P Jain. The complex also provides temporary working space for traditional and contemporary artists, who can interact with one another, thereby helping to develop the artistic and cultural expression of India.

The spaces among the buildings in the sprawling complex have a distinct character, resembling areas in a rural housing complex. The levels of the rocky land have been moulded so as to create varied small sites that lend themselves to the display of terracotta artefacts and objects from the everyday life of traditional Indian families.

Water is a linking element throughout the buildings and the garden areas. It features in ponds, while locally available slabs of quartzite and locally made bricks have been used to create areas of hard landscaping. Because of its natural ruggedness, such material blends well with the brick buildings and enclosed spaces; it is also reminiscent of rural Indian communities.

A large number of trees and shrubs – there are about 100 species of tree, including numerous figs and species of plumeria, as well as myrobalan (*Prunus cerasifera*) – have been planted informally throughout the complex, and attract many birds and other wildlife. The landscape is also dotted with planters, although these can be rather distracting. A banyan tree (*Ficus religiosa*) near the entrance will, when fully grown, lend the appropriate scale.

Building began on the complex at Sanskriti Kendra in 1985. Its rocky site lies against the backdrop of the Aravalli Hills and has a humid, subtropical climate. The garden is private but is open to the public.

1, 2—The areas around the Museum of Indian Terracotta show how the spaces of the garden have been carefully contrived to resemble the kind of domestic areas familiar from traditional Indian homes.
3—Streams and lotus ponds are integrated throughout the garden, and help attract birds and other wildlife.

# Mughal Sheraton

Agra, Uttar Pradesh, India

ARCOP Design Group, Ramesh Khosla, Ranjit Sabikhi, Ajoy Choudhury, Ray Affleck (architects), Ravindra Bhan (landscape architect)

20th century

6 hectares / 15 acres

Dry Semiarid

Courtyards / Formal / Islamic / Modern

Built almost in the shadow of India's most famous garden – the Taj Mahal (see page 56), only a kilometre or so down the road – the gardens of the Mughal Sheraton hotel in Agra are a late-twentieth-century interpretation of a traditional garden by the leading Indian landscape architect and garden designer Ravindra Bhan. His skill was recognized when the hotel and garden together won the Aga Khan Award in 1980 as one of the fifteen best buildings built in the previous twenty years.

Bhan's design reflects the central role of the garden in Mughal culture as a space to socialize, with three interlinked landscaped courtyards housing the two-storey guest wings of the hotel. A series of landscaped terraces, pools and fountains act as buffer zones between the private and public areas, while a formal Mughal garden provides a vista for the central buildings and a focal point for the walkways. The guest wings are connected to one another and to the central block by roofed pedestrian bridges. In the central block, guests are led from the entrance to the lobby by a bridge across a large reflecting pool with fountains. On the mezzanine level an observation area offers views of the Taj Mahal, while activities in the ground-floor restaurants and ballroom can spill out on to the garden terraces.

The walls that enclose the landscape courtyards support wide planters at their base, providing a privacy screen to the rooms. From room level the courtyards gradually descend some 3.7 metres (10 feet) through a series of step terraces, planters, pools and fountains, which introduce the cooling presence of water – a concept familiar to the Mughals. In the centre of the garden, on an axis with the Taj Mahal, is a formal garden where cypress trees line a terraced water channel set with fountains and enclosed at the far end by a sandstone wall with lantern niches.

Surrounding the formal garden are 2 hectares (5 acres) of informal gardens, which offer further space for recreation, including putting, archery and croquet. The entire site is bounded, not by a wall, but by thick bougainvillea embankments that help to make this garden a cool haven from the hot, dusty Agra climate.

1, 3—The sunken courtyards are home to dozens of terraces with wide planters set into the walls that support carefully proportioned and neatly shaped trees and shrubs.
2— Cypress trees line the terraced water channel in the formal part of the garden.
4— A large reflecting pool is crossed by a walkway that takes guests from the entrance to the lobby.

# Taj Mahal

Agra, Uttar Pradesh, India

| |
|---|
| Shah Jahan, Ustad Ahmad |
| 17th century |
| 40.5 hectares / 100 acres |
| Dry Semiarid |
| Islamic / Mughal / Tomb |

Some images are so familiar that the real thing threatens to be an anticlimax – but with the Taj Mahal the opposite is true. The reality far exceeds expectation. Built between 1632 and 1654 by Shah Jahan, the fifth Mughal emperor, the white-marble mausoleum and its garden are a memorial to his favourite wife, usually known by the title 'Mumtaz Mahal' ('the exalted one of the palace').

The garden in front of the tomb is in the style of a classic Islamic *chahar bagh* (paradise garden). It is a large square divided into four equal quadrants by two intersecting and perpendicular *nahr* (shallow canals) flanked by *khiyaban* (walkways). The *nahr* are fed from the *hauz* (a raised marble water tank) at the garden's centre, and each of the quadrants is further subdivided into four beds by smaller walkways. Today, grass has replaced what were once sixteen flower beds planted with a riot of floral colour and scent, with plants brought from all over the Mughal empire. The modern lawns are a poor foil to the architecture. Additional tree planting by the British in the nineteenth century has also reduced the formality of the garden structure.

The mausoleum, positioned on a raised platform above the garden, overlooks the River Yamuna beyond. Despite initial appearances, it is sited at the centre of the garden complex. Across the river, on the north bank, the recently rediscovered and renovated Mehtab Bagh (Moonlit Garden) shares the same alignment, aesthetic and proportion as the more celebrated garden in front of Mumtaz Mahal's tomb. The square, quadripartite garden has one notable difference from its counterpart. At the southern end of its north–south *nahr* is a large, sunken octagonal pool positioned to reflect the Taj Mahal. The pool is now empty, but the effect would have been ethereal on a moonlit night, when the white building was reflected in the black water. The Mehtab Bagh has been replanted with more than forty species, including fruit trees, making it more historically accurate than the more-visited gardens south of the mausoleum.

1—At the end of the day the white marble of the Taj Mahal glows as its gardens fall into shadow.
2—The water rills of the *chahar bagh* – this one looks north towards the Darwaza, or Entrance Gate – symbolize the four rivers of Jannah, the Islamic Paradise.
3—The view south from the Darwaza over the *chahar bagh* towards the tomb.
4—The garden was originally planted with fruit trees signifying life; in contrast, today's cypress trees signify eternity.
5—The Mehtab Bagh, 'Moonlit Garden', was designed as an integral part of the complex to give views of the Taj Mahal from across the River Yamuna.

3

4

5

# Halfway Retreat
Ahmedabad, Gujarat, India

| |
|---|
| Aniket Bhagwat |
| 21st century |
| 4 hectares / 10 acres |
| Dry Semiarid |
| Courtyard / Grasses / Natives / Water |

When the Indian landscape architect Aniket Bhagwat joined the landscape design firm started by his father, he had evolved his own ideas about the direction Indian architecture and landscaping should take. Rather than follow his contemporaries who worked in Western traditions, Bhagwat turned back to India itself – to the shapes and materials of its indigenous buildings, the patterns of its traditional land use.

One of the finest expressions of Bhagwat's philosophy is Halfway Retreat, a luxurious escape from the crowds and bustle of nearby Ahmedabad. The elements of India's Hindu and Mughal gardening tradition are here – water channels, terraces, vistas, a formality created by defined strips of planting and a grid of trees – but they are merely the starting point for a thoroughly modern Indian garden.

Not only did Bhagwat draw on indigenous planting, he also used plants that few Indian gardeners would think of using – the kind of hardy grasses and reeds that usually grow on verges and neglected patches of ground. Bhagwat distributed these plants around the undulating site in strips that deliberately recalled the strip agriculture traditionally practised in this part of India, linking the garden with the local culture. There are also extensive lawns that stretch away outside the large glass windows of the main living rooms. The strong horizontal lines of the garden are overlaid and broken up by a grid of trees that adds an element of formality as well as vertical interest. The echoes of Eastern nonlinear perceptions of space allow varied and complex readings of the site.

The house itself is equally at home in the existing landscape and the local culture, using a limited palette of stone, steel and brick that seems indigenous. The parking court is broken up by local boulders, as if visitors were parking in a rural lot. Upright fountains recall village standpipes, pouring water into a pool, while a system of sprinklers fills the air of a sunken courtyard next to the house with a fine, rising mist that coats the dense planting around the courtyard's edge with moisture in a manner reminiscent of a steamy rainforest. At Halfway Retreat, Aniket Bhagwat shows what a detailed understanding of Indian traditions and materials can achieve when allied with a gardening approach that is truly of the twenty-first century.

1—Native grasses and rushes grow in front of the house and also on its roof.
2—A veranda juts out over a sunken courtyard where sprinklers send clouds of fine mist over banks of lush shrubs.
3, 4—Water is at the heart of the garden, either in a tranquil hidden water 'room' or in irrigation channels that collect rainwater.

# Amber Fort Garden

Amer, Jaipur, Rajasthan, India

Raja Man Singh I, Raja Jai Singh, Sawai Jai Singh

17th century

0.2 hectares / 0.5 acres

Dry Semiarid

Formal / Islamic / Terraces / Water

Amber, or Amer, Fort sits on a rocky promontory overlooking Lake Maota, where an artificial peninsula is home to a remarkable terraced garden of geometrical beds. These were once swathed in white plants to create a moonlight garden for the ladies of the harem to enjoy after dark. The women were conveyed from the fort by an elaborate system of ropes and pulleys.

The Amber Fort was built by Man Singh I, a warrior of the warlike Rajput clan of Rajasthan, whose military might supported the Mughal Empire in India. In return for their military service, the Rajput leaders became wealthy. While they did not adopt the Mughals' Islamic faith – the Rajputs remained Hindu – they nevertheless adopted Mughal ideas about beauty, sophistication and art.

Within the fort itself is one of four courtyards Singh created. It is a rectangular sunken garden based on the traditional Islamic quadripartite *chahar bagh*. The pattern is more elaborate than a simple fourfold division, however. The central pool is octagonal, and laid over the four beds is a hexagonal pattern that creates a series of geometric divisions. This highly ornamental design can be viewed from one of the buildings above – the courtyard is outside the most magnificent building in the palace, the Jai Mandir (Hall of Victory).

The detached, rectangular garden on the lake is built on three terraces. On the upper terrace, the form of the beds echoes that of the fort courtyard garden, but with an overlaid octagonal pattern. The beds on the lower terraces are also ornately divided, but with a less complex pattern. As with many Islamic-inspired gardens, water is the unifying theme. Here it would have flowed from the (now-empty) scalloped pool on the upper terrace into four perpendicular rills and across the terrace before cascading down to the second and third terraces, and out into the lake. The whole garden is especially ornate when viewed from above.

Today both the lake and courtyard gardens are planted with low-maintenance shrubs, but in their heyday the beds would have been filled with rich displays of scent and colour.

1—The gardens are laid out in sunken beds that follow patterns based on both Islamic and Hindu symbolism: the star patterns on the top terrace of the Lake Garden are linked to the Seljuk Turks, for example. The Kesar Kyari (Saffron Garden) lies in the centre of the lake, laid out like a Persian carpet. The garden was planted with saffron for the fragrance to waft into the palace above.
2—The *chahar bagh*, or paradise garden, within the fort surrounds an octagonal fountain from which water-filled channels lined with marble ran throughout the courtyard.

# Lunuganga

Bentota, Sri Lanka

Geoffrey Bawa

20th century

10 hectares / 25 acres

Tropical

Coastal / Informal / Modern / Water

Lunuganga was the country home of the influential Sri Lankan architect Geoffrey Bawa, who fused buildings and landscape to transform an old rubber plantation into a stunning theatrical space. Shades of green dominate: trees, vines, palms, ferns and bamboos are densely planted to suggest a garden carved from the jungle.

Bawa was quick to appreciate the beauty of common objects. Long before architectural salvage was chic, he rescued and redeployed old shutters, windows and doors to add an air of age to his garden pavilions. He also promoted the use of Chinese water urns as sculpture and popularized frangipani trees, formerly grown mainly in temples, where their blossoms were used as votive offerings.

The entrance to the estate is through heavy iron gates, creating an air of mystery before the road rises to an open plaza surrounded by outbuildings: an overhead guest house presides like a portal, screening the view beyond. A staircase draws visitors to the central bungalow, where open porches, terraces and courtyards blur the distinction between interior and exterior space. On the terrace above the lake, Bawa extended the tilework of the living room to the lawn by setting concrete squares into the grass. The seating area is flanked by fragrant frangipani trees. The curving wall of the terrace echoes the line of the seashore below.

To the east a grid of rice paddies recalls the agricultural history of the region, while a reservoir planted with lilies creates a Water Garden. To the west the Field of Jars features large ceramic pots. Cinnamon Hill, to the north, was a wooded slope that Bawa cleared to create a vista. He placed a large urn on the slope, and its curves echo the dome of a distant Buddhist shrine. Paths and stairs traverse the hill, while classical nudes, lascivious satyrs, Hindu gods and stone lingams linger in the undergrowth. Although the statuary and pavilions assert the influence of the human hand on the landscape, these formal elements have an organic quality, creating an exotic and surreal garden.

1—The overhead guest house acts as a portico, while concealing the garden beyond.
2—The skeletal shapes of frangipani trees are reflected in the Water Garden.
3—Trees grow in the open courtyards of the house, helping to blur the distinction between indoors and outdoors.
4, 6—Concrete slabs set into the Western Terrace refer to the tilework inside the house; a sinuous wall along the terrace edge echoes the shape of the coastline below.
5, 7—The Southern Terrace outside the main entrance provides a quiet place to relax, presided over by a classical bust.

# Qunli National Wetland Park

Haerbin City, Heilongjiang, China

| Turenscape (Kongjian Yu) |
| 21st century |
| 34 hectares / 84 acres |
| Humid Continental |
| Ecological / Grasses / Landscape / Urban / Wetland |

Qunli National Wetland Park, it might be objected, is not so much a garden as a civil engineering project. But in its use of aesthetic landscaping and planting to solve drainage problems in the city of Haerbin, in northeast China, it belongs squarely to the tradition of eighteenth-century landscape gardening.

Qunli is a new suburb of Haerbin, a huge conurbation on the Songhua River about 1,200 kilometres (750 miles) northeast of Beijing. The local environment is challenging. So far from the coast, winter temperatures drop to –18°C (0°F), while at the height of summer they rise to 25°C (77°F). The monsoon brings 50–60 centimetres (20–24 inches) of rain in late summer.

When the rains hit Qunli's extensive concreted terrain, the water needs somewhere to go. Turenscape, the Beijing-based architecture, landscaping and urban planning practice founded in 2000 by Kongjian Yu, was tasked with solving Qunli's water problem and at the same time preserving a delicate wetland area in the heart of the new suburb. Its solution was to turn the wetlands into a giant sponge for the city, drawing away, filtering and returning storm-water to the water table, while providing the city with a wild, green space.

Rainwater from the streets is piped to the edge of the park, where Turenscape dug a ring of ponds, piling up the excavated earth into mounds. The mounds are planted with silver birches (*Betula pendula*), while the ponds feed excess water into the park's centre. The landscapers did not interfere with the wetlands themselves, leaving local marsh and meadow grass species to thrive. This local flora is rather dreary during the winter, but in the early summer the park comes alive with verdant growth, which residents can enjoy as they stroll along paths among the outer ring of ponds and mounds or enjoy views from pavilions or towers. There is also an elevated walkway, or skywalk. These are all built in part from local materials, such as wood, bamboo and stone – a reminder that, while the park was created to solve human-made problems, it also serves as a vital link with nature.

1 — A view northeast along the edge of the park shows how the wetland sits right beside the suburb of Qunli, providing easy drainage into the perimeter ponds.
2 — The ramp leading to the skywalk is integrated into a service building at the edge of the wetland; like the other structures, they are built from local materials.
3 — In the east, the skywalk cuts through the silver birch forest above the contoured landscape and offers views of the wetland.
4 — Sawn-through sections of tree trunks are used to create one of the two viewing towers, which give visitors views across the whole of the park.

# Yi-He-Yuan

(Garden of Preservation of Harmony)

Beijing, China

| |
|---|
| Unknown |
| 18th & 19th centuries |
| 300 hectares / 741 acres |
| Humid Continental |
| Classical / Imperial / Water |

One glance at the huge Vast Bright Lake (*Kunming Hu*) of Yi-He-Yuan makes it clear that this is a landscape created by Imperial ambition. The Summer Palace and its garden was a short journey for the Imperial court from Beijing's Forbidden City and was a means of escaping its claustrophobic atmosphere and summer heat.

The site was used from 1153 as a temporary residence to appreciate a flowing stream which was used to create a lake. The area supported crops until 1749, when the Emperor Qianlong, an enthusiastic garden-builder, built the Garden of Clear Ripples (*Qingyi Yuan*) by enlarging the lake, landscaping the topography and adding residential and garden buildings. The garden celebrated the emperor's mother, who was then sixty. Many of the features reflect this in their names, such as Longevity Hill, covered in flowering almond, cherry and plum trees.

The garden was ransacked and burnt in 1860 by British and French troops and again in 1900, to the annoyance of the Dowager Empress Cixi. In 1886 and 1902 she rebuilt the features and gave the garden the name we know today. It is said that she paid for it using money originally intended for the Navy, so it is suitable that she had a bizarre Western paddle steamer created from marble to replace an earlier wooden boat pavilion. The imagery of boats is an important feature of Chinese gardens; they allude to family power and stability.

Cixi visited the garden 'from the flowering of the magnolias to the withering of the chrysanthemums', and these plants can still be appreciated, along with the spring blossom, later wisteria and peonies, and the summer lotus flowers in the lake.

In 1924 the garden opened as a public park. Visitors come to marvel at the lake's Seventeen Arched Bridge or the Long Corridor, which stretches 700 metres (2,300 feet) along one side of the lake, each beam painted with different scenes. In quieter areas smaller gardens include a fan-shaped pavilion, 'mountains' created from rockwork and an imitation of the canals of Suzhou, complete with 'shops' where courtiers could pretend to buy things. This vast garden needs time to be understood, but it is worth the effort.

1—Kunming Lake is at the heart of the huge garden of the Summer Palace.
2—The Dowager Empress Cixi had a marble boat pavilion built in 1893 to replace a wooden one destroyed by fire.
3—The Seventeen Arched Bridge links islands and causeways in the lake.
4—The Long Corridor is illustrated with hundreds of scenes from classical Chinese stories and folk tales.
5—Part of the garden is a miniature version of the canals of Suzhou.

# Liu Yuan

(The Lingering Garden)

Suzhou, Jiangsu, China

| |
|---|
| Xu Taishi, Liu Rongfeng, Sheng Xuren |
| 16th, 19th & 20th centuries |
| 2.5 hectares / 6 acres |
| Humid Subtropical |
| Classical / Naturalistic / Rooms / Water |

As with all classical Chinese gardens, the entrance to Liu Yuan is modest: a doorway opens into a plain courtyard. But pass through the warren of dark rooms and one emerges into a rural idyll. This naturalistic but contrived scene was the site of the court official Xu Taishi's East Garden and is now the middle part of the expanded garden. It is almost square and enclosed, yet the visitor barely notices the surroundings because all the vistas lead the eye to the artfully contrived scenes of the lake, the artificial mountain, the wisteria-clad bridges and pavilions such as the Refreshing Breeze Pavilion.

Liu Yuan, which is one of the larger classical gardens in Suzhou, was created by Xu in the late sixteenth century. It was expanded in the early nineteenth century, and has been restored twice since, most recently after the Sino-Japanese War (1937–45).

The great delight of the garden is the sense of disorientation created by the twisting galleries: the visitor stumbles across new garden spaces between the buildings. The plantings of trees, evergreen shrubs, bamboos, bananas, peonies and vines add to the sense of natural landscape, while the shades of green contrast with the white walls and dark wood of the buildings.

To the west, beyond the wall of the Middle Garden, the Extended Garden features a naturalistic landscape with pavilions, a large artificial hill and a collection of more than 500 *penzai* (Chinese bonsai). The focus of the eastern part of the garden is the Three Peaks set in a courtyard. These valuable Taihu stones come from Lake Tai, whose waters have eroded them into fantastical shapes. Such rocks are avidly collected. Along the bamboo-lined path and through the moon gate one enters the Small Garden of Stone Forest – more sculptural rocks set about with evergreen shrubs.

Liu Yuan is also justly famous for its collection of stelae. Scattered around the garden, these are inscribed with the works of more than a hundred calligraphers, and they chart more than a thousand years of evolution of this most Chinese of art forms.

1—Looking across the lake to the Pellucid Tower and other buildings; buildings cover a third of the area of the garden.
2, 3—Evergreen shrubs and grasses grow among the sculptural rocks of the Small Garden of Stone Forest, which is entered through a moon gate approached by an avenue flanked by bamboo.
4—At 6.5 metres (21¼ feet), the Cloud Capped Peak is the tallest of the prized Taihu stones in all of Suzhou's gardens.
5—A doorway frames an example of *penzai* or *penjing*, the Chinese form of bonsai.
6—The Passable Pavilion stands on top of the rocky bank of the lake.

3

4

5

6

# Wang Shi Yuan

(The Master-of-the-
Fishing-Nets Garden)

Suzhou, Jiangsu, China

Song Zongyuan

12th & 18th centuries

0.5 hectares / 1.5 acres

Humid Subtropical

Classical / Rock / Rooms / Water

In a city renowned for its classical gardens, this is arguably the finest. Although relatively small, Wang Shi Yuan is a seamless union of nature, art and architecture, full of dynamic change, with a sense of boundlessness generated by the subtle and ingenious use of dimension and proportion, asymmetry and contrast, particularly the use of light and shade.

A garden was created here in 1140, but it had fallen into decay by the time Song Zongyuan acquired it in 1785. While retaining the spirit of the original, Song extensively redesigned the garden in three areas – a residential area, a central main garden and an inner garden – and added many buildings. The garden today largely follows Song's design.

The central garden, northwest of the residential area, is focused on the informal Rosy Cloud Pool. The yellowstone boulders of the shoreline are arranged to suggest mountains and grottoes. Overlooking the pool and rocks are carefully proportioned structures: the Moon Comes with Breeze Pavilion, the Washing-My-Ribbon Pavilion, the Bamboo Protruding Corridor and the Duck-Shooting Corridor. Using an approach known as 'close to the water', small buildings are set on rocks or piers directly over the water and larger buildings are set at a distance from it, with trees planted to obscure their size, thus creating the illusion that the pool is larger than it actually is. In this central garden the planting includes ornamental shrubs and groundcover plants trailing over the rockwork. Especially notable are the centuries-old sculptural Lacebark pines (*Pinus bungeana*) and a cypress planted in the Ming Dynasty (1368–1644).

Accessed by a roofed corridor, the shady courtyards and buildings south of the Rosy Cloud Pool were used for social activities, while those to the north were used for intellectual activities. As the visitor progresses through the studies, studios and associated garden courts, the combination of architecture, white-washed walls, ornate mosaic floors, arrangements of sculptural rocks and plantings of banana, bamboo, ornamental grasses, evergreen shrubs and Chinese plum or apricot (*Prunus mume*) combine to create a succession of tranquil and picturesque scenes.

1—The central area of the garden, the Place for Gathering Breezes, is the Rosy Clouds Pool with the Washing-My-Ribbon Pavilion (left) and the Moon Comes with Breeze Pavilion.
2, 4—Arrangements of ornamental rocks and trees are a constant companion as the visitor moves through the maze of pavilions, courts and gardens.
3—A moon gate leads from the Late Spring Cottage courtyard towards the Peony Study.
5—A twisting covered walkway leads to the Daohe House.

# Zhuo Zheng Yuan

(The Humble Administrator's Garden)

Suzhou, Jiangsu, China

| | |
|---|---|
| Wang Xiancheng, Wang Xinyi, Zhang Luqian | |
| 16th century | |
| 6.5 hectares / 16 acres | |
| Humid Subtropical | |
| Classical / Naturalistic / Vistas / Water | |

This, the largest garden in Suzhou, has a chequered past. It was created between 1513 and 1526, and its design was strongly influenced by Wen Zhengming, a Ming dynasty artist and scholar. In the following centuries the garden was divided into three and each section remodelled. In 1949 the Chinese government rejoined the parts, but, while the garden has a restored sense of unity, in reality it still consists of the eastern, western and central sections.

Facing the main entrance is the Eastern Garden. This is a sequence of delicate vistas of ponds and islands encircled by winding streams, pavilions (the main one being the Hall of Orchid and Snow), verdant 'mountains' clad with pine and bamboo, and a large lawn surrounded by crepe myrtle (*Lagerstroemia indica*).

Beyond is the central section: the heart of Zhuo Zheng Yuan. Covering a third of it is the sinuous Surging Wave Pond, with its three connected, 'mountain'–capped islets and inviting inlets and bridges. Around the perimeter, roofed corridors link pavilions, key among which is the Hall of Drifting Fragrance, which takes its name from the lotus in the pool, the pink flowers of which perfume the air in summer. Branches of forsythia on the lakeside stroke the water's surface, while bamboo groves line the paths and willow trees provide welcome shade.

A moon gate in the Western Half Pavilion leads to the smaller western part of the garden. Arranged around a pond and waterways are rockworks, wooded 'mountains', undulating roofed corridors and pavilions (including the thirty-six-roomed Mandarin Duck Hall). The buildings are more lavishly decorated than in the central section, and their layout remains much as when it was remodelled in the Qing dynasty.

Taken as a whole, the gardens at Zhuo Zheng Yuan create a 'natural' landscape and waterscape that present an ever-changing succession of vistas and reflections. This technique (called 'borrowed view from afar') imbues the garden with a sense of scale and ambience reminiscent of the scenery in the south of the Lower Yangtze Valley.

1—Lotus leaves carpet the Surging Wave Pond next to the Mountain-in-View Tower.
2—The artful arrangement of buildings, covered walkways, water and planting combines intimacy with a feeling of space, giving the garden a sense of scale.
3—The view across a lotus-covered lake features the fan-shaped With Whom Shall I Sit? Pavilion in the Western Garden.
4—A small courtyard demonstrates just how less can be more: a pool with koi carp, a banana plant and artfully arranged rocks.
5—The Western Garden is more intimate than the Eastern Garden: walkways and narrow paths snake among rocks, streams, bamboo and pavilion-topped hills.

# Maggie's Cancer Caring Centre

Tuen Mun, Hong Kong, China

| |
|---|
| Frank Gehry, Lily Jencks |
| 21st century |
| 0.016 hectares / 0.04 acres |
| Humid Subtropical |
| Courtyard / Healing / Modern / Rooms |

It is rare for a Hong Kong garden to have much of a view, so the landscaping around Maggie's Centre is remarkable, not least because its southern lawn has a great vista – even if the grass, very occasionally, also serves as a helicopter landing pad. This single-storey cancer support centre, designed by the Pritzker Prize laureate Frank Gehry and opened beside Tuen Mun Hospital in 2013, creates a haven of tranquillity beside a hive of medical industry. Throughout its creation, Gehry worked closely with the landscape architect Lily Jencks, daughter of the late writer and garden designer Maggie Keswick Jencks, in whose name the Maggie's Centres were founded.

As with other such centres, the garden is intended to offer a tranquil respite from the stress and the bright efficiency of the hospital. Set among mature trees, ponds lend an air of serenity to the building, as if it were floating on water. Beside the ponds Jencks has laid out four 8 × 5-metre (26 x 16-foot) spaces, augmented with arrangements of traditional Chinese rocks and planted with plumerias and red bottlebrush trees. Jencks describes the centre's interior and garden spaces as having a certain synchronicity, and it is easy to see how, in such a favourable climate, that these spaces could be seen as a set of outdoor rooms.

There is a small Herb Garden, installed by the centre's visitors, but most of the landscaping was undertaken by a local firm, Urbis, which also planted the Hong Kong Wetland Centre and understood exactly which plants thrived in such a setting.

Although there is not a great deal of seasonal variation in the garden, there are some changes worth looking out for, such as the plumerias losing all their leaves before bursting into flower during the dry season. These blooms are red, as are many of the other flowers – the colour choice being apt for a garden that tries to reflect local horticultural traditions. Much of Jencks's inspiration came from her mother's book *Chinese Gardens* (1978) and, while the garden might serve as private tribute from Jencks to her mother, its service in helping to make cancer a little more bearable is an equally fitting legacy.

1—Rocks reminiscent of those used in classical Chinese gardens in Suzhou were imported from mainland China to complement the garden's plumeria and other flowering plants.
2, 3—Lily Jencks worked closely with the architect Frank Gehry to create a series of garden rooms, with colour schemes for the buildings to match those of the garden.
4—Wherever possible, the garden was designed to incorporate existing trees, such as this clump of palms.

# Tokachi Millennium Forest

Hokkaido, Japan

Dan Pearson, Fumiaki Takano, Mitsushige Hayashi

21st century

240 hectares / 593 acres

Humid Continental

Naturalistic / Sustainable / Woodland

The northernmost island of Japan, Hokkaido is a challenging environment, with some six months of snow each year and winter temperatures as low as −14°C (7°F). It is partly for that reason that the mountains of Hokkaido remain relatively remote, with wild bears and wild ponies in the extensive woods, although here as elsewhere in Japan extensive agriculture comes up to the very borders of the woods. There has been extensive logging, and the original forests have been replanted with larch, allowing a low-growing bamboo to colonize the forest floor. It was here that Mitsushige Hayashi bought a huge tract of land in a bid to offset the carbon footprint of his Japanese newspaper business, Tokachi Mainichi.

Mitsushige brought in the local designer Fumiaki Takano to begin restoring and protecting the original landscape in order to provide a place where Japanese city dwellers could interact with nature. The next call was further afield—to the British garden designer Dan Pearson.

Together, Fumiaki and Pearson worked to cut down the bamboo by years of strimming in order to allow the seeds of former plants held in the ground to renaturalize. There is a wide range of low plants, accessible by wooden walkways raised off the forest floor. They include marsh marigold, candelabra primulas and pale green cardiocrinum lilies.

Large areas of the forest had been felled, and these represented more of a challenge. The open ground was somewhat daunting for visitors, so Pearson set out to link them more closely with the mountains with a series of earthforms based on rolling hills. This area is known as the Earth Garden, its undulating, grass-coated earthforms like a series of dynamic waves.

Pearson also created the Meadow Garden, introducing an ornamental element to the natural landscape in order to underline the connection between wild plants and those that gardeners use at home. Pearson's massed planting includes ornamental shrubs and 35,000 perennials.

1—The Meadow Garden's massed plantings imitate the succession of natural plants that bloom together during the short summer season.
2—Near the cafe is a more structured area, with broad walkways and raised beds.
3—The undulating landforms of the Earth Garden provide striking contrast to the planting in the Meadow Garden.
4—Moisture-loving plants line one of the many streams that carry water off the nearby mountains.
5—Wooden walkways guide the visitor through the heart of the new growth in the forest without damaging the fragile natural environment that surrounds.

# Katsura Rikyu

(Katsura Imperial Villa)

Kyoto, Kyoto Prefecture, Japan

| |
|---|
| Prince Toshihito, Prince Toshitada |
| 17th century |
| 6.5 hectares / 16 acres |
| Humid Subtropical |
| Naturalistic / Stroll Garden / Water |

By the early Edo Period (1603–1867) Japan was ruled by warlords – the shoguns – and the emperors were reduced to being custodians of Japanese scholarship and aesthetics. Yet it was a role they filled superbly. The garden south of the Katsura Imperial Villa is considered the epitome of the stroll garden style, and is notable for its intimacy, detailing and complexity.

The villa was begun in the 1620s by Prince Hachijo no Miya Toshihito and completed in 1645 by his son Prince Toshitada, aided by the garden designer Kobori Masakazu (Enshu), as a retreat for refined living. The garden was originally conceived as a very large *roji* (tea garden), with teahouses, flagstone and stepping-stone paths, stone lanterns and *tsukubai* (stone washbasins), which still exist. In essence, this type of garden selects picturesque forms of nature and places them in a new context. The garden combines the beauty of the natural and the perfection of the artificial to epitomize *kirei sabi* (elegant beauty infused with a weathered rustic quality).

The garden is aligned in order best to observe the rising of the moon, for which a viewing platform was created. Surrounded by winding paths, the lake holds many islands, including a group of three that may have represented the Isles of the Blessed, which have their origin in Chinese mythology and Pure Land Buddhism. A clockwise route around the lake reveals a series of beaches and promontories, inlets crossed by stone-slab bridges and islets planted with specimen trees, stone lanterns, ornamental shrubs and carefully sculpted pines. There is also a miniature version of Amanohashidate – one of the Three Views of Japan, the celebrated scenic sights as defined by scholar Hayashi Gaho in 1643. The original is a long pine-covered sand bar, which connects two sides of Miyazu Bay in northern Kyoto Prefecture.

The planting combines to present a succession of carefully contrived views reflected in the still water. The garden also contains literary images from *The Tale of Genji*, a wistful evocation of the Heian Era (794–1185), when the Imperial family still had power. Although the lake has lost one of its islands and a long bridge, Toshihito would still recognize the garden very much as his.

1, 3—The lake at Katsura is framed with carefully shaped pine trees and teahouses; as the visitor follows the path, the view of the water changes constantly.
2—Part of the lake is a reconstruction of the famous causeway of Amanohashidate.
4, 5—Stone lanterns throughout the garden were used to guide visitors to teahouses or across earth-covered bridges, called *tsuchibashi*.

3

4

5

# Kenroku-en
(Garden of the Six Sublimities)

Kanazawa, Ishikawa, Japan

| |
|---|
| Maeda Family |
| 17th–19th century |
| 11.5 hectares / 28 acres |
| Humid Subtropical |
| Landscape / Stroll Garden / Vistas / Water / Woodland |

The Western impression of Japanese gardens is often restricted to dry Zen gardens or stroll gardens, but the Japanese also made landscape gardens, and Kenroku-en on the west coast of Honshu is arguably the finest example. Its name means 'Garden of the Six Sublimities' and was derived from *Famous Gardens of Luoyang*, written by the Chinese poet Li Gefei in the eleventh century. Kenroku-en embodies the six sublimities that Li Gefei believed comprised the perfect garden: antiquity, artifice, panoramic views, seclusion, spaciousness and abundant water.

Dating from the Edo Period, the garden was created by the fifth Lord Maeda Tsunanori between 1673 and 1681. Destroyed by fire, it was restored in 1774 by the eleventh Lord Harunaga, who also made the Emerald Waterfall, the oldest such feature in Japan.

Today the Kasumigaike Pond sits in the centre of a garden of variety and subtlety. Surrounding it are smaller ponds linked by intertwined paths and streams added by the twelfth Lord Naringa. Highlights of ornamentation include the Kotoji-toro, a two-legged stone lantern, and the Ganko-bashi (Flying Geese Bridge), eleven red stones laid out to resemble flying geese. Hills and valleys create views and vistas and provide the setting for buildings including the Kaiseki Pagoda and the teahouse Yugao-tei (1744), which is the oldest building in the garden.

But Kenroku-en is as much about its plants as its buildings. The garden boasts some 8,750 trees of 183 species, including ume or Japanese apricot (*Prunus mume*), whose flowers herald the arrival of spring. In April, 400 ornamental cherries together put on a show of blossoms. They are followed in summer by azaleas and in autumn by the coloured foliage of Japanese zelkova (*Zelkova serrata*) and maples (*Acer palmatum* cvs). The effect of the fallen leaves lying on the carpet of green moss is beautiful. In winter the garden is notable for its *yukitsuri*, a system of ropes attached to the top of the pine trees and tied to the lower branches to maintain their shape and protect them from damage by the weight of snow.

1 — Kenroku-en is dominated by the colours of foliage from trees and shrubs: a palette of varied greens in spring and summer, and reds and golds in autumn.
2 — The garden is notable for its extensive use of *yukitsuri*, or snow hanging, a system of ropes to protect trees from collapsing under the weight of snow in winter.
3 — Early pink cherry blossom catches the light in an unseasonable spring snow shower; the garden contains forty species of cherry tree.

1

4—The graceful pavilion and its
surrounding woodland are reflected
in the still waters of the lake.
5—Leaves litter the ground beneath
Japanese maples in early autumn. The path
leads visitors around the lake, revealing a
series of carefully constructed views.
6—The fountain plays next to a *yukitsuri*,
or snow hanging, against the glowing,
coppery colours of autumn foliage.
7—The shape of the two-legged Kotoji-toro
lantern that stands by the Kasumigaike
Pond is based on that of the Japanese harp.
8—Sekirei-jima ('Wagtail Island') takes its
name from a Japanese myth. The island has
a *tori* gate and three stones that represent
birth, marriage and death.

76

# Tofuku-ji

Kyoto, Kyoto Prefecture, Japan

| | |
|---|---|
| Mirei Shigemori | |
| 13th & 20th century | |
| 0.7 hectares / 1.75 acres (garden); 6.5 hectares / 15 acres (temple complex) | |
| Humid Subtropical | |
| Dry / Modern / Zen | |

Founded in 1236, Tofuku-ji is one of the great Zen Buddhist temple complexes of Kyoto. In 1939 the abbot requested the then unknown garden designer Mirei Shigemori to produce a master plan to improve the temple grounds over the next century. Shigemori was so inspired by the area around the *hojo* (abbot's residence) that he worked without a fee. In keeping with Zen beliefs, existing stones were used whenever possible, and waste was avoided. The result was an early Modernist masterpiece that carried Japanese garden design into the twentieth century.

Around the temple Shigemori created three distinctive gardens that blended Japanese traditions with an appreciation of Modernism. On entering the gardens on a raised walkway, the visitor comes first to an area featuring pillars from the temple's foundations, now arranged in the shape of the constellation of the Plough (the Big Dipper). Circles of raked gravel radiate from the pillars like cosmic waves.

The next garden is a sea of gravel, a *kare-sansui* (dry landscape), set within which are rock groupings that symbolize islands and take the form of cranes flying above spiral whirlpools raked into the gravel. At the northwest corner of this white-walled garden is a strong contrasting diagonal made by a moss-covered 'mountain range' that projects into the gravel ocean.

The third garden lies at one end of the building. It reinterprets the paddy fields of Japan by using azaleas pruned into squares and placed in a grid. The beds are defined by recycled kerbstones. On the north-facing aspect the grid design is repeated in what has become an iconic Shigemori design. Square grey paving stones formerly used for an entrance path are placed in a geometric pattern contrasting with the green moss, fading into the groundcover.

Tofuku-ji has other significant features, including a long wooden bridge overlooking a valley of maple trees, which provide spectacular autumn colour. There are other subtemples with gardens, but it is the groundbreaking work of Shigemori that truly inspires the visitor.

1—Rocks representing cranes on the wing fly above 'whirlpools' raked into the gravel in the Dry Garden.
2—In the garden near the entrance, pillars from the former foundations of the temple are arranged in a sea of raked gravel.
3, 4—A grid pattern is formed by paving stones that fade gradually into the moss groundcover; it echoes squares of clipped azaleas that reflect the paddy fields of Japan.
5—Moss-covered 'mountains' project into the gravel of the Dry Garden.

# Saiho-ji

Kyoto, Kyoto Prefecture, Japan

| |
|---|
| Muso Kokushi (Soseki) (attrib.) |
| 14th century |
| 2 hectares / 4.5 acres |
| Humid Subtropical |
| Dry / Moss / Water / Woodland / Zen |

Great gardens are about atmosphere: to enter the velvet-textured woodland garden of Saiho-ji is to be engulfed in another world. Muso Kokushi (Soseki), the priest who created the first garden here, believed gardens could provide the means by which Buddhist enlightenment might be achieved. It has been said of Saiho-ji, also known as Koke-dera (moss temple), that a visitor can contemplate not only 'the existence of nature but the nature of existence'.

This is not a garden of instant gratification; a visitor must reserve a place in advance by contacting the abbot. On arrival guests are welcomed to the temple to copy sutras or perform other calming activities that will leave them ready to experience the garden fully. There is a limited plant palette, with many maples and azaleas (for spring interest) as well as lotuses (for summer display) in the lake. All these contrast with the groundcover, which features anything up to 120 species of moss, depending on the sources consulted.

Most of the temple buildings that once dotted the landscape were destroyed in the fifteenth-century civil wars. In contrast to this destruction, the garden presents a version of the Western Paradise of the Amidha Buddha, and has a central pond in the shape of the calligraphic character for 'heart' or 'mind'. The water seems to gleam through the forest, illuminating the green world. Mosses and lichens cover every surface, although they are removed from the maple trunks by the gardeners to allow the grey bark to contrast with the green background. Kyoto provides the perfect climate of high humidity, rainfall and mild winters for a patina of green to accumulate and thrive.

There is a deep sense of mystery in the garden. A bamboo grove screens an important historic feature: a dry waterfall that is considered the first example of *kare-sansui* (dry landscape) in Japan, and which had a major influence on later gardens. The step-like horizontal stones are perfectly placed to resemble a cascade, and the viewer can readily imagine tumbling water.

Green is truly the colour of this garden for much of the year – so much so that the light itself seems to take on a greenish hue. However, in autumn the senses will instead be assailed by the vibrant contrast of the reds and oranges of the transforming maple leaves.

1—The pond forms the central feature of the garden and its representation of the Western Paradise of Amidha Buddhism.
2—The rich greens of the mosses seem to lend a greenish hue to the light.
3—The historic dry waterfall with its series of horizontal stones is considered the first example of a dry-landscape garden in Japan.

# Ryoan-ji

Kyoto, Kyoto Prefecture, Japan

| |
|---|
| Soami (attrib.) |
| 16th century |
| 0.02 hectares / 0.75 acre (courtyard); 48.5 hectares / 120 acres (gardens) |
| Humid Subtropical |
| Courtyard / Dry / Moss / Temple / Zen |

The raked-gravel *kare-sansui* (dry landscape garden) in front of the *hojo* (abbot's hall) at Ryoan-ji is one of the most compelling gardens in the world. This garden is one of the few that is instantly recognizable; not only does it live up to its hype, but also it exceeds all expectations. Its design combines simplicity and complexity and draws in both the eye and the mind.

The *kare-sansui* is used as an aid to meditation by the monks of the Myoshin-ji school of the Rinzai sect of Zen Buddhism. The earliest temple recorded on this site dates from 983, but it was destroyed during the Onin Wars and reconstructed near the end of the fifteenth century. It is generally believed that the *kare-sansui* dates from soon after. No one knows who laid out the garden, although Soami often receives credit. Being a flat, rectangular area measuring 23 × 10 metres (75 × 33 feet), the *kare-sansui* is far more abstract than other Zen gardens. Its tranquil arrangement of fifteen beautiful boulders encircled by moss and set within a bed of white, raked gravel is enhanced by buildings on two sides and by clay walls on the remaining sides. The earthy hues and abstract patterns of the walls were created by mixing sesame oil into the clay, which continues to exude it. The boulders are arranged so that, when viewing the garden from any angle, only fourteen are visible at one time. In the Buddhist world the number fifteen denotes completeness, and the fifteenth boulder becomes visible only when the viewer has reached 'Enlightenment'.

Sometimes deemed the highest expression of Zen art and teaching, and perhaps the single greatest masterpiece of Japanese culture, Ryoan-ji offers a more profound experience than a mere garden visit. All who go there, albeit briefly, enter another world. Yet there is more to Ryoan-ji than the *kare-sansui*. To the side of the *hojo* is a tranquil moss garden studded with towering bamboos, and in the landscape beyond are scenic hill views and the *oshidori-ike* (pond of mandarin ducks), created in the twelfth century. On the larger of the two islands, reached by a small bridge, is a shrine to Benten, the Shinto goddess of good luck.

1 — The fifteen stones in the *kare-sansui* are composed in five groups: one of five stones, two of three, and two of two stones. The stones are surrounded by moss and gravel, which is raked by the monks every day.
2 — The wall behind the garden has been stained by the oil leaching from the clay to create subtle brown and orange tones. In 1977 the tiled roof was restored using tree bark, as in the original. The former view of the mountain scenery beyond is now blocked by trees.

1

2

# Kinkaku-ji

(Temple of the Golden Pavilion)

Kyoto, Kyoto Prefecture, Japan

Shogun Ashikaga Yoshimitsu

14th century

4.5 hectares / 11 acres

Humid Subtropical

Historic / Stroll Garden / Zen

The most striking sight of Kinkaku-ji is appropriately the golden three-storey pavilion that stands at the heart of the reflecting Kyoko-chi (Mirror Pond). The Chinese-inspired *shariden* (a pavilion for viewing and relaxing) is the only structure remaining of the buildings and strolling garden created by Shogun Ashikaga Yoshimitsu for his retirement in 1394. Even the pavilion itself is a reconstruction from 1955 of the historic structure, which was destroyed in a fire. There are doubts as to whether the original pavilion was actually gilded in gold leaf, but the modern structure makes a striking sight regardless, and is especially beautiful on a sunny day or after a fall of snow.

The composition of building and pool is testament to the highly developed aesthetic of Yoshimitsu, Japan's military ruler. Kinkaku-ji is a supreme example of the use of scale and perspective to increase the apparent size of a garden – a technique pioneered in early Chinese gardens and perfected in Japan. The foreground of rocks and exquisitely pruned trees – mainly pines and maples – is of small scale, merging seamlessly into and reflected by the sinuous peninsulas and bays of the pond. The rocks and islands with their trees create a mid-ground that blends into the wooded background, and the whole contrived composition unites with the borrowed landscape of Mount Kinugasa, which rises beyond the garden.

The pond may have been part of an earlier thirteenth-century *shinden* (main hall) garden, but Yoshimitsu augmented it with rocks and ten small islands. He thus created a landscape that evoked the Chinese iconography of Pure Land Buddhism, with its seas and mountain ranges: Mount Horai (home to the Taoist immortals); *kame-jima* (the turtle island); and *tsuru-jima* (the crane island). After Yoshimitsu's death the complex became a temple of Zen Buddhism, officially known as Rokuon-ji (Deer Garden Temple).

The visitor can walk around about half of the lake's perimeter and enjoy the ever-changing vistas from established vantage points. A woodland walk enlivened by streams and a lake winds up the hill behind the temple to a teahouse at the garden's summit.

1 — Beside small-scale, carefully pruned trees, the golden pavilion is reflected in the Mirror Pond on a still day, creating a feeling of harmony between heaven and earth.
2, 3 — The carefully scaled trees and typology of the lake and its islands reflect the principles of Pure Land Buddhism, which influenced Japanese garden design before Zen Buddhism.

# Ginkaku-ji

(Temple of the Silver Pavilion)

Kyoto, Kyoto Prefecture, Japan

| |
|---|
| Soami (attrib.) |
| 15th century |
| 3 hectares / 7.5 acres |
| Humid Subtropical |
| Dry / Stroll Garden / Vistas / Zen |

The black-and-white Silver Pavilion might appear to be something of a misnomer – it never received its intended covering of silver leaf – but the buildings and the celebrated *kare-sansui*, or dry, garden were both designed to take advantage of nights when they are bathed in moonlight. Shogun Ashikaga Yoshimasa created the Moon Viewing Garden to spend his retirement away from the hurly-burly of Kyoto. There he could indulge in artistic pursuits, write poetry and enjoy Noh theatre. In his will Yoshimasa arranged that the villa be converted to a Zen temple, Jisho-ji ('Temple of Shining Mercy').

The visitor enters the garden near the *hon-do* (main hall) and the Togu-do Hall. The latter contains a room considered to be a prototype of the teahouse, a fashionable garden feature from the late fifteenth century onwards. In front is the dry garden, a later addition from the Edo period. The taller of the two sculptured mounds of sand is the Moon-Viewing Heights, a truncated cone whose shape echoes that of Mount Fuji or perhaps Mount Shumisen, the iconic mountain of Buddhism. Or does the shape simply represent a mound of rice? The larger, horizontal expanse is the carefully raked Sea of Silver Sand, which sparkles in the light of the sun and moon.

The two-storey Silver Pavilion is positioned in front of a strolling garden that forms an interesting and unusual contrast with the dry garden. The naturalistic miniature landscape – attributed to the painter and garden designer Soami – is a succession of picturesque scenes inspired by Japanese and Chinese literature and is centred on an informal, sinuous pool with rocky shores and stone-slab bridges. The pool is planted with a combination of artistically shaped pines that arch out over the water, spring-flowering azaleas, and maples that imbue the garden with flaming hues in autumn. The lush groundcover is a garden of different types of moss. A path leads the visitor up through the wooded hill behind the temple complex, where a series of viewpoints offer elegant vistas down over the gardens and out across the city beyond.

1, 2—The strolling garden is arranged around an informal pool, which forms the centrepiece of a miniature landscape, with carefully shaped pines and azaleas growing close to the rocky banks.
3, 4—The Sea of Silver Sand is carefully raked into sinuous strips of contrasting textures. Rising above it is a truncated mound whose shape may be intended to represent a mountain or possibly a bowl of rice, a key symbol of health and prosperity.

# Awaji Yumebutai, Hyakudanen Botanical Gardens

Awaji City, Hyogo Prefecture, Japan

| | |
|---|---|
| Tadao Ando | |
| 20th century | |
| 0.7 hectares / 1.7 acres | |
| Humid Subtropical | |
| Botanical / Memorial / Modern / Terraces | |

No set of gardens looks quite like Awaji Yumebutai, and no other gardens serve quite the same purpose. Yumebutai ('stage of dreams') is an international seaside conference centre and garden as well as a memorial to the 6,000 victims of the great Hanshin earthquake of 1995. Although the disaster is best known for destroying much of the city of Kobe, its epicentre was actually at the northern end of Awaji Island, in Osaka Bay. The land there had already been heavily disturbed a few years earlier by excavations undertaken to build an artificial island to support the new Kansai International Airport, some 20 kilometres (12 miles) away.

When the famous Japanese architect and Pritzker Prize laureate Tadao Ando took over the development, he replanted the region with indigenous saplings before imposing his singular vision of a highly architectural series of horticultural spaces. The most striking of these is the Hyakudanen – a terraced flower garden of 100 square beds each of 4.5 square metres (48 square feet) arranged to fit the topography of the hillside. The design is so distinctive that it can be made out clearly on Google Earth. In person visitors can wander between the plots, enjoying a wide variety of flowering plants, including an extensive selection of chrysanthemums, which are kept in bloom all year round.

Yumebutai is also home to Japan's largest greenhouse. Known as the Miracle Planet Museum of Plants, this botanical hothouse takes human's coexistence with nature as its theme, and prides itself on its range of ferns, succulents and tropical plants. However, it also displays a series of houseplants in domestic settings, and has another area that is dedicated to demonstrating various ways in which plants can be cultivated in urban environments.

Rather than being set aside as a distinct pleasure for garden-lovers, horticulture is a key part of the whole Yumebutai development. The gardens are worked in among restaurants, theatres and luxury hotels, just as a cinema or golf course might be included in less attractive, less ambitious leisure developments. Because it was opened on 9 March 2000, Awaji Yumebutai is strictly speaking a twentieth-century garden, yet Ando's vision and scope place it decades ahead of its time.

1—Ando's design for the Hyakudanen covered a devastated hillside with 100 linked terraces planted with species from around the world. In general, African and Asian specimens grow on the lower terraces, American and tropical plants in the middle and European plants near the top.

# Adachi Museum of Art

Yasugi City, Shimane, Japan

| | |
|---|---|
| Adachi Zenko | |
| 20th century | |
| 16.5 hectares / 40 acres | |
| Humid Subtropical | |
| Modern / Tea Garden / Viewing / Zen | |

Established in 1970, the Adachi Museum of Art is not visited by many Western tourists. This is a pity, because not only is Adachi Zenko's private art collection superb, but also the five separate gardens surrounding the buildings represent an entirely modern expression of Japan's long heritage of garden-making and painting.

The Adachi Museum takes the concept of the 'viewing garden' to its natural conclusion. Like the paintings inside, the gardens (with the exception of the Juryu-an Garden) are only to be looked at. They are works of art to be contemplated, not to be experienced by being in. This effect is heightened by the architecture, which often frames specific views from the buildings.

Adachi crafted five individual gardens that merge seamlessly, although each has its own character. The White Gravel and Pine Garden is a landscape of gnarled Japanese black pine (*Pinus thunbergii*), dome-shaped azaleas, sculptural rocks and white gravel against the backdrop of the 15-metre (50-foot) Kikaku-no-taki waterfall. The Kyoto-style Moss Garden, by the designer Saichi Kojima, contrasts Japanese red pine (*Pinus densiflora*) with a white-and-black *namako* wall. The Juryu-an (teahouse) Garden, with its traditional pavilion, features flaming red maple foliage in the autumn, while the Pond Garden is dominated by a pool with carp and a slab bridge. The Dry Landscape Garden acknowledges the meditative *kare-sansui* gardens of Zen Buddhist temples, and uses white gravel to symbolize a river fed by a central waterfall represented by three standing rocks circled by azaleas.

Adachi Zenko was as fastidious about his garden as his art, and travelled all over Japan to seek out trees and rocks that had especially eye-catching and artistic shapes. The spring- and summer-flowering azaleas are evergreen and provide year-round contrast to the conifers, while in autumn the foliage of the Japanese maples (*Acer palmatum* cultivars) adds a seasonal and contrasting fiery note.

1—In the White Gravel and Pine Garden the architectural forms of the black pines contrast with the soft mounds of azaleas and water-worn rocks against the backdrop of an artificial waterfall.
2—The stone bridge, rock formation, and trees in the Pond Garden were positioned so that they can be seen from every direction.
3—In the Dry Landscape Garden, rocks surrounded by azaleas symbolize a waterfall feeding a river of gravel.
4—The red pine trees in the Moss Garden grow at the same slanted angle they grew at in their original mountain home.

3

4

# Gotanjyou-ji

Takefu, Hukui Prefecture, Japan

Shunmyo Masuno

21st century

Less than 0.2 hectares / 0.5 acres

Humid Subtropical

Gravel / Moss / Temple / Zen

In this gem of a contemporary Japanese temple garden, the life of a Zen monk is celebrated in moss, gravel, stone and trees. Its designer, Shunmyo Masuno, is head priest of Kenko-ji in Yokohama. As part of his Zen practice he creates internationally renowned gardens. At Gotanjyou-ji, he designed an L-shaped garden to form a physical connection between the temple buildings as well as a place to stimulate reflection.

The informally shaped, moss-covered mounds with carefully embedded rocks are cut through by a grey gravel 'stream' seemingly flowing from a large upright rock. The latter represents the priest Keizan Zenji, who disseminated Zen teaching throughout Japan, while the stream refers to his words reaching out to his disciples. Two more standing stones, colonized by mosses and ferns, are further representations – one of the Kannon Bosatsu (the personification of mercy) and the other of Keizan Zenji's mother, as if bent in prayer to the Kannon Bosatsu. In this gently rolling moss landscape, five different species of tree have been positioned to lead the eye up to the eaves of the grey-tiled roofs of the surrounding buildings. These trees create height in the planting and provide a contrast of foliage textures with the moss groundcover, while the forms of their trunks are outlined against the white walls of the buildings.

The most dramatic feature of the space is the pathway that cuts through the design. Its formality emphasizes the informality of the rounded mounds and curving gravel. The path has a narrow curb of grey stone, which frames the black pebbles through which are placed rectangular stone pavers in pairs; these are laid as diamonds, controlling the users' pace and direction of travel through the courtyard. The path changes direction twice in order to present a view of the Keizan Zenji stone beneath a red-leaved maple. This tree's foliage contrasts with the dominant green plantings in order to show the importance of the stone in the story being revealed by the garden.

This garden is a quiet place with a subtle palette of materials enlivened by the glistening of water on the stones and black pebbles of the path, the scent of the damp ground, the velvet texture of mosses and the different tree shapes. As Shunmyo Masuno has said, 'The garden is a special spiritual place where the mind dwells.'

1 — The main path provides straight lines and angular turns to contrast with the contours of the grassy mounds and the sinuous stream of gravel that represents the priest Keizan Zenji's teachings spreading out into the world.

# The Jim Thompson Garden

Bangkok, Thailand

| |
|---|
| Jim Thompson |
| 20th century |
| 0.2 hectares / 0.5 acre |
| Tropical |
| Foliage / Urban / Water |

In a city as crowded as Bangkok, it's no mean feat to create a tranquil, restorative garden. But on the banks of a *klong*, or canal, in the heart of the city, Jim Thompson created a compound filled with a calm and contemplative atmosphere that has resisted the impact of surrounding development for more than half a century. The charismatic American expatriate also did much to revive a flagging Thai silk industry before he mysteriously disappeared on a weekend excursion.

Now a museum, what Thompson called his House on the Klong comprises six antique teak buildings relocated from the Thai countryside. Interior and exterior are seamlessly linked by covered patios, balconies and colonnades; many of the smaller outdoor terraces are edged by low brick walls and foliage plants that most Westerners know only as houseplants, such as philodendron, anthurium, caladium, dieffenbachia, scindapsus, rhaphidophora and figs.

With an expat's enthusiasm for his adopted culture, Thompson set out to create the feeling of a jungle rather than replicate his Thai friends' preference for topiary and cultivated lawns. But this urban jungle is never allowed to revert to a true natural state: the abundance of growth embraces rather than suffocates, thanks to careful maintenance and the space-enhancing palms (betel nut, footstool and fan), flowering bananas and a giant rain tree (*Albizia saman*) that have grown here since before Thompson bought the property. Beneath the canopy, brick paths lead to unexpected *plein-air* displays of Thompson's art collection, ranging from the traditional spirit house that anchors the northeastern corner of the property to a seventh-century limestone Buddha and the 600-year-old ceramics grouped on terraces or used to house miniature ponds.

Water is a central feature of the garden, which was renovated several decades ago by luxury-resort designer Bill Bensley and garden expert William Warren. Urns hold baby koi, water lettuces and water-lilies, and larger, sunken ponds are home to carp, turtles and fountains that introduce the calming sound of water in motion.

1 — Layers of shade-tolerant plants with broad leaves crowd around a pond. The green foliage contrasts with the red paint used to preserve the wood of the buildings.
2 — Brick paths set off the colours of the foliage and allow for changes in the hardness of the ground beneath.
3 — Red *Heliconia* bracts and tree ferns form an intermediate layer between the groundcover and the tree canopy.
4 — A traditional spirit house is meant to protect the property and its inhabitants.

# Howie's HomeStay

Chiang Mai, Thailand

Bill Bensley, Jirachai Rengthong

21st century

2 hectares / 5 acres

Tropical

Exotic / Sculpture / Water

Most good gardens respond to local geography, history and culture, but few have a founding myth. The garden surrounding this northern Thai dream home in the eastern foothills of the Himalayas is unique in that respect. Here the US-born, Thailand-based landscape architect Bill Bensley has constructed a private Shangri-La, based on the fabled land of pleasure and perfection. Pedants might point out that this mythical haven was supposed to be at the western end of the Himalayas, rather than the eastern, yet Bensley's creations are less about historical accuracy than aesthetic enjoyment. The designer, who is best known for his resort designs, collaborates closely with his head horticulturalist, Jirachai Rengthong, to create 'ruinscapes': charming, cheerful gardens that sit somewhere between a sculpture garden, an adult play park and an Indiana Jones film set.

This private commission, for a house-cum-guest house in the Mae Rim district of Chiang Mai, close to the border with Laos and Burma and about 700 kilometres (435 miles) north of Bangkok, takes advantage of the region's warm, wet conditions. A river runs along the front of the seven-structure, open-plan home, and a series of fish ponds, swimming pools and water features occupies much of the grounds at the rear. The ponds are planted with lotuses and crisscrossed with bridges fashioned from railway sleepers, while yellow and giant bamboo, heliconias, plumerias, sage flowers, banana trees, betel nut palms and fig trees grow in the grounds, surrounded by sculptures and garden ornaments, winding paths and magnificent *salas* (gazebos). In the distance, visitors might make out a herd of elephants or water buffalo – traditional agriculture in the local paddy fields – or the outline of the Mae Rim Mountains.

The warm temperatures mean that plants always thrive in the garden, although visitors might want to avoid the rainy season, which lasts from July until October. As owner Howard Feldman told *Architectural Digest*, 'What happens when it rains? You get wet!'

1, 2, 4—The entire western part of Howie's HomeStay is given over to a large water garden, which is surrounded by a series of traditional *salas*, or gazebos, whose shape is echoed in the traditional lanterns that light the garden after dusk. The buildings are made from yellow teak, which is said to repel insects.
3, 5—The garden combines strikingly modern decoration with traditional Thai vernacular forms, such as the wooden bridge. The garden features 350 different species – and Bill Bensley and his partner Jirachai Rengthong bought and installed each plant individually.

# Bang Pa-in

Ayutthaya, Thailand

| |
|---|
| King Chulalongkorn |
| 19th century |
| Tropical |
| Landscape / Palace / Water |

Still a residence for the Thai royal family, the Bang Pa-in Palace is surrounded by a vast landscaped garden with manicured lawns, promenades shaded by tall hopea and banyan trees, and vibrant plantings of lotus and ginger, all surveyed by entire topiary families of elephants and other animals.

The complex is a wonderland of ornate buildings, lakes and 'floating' temples built on a sliver of land beside the Chao Phraya River, which forms an artificial island owing to a canal dug along the eastern side. The first royal residence was constructed here in the seventeenth century, outside the then capital, Ayutthaya. The site later became home to a Buddhist monastery built in the form of a Gothic church. However, when Ayutthaya was razed by Burmese invaders in 1767, the ruined palace was returned to the forest.

The garden complex seen today has been in development since 1872, first under the auspices of King Chulalongkorn and then maintained and added to by his heirs. It comprises ten main buildings, divided between Inner and Outer palaces. Chulalongkorn's vision was a summer palace that would rival Versailles and the Forbidden City in its splendour, and he commanded his architects to use a range of building styles. The royal residence is in a Western classical style, while across a covered bridge is a reception hall in the style of a Swiss chalet. In places, the careful landscaping, the balustraded canals and the series of artfully contrived reflections in the lake are reminiscent of a grand English country estate from the eighteenth century.

Other sites include the pagoda tower and a Chinese-style throne room. One of the first buildings visitors come across is a Khmer shrine carved from stone and shaded by a mighty banyan tree. It stands near the entrance in a place where similar shrines have stood since antiquity. Further into the park, in a sheltered area of the Inner Palace near the eastern boundary, are some simple stone obelisks in a quiet, unfussy garden. The largest is a memorial to Queen Sunantha Kumarirat, the favoured wife of King Chulalongkorn.

1, 4—Simple arrangements of green lawns and low clipped planting define walkways through the park that take visitors past reflected views of the palace and the many pavilions.
2—The Sage's Lookout and the Chinese Pavilion stand at the edge of the water.
3—A family of topiary elephants stands on a lawn near the palace; elsewhere, topiary rabbits nibble the grass near a pool.
5—A gazebo festooned in climbing plants provides some shade in the gardens.

# Bay South, Gardens by the Bay

Singapore, Singapore

| | |
|---|---|
| Grant Associates | |
| 21st century | |
| 54 hectares / 130 acres | |
| Tropical | |
| Conservatory / Display / Park / Sustainable / Urban / Water | |

Gardens by the Bay is an appropriately cutting-edge garden for Singapore, a leader of Asia's twenty-first-century economic boom. Part-national conservatory, part-theme park, the two gardens – they will eventually be linked by a third – are a startling combination of planting and architecture.

The idea of creating a sustainable garden on Singapore's waterfront was announced in 2005, and contracts were awarded after an international design competition. The Bay East Garden by Gustafson Porter opened in 2010 but remains work in progress. The series of leaf-shaped gardens will eventually be based on the theme of water.

The Bay South garden by Grant Associates, in contrast, made a bold statement as soon as it opened in 2012 to showcase tropical horticulture. Its layout is based on a tropical vanda orchid flower, the national flower of Singapore, with a focus on two vast conservatories near the waterfront. The Flower Dome is home to seven different gardens representing microclimates from the Mediterranean and semiarid tropical regions. In the other dome, the Cloud Forest incorporates the 42-metre (138-foot) Cloud Mountain, with its 35-metre (115-foot) waterfall; it is suitable for plants native to cool, moist, tropical montane regions.

In addition to the two domes, there are numerous so-called Supertrees around the garden. These splaying structures – like mature trees without the wait – are up to sixteen storeys tall and support a living 'skin' of plants such as bromeliads. They also play a key role in the garden's sustainability, harvesting solar energy by means of photovoltaic cells. At night they come alive with sound and light.

Another part of the garden is the Heritage Gardens. These four themed gardens introduce the visitor to the history and culture of the main peoples in Singapore's history. They comprise the Malay Garden, which highlights traditional fruit and medicinal plants; the Colonial Garden, which displays the crops and plants on which Singapore's wealth was based; and the Chinese and Indian gardens, which reflect Singapore's various ethnic influences.

1—An aerial walkway in the Supertree Grove gives visitors a spectacular view over the garden.
2, 5—The Flower Dome replicates a cool-dry environment, allowing it to grow plants from arid and desert regions around the world.
3, 4—Inside the Cloud Forest Dome, an artificial mountain has been densely planted with orchids, ferns, bromeliads, begonias, pitcher plants and other epiphytic species that usually grow in tropical highlands up to 2,000 metres (6,500 feet) above sea level.

1

# Villa Bebek

Mertasari, Sanur, Bali, Indonesia

| Made Wijaya |
| 20th century |
| 0.3 hectares / 0.7 acres |
| Tropical |
| Courtyard / Exotic / Water |

Australian-born garden designer Made Wijaya has lived in Bali since 1973, but the garden he has created at his own home, Villa Bebek, reveals his intuitive understanding of and empathy with the lush tropical growth of the island's natural rainforest. Wijaya's garden – dominated by an intense palette of jungle greens – is ornate and planned, yet retains a highly naturalistic feel. Despite the garden's suburban setting, it feels as if the space has merely been borrowed from the natural vegetation.

In fact, like many of the more than 700 gardens Wijaya has designed since establishing his business, Villa Bebek can be maintained only through a level of control as demanding as in any traditional Western garden. Wijaya's own garden influences stretch far beyond Southeast Asia to include English country gardens – he has referred to his own style as 'the tropical Cotswolds look' – formal gardens in France, Spain and Italy, designers such as Roberto Burle Marx (see pages 448 and 453) and the Wirtz family (see pages 129 and 210), and the botanical gardens of his native Australia.

The villa – which is also Wijaya's studio and office – is based on a characteristic Balinese arangement of thatched buildings, courtyards for outdoor living and ponds to keep the surroundings cool. Although the garden is relatively small, it has forty-eight different courtyards that Wijaya uses to experiment with ornamental trees and shrubs that reflect Balinese traditions. Around the swimming pool, the vegetation is kept low in order to admit more sunlight, but elsewhere taller trees blend in with the coconut palms of the plantation outside the garden. The ponds are full of water lilies. Colourful bougainvillea climbs over the house, and the pergola by the pool is swathed in white *Thunbergia grandiflora*.

Throughout the garden traditional sculptures collected by Wijaya and contemporary works commissioned from Indonesian artists add fascinating detail. There are many thatched-roof lanterns that create a magical atmosphere at dusk, when the air in the garden and on the veranda of the house is thick with the scent of plumeria and other shrubs.

1—A lily pond by the house is framed by pink bougainvillea and spiky *Pandanus veitchii* that grows behind one of the garden's many traditional lanterns.
2—Wijaya uses traditional Balinese materials and breaks up the garden with local artworks of various dates.
3—The area around the swimming pool is left relatively open to admit more sunlight.
4—The dense planting at the edge of this pool may appear naturalistic but is in fact carefully orchestrated to create depth and a variety of shape, size and texture.

# Goa Gajah Temple Garden

Near Ubud, Bali, Indonesia

| Unknown |
| 9th century |
| Tropical |
| Historic / Rainforest / Religious / Water |

The garden at Goa Gajah is in some ways not really a garden at all. It is a sacred haven. But, like a garden, it is separated from the landscape around it, and its ornament and architecture combine to provide a heightened appreciation of nature as it is and as it can be controlled. The ancient buildings – the temple was carved out of the rock by Buddhists in the ninth century AD but later became a Hindu shrine – are a spiritual space. For the Balinese, being outdoors in gardens is not simply a matter of recreation or aesthetics: it is deeply connected with a spiritual experience. The Balinese form of Hinduism – about 95 percent of the population are Hindu – is closely related to the idea of open-air worship. Balinese temples – or *pura* – use walls to define a series of enclosures.

The shrine at Goa Gajah is situated in a ravine near the meeting of two streams, a confluence that the Balinese believe produces a positive, magical energy. Its main feature is the so-called Elephant Cave, an opening in a rock wall carved into a face of which the cave forms the mouth (the effect is similar to that of the Renaissance grotto at Bomarzo in Italy, see page 300). The carved 'elephant' that may have given the cave its name is more probably the Hindu earth god Bhoma, as befits a site bordered by paddy fields where the massive roots of ancient figs spread over the ground. The cave contains a statue of the elephant god, Ganesh, and *lingams* representing Shiva.

Nearby is a pool that was probably used for ritual cleansing or gathering holy water. It is fed by the water from six fountains carved in the shape of female angels. Beyond the immediate area of the cave, however, the garden holds far more attractions. A long staircase twists and turns as it climbs down into a valley shaded by the canopy of tall vine-tangled trees. The path leads between moss-covered rocks and red-flowered shrubs to a bridge that crosses the river where it rushes over a rocky waterfall near the ruins of a Buddhist temple. Here the crowded area near the cave seems like another world, and visitors and worshippers alike enjoy the tranquil landscape of emerald green lawns and moss, paths and stairs and venerable trees.

1, 5—The ample water is harnessed to create a variety of formal and informal pools within the rocky valley.
2—The terrifying face carved into the rock has been identified as either the Hindu god Bhoma or a Balinese demon named Rangda.
3—The pool where worshippers collect holy water was fed by six fountains – five have been restored – shaped as Hindu angels.
4—The roots of an ancient fig tree spread over the ground in a characteristic tangle.

# Arctic-Alpine Botanic Garden

Tromsø, Norway

| | |
|---|---|
| Dr Finn Haugli | |
| 20th century | |
| 2 hectares / 5 acres | |
| Subarctic Continental | |
| Alpine / Botanical / Modern / Naturalistic / Rock | |

This garden owes its existence to the warming Gulf Stream, without which growing conditions would be even more challenging. Some 355 kilometres (220 miles) inside the Arctic Circle, this is the world's most northerly botanic garden. It focuses extensively – although not exclusively – on plants from northern polar regions and alpine habitats that are adapted to two months each year of constant darkness and a short, intensive growing season.

The Tromsø University Museum opened this small garden in 1994 and decided that, although it was primarily a botanical collection, it should look as natural as possible. The garden creates appropriate conditions for the plants while also re-creating their natural habitats in settings made even more attractive by the rock formations clearly visible among the plants. As an adaptation to their climate, alpine plants tend not to be very tall, although many have brightly coloured and elegantly shaped flowers.

The garden stands on an east-facing slope, with views over the Tromsdalen valley and across the sea to Tromsdalstinden Mountain. Beyond the formal beds at the entrance, gravel paths wind up the hill, leading the visitor through a variety of habitats created to provide each plant collection with its favoured growing conditions – nestled between rocks, on a scree slope, near a stream and so on.

In spring a striking show of saxifrages lights up the garden while snow still lies on the ground, before summer brings a spectacular riot of blooms. The garden is especially renowned for its collections of chirpy lewisias, gentians, vibrant primulas, elegant and refined *Meconopsis* and, everywhere, drifts of Arctic poppies in orange, yellow and white. From the top of the garden there is a spectacular panoramic view with no boundary to mark the terminus. The garden seamlessly blurs into a patch of natural sorbus woodland, with a dense understorey of grasses and wild flowers.

1 — As primulas peek through in early summer, the Rock and Stream Garden at the top of the hill offers spectacular views of Tromsdalstinden Mountain.
2 — *Meconopsis punicea* provide a striking show of colour among the neutral rocks and mosses.
3 — Mixed alpine poppies, *Papaver alpinum*, grow in colourful drifts in a rock field.
4 — The gardens are renowned for their collection of saxifrages, such as this delicate *Saxifraga burseriana* 'Ganymede'.
5 — The sculptural forms of *Saxifraga* x *arendsii* 'Purple Robe' and other low-growing saxifrages add softness to the dramatic natural landscape.

# Villa Mairea

Noormarkku, Finland

Alvar Aalto

20th century

0.6 hectares / 1.5 acres

Subarctic Continental

Modern / Naturalistic / Water / Woodland

Set amid a forest of dark green pines and silver birch, Villa Mairea was designed and built between 1937 and 1939 by the Finnish Modernist architect Alvar Aalto as a guest house and rural retreat. The commission was an opportunity for Aalto to experiment with thoughts, styles and materials, but the result is surprisingly cohesive. Not so revolutionary, however, is the 'L' shape ground plan – a form common in Scandinavian aristocratic homes. The house encloses the courtyard garden in its angle on two sides. The sauna is connected to the house by a canopy walk; both are grass-roofed, which helps to define the form of the garden, extends the link between garden and domestic space, and generates a sympathetic transition between the house and the natural forest surroundings.

Both house and garden make full use of rigid angles and contrasting wave-like forms. In the garden this free-form motif is found in the shape of the swimming pool. This close to the Arctic Circle, a pool may seem an unlikely feature, but it provides perfect balance within the composition. It also influenced another famous pool – that created at El Novillero in California by Thomas Church (see page 364), who visited Aalto in 1937.

The interior and garden are also united in other ways, such as the large glass door that opens from the living room and the outdoor fireplace, the chimney of which forms the stairs to the roof terrace. Here a sinuous white metal rail – a typical Modernist feature – borders slate stepping stones set in gravel. The area offers fine views over the garden and surrounding forest, and is a curious variation on the Japanese *kare-sansui* (dry garden).

There are other traditions of outward-looking gardens that unite a house and its surroundings, such as those of the Italian Renaissance, as at Villa d'Este (see page 302), and the English landscapes of Lancelot 'Capability' Brown such as Blenheim, where the country house is adrift in a sea of sward (see page 153). However, the subtle unity that Aalto achieved on a small scale here is as sublime as it is effective.

1—The L-shaped villa is intimately set into a garden that both unifies and celebrates the opposition of the artificial and the natural. Slender poles holding up the entrance porch echo the trunks of the tall pines that surround the garden, so that the sensation of being within the forest remains even inside the house.
2—The grass-roofed sauna stands behind a swimming pool designed to echo the curves of a natural lake.

1

2

# Wij Garden

Ockelbo, Sweden

Simon Irvine, Lars Krantz, Ulf Nordfjell

21st century

0.1 hectare / 0.3 acres

Humid Continental

Formal / Modern / Rooms / Roses / Woodland

For Ockelbo, 225 kilometres (140 miles) north of Stockholm, the seventeenth-century estate of Wij (pronounced *vee*) is far more than its two gardens. Wij has revived the community and put it on the map. Since 2000 the biodynamic gardener Lars Krantz has been instrumental in creating a horticultural centre in a region known for iron-ore mining rather than gardening. Despite long winters and short summers, Krantz has showcased what can grow in the local acidic soil, and made the area an inspiration to its many visitors.

Krantz's first commission was the Rose Garden by Simon Irvine. Its formal layout is given a contemporary twist with perennials, grasses and clematis, adding layers of planting interest. Slatted-timber screens protect the plants during the harsh winters. Supports for climbing plants and border edges are made from iron and steel, as a link to the region's natural resources.

In 2004 Krantz invited the landscape architect Ulf Nordfjell to design the Forest Garden. Inspired by Sweden's native landscape, Nordfjell combined strong-lined plane trees with modern features made from timber, steel and granite. The Forest Garden embodies both Nordfjell's and Wij's philosophy of relating gardens to the surrounding landscape. It is rich with references to the culture of northern Scandinavia and its past inhabitants.

Seven rooms represent different aspects of Sweden's landscape: heath, bog, tarn, forest margin, birch, pine trees and open sky. Hardscaping materials are used: wood, stone, steel, glass, clinker and gravel. Pale grey timber walls partition the space, echoing vernacular architecture, while openings frame vistas and views inside and beyond the garden. Steel structures form larger arches that support climbing plants, frame views of the sky or focus the eye on garden views.

Steel-sculpted, obelisk-like trellises support clematis and resemble small, parasol-canopied trees amid real pine trees. Shallow steel tanks of dark water represent the tarns of northern Sweden, while other simple metal vessels create contemporary containers for mosses and other low-growing plants.

At Wij the beauty of the landscape is enhanced by modern garden design that uses native materials to create a remarkable understated elegance.

1, 2, 3—Simon Irvine's Rose Garden gives the formal garden a contemporary slant, with iron and steel supports, slatted fences and plantings of perennials and grasses that are tied to keep them upright.
4, 5, 6—Ulf Nordfjell's Forest Garden uses traditional Scandinavian materials that help link the garden to the landscape beyond.

4

5

6

# Enköpings Parker

(Enköping Parks)

Enköping, Uppsala, Sweden

| |
|---|
| Various |
| 20th century |
| Various sizes |
| Humid Continental |
| Naturalistic / New Perennial / Parks |

Enköping is less a garden than a whole town, with twenty-five parks unified by the same type of plants. Parks are expensive, and in the early 1980s, at a time when it planted more than 35,000 annuals each year, Enköping Parks and Sports Department decided to adopt a new strategy. It would plant mainly perennials, and in doing so create parks of greater inspirational and visual impact. In 1982 the first 400 perennials were planted; by 2004 they covered 20,000 square metres (24,000 square yards), and today some of Europe's outstanding garden designers have helped to give the parks the ambience of private gardens. Set within a designed and structured framework, each border is planted with 'planting communities'. These are not traditional borders but a harmonious combination of bulbs, perennials and ornamental grasses, shrubs and trees. The mixture results in the longest possible season of interest, with naturalistic planting sympathetic to natural habitats.

The parks are as varied as they are numerous. They have breathed new life into existing public spaces, such as the nineteenth-century Afzelius Place. The famous Drömparken (Dream Park) was designed by Piet Oudolf in 1996 and enlarged in 2002. It features blue streams of three kinds of *Salvia nemorosa* complemented by 217 other types of perennial and ornamental grass, while the tall, cylindrical beech hedges give height and form in winter. The Railway Park was designed by the Swedish landscape architect Ulf Nordfjell with a pergola, water and perennials, while the Herbal Garden stimulates the senses: pride of place goes to the humble horseradish – the old symbol of the town.

Enköping is always looking to the future, and its latest additions are the pocket parks, such as the peony-filled Kölnback's Park. Adapted to their locality and clearly defined as 'rooms' by clipped hedges, the pocket parks are smaller, more intimate places, with planting intended to be dynamic and inspirational. Taken collectively, Enköping's parks make for a charming town and help to fulfil the authorities' aims of 'attractive living and education', 'stimulating experiences' and 'democracy and participation'.

1, 2—In the Dream Garden, tall, cylindrical beech hedges grow among 220 perennials, including blue streams of *Salvia nemorosa*.
3— The Blue Garden was created in 1998 in honour of Stockholm being made European Capital of Culture.
4—In the Herbal Garden, pride of place goes to a white-flowering radish, which is the emblem of the town.
5—Autumn leaves lend colour to Fish Market Square, an old marketplace where paved areas are surrounded by romantic planting.

# Linnaeus Home and Garden

Hammarby, Uppsala, Sweden

| | |
|---|---|
| Carl Linnaeus | |
| 18th century | |
| 340 hectares / 840 acres (estate) | |
| Humid Continental | |
| Botanical / Historic / Naturalistic / Plantsman / Woodland | |

Hammarby is steeped in botanical history: it was the home of one of the most influential of all plant enthusiasts: Carl Linnaeus. In 1741, when he became professor of medicine at Uppsala University, medicine was a plant-based science. To avoid confusion about plant types, Linnaeus developed the two-word (binominal) Latin naming system in 1753. It is still used today. The naming system made it possible to communicate internationally in all languages, helped the understanding of plant reproduction and cultivation, and aided conservation.

In 1758 Linnaeus chose a farm at Hammarby as a retreat where he and his family could escape the unhealthy conditions in Uppsala. Boulders, woodland and the beauty of the sloping site create a timeless atmosphere. What is now the main building was added a few years later, with a small museum to house Linnaeus's large natural history collections. In the garden, Linnaeus indulged his thirst for knowledge about cultivation. His plants included the Hammarby houseleek (*Jovibarba globifera*) – commonly used (along with other plants) for covering roofs in various parts of Sweden. As Linnaeus grew older, it was invaluable for him to have his personal outdoor laboratory and plant collections close at hand.

In front of the house, two flower borders have been re-created from his sketches. Introducing plants originating from similar climates to Sweden was one of Linnaeus's major interests, and a Siberian crab apple (*Malus baccata*) is the central plant in the courtyard. It was originally planted as one of a pair in the 1760s. In late spring it is a mass of white blossom, but the fruits are very small.

In the second courtyard, the Uppland Garden dates from the 1880s. Its formal design and planting also demonstrate the horticultural practices of the eighteenth century. Russian pea shrub (*Caragana frutex*) makes a hedge on the south side; it is grown from plants originally cultivated by Linnaeus. In the parkland beyond the house, Linnaeus laid out the Siberian Garden to cultivate a large consignment of seeds gifted by Empress Catherine II.

1 — Two borders of the Uppland Garden frame a view of the house.
2 — Linnaeus called the small natural history museum where he kept his botanical collection, 'My palace in the sky'. The building was fire- and floodproof.
3 — A view towards the open countryside over the Uppland Garden shows planting based on Linnaeus's writings of the 1730s.
4 — A path winds through natural woodland and boulders towards the main house.

# Skogskyrkogården

(Woodland Cemetery)

Enskede, Stockholm, Sweden

| | |
|---|---|
| Erik Gunnar Asplund, Sigurd Lewerentz | |
| 20th century | |
| 100 hectares / 247 acres | |
| Humid Continental | |
| English Landscape / Modern / Naturalistic | |

A cemetery might not be the first form of land use that one would associate with the highest levels of garden art, but Skogskyrkogården is exactly that and has influenced cemetery design around the world. In 1912 a competition was held to design a new cemetery for Stockholm, to be sited on a disused gravel quarry and pine forest. The joint winners were the two young Swedish architects Erik Gunnar Asplund and Sigurd Lewerentz, who together created not the kind of Modernist design that might have been expected in the 1910s but a timeless place that embraces all denominations, even though it was consecrated as Lutheran. Skogskyrkogården is imbued with a deep sense of reverence for the Swedish wilderness and pagan Norse traditions, but simultaneously references classical antiquity.

Almost like a Greek procession, visitors and mourners enter the cemetery up a walled ramp that subtly constricts their view and focuses the mind. Then the experience opens up and the buildings and landscape can be seen. The Chapel of the Holy Cross (Asplund's last building, 1935–40), the site of the underground crematorium, is set into the contoured landscape. Nearby a giant black granite cross is juxtaposed with an outdoor catafalque surrounded by blazing braziers. These both give a pagan feel – especially in snow – and provide the foreground to the sweep of a small hill that climbs to the square of birch trees known as the Grove of Remembrance.

Further out in the landscape the graves are fitted among the trees rather than arrayed in serried ranks. It is a moving experience to wander the paths when the groves are illuminated with candles on a dark Swedish night. Here too at the end of a path is Asplund's first building – the small Woodland Chapel – which encapsulates the essence of Skogskyrkogården. It is a mix of vernacular and naturalism, nature and buildings, topography and trees. Cemeteries are often melancholy, but the atmosphere at Skogskyrkogården, while laden with dignity, is also completely in tune with the cycle of life and death that is nature.

1 — The open portico of the Chapel of the Holy Cross is reflected in the glassy lake.
2 — The Grove of Remembrance is a still space formed by a square of birch trees.
3 — The black granite cross was intended as a non-denominational symbol.
4 — An avenue known as Seven Springs Way leads to the site's third chapel, the classical Chapel of the Resurrection.
5 — Graves fit comfortably into the natural arrangement of trees in the woodland.

# Millesgården
Lidingö, Stockholm, Sweden

| |
|---|
| Carl Milles, Evert Milles |
| 20th century |
| 2 hectares / 5 acres |
| Humid Continental |
| Coastal / Naturalistic / Sculpture / Terraces |

This sculpture garden from the first half of the twentieth century lies on an island but is not at all isolated: it is only ten minutes' drive northeast of central Stockholm. The city skyline provides a backdrop to Millesgården, and the sea the foreground. The garden itself is an unusual yet successful hybrid of an Italianate style and an elegant, simple, Nordic style.

In 1906 the Swedish artist Carl Milles and his Austrian wife, Olga, purchased a plot on Herserud Cliff and had a home and studios built. Over the ensuing half century Milles dedicated himself to developing the garden and its display of sculpture. Despite his love for the Italianate, the garden has none of the axial formality the Italians applied to their gardens. Millesgården feels as if it has evolved organically, with the buildings, changes in level and different areas juxtaposed and linked by an ingenious use of asymmetric geometry.

The first addition to the garden was the loggia designed by Milles's half-brother, the architect Evert Milles, as an open-air studio. Today the Upper Terrace is surrounded by buildings and is open only to the water, but the enclosure creates a tranquil setting for artworks including *The Little Triton* (1916) and *William Penn with Angel* (1948). Originally a kitchen garden, the Studio Garden boasts two notable works: *The Wings* (1908), on top of a tall column, and the fierce-looking *Eagle* (1919).

In the 1920s Milles bought adjoining properties and created the Middle Terrace. Highlights there today are the *Venus and the Shell* fountain and *The Sun Singer* (1926), a naked male body without head and arms. One particularly personal garden room is *Little Austria* (1924). Aware of his wife's homesickness for Austria, Milles conceived this steep, stony hollow with plantings of alpine flora as a surprise to celebrate her fiftieth birthday.

There was a nineteen-year hiatus when Milles taught in the United States, but the spacious Lower Terrace was begun in 1950. It was almost complete when Milles died in 1955. Paved with red sandstone, the open space has echoes of an Italian piazza, with numerous sculptures and the garden's largest fountain, *Europa and the Bull* (1926).

1 — The Italian-inspired Lower Terrace features *Europa and the Bull*, the largest fountain in the garden.
2 — Large isolated topiary spheres provide geometric interest on the Lower Terrace, in front of a sculpture named *Angel Musicians*, which represents fountains around the world.

103

# Anne Just Garden

Hune, Blokhus, Jutland, Denmark

| |
|---|
| Anne Just |
| 20th century |
| 0.5 hectares / 1 acre |
| Humid Continental |
| Artistic / Informal / Plantsman / Rooms |

The artist Anne Just specialized in cheerful paintings and ceramics of flowers. This was entirely appropriate given that her studio was surrounded by the garden she created. When she bought her workshop in 1991, it was in the middle of a pine-tree plantation and on soil that was almost pure sand, but over the next eighteen years Just and her husband, the architect Claus Bonderup, created one of the most surprising gardens in Denmark.

This is a garden of compact rooms added one after another. The first, created in 1993, was the South Garden; it has geometric beds defined by low metal edging and box hedging filled with a profusion of perennials, herbs and roses, in which the flowers accentuate the various shades of green foliage. There followed the North Garden, with its rectangular pool and statue; the curved, raised Mirror Pool, which winds away from the house through the pine trees; the Iris Hill; the Skovbunden; the Olympic Garden; and the Yellow and Pastel gardens, which are filled with plants of the appropriate tints and tones.

The rooms are laid out and juxtaposed with a designer's eye. The narrow paths slow the pace, forcing the visitor to become immersed in each room's structure, planting and ornamentation. Moving through the garden, the visitor encounters a constantly changing series of stimulating and occasionally amusing vistas and experiences, including the former pigsty ornamented with three towers and a porcine statue and renamed 'Pig Castle'. Yet while the rooms' structure – formal, informal or playful – is always clear and is part of the visual experience, what is striking is their balance with planting that is both profuse and carefully controlled, seemingly artless but in fact designed with an artist's eye. The genius of the garden is that, in such a small area, Just combined so many distinct areas in such a way that, while each is enjoyable in itself, a sense of continuity and continuation comes as the visitor moves through the garden, giving the feeling and experience of a much larger garden.

1 — Profuse planting in the South Garden, next to Just's studio, is typical of the lush vegetation throughout the site.
2, 3 — Reflections in the irregular, elongated Mirror Pool help to integrate the different parts of the garden; the pool curves around a corner, creating a sense of mystery and drawing the visitor on.
4 — This small verdant courtyard towered over by the statue of the *Gris Slot* or 'Pig Castle' is a tongue-in-cheek tribute to one of Denmark's biggest exports.
5 — The Gran Via or main path – like other narrow, enclosed paths – encourages visitors to move through the garden slowly, taking more time to absorb the full impact of the varied planting.

4

5

# De Runde Haver

(The Oval Gardens)

Nærum, Zealand, Denmark

| | |
|---|---|
| Carl Theodor Sørensen | |
| 20th century | |
| 3.5 hectares / 8.5 acres | |
| Humid Continental | |
| Communal / Edible / Modern / Rooms | |

On paper, there is something childishly simple about De Runde Haver's elliptical, hedge-enclosed 'round gardens' set like islands on a sea of sward, but in the hands of Carl Theodor Sørensen – the most influential twentieth-century landscape architect and garden designer in Denmark – the relationship between the gardens and the contours of the site creates something far more special. Sørensen is little known outside his home country because his publications were not translated, but he was a Modernist who in the 1940s pioneered 'adventure playgrounds', inspired by children playing with leftover materials on construction sites. 'Children's playgrounds are the city's most important form of public plantation,' he claimed, and the same community approach underlines his gardens for grown-ups, of which De Runde Haver is the most famous example.

In 1948 Sørensen drew plans for forty-four elliptical allotment gardens on a sloping field on the edge of the town of Nærum (six more were added later). Although there appears nothing remarkable about the design, a visit to the site reveals how Sørensen arranged the gardens so that the collective curves of the hedges create an attractive vista as the visitor enters the field. The gardens each enjoy maximum privacy and the most generous aspect, and the curving grassy corridors between them are aesthetically pleasing both to view and to walk along. Even knowing that all there is around the next bend is another garden hedge, the visitor cannot help a sense of anticipation.

De Runde Haver sums up Sørensen's approach to the modern garden, which he believed should be both sculptural and personal, applying strong spatial expression to create well-defined forms and often introducing geometry and clipped planting to provide structure. He drew four blueprints for how the individual gardens might be laid out, but left it up to the garden owners to express their creativity. With their different pavilions and varied mixtures of ornamental and vegetable planting, the personalized gardens are a counterbalance to the controlled structure of Sørensen's overall design.

1—From the air the fluid shapes of the allotments and the organic spaces between them become clear. Although the cottages are situated differently within the plots, they all conform to the overall plan. Sørensen advocated a range of hedging plants for the enclosures, such as sweetbriar, hazel and lilac, some to be clipped, others not; today most are clipped hawthorn and privet.
2, 3—Within the plots, varied planting by the individual gardeners that includes fennel, beans, carrots, kale and rhubarb provides a wide range of colour, texture and scale.

# Fredensborg Slotshave

(Fredensborg Palace Gardens)

Fredensborg, Zealand, Denmark

| |
|---|
| Johan Cornelius Krieger, Nicolas-Henri Jardin |
| 18th century |
| 121 hectares / 300 acres |
| Humid Continental |
| Baroque / Historic / Woodland |

Like other Danish gardens of the early eighteenth century, the royal palace at Fredensborg reflects the influence of Versailles, but with a Danish take that makes it smaller and less intricate. Like Versailles, Fredensborg began life as a royal hunting park but in 1720 King Fredrik IV had the architect Johan Cornelius Krieger design a Baroque palace, which was named the Castle of Peace to commemorate the signing of a treaty to end the Great Northern War between Sweden and Russia.

In 2013 the Baroque garden behind and north of the palace was restored to Krieger's 1720s' design, with some later elements by the French architect Nicolas-Henri Jardin. Juxtaposed with the palace, the Half Moon Terrace is again divided into six wedge-shaped compartments. The two central, most ornate compartments are laid out as *parterres anglais* – grass plats edged with clipped box hedges to pick out the scrollwork patterning. Enclosed by beech hedges that also line the paths running through them, the remaining grassy compartments echo Versailles's *bosquets* (formal tree groves). Beyond the Half Moon Terrace are four larger compartments, defined in part by tree-lined allées that radiate out into the woodland: to the west the Great Balloon Square, to the east the Ships' Hill and in the middle the pair that feature the Denmark and Norway monuments.

Under Frederik V, Jardin developed the French theme, adding a main axis – the Brede Allé – with a central band of grass flanked by avenues of common lime (*Tilia* x *europaea*). The woodland beyond the formal garden and between the allées is pierced by winding paths. It is particularly lovely to walk along the lakeside, with its extensive views over to Gribskov Wood on the far shore.

Another highlight of Fredensborg Slotshave is the *Nordmandsdalen* (Norwegian Valley). Set in an artificial amphitheatre are seventy statues depicting Norwegian and Faroese farmers and fishermen. The Kitchen Gardens and the Orangery (1995) are open to the public when the royal family is not in residence.

1—View across the newly restored *parterres anglais* and along the garden's main axis, the Brede Allé.
2—The Reserved Garden, the Queen's private garden, is open to the public only in the summer.
3—This is one of two monuments in the garden that celebrate the then-kingdom of Denmark and Norway.
4—An avenue of common lime gives a distant view of the Esrum Lake.
5—Unusually for the time, the statues by the Danish sculptor J G Grund in the Norwegian Valley depict fishermen and peasants rather than classical figures.

# Dillon Garden

Dublin, Ireland

| |
|---|
| Helen Dillon |
| 20th–21st century |
| 0.4 hectares / 1 acre |
| Temperate Oceanic |
| Borders / Containers / Exotic / Rooms / Water |

Perhaps more than with any other contemporary garden, here garden and gardener are inseparable: one is inconceivable without the other. Helen Dillon's town plot has helped to spearhead a new movement in Irish gardening, partly because Dillon is very good at what she does and partly through the sheer force of her personality. An effective writer and lecturer, Dillon is also creative and experimental, and pushes constantly at the boundaries of the possible. As a consequence, hers is a garden that has gone through many changes – and will probably continue to do so.

A career on *Amateur Gardener* magazine introduced Dillon to many personalities of the garden world, so that when she began her own garden in the 1970s she was remarkably well informed. By the 1990s her garden had gained a reputation for striking colour schemes and immaculate maintenance, as well as its wide range of plants. The Dublin climate allows for mixing plants from different climate zones. Dillon exploits this advantage in a selective way, always considering plants' visual relationships with their neighbours.

Until 2000 the centrepiece of the back garden was a lawn, but its replacement – a canal surrounded by limestone paving – creates a more formal effect. It is flanked by the borders that made Dillon's name as a planting designer. The rear of this area includes intimate spaces defined by hedges, shrubs and foliage plants, and an apple tree pruned to look like a Mediterranean stone pine. The front garden, dating in its current form to 2005, is dominated by a grove of *Betula utilis* 'Fascination', with grasses and cool, relatively naturalistic planting.

The main emphasis, however, is the rear garden, and the excitement of its strong colours and forms. Dillon practises the kind of high-energy gardening that involves growing some plants in containers, such as lilies and dahlias, and moving them around for short-term effect. Plants are regularly dug up and repositioned. This is a garden that above all celebrates the '-ing' of gardening.

1, 3—The former lawn in the back garden has been replaced by the Canal, edged with cool limestone paving; among others, the wide herbaceous borders feature *Filipendula rubra* 'Venusta', *Ferula communis* (giant fennel), agapanthus, dahlias, miscanthus, *Dierama pulcherrimum* (angel's fishing rod) and *Tetrapanax* spp.
2—A tunnelled walk is covered in Banksian rose (*Rosa banksiae*); beyond, a statue and box topiary form a terminus to the vista.
4—A Cupid fountain stands in a small courtyard with low-level planting that combines naturalistic *Alchemilla mollis* with sculpted box (*Buxus sempervirens*).

1

2

3

4

# Ilnacullin

## (Garinish Island)

### Glengariff, County Cork, Ireland

| |
|---|
| Annan Bryce, Harold Peto |
| 20th century |
| 15 hectares / 37 acres |
| Temperate Oceanic |
| Arts & Crafts / Exotic / Italianate / Landscape / Woodland |

A boat trip adds a sense of anticipation to a garden visit – and Ilnacullin does not disappoint. This jewel on Garinish Island adds to the beauty of its setting in Bantry Bay. Ilnacullin Garden and Garinish Island are interchangeable names: the island *is* the garden. When Annan Bryce bought the island from the British War Office in 1910, it was a bare, exposed, rocky moorland, with only a Martello tower and the ruins of a fort and military garrison. Bryce commissioned the architect Harold Peto to design a house and create a garden. Peto's approach combined Arts and Crafts ideas with Italianate architecture and style. Ilnacullin was to be his masterpiece (although the planned mansion was never built).

Creating conditions suitable for making a garden on such an exposed site involved blasting rocks to improve planting spaces, and planting a shelter belt, primarily of conifers. The garden works with the site's topography to provide a series of vistas that are enjoyed from a network of circular routes. Stopping points appear 'natural', a sign of good design.

A fine *casita*, or tearoom, overlooks the Italian Garden. Shallow steps lead down to a rectangular pool that is perfectly proportioned in relation to the *casita* and the temple beyond, which marks the end of this garden room and complements the view to the Caha Mountains on the mainland beyond.

On another promontory, wide stone steps climb to an avenue of Italian cypresses (*Cupressus sempervirens*), which ends at a classical temple. Its simple columns and open roof retain the expansive view of mountains beyond as the dominant feature.

The whole garden benefits from the warming Gulf Stream, but in the more formal central area, a walled garden provides its own microclimate for a different range of plants, including acacia, leptospermum, clematis, camellia and roses. Ilnacullin has a sense of theatre and magic, not least because its mysteries are offered up only after the adventure of a boat trip.

1—The view from the *casita* across the architectural Italian Garden terminates in a temple with columns of dark coloured 'antico rosso', through which can be seen the Caha Mountains beyond.
2—Rhododendrons and azaleas blend with autumn colours on a sunny day.
3—A gate opens into the Walled Garden, where the microclimate supports plants from a wide range of Mediterranean-type climate regions including South Africa and Western Australia.
4—The Italianate *casita*, draped in wisteria, stands between the Lawn and the Italian Garden. Peto's combination of Italianate architecture and Arts and Crafts planting reached its peak at Ilnacullin.

# Mount Congreve

Kilmeadan,
County Waterford, Ireland

| | |
|---|---|
| Ambrose Christian Congreve | |
| 20th century | |
| 30 hectares / 74 acres (garden); 80 hectares / 198 acres (woodland) | |
| Temperate Oceanic | |
| Naturalistic / Plantsman / Woodland | |

Ambrose Christian Congreve was just eleven when he was inspired by a visit to the garden created at Exbury in Hampshire by Lionel de Rothschild (see page 187) to begin making a garden at the family home in Kilmeadan. Rothschild sent truckloads of plants, and Congreve grew to share his mentor's passion for rhododendrons, magnolias, camellias and other exciting plants arriving from China thanks to plant hunters such as George Forrest and Frank Kingdon-Ward. One of Congreve's original plantings still stands below the Terrace Garden: a stately *Rhododendron sinogrande* whose large limbs rest on the woodland floor.

Congreve continued to develop his gardens until his death in 2011 at the age of 104. The Walled Garden boasts collections of iris and peony, as well as edibles, and the Victorian conservatory is home to rare hothouse flowers. But his passion was the Woodland Garden. Within its 28 hectares (70 acres) above the River Suir, he carved out clearings to create the necessary environment for plants. Today the collection has more than 2,000 varieties of rhododendron, 600 camellias, 600 conifers and 1,500 herbaceous taxa. Trees include the handkerchief tree (*Davidia involucrata*) and the silver beech (*Nothofagus menziesii*) from New Zealand.

Mount Congreve is more than just a botanical collection, however. Congreve had an eye for landscape design, and the paths that wind through the woodland lead the visitor to contrived views of the plantings and the surrounding landscape. They also reveal surprises such as the old quarry, with its Chinese Pagoda, and the Waterfall Garden with its rocky slopes. Another factor that makes Mount Congreve stand out is its diversity and intensive planting. Most gardeners use single specimens, but Congreve planted in groups of up to fifty. This approach created a breathtaking display of flowers, which look their best in early to mid-spring when the woodland is carpeted with drifts of bulbs including bluebells, crocuses, daffodils, glory of the snow, grape hyacinths and snowdrops. It also imbues Mount Congreve with a more natural feel.

1, 2 —Congreve's philosophy of creating sweeping groups of plants can be seen in the azaleas in the Woodland Garden, and clusters of rhododenrons around a water feature.
3—Bluebells bloom among tree ferns beneath a foxglove tree (*Paulownia tomentosa*).
4—Dahlias flower in the Walled Garden, which contains fruit and vegetables as well as borders planted to flower at different times of the season.
5—One of the garden's many surprises: the Chinese Pagoda in the Old Quarry.

# Powerscourt

Enniskerry, County Wicklow,
Ireland

| | |
|---|---|
| Daniel Robertson | |
| 19th century | |
| 18 hectares / 45 acres | |
| Temperate Oceanic | |
| Formal / Japanese / Terraces / Water | |

Set in the picturesque surroundings of the Wicklow Mountains, Powerscourt is one of Ireland's great horticultural showpieces. The Palladian mansion was built for the first Viscount Powerscourt between 1731 and 1741, while the formal garden as seen today dates from a century later. Both mansion (now a shopping complex) and high terrace enjoy a magnificent view across the River Dargle to Sugar Loaf Mountain. It was Richard Wingfield, 6th Viscount Powerscourt, who commissioned Daniel Robertson to remodel the gardens in 1841. A talented garden designer, Robertson had one weakness, as recalled by Mervyn, the 7th Viscount: 'He was much given to drink ... [and] suffered from gout and used to be wheeled out on the terrace in a wheelbarrow, with a bottle of sherry, and so long [as] that lasted he was able to design and direct the workmen but when the sherry was finished he collapsed and was incapable of working till the drunken fit evaporated.'

Yet Robertson created a triumph of art over nature: the Italian Garden. This amphitheatre of six grass terraces has formal beds that are filled with roses and bedding plants in summer. Aligned on the main axis is a wide path on the upper terrace, which is composed of black-and-white pebble mosaics and ornamented with classical figures. This leads to a twin stairway that surrounds the water feature on the second terrace, where statues spout water into a pool. At the foot of the Italian Garden is the Triton Pool, with a boathouse guarded by two winged statues of Pegasus. The Triton fountain sends up a jet 21.3 metres (70 feet) into the air.

To the west of the house is the large Walled Garden, now planted with a long, double herbaceous border. Beyond is the Dolphin Pond, the Pets' Cemetery and the terminus of the Triton Pool. From there a path descends to the Japanese Garden (added in 1908) before climbing through a woodland richly planted with North American trees and rhododendrons and leading via the Pepperpot – a fortified folly – back to the mansion. The contrast between the formal, woodland and Japanese gardens is delightful, but the lingering memory of Powerscourt is the view from the upper terrace.

1 — The Sugar Loaf mountain rises spectacularly behind the Italian Gardens.
2 — The fountain in the Triton Pool in front of the house is based on an original in the Palazzo Barberini in Rome.
3 — In spring the Japanese Garden is full of the colours of flowering azaleas and in autumn with the foliage of Japanese maples.
4 — A fountain plays in the middle of the double herbaceous border in the Walled Garden.

# Mount Usher

Ashford, County Wicklow, Ireland

Edward Walpole

19th & 20th century

8 hectares / 22 acres

Temperate Oceanic

Naturalistic / Plantsman / Water / Woodland

The Walpole family acquired Mount Usher in 1868 and for five generations developed the garden around an old mill, which lay in a sheltered valley on both sides of the River Vartry. Although the family took much expert advice, the garden's informal style is most closely linked to the design ethos of William Robinson. The Robinsonian style, as developed in Robinson's own Gravetye Manor garden (see page 198), essentially envisioned a garden that preserved the landscape. It delighted in the natural beauty of flowers and trees, while hardy plants were arranged so that their qualities could be admired both individually and as part of a whole composition.

The gardens of Mount Usher tick all these boxes. Passing through the hedge from the entrance, the visitor meanders downstream as the river babbles over weirs. The meadow, studded with wild flowers and ornamental species, leads to the shaded Woodland Garden, with its collection of unusual trees and camellias. The Azalea Walk glows with fiery tints in spring, and has notable specimens of the Handkerchief tree (*Davidia involucrata*), Chilean lantern tree (*Crinodendron hookerianum*) and Japanese big-leaf magnolia (*Magnolia obovata*). In all, the garden boasts 5,000 species and cultivars, including the tallest *Cornus capitata* (at 18 metres/59 feet) in the British Isles. Passing through the Eucalyptus Grove, with its carpet of bluebells, a bridge crosses the river, where a vast kiwi-fruit vine (*Actinidia deliciosa*) twines into the branches above.

On either side of the Palm Walk – a lawn flanked by an avenue of *Trachycarpus fortunei* – are the garden's two national collections, one of the genus *Nothofagus* and the other of *Eucryphia*, both of which thrive in the munificent climate. Behind the (private) house the visitor reaches The Island, with its bog garden filled with candelabra primulas, meconopsis and gunnera as well as island beds crammed with rhododendrons. As throughout the garden, the foreground is filled with interesting plants, and when one raises one's eyes these combine to create a picturesque ensemble, all enhanced by the natural beauty of the setting.

1—In late summer the Azalea Walk is lined with rhododendrons, davidias and azaras, the fragrant white-flowering *Magnolia salicifolia* and *Eucryphia glutinosa*.
2—The grassy Palm Walk is flanked by *Trachycarpus fortunei*.
3, 4—The River Vartry tumbles over a series of waterfalls as it flows through the garden.
5—Candelabra primulas flower in the bog garden, where many water-loving plants are grown, including primulas, astilbe, kingcups (giant buttercups) and hostas.

4

5

# Mount Stewart

Newtownards, County Down, UK

Edith, 7th Marchioness of Londonderry

20th century

39 hectares / 97 acres

Temperate Oceanic

Formal / Landscape / Plantsman / Rhododendrons / Woodland

The highly personal garden at Mount Stewart did not have promising beginnings. On visiting the run-down country house that her husband, the 7th Marquis of Londonderry, inherited in 1917, Lady Edith noted: 'I thought the house and surroundings were the dampest, darkest and saddest places I had ever stayed in.'

Nevertheless, in 1921 Lady Edith set about creating a garden in two parts: formal gardens around the house, and naturalistic pleasure grounds beyond. Out of sight of the house, a 2-hectare (5-acre) lake nestles in a small valley, from which paths take the visitor into the ornamental woodland. There Lady Edith took fullest advantage of the undulating topography and the mild microclimate (owing to Mount Stewart's location on the shores of Strangford Lough) to create a series of changing vistas. As she was free to experiment with a wide palette of plants, Lady Edith integrated exotic trees into the native woodland and planted a collection of rhododendrons and exotic shrubs, such as the New Zealand Christmas tree (*Metrosideros* spp.) and Chilean firebush (*Embothrium coccineum*). Here too is the Tir Nan Og, the family burial ground.

Lady Edith's gardens reflect interests ranging from classical and Celtic mythology to Italian and Moorish gardens and her own family history. In front of the house, the paved terrace leads to the Italian Garden, with statuary drawn from the *Odyssey*, and the Spanish Garden, which has an elegant pavilion and pool. West of the house is the Lutyens-inspired, pergola-framed Sunk Garden as well as the Shamrock Garden, with its iconic harp topiary. To the east is the Mairi Garden, named for Lady Edith's daughter, planted in blue and white.

In style, Mount Stewart blends the structural formality of the Italian Baroque with the flowery exuberance of the Arts and Crafts movement. Yet Lady Edith's sense of humour shines through everywhere – especially in the animal statuary of the Dodo Terrace. Not far from the main garden, the Neo-classical Temple of the Winds (1785) overlooking the Lough is well worth the walk.

1, 4—The formal Italian Garden, near the Dodo Terrace, displays sculptural features based on Baroque gardens such as Palazzo Farnese and Villa Gamberaia.
2, 3—Lady Edith's sense of fun is clear from the statuary found throughout the garden.
5—Wisteria blossoms in front of arches of *Cupressocyparis leylandii* in the Spanish Garden.
6—Planting of flame-coloured azaleas and blue delphiniums in the Sunk Garden follows one of Lady Edith's garden books from 1926.
7—The woodland around the lake near the Tir Nan Og, the family burial ground, contains majestic specimen trees, while rhododendrons abound both here and en route to the house.

# Inverewe

Poolewe, Wester Ross,
Highland, UK

Osgood Hanbury Mackenzie,
Mairi T Sawyer

19th & 20th century

20 hectares / 50 acres

Temperate Oceanic

Coastal / Edible / Naturalistic /
Plantsman / Woodland

On a promontory overlooking Loch Ewe, Inverewe occupies one of the most enviable locations in Scotland. It also benefits from the warming effect of the Gulf Stream, which bathes the west coast. This benefit, however, is limited by the strong, salt-laden winds, so the first job Osgood Mackenzie did when he began his garden in 1862 was to plant the headland with woodland. He waited twenty years until the sheltering effect was enough to allow him to introduce other plants. Mackenzie planned a maze of paths through the woodland and carved out niches of plants that are unexpected this far north, originating in China, the Antipodes, South America and the Himalayas.

From the terrace, visitors enjoy views across the loch and down over the Walled Garden. A path descends to this haven on the foreshore, which is filled with edible crops and flowers, with soil fertilized with seaweed from the beach. At the western extremity, a steep flight of steps up through a display of New Zealand flora leads back to the terrace and the white-painted house.

South of the house is the Rock Garden, while behind it to the north and west is the Woodland Garden. Here highlights include the Pond Garden, the Peat Banks planted with ericaceous species and the Bambooselem. Spring and early summer are the best times to see blue and red Himalayan poppies, Chilean lantern trees, Chatham Island forget-me-nots and the Wollemi pine, but the highlight is the collection of rhododendrons. Strolling along the Rhododendron Walk, the Niveum Walk and the Barbatum Walk under the tall trees smothered with trusses of flowers in all hues is a true delight.

Osgood died in 1922 and the garden passed to his daughter, Mairi, who continued to develop her father's masterpiece. Upon her death in 1953 this gem of a garden was bequeathed to the National Trust for Scotland.

1—The Walled Garden hugs the shore of Loch Ewe. The beach was excavated and soil imported to create the fruit, vegetable and flower garden.
2—The Peat Bank pond has an 'insectivorous island', where *Darlingtonia californica* and *Sarracenia purpurea* help to control Inverewe's biting midges.
3—In spring and early summer Inverewe is home to a spectacular show of rhododendrons and flowering shrubs.
4—A colour clash of Karume azaleas and other azalea cultivars, with the groundcover of *Epimedium* and a scarlet-flowering *Embothrium coccineum* above.
5—The path winds through the structural forms of Japanese maples and smaller rhododendrons, the flowers of which add to this rich tapestry. Here 'America' is in full bloom in spring, with the blue Himalayan poppy below.

# Drummond
# Castle Gardens

Crieff, Perthshire, UK

Charles Barry, Lewis Kennedy

19th & 20th century

7.3 hectares / 18 acres

Temperate Oceanic

Baroque / Formal / Parterre / Terraces

The obelisk sundial at the heart of Drummond Castle Gardens recalls the first great period of a castle and gardens that today present a rich amalgam of architectural and garden styles from the mid-seventeenth to mid-twentieth centuries. The castle on the rocky knoll was already nearly 150 years old when James Drummond, 2nd Earl of Perth, transformed the gardens in the 1630s and added the obelisk. The Drummonds were ardent Royalists, and the castle was devastated by Oliver Cromwell's Parliamentarians in the 1650s, setting the tone for a history of oscillating fortunes.

Early evidence of a formal garden comes from a military survey from the mid-eighteenth century. It describes four grass platts (plots) arranged on an axis south of the castle, with a central avenue across the undulating policies (grounds). In the nineteenth century this terrace formed the canvas for the current garden, an outstanding formal revival initiated by Clementina Drummond, daughter of the 11th Earl, and her husband, Peter Burrell. Paintings exhibited in 1828 by revivalist designer Charles Barry show a richly planted parterre, possibly undertaken in collaboration with the noted landscape gardener Lewis Kennedy. A plan by Kennedy's son George, a decade later, shows the completed formal garden alive with richly coloured beds, shrubs and conifers, all set in the pattern of the Saltire, the national flag of Scotland.

Now, as then, the obelisk sundial sits amid an intricate pattern of low box hedges, gravelled compartments, shrub beds, clipped conifers and lawns. The north–south path extends over the horizon through a woodland vista. While this reflects French inspiration, the overall design retains an Italianate feel, with its balustraded terraces, grand flight of steps, and statuary. The garden was largely renewed in the 1950s, carefully maintaining earlier features while simplifying some nineteenth-century excesses. Today the impression is one of formal grandeur: historically based yet freely worked and vibrant, a foil to the austere grey stonework behind.

1—The famous obelisk sundial stands in the heart of the Parterre, while the diagonal cross of the saltire is picked out in blue lavender and silver anaphalis.
2—Autumn foliage of *Acer palmatum* (Japanese maple) is a backdrop to a grass path lined with clipped hollies and maples, underplanted with anaphalis.
3—The garden provides views to the castle above; the garden includes box hedges, topiary holly and yew.
4—Autumn highlights the structure of the Parterre, which was probably a collaboration between the celebrated designers Charles Barry and Lewis Kennedy.

# Little Sparta
Dunsyre, South Lanarkshire, UK

Ian Hamilton Finlay, Sue Finlay

20th century

1.6 hectares / 4 acres

Temperate Oceanic

Allegorical / Artistic / Naturalistic / Sculpture

When Ian Hamilton Finlay bought the old farmhouse in the Pentland Hills in 1966 it was surrounded by heath. But over the forty years until his death, the poet and sculptor and his wife, Sue, created one of Scotland's most interesting gardens. Little Sparta is not just an attractive setting for an eclectic collection of sculptures; the garden is also laden with meaning and allegory.

Little Sparta shares parallels with Stowe (see page 156) – the archetypal English Landscape garden – in its use of allegorical symbols to encourage the visitor to 'read' the garden. Little Sparta is also an iconoclastic garden. Hamilton Finlay shared with Stowe's creator, Lord Cobham, a commitment to personal freedom and virtue. Little Sparta both expresses the Finlays' deep belief in social justice and challenges visitors to review how they live their lives.

The farm garden has become the intimate and enclosed Front Garden with its stone tortoise nestling among hostas; the farmyard behind has been transformed into the Temple Pool Garden, overlooked by the Temple of Apollo (a former outbuilding). The pools and glades of the Woodland Garden are the setting for many sculptural elements. The Wild Garden climbs behind the house to the hills beyond, blurring the boundary between the garden and the natural landscape.

Originally called Stonypath, the garden was renamed in 1978 after a battle with the local authority over tax. Hamilton Finlay introduced a number of martial features – including tank tracks – to symbolize his battle for his art. In stark contrast, much of the poetry carved into stones or sculptures has a lyrical quality. Again as at Stowe, Little Sparta uses the borrowed landscape to provide views, but here the climate also shapes the visitor's emotional response to the garden.

Hamilton Finlay claimed: 'Superior gardens are composed of Glooms and Solitudes, not of plants and trees.' Little Sparta is not a garden for simply enjoying. It emphasizes the cerebral and emotional impact gardens should have, and the complex relationship between the wildness of nature and artistic attempts to control it that encapsulates all garden-making.

1, 2—The Temple Pool Garden is in some ways the heart of Little Sparta, featuring 'The Temple of Baucis and Philemon' and the 'Columns of the Revolution' in one corner. In another *Aruncus dioicus* grows behind a planter bearing the motto 'Semper Festina Lente – Hasten Slowly', accompanied not by the usual image of a tortoise but by a tank using a flail to explode buried mines.
3—The flagstones of the path through the Front Garden are each inscribed with a word related to boats or sailing.

4—On the bank of Lochan Eck, granite slabs are carved with a quotation attributed to the French revolutionary Antoine de Saint-Just – 'The Present Order is the Disorder of the Future'.
5—On the sloping Wave Lawn in the English Parkland, five small artificial ridges each bear a stone block carved with the word 'wave' in a different language.
6—The gilded head of Apollo in the Wild Garden shows the Greek god with the features of Antoine de Saint-Just.
7—The broken stone column of 'Tragedies of the Dido Class' in the Wild Garden is a memorial to cruisers of this class sunk in World War II.
8—An inscribed bridge spans the stream that separates the Wild Garden from Lochan Eck.

5

# Mellerstain

Gordon, Berwickshire, UK

| |
|---|
| Reginald Blomfield |
| 20th century |
| 2 hectares / 5 acres (garden); 82 hectares / 203 acres (park) |
| Temperate Oceanic |
| Formal / Parterre / Renaissance / Terraces / Water |

Mellerstain is the creation of the architect Reginald Blomfield, who with William Robinson was a protagonist in the so-called Battle of Styles in the late nineteenth century, when both sought to shake off the High Victorian garden and forge a new British garden style. While Robinson developed his vision at Gravetye Manor (see page 198), Blomfield worked at Mellerstain from 1909 for Lord and Lady Binning. The house in the Scottish borders had been designed by the architects William Adam and his son Robert between 1725 and 1778, but nothing of the Adam garden remained except for the lake, which Blomfield enlarged and reshaped.

Blomfield's garden vision was inspired by the formal seventeenth-century garden, with raised terraces and a series of spaces divided by walls or clipped hedges, simply planned and proportioned and incorporating gazebos, broad walks and lawns. He superimposed his most grandiose scheme – three balustraded terraces – on William Adam's Dutch-inspired garden to take advantage of the superb vistas out to woodlands dating from 1725, to the *cottage orné* added a century later and towards the Cheviot Hills beyond. A divided flight of steps descends from the top terrace with its lawns and topiary yews to meet in front of the cryptoporticus (pillared loggia) in the middle of the largest terrace. In front of the cryptoporticus and aligned on the main axis, a wide flagged path leads to a second divided flight of steps – this time curved – that embraces a formal pond on the lowest terrace. Either side of the path is an intricate parterre of tightly clipped box forms and flower beds planted with catmint (*Nepeta* spp.) or a single type of rose: *R*. 'Baby Faurax', Bonica, Cardinal Hume, 'Gruss An Aachen', 'Little White Pet', 'De Resht' and 'The Fairy'. Like the middle terrace, the third terrace has mixed beds of herbaceous perennials and climbing roses growing against the wall. Beyond it, the lawn with its statue of Mercury slopes down to the lake.

Blomfield's original design called for a far larger garden, but it proved too expensive. The result is that the partly finished gardens look splendid when viewed from the house, but rather peculiar when viewed from the lake back towards the house.

1, 2, 3—The planting on the middle terrace has intricate parterres of clipped box, lavender and many old roses planted in the 1990s. They end in mixed borders of geraniums, delphiniums and *Cimicifuga* (*Actaea*) with a backdrop of climbing roses.
4—The main axis of the terraces leads to a lawn with a statue of Mercury and a distant lake.

# Garden of Cosmic Speculation

Portrack, Dumfries and
Galloway, UK

Charles Jencks, Maggie Keswick

20th–21st century

12 hectares / 30 acres

Temperate Oceanic

Artistic / Landscape / Modern /
Sculpture / Water

This modern landscape garden set in the rolling hills of southwest Scotland is truly eighteenth-century in its scale, ambition and intellectual intent. It takes the visitor on nothing less than a journey through the underlying principles of the universe. It can be overwhelming: time or, even better, repeat visits are needed to take it all in.

The Portrack garden presents a series of concept areas, each of which outlines a particular aspect of the cosmos. The Universe Cascade, for example, traces the development of the universe since the Big Bang; the mounds and lakes outline key ideas of fractal geometry; and the Black Hole Terrace illustrates theories about these cosmic phenomena and the possibility of worm holes in space-time. What appears to be a conventional Parterre Garden is also a celebration of the senses and DNA. There is no respite. Everywhere one looks quotations and equations underline the garden's meaning – even on the roof ridges of the greenhouses. The impression is of being inside a library, or the brain of a polymath.

No expense has been spared in building, carving, digging, etching, casting, bolting and all the other myriad artisan operations needed to build the many sculptures, inscriptions, installations and functional features to a very high quality. As much as anything, the garden stands as a monument to British craftsmanship.

The germ of the idea for the Garden of Cosmic Speculation began with Charles Jencks's late wife, Maggie Keswick, who designed the lakes. With her death in 1995, Jencks carried on developing the garden alone. The great grass-covered landforms at the centre are the original core of the garden; they provided the model for a landscape concept that has become an important part of Jencks's career. Standing in the breeze atop the mounds is a wonderful way to refresh the mind and appreciate the surrounding landscape before plunging back into the intellectual challenges presented by the garden. Jencks is now a designer of landforms around the world – and it is intriguing that this, the most restful of his works, has proved his most adaptable and engaging.

1, 2—Snail Mound gives a view over the conical Snake Mound; the wave-like landforms and lakes reflect ideas in fractal geometry.
3—The twenty-five steps of the Universe Cascade represents the development of the cosmos from a point before space and time, at the bottom, and the future, at the top.
4—On the Black Hole Terrace a plasma-jet sculpture forms a backrest for the bench and a climbing frame for plants.
5—The former kitchen garden is now the DNA Garden, with a sculpture of the double helix at its centre.

# Bodnant

Tal-y-Cafn, Conwy, UK

Aberconway Family, Edward Milner

19th–20th century

32 hectares / 80 acres

Temperate Oceanic

Arts & Crafts / Informal / Plant Collection / Terraces

The garden at Bodnant is the work of four generations of the family of Henry David Pochin, the industrial chemist who bought the estate above the River Conwy in 1874. Pochin remodelled the house and had the designer Edward Milner lay out the gardens to take advantage of the spectacular views over the valley to distant mountains.

Today the garden comprises two main sections: the Upper Garden around the house and the Dell. Pochin's son-in-law Charles McLaren, who became the 1st Baron Aberconway in 1911, created the Upper Garden with a strong Arts and Crafts feel to its formal terraces, wooden pergolas, sweeping lawns, rose garden and displays of herbaceous plants. Two highlights are the 55-metre (180-foot) laburnum tunnel, which looks spectacular in early summer when its flowers hang like a shower of gold, and the Canal Terrace, with its large lily pool set in a verdant lawn and headed by a picturesque pin mill, which was imported from the Cotswolds in 1938 for use as a garden pavilion.

The 2nd Baron Aberconway had an enthusiasm – passed on to his son – for collecting rhododendrons and magnolias, many of which were new introductions found by plant-hunters whose expeditions he supported. Much of his collection is found in the Dell, an informal woodland garden on the steep slope down to the River Hiraethlyn, with its associated mill, pond and race. The collection of conifers is notable for the tallest redwood (*Sequoia sempervirens*) in Britain, a Douglas fir (*Pseudotsuga menziesii*) that is 48 metres (157 feet) tall and a Wellingtonia (*Sequoiadendron giganteum*) that is only slightly shorter. Beneath these conifers the slopes are smothered with magnolias and brightly coloured rhododendrons, themselves underplanted with ferns, *Meconopsis*, primulas and other exotic hardy perennials. Above the Dell is the Poem, the family mausoleum from where paths wind through shrubberies to the Rosemary Garden, the lawn, the Round Garden and the ha-ha, which gives access to views of the parkland beyond.

1 — The view across the Upper Garden stretches to the mountains of Snowdonia.
2 — The summerhouse at the end of the rectangular lily pond is a former pin mill brought from the Cotswolds in England.
3 — A sphinx guards steps down to the Canal Terrace.
4 — A stream runs through the Rock Garden to the Dell below.
5 — Colourful rhododendrons in the Dell show a mix of red, pink and white flowers on either side of a stream.
6 — The famous Laburnum Tunnel (*L.* x *watereri* 'Vossii') is at its best in early summer, when it is swathed in racemes of yellow pea-like flowers.

4

5

6

# Powis Castle Gardens

Welshpool, Powys, UK

| |
|---|
| William Winde, Adrian Duval, William Emes; Violet, Lady Powis; Jimmy Hancock |
| 17th–21st century |
| 9.7 hectares / 24 acres |
| Temperate Oceanic |
| Borders / Exotic / Historic / Terraces / Topiary / Vistas |

Many British enthusiasts cite Powis Castle as their favourite garden. It has everything: splendid old trees, flowering shrubs, herbaceous borders, clipped hedges and a walled garden. It also has one of the most spectacular situations of any British garden, which since the 1970s has been used to grow an exotic range of plants.

Looming over the landscape, the castle sits on a bluff that soaks up the sun and allows cold air to roll off it. That this would be a superb location for a garden was recognized by the 1st Marquess of Powis in the 1680s. He commissioned the architect William Winde to create terraces and grass slopes, while his successor brought in Frenchman Adrian Duval to create a formal garden. Much of this was swept away in the next century by William Emes (a follower of 'Capability' Brown), although much of the yew hedging and clipped trees on the terraces was kept. Today the garden's mass of clipped foliage occasionally smothers the terrace balustrades.

In the early twentieth century Violet, Lady Powis, relocated the Kitchen Garden, putting a new Formal Garden in its place and creating borders on the terraces to take advantage of the warm microclimate. After passing into the care of the National Trust in 1952, the garden was given a new lease of life by Jimmy Hancock, head gardener from 1972, whose choice of planting was vindicated by the increasing acclaim the garden received in the 1980s. Hancock's focus was the growing of borderline hardy species on the castle terraces. Today, the top terrace is one of the most spectacular borders in Britain, with colourful and dramatic planting rearing up at a formidably steep angle.

The lower terraces feature more conventional early twentieth-century herbaceous planting enclosed by box hedging. Lower still, there is meadow grass with wild flowers and mature trees and shrubs. The old Formal Garden is now much reduced, but still features some venerable apple trees with innovative groundcover plantings. Powis Castle remains a splendid place to relish horticultural excellence.

1—The view from the Fountain Garden shows the castle rising on its rocky bluff above the terraces of the garden.
2—Autumn sunshine bathes the view over the Formal Garden to the Severn Valley.
3, 5—The Orangery was built in the 1740s. In July salvia, sunflowers, achillea, *Kniphofia* (red-hot poker) and *Crocosmia* 'Lucifer' colour the borders on the Orangery Terrace.
4—The yew hedges buttressing the terraces have swelled out of their original shape.

3

4

5

# Veddw
# House Garden

Devauden,
Monmouthshire, UK

Charles Hawes, Anne Wareham

20th century

1.6 hectares / 4 acres

Temperate Oceanic

Artistic / Parterre / Rooms

Veddw has been called an Alice in Wonderland garden, for its embracing woodland and high hedges surround many surprise gardens and the effect is occasionally disorientating. Yet for all its undoubted fairytale qualities, this is a garden rooted in reality. With its powerful design, generous sweeps of plants and dramatic views over the hedges, Veddw sets out to honour the people who lived and worked there in the past. This was no glamorous country house, but a home in the eighteenth century for agricultural workers living in turf-and-mud huts. The garden's owners have set out to remind visitors of those hard lives and the way the garden and the land have been shaped by the past as well as the present.

Veddw is part living sculpture and part celebration of the colours and forms of planting. The garden features robust plants, happy mostly to look after themselves, living together in some mild disorder but made effective by their containment within the strong lines of hedges and paths. This is a country garden, intended to look comfortable in its setting and to reflect the surrounding countryside. Old, unploughed grassland is now conserved as meadow. A large parterre filled with ornamental grasses is contained in a pattern of box hedging based on the 1841 tithe map of the area. The plants may not be unusual – few if any are labelled – but they do take a succession of starring roles, one prima donna following or playing with another to dramatic effect right into the autumn.

The landscape of the surrounding Monmouthshire countryside is referenced in the low curves of some of the hedges, in particular the Hedge Garden beyond the black Reflecting Pool, which can create a somewhat sinister effect. The curved hedges play against one another, creating a maze-like effect, while the pool offers dramatic reflections of hedges, trees and sky, which often encourage visitors to be quietly appreciative for a while.

1—A view across the garden reveals something of the structure created by the clipped yew hedges, in contrast to the 'borrowed' landscape beyond.
2—A hornbeam tunnel and clipped box domes give structure and vertical interest to a perennial border.
3—The curved waves of the Hedge Garden create a theatrical backdrop for the sinister black waters of the Reflecting Pool.
4—A black-painted fence made from irregular lengths of timber provides an unusual boundary.
5—An avenue of *Corylus colurna* stands in the Wildflower Meadow.

# The Alnwick Garden

Alnwick, Northumberland, UK

Wirtz International

21st century

17 hectares / 42 acres

Temperate Oceanic

Formal / Rooms / Roses / Water

The new gardens surrounding Alnwick Castle are not without controversy. When the Duchess of Northumberland opened them in 2001, English Heritage accused her of destroying one of Britain's most important historic gardens: an eighteenth-century 'Capability' Brown landscape modified in the nineteenth century with a formal Italianate garden. In fact the historic garden was a neglected ruin until 1997, when the duchess decided to create her new garden, working closely with the Belgian father-and-son design team of Jacques and Peter Wirtz.

The centrepiece of the first phase was the Grand Cascade. Every minute some 33,000 litres (7,259 gallons) of water tumble down a series of twenty-one weirs made from local Darney stone, and an exuberant fountain show plays every half hour. The visitor climbs steps lined by the sinuous curves of the cascade on one side and on the other by an arched tunnel of hornbeam. Through the Venetian gates at the top of the slope, the walled Ornamental Garden reveals the Wirtz signature style: a formal green structure with a Belgio-Dutch feel defined by hornbeam-covered pergolas, yew topiary, and box and beech hedges. The intricate arrangement of small formal beds filled with a mix of roses, perennials and bulbs, pleached crab apples and paths interspersed with rills fed from a bubbling pool creates an environment that is both tranquil and stimulating.

With a flair for the theatrical, the duchess added one of the largest tree houses in the world in 2004, and a year later she opened the Poison Garden to grow plants such as cannabis and opium poppy as a fun yet educational experience for children. Another children's favourite is the Serpent Garden, with its water sculptures hidden within the coils of a holly-topiary serpent. In spring the Cherry Orchard is a breathtaking experience, with more than 300 great white cherry (*Prunus serrulata* 'Tai Haku') trees underplanted with 600,000 pink tulip 'Mistress'; and in summer the focus moves to the Rose Garden, with more than 3,000 English roses bred by David Austin.

1 — The stunning Grand Cascade – the UK's largest water feature – is controlled by computers from underground pump rooms.
2 — *Delphinium* 'Cristella' frames a rill in the Ornamental Garden.
3 — A modern fountain plays in the Serpent Garden, where the coils of a topiary snake each hold a water feature.
4 — A tunnel of ivy leads to the Poison Garden, full of potentially harmful plants.
5 — The Cherry Orchard is planted with over 300 cherry trees and underplanted with pink *Tulipa* 'Mistress'.

1

2

4

3

5

# Rydal Hall

Rydal, Cumbria, UK

| |
|---|
| Thomas Mawson, Sir Daniel le Fleming |
| 17th, 19th & 20th century |
| 0.6 hectares / 1.5 acres (terrace garden); 6 hectares / 15 acres (park) |
| Temperate Oceanic |
| Formal / Picturesque / Terraces / Water / Woodland |

Rydal Hall combines formal terraces with the romantic landscape of the Lake District and the rushing waters of the beck tumbling down the hillside. Thomas Mawson, whose family owned a nursery in nearby Windermere, was asked in 1909 to design a new garden for the south range of Rydal Hall. Mawson's designs were often in the same vein as the Arts and Crafts fashion. He favoured a formal structure of garden compartments combined with expert planting. Whereas Lutyens and Jekyll drew on the local vernacular, Mawson was inspired by the revival of interest in the gardens of the Italian Renaissance. At Rydal Hall he created a series of Italian-inspired terraces linked by twin flights of steps, the lowest of which embraces a semicircular portico.

By the 1950s the terraced gardens had fallen into decay, but they were restored in the mid-2000s and once again feature manicured lawns set with formal flower beds edged with low box hedges and planted with a period-correct display. There is ornament in the form of topiaried golden yew and planted urns on pedestals, pergolas set over benches, herbaceous borders against the terrace walls and fountain jets playing in the circular pool. Mawson used exposed precast concrete for the balustrading, stairs, urns and other features – an early use of the material – but it did not weather well, and many features have been recast using moulds found in the basement of the house.

Rydal Beck flows to the west of the terraced garden to a waterfall. Beside the pool at its base stands the Grot – now called the Grotto – a little stone building with a window designed for viewing the waterfall. The Grot was part of a mid-seventeenth-century Picturesque landscape created by Sir Daniel le Fleming and later described by William Wordsworth in his poem 'An Evening Walk'. The Walled Garden has also been restored and is once again productive as a vegetable garden, while scattered throughout the park is a collection of sculptures.

1 — The circular pool at the heart of the terraced gardens is aligned on the central axis of Mawson's garden.
2 — The tall flowers of alliums rise above the verdant, richly planted beds that soften the overall formality of the terrace garden.
3 — The nineteenth-century Walled Garden at the end of a woodland walk has been restored as a productive vegetable garden.
4 — A bench in a niche in a wall of one of the terraces allows the visitor to take in the surrounding planting.
5 — Rydal Beck tumbles down a waterfall into a pool beside the Grotto, a small summerhouse built for viewing the falls.

# Holker Hall

Cark-in-Cartmel,
Grange-over-Sands,
Cumbria, UK

Lord George Cavendish,
Thomas Mawson, Kim Wilkie

19th, 20th & 21st century

10 hectares / 25 acres (garden);
81 hectares / 200 acres (park)

Temperate Oceanic

Arts & Crafts / Italianate / Landscape /
Plant Collection / Woodland

More than 200 years ago, Lord George Cavendish created what he described as a 'contrived natural landscape' at Holker Hall. Today the gardens continue to evolve under the Cavendish family stewardship. Holker (pronounced Hooker) has many acres of 'natural' parkland, award-winning walks through rhododendrons and azaleas, and woodlands planted with collections of unusual specimens.

More formal gardens lie close to the sixteenth-century house. The designer, Thomas Mawson, was a local landscape architect and nurseryman who understood the climate and other site conditions. Closely trimmed hedges of yew and box add a traditional formality to the design. Many areas are Italianate in style, from the balustraded terrace to the Sunken Garden (once a rose garden, but now with many subtropical plants) to the Cascade, which resembles the Renaissance example at Villa d'Este (see page 302). A new Neptune Cascade was added in the early 1990s.

A labyrinth and wild-flower meadow were added in the early 2000s to link the formal gardens with the parkland and surrounding landscape. The labyrinth design is based on Hindu temple motifs combined with a contemporary version of a Cumbrian stone circle. Twelve monoliths, seats and gravel paths are all made from local slate. It is a place for peaceful reflection.

Change at Holker is a continuous process. In 2014 Kim Wilkie designed the Pagan Grove, which reshaped parts of the formal gardens to create an oval amphitheatre that sinks into the ground. Elsewhere, other features are timeless: the Great Holker Lime tree is more than 400 years old, and the trunk has highly sculptural qualities. The Gulf Stream climate allows many choice trees, shrubs and tender perennials to thrive.

Holker Hall combines parkland, woodland, plant collections and formal gardens overlaid with typically English planting with topiary, herbaceous perennials and roses. With a great sense of place and history, it is a garden that has developed in ways that are perfectly suited to its site.

1 — Evening light falls across a lawn and part of the formal Italianate gardens near the house.
2 — The Great Holker Lime was listed in 2002 as one of the fifty great trees of Britain.
3 — The labyrinth was designed by Jim Buchanan and Grania Cavendish based on designs from a Hindu temple.
4 — Rhododendrons add splashes of colour to a shady fountain and pool.
5 — Two obelisks mark the entrance to the Neptune Cascade.

# Biddulph Grange Garden

Biddulph, Stoke-on-Trent,
Staffordshire, UK

James Bateman, Maria Bateman,
Edward William Cooke

19th century

3 hectares / 8 acres

Temperate Oceanic

Arboretum / Historic / Plant
Collection / Plantsman / Rooms

In their influence on garden design and
fashion in Victorian Britain, especially
on the villa gardens of the spreading
suburbs, two gardens reigned supreme.
One was Chatsworth in Derbyshire
(see page 136); the other was Biddulph
Grange. Biddulph was created at a time
when the fashion was for the artistic:
gardens reflected the visible hand
of Man rather than being an imitation
of Nature. If Chatsworth demonstrated
how art and nature could coexist,
Biddulph Grange was the masterclass
in demonstrating how they could clash.

James Bateman, who inherited
both money and land, was a devoted
horticulturalist with a passion for
orchids. His work *The Orchidaceae of
Mexico and Guatemala* is one of the rarest
books on botany ever published – and
physically the largest. Bateman and his
wife, Maria, moved to Biddulph in 1840
and created their garden from 1849 with
help from their friend Edward Cooke,
a well-known painter of seascapes.
The plantaholic Bateman set out to
create a garden in which to display
his extensive plant collections from
all over the world, grouping them
either geographically or botanically.

In order to achieve this, the garden
was designed as something of a
horticultural theme park, in a succession
of more than a dozen linked compartments,
the most famous of which are China,
Egypt, Cheshire Cottage, the Glen
and the Rhododendron Ground. Each
compartment has its individual character,
features and collection of plants. When
walking through the garden the visitor
is constantly surprised and amused
by the brilliantly contrived ways in which
the compartments are linked. The design
is also deliberately inward-looking.
The visitor's attention is focused on
the immediate surroundings – especially
the plants – rather than being drawn to
distant vistas.

Such was the Batemans' passion
for garden-making that their money
ran out, and in 1861 they were forced
to move. The gardens subsequently
fell into decay, but have been faithfully
restored since 1988.

1 — The yew-lined Dahlia Walk – seen
here from the Shelter House – was laid
out by James Bateman in 1842 and restored
in 1988.
2 — A view from the Terrace shows a
colourful display of rhododendrons in June.
3, 4 — The Chinese Garden, complete with
its bridge and pavilion, is entered through
an oriental stone gateway.
5 — Twin sphinxes guard the entrance to
the Egyptian Garden with its pyramid of
clipped yew.
6 — The Glen, the work of Edward William
Cooke, is an outstanding example of a
Victorian rock garden.

# Trentham Estate

Stoke-on-Trent, Staffordshire, UK

Sir Charles Barry, Tom Stuart-Smith, Piet Oudolf

19th & 21st century

3 hectares / 9 acres (garden); 121.5 hectares / 300 acres (park)

Temperate Oceanic

Grasses / Italianate / Terraces

The story of Trentham is one of beauty, decay, near destruction – and eventual restoration. When he remodelled Trentham Hall in the 1830s for the Duke of Sutherland, Sir Charles Barry – best known as the architect of the Gothic Revival Houses of Parliament in London – used a very different approach that he had devised. Although it was called Italianate, the garden he created in fact plundered from the English Tudor, the Italian Renaissance and the French and Dutch Baroque. On terraces leading down to the informal lake created by Lancelot 'Capability' Brown in the eighteenth-century, Barry laid out a series of formal parterres, with pools and fountains separated by paths and ornamented with statuary and topiary.

When, however, the local pottery industry polluted both the air and the River Trent (which fed the garden), later in the nineteenth century, the duke moved away. In 1911 much of Trentham Hall was demolished, and the gardens left to decay. It was nearly a century later, between 2003 and 2012, that they were restored when the estate was redeveloped as a leisure facility.

The Italianate terraces, now called the Italian Garden, were restored to the formality of Barry's original plan. Rather than refill the flower beds with seasonal displays, Tom Stuart-Smith reworked the planting in a contemporary, naturalistic design. The result is a beautiful show in high summer, with drought-tolerant species in hot colours on the upper terrace running to cooler colours and species that prefer moister soil nearer the lake. Seventy flower beds contain 80,000 plants of 400 types.

Flanking the formal terrace, an informal contrast comes from two new areas designed by Piet Oudolf. The Floral Labyrinth at the garden's entrance is a maze of paths meandering through three beds of tall perennial plantings of strong colours and scents. Juxtaposed with it is the Rivers of Grass, a tapestry of ornamental grasses and perennials growing *en masse*. In the wider estate a woodland of 200,000 native oak trees has been planted as a Royal Diamond Jubilee wood.

1 — The contemporary Italian Garden created by Tom Stuart-Smith on the lower terrace uses naturalistic planting of perennials and ornamental grasses.
2 — The upper terrace of the Italian Garden is a more traditional, formal arrangement of parterres.
3 — A gravel path runs through the Floral Labyrinth, designed by Piet Oudolf, with borders of tall perennials and ornamental grasses, including sedum and monarda.
4 — A border designed by Oudolf is filled with *Eupatorium, Solidago, Helenium, Phlox* and *Datisca cannabina*.

# Cottesbrooke Hall

Northampton,
Northamptonshire, UK

Robert Weir Schultz, Geoffrey Jellicoe,
Sylvia Crowe, James Alexander-
Sinclair, Angela Collins, Arne Maynard

20th & 21st century

12 hectares / 30 acres

Temperate Oceanic

Arts & Crafts / Italianate /
Modern / Rooms

Said to be the pattern for Jane Austen's
*Mansfield Park*, Cottesbrooke Hall is
a near-perfect example of Queen Anne
architecture, but its gardens are far
newer and feature work by many of the
twentieth century's finest practitioners.
They were begun in the 1930s, when
the then-owners engaged the Scottish
architect Robert Weir Schultz to
introduce an Arts and Crafts feel.
Part of Schultz's legacy is the pergola
beneath the spreading branches of
the ancient cedars of Lebanon, and
the long paved terrace walk with its
double herbaceous borders.

In 1937 the new (and current) owners,
the Macdonald-Buchanan family, had
Geoffrey Jellicoe (see Shute House,
page 194) add a Renaissance-style
balustraded forecourt. Boasting statues
and topiaried yew and golden yew,
the box-edged parterre was later
softened using herbaceous plantings.
In the 1950s Sylvia Crowe remodelled
the walled Pool Garden, replacing
Schultz's rose garden with sunken
grass with a circular pool, and trees
and shrubs including *Cercidiphyllum
japonicum*, *Cornus macrophylla* and
magnolias. Crowe's arbour has a vista
to the statue of the Gladiator defined
by twin avenues of pleached limes (*Tilia
x europaea*). Classical statues that once
graced the Temple of Ancient Virtue
at Stowe (see page 156) now line the
Statue Walk, where Arne Maynard
has designed borders that mix informal
herbaceous plants and rose domes
that appear like topiary.

Several areas had to be replanted
after an outbreak of box blight in 2009.
In the Philosopher's Garden, the beds
are now edged with Lady's mantle
(*Alchemilla mollis*). The Secret Garden
is now planted with a mix of bulbs,
hornbeam topiary and oak-leaved
hydrangeas, while the Dutch Garden
was redesigned by Angela Collins as a
riot of cornflowers, *Echium* and dahlias.
Other highlights include the Herb
Garden, with its naturalistic planting
of grasses, bulbs and perennials, and
the Wild Garden, with its shows of wild
flowers in the meadow areas followed
by rhododendrons with bamboos,
gunneras and Japanese maples.

1—The borders on Schultz's terrace walk
were replanted by James Alexander-Sinclair.
2, 3—Sylvia Crowe's Pool Garden is a
peaceful space with a central pool, a gazebo
and a pergola that offers views across the
pool and lawn.
4—On the Statue Walk, Arne Maynard's
broad border contains red dahlias, *Anemone
japonica*, chleome and *Macleaya cordata*.
5—A bridge provides a focal point in the
Wild Garden beyond *Darmera peltata* and
*Ligularia dentata* 'Desdemona'.

# Chatsworth

Bakewell, Derbyshire, UK

| |
|---|
| George London, Henry Wise, Lancelot 'Capability' Brown, Joseph Paxton |
| 17th–20th century |
| 42.5 hectares / 105 acres |
| Temperate Oceanic |
| English Landscape / Formal / Kitchen / Rock / Water |

Chatsworth is unique in its harmonious incorporation of features from five centuries of garden-making. In gardens so old, it is usual for the new to sweep away the old. That is not the case at Chatsworth, which has a history that stretches from the Baroque garden laid out by the famous seventeenth-century designers George London and Henry Wise to a Sensory Garden opened early in the third millennium.

Vestiges of London and Wise's design include the Great Cascade and the Canal Pond, the 1st Duke's greenhouse, the Temple of Flora and the Willow Tree fountain. The greatest legacy of the eighteenth century is the 'Capability' Brown landscape, which emphasizes the natural landscape from near the house and provides the perfect setting for the house when seen from afar.

Chatsworth reached its zenith in the nineteenth century, when the 6th Duke and his head gardener, Joseph Paxton, created one of the two most influential English gardens of the century (the other was Biddulph Grange, see page 132). Chatsworth's eclectic features became the backdrop for a garden that showed how art and nature could coexist harmoniously. Paxton planted the Arboretum (1835), erected the Great Conservatory (1836) and arranged boulders to construct a huge rockery (1842). He also built the Conservative Wall (c.1832) for growing fruit and camellias, turning it into a series of stepped greenhouses in 1848–50. For a planned visit of Tsar Nicholas of Russia, he installed the Emperor Fountain, with its 84-metre (276-foot) gravity-fed jet.

Many of Paxton's features remain in the grounds around the house, but the Great Conservatory and the bespoke glasshouses – including the Water Lily House, where he achieved the first garden flowering of the giant water lily *Victoria amazonica* in 1849 – have all gone. But new features have been added: the Serpentine Hedge (1953); the Maze (1962), with 1,209 yews; and more recently a new Kitchen Garden. Modern sculptures introduce a contemporary feel to the historic garden, helping to bring it into another century of fascinating evolution.

1—The magnificent Emperor Fountain plays on the Canal Pond in front of the house.
2—The Willow Tree Fountain takes the shape of a deceptively naturalistic tree, but sprays unsuspecting passers-by with water.
3—The Serpentine Hedge is a yew avenue planted in the 1950s to join the Ring Pond to a bust of the 6th Duke.
4—The glasshouses of the Conservative Wall contain a remarkable collection of camellias.
5—The setting sun casts a glow over the Great Cascade; steps of different sizes produced different notes of water 'music'.

4

5

# The Bressingham Gardens

Bressingham, Norfolk, England

Alan Bloom, Adrian Bloom, Robert Bloom

20th–21st century

7 hectares / 17 acres

Temperate Oceanic

Bedding / Informal / Nursery / Perennials /Plantsman

At Bressingham some of the outstanding plant combinations in Europe create a vibrant garden with a use of colour that is unparalleled in its extragavant use of flowers. Founded by Alan Bloom in 1946, the gardens also contain a famous nursery.

Bloom was one of the most famous of British gardeners of his era – his achievements were acknowledged with both an MBE and awards from the Royal Horticultural Society. He was the first person to grow herbaceous plants in island beds separated by grass paths but connected by a clever use of colour and texture. Bloom's enthusiasm for this style of gardening would eventually lead to the creation of the Dell Garden, forty-eight beds covering almost 2.4 hectares (6 acres). The beds are a world in themselves, where the visitor can spend days enjoying their complexity.

The island beds are just one element of the garden, however. In 1996, Bloom's son Adrian created a second garden he called Foggy Bottom. It was one of the first gardens – if not the first – to use conifers for colour, mixing 500 different species with heathers and ornamental grasses. It remains a dynamic garden today, even though many of the 'dwarf' conifers are now huge.

There are numerous other gardens at Bressingham. The Summer Garden is full of *Miscanthus* spp. and summer-blooming perennials. The Woodland Garden, which has a central feature of giant redwoods (*Sequoiadendron giganteum*) that are now over 24 metres (80 feet) tall, has been planted with North American species.

The sweetest garden is the Fragrant Garden, which mixes plants that have fragrant flowers and foliage. It is well placed next to a picnic area. A dramatic Winter Garden sets early-flowering bulbs against a backdrop of the coloured stems of cut-back shrubs.

In all, Bressingham offers the visitor much to explore, much to ponder and much to take home.

1, 2—The Dell Garden features the island beds championed by Alan Bloom. Among the plants providing contrasts of colour, texture and shape in a mixed border are evergreen conifers, silver birch, feather reed grass (*Calamagrostis* x *acutiflora* 'Overdam'), eastern redbud (*Cercis canadensis*) and dwarf silver grasses (*Festuca glauca*).
3, 4—Adrian Bloom's Winter Garden retains interest through the year, and mixes woody plants with bold coloured bark such as silver birch, red and orange dogwoods (*Cornus sanguinea* 'Midwinter Fire'), and perennials, grasses and conifers.
5, 6—The Summer Garden reaches a peak in August, when a riot of colour comes from dozens of species, including varieties of agapanthus, echinacea and *Miscanthus*.

138

3

4

5

6

# East Ruston Old Vicarage Garden

East Ruston, Norwich,
Norfolk, UK

| |
|---|
| Alan Gray, Graham Robeson |
| 20th–21st century |
| 12.9 hectares / 32 acres |
| Temperate Oceanic |
| Dry / Informal / Plantsman / Rooms / Vistas / Water |

The garden that Alan Gray and Graham Robeson began at East Ruston in 1973 was just a sixteenth of its size today. Constant development has created a highly varied plot crammed with horticultural treasures and exciting plant combinations. Key to the garden's survival was the early establishment of shelter belts, to protect it from wind. The outer boundaries are Monterey pines (*Pinus radiata*), Italian alder (*Alnus cordata*), Tasmanian snow gum (*Eucalyptus coccifera*) and holm oak (*Quercus ilex*), with inner defences of evergreen shrubs. Hornbeam and beech are used for some inner hedges.

Next, Gray and Robeson made several ponds. The pools, hedges, banks and wild areas are attractive to wildlife, so the garden is now a haven for a wide range of birds, insects and mammals. Close to the house are intimate enclosed areas, such as the walled Gravel Garden, while nearer the boundaries are more expansive plantings, such as the breathtaking meadow, the cornfield, the Desert Wash and the California Garden.

The Desert Wash, one of the more recent areas, was inspired by an Arizona desertscape. It is filled with drought-loving plants from California, Mexico, South Africa and Australia. Although it may look rather like a heap of stones, a carefully engineered system drains water away deep below the surface.

Colour in the borders, containers and extensive Vegetable Garden provides seasonal interest, as does foliage shape and texture. Statuary and borrowed features, such as the Happisburgh Lighthouse and the church, offer focal points at the end of long vistas.

Both Gray and Robeson have great plant passions, and both are involved in all aspects of this high-maintenance garden, planning new developments. The latest areas include the Diamond Jubilee Walled Garden, a new Fruit and Vegetable Garden, an orchard of heritage fruit trees and extensive planting in the East Park. In addition, as the garden matures, choices need to be made about cutting back or removing overgrown plantings – hence the decision to build decorative wood piles.

1 — Golden California poppy (*Eschscholzia californica*) self-seeds all through the Desert Wash, where agapanthus, agave and other succulents thrive.
2 — In May the woodland fills with bergenia and delicate forget-me-nots (*Myosotis*).
3 — The Dutch Garden has geometric box pyramids, balls and hedges around a central *Ilex* x *altaclerensis* 'Golden King'.
4 — In the Tree Fern Garden *Dicksonia antarctica* is underplanted with maples, narcissi and hellebores.
5 — In late summer the Red and Purple Border is bursting with standard ligustrum, dahlias, phormium, hydrangea and fuchsia.

1

2

3

4

5

# The Laskett Gardens

Much Birch, Herefordshire, UK

| |
|---|
| Roy Strong, Julia Trevelyan Oman |
| 20th century |
| 1.5 hectares / 4 acres |
| Temperate Oceanic |
| Formal / Individualistic / Rooms |

This is among the most important formal gardens of the last forty years, but it provokes mixed responses: some visitors love it, while others are less than impressed. Perhaps this reflects the personality of Roy Strong, the garden's co-creator, who holds strong opinions about which historical garden styles are a suitable inspiration – and which are not. He abhors the naturalism of 'Capability' Brown but rejoices in the formal gardens of the Italian Renaissance, English gardens of the Tudor and Stuart eras, and gardens created in England before World War I, such as Hidcote Manor (see page 148). Their influence is clear at The Laskett Gardens, not only in the extensive use of topiary, building, statuary and ornamentation, but also in the strong architectural structure.

The gardens are laid out in a series of twenty or so 'rooms', including a rose garden, a knot garden, a kitchen garden, a pleached lime avenue and the Colonnade Court. The aim is to thrill the visitor, and to offer dramatic vistas.

The gardens, set on a triangular plot, were begun in 1973. They are highly individual, with a number of features that recall the couple's friends and various jobs. An armillary sphere from the garden of Sir Roy's friend Sir Cecil Beaton graces the Jubilee Garden; an arbour honours Sir Frederick Ashton, the choreographer, two of whose most famous ballets Trevelyan Oman designed; while the Victoria and Albert Museum Temple testifies to Sir Roy's directorship of that institution.

After thirty years, Sir Roy decided that the infrastructure was over-mature, and so the hedges were recut, vistas out to the borrowed landscape were opened up and the planting was reconditioned. The design is not without its critics; some find the layout of the rooms cramped, for example. Yet The Laskett Gardens are still evolving under the direction of Sir Roy (Trevelyan Oman died in 2003) for his own pleasure, not that of the critic or visitor. The gardens are a lesson in how garden history can be brought up-to-date to create a place that owes its inspiration to the past but is also very much a part of its own *Zeitgeist*.

1 — This platform in the Howdah Garden provides views across the site.
2 — In the heart of the Kitchen Garden stands a modern copy of an eighteenth-century statue of a gardener.
3 — An urn in the Christmas Orchard, first planted in 1974, holds the ashes of Julia Trevelyan Oman and will eventually hold those of Sir Roy Strong.
4 — An armillary sphere from the garden of Cecil Beaton stands in the Silver Jubilee Garden. In the background stands the Triumphant Arch in the Rose Garden.
5 — The arms of Edward I, a fragment from the medieval Palace of Westminster, is displayed in the Christmas Orchard.

1

# Montpelier Cottage

Brilley, Herefordshire, UK

| |
|---|
| Noel Kingsbury |
| 21st century |
| 1.5 hectares / 4 acres |
| Temperate Oceanic |
| Grasses / Informal / Meadow / Naturalistic / New Perennial |

Noel Kingsbury began the garden at Montpelier Cottage in 2005 as an experiment in naturalistic planting. It had to be both decorative, to use for entertaining, and functional to trial planting, particularly for low-maintenance public spaces. The planting was to respect the 'visual ecology' of a landscape dominated by native deciduous trees; evergreen, woody plants or any colours or shapes that might detract were avoided. The garden blends seamlessly into a wilder, semi-natural landscape.

The planting is dominated by summer-flowering perennials, with spring interest provided by daffodils, *Helleborus* x *hybridus* and primulas. Ornamental grasses play a major decorative role in winter. With fertile soil and high rainfall, growth tends to be lush, with high levels of weeds, so there is an emphasis on strongly growing, competitive plants, particularly those from North American tall-grass prairies and Eurasian 'tall-herb' flora. Wide borders around a lawn are managed to a relatively conventional standard, while a lower area – the Wild Garden – receives much less attention. A range of robust summer-flowering perennials coexists there with spontaneous native flora. Self-seeding and spreading are encouraged as part of a process of continuous, natural regeneration.

The Wild Garden blends into a Bog Garden with two ponds, and then into meadow grassland. The meadow is unimproved rush pasture, a species-rich survival of old farming practices. Unlike most British grassland, the main season of ornamental interest is late summer, when it is dominated by the yellow of fleabane (*Pulicaria dysenterica*).

The remainder of the cultivated portion of the property is given over to a series of research and trial plots. New plant species and cultivars are trialled, and perennial combinations are assessed for their viability and potential in reducing maintenance. One current project is the use of sedges (*Carex* spp.) as 'living mulches' around perennials.

1 — The border around a natural pond includes *Filipendula* (meadowsweet), asters and *Gunnera*. A line of willow trees leads to the yurt and the meadow beyond.
2, 3 — The borders near the cottage include *Stipa tenuissima* and *Verbena bonariensis*, as well as *Persicaria microcephala* 'Red Dragon', *Astrantia major*, geraniums and *Calamagrostis* x *acutiflora* 'Karl Foerster'.
4 — Robust perennials flower in the Wild Garden in late May, including *Rhododendron occidentale*, *Persicaria bistorta* and *Anthriscus sylvestris*, with *Iris sibirica* and *Ranunculus acris* subsp. *acris* 'Stevenii' in the distance.
5 — The main border in August is rich in interest, with *Persicaria amplexicaulis* 'Rosea', *Cirsium canum*, *Acanthus spinosus* hybrid and *Eupatorium fistulosum*.

# Upton Wold

Moreton-in-Marsh,
Gloucestershire, UK

| |
|---|
| Brenda Colvin, Hal Moggridge |
| 20th century |
| Temperate Oceanic |
| Arboretum / Borders / Edible / Formal / Water / Woodland |

When Mr and Mrs Ian Bond bought the old manor house at Upton Wold in 1973, there was no garden, just two old yew trees, a holly and some old apple trees. Since then, helped by the garden architects Brenda Colvin and Hal Moggridge and sustained by their own energy and flair, the Bonds have created an original and intriguing garden.

Approaching the house down the long drive through woodland, the visitor has no inkling of the surprise that awaits. Even standing by the oak front door, the secret is still not revealed. But dart through a path in the yew hedge, stand on the terrace – and look. You are facing east over a fine garden and a wide valley. The central axis runs away in front of you, leading your eye down into the valley and up over the woods and fields beyond.

The axial Broad Walk is bordered by two massive yew hedges, with windows (*clairvoyées*) cut into them to offer glimpses of a colourful herbaceous border, and a long iris walk. The right-hand hedge has a dark, scary tunnel running through its centre – a child's wild delight. Up a bank sits the Secret Garden, with magnolias and a fine *Davidia involucrata*, underplanted with bulbs.

Elsewhere are a pond with bog plants and a wild-flower meadow. There is a large kitchen garden with fruit, vegetables and flowers arranged each side of a pleached hornbeam path; clipped standard cones of holly, box hedges and espaliered apples and pears are underplanted with hellebores. Stone pillars at the end of the Hornbeam Path lead into the Woodland Garden, with an essential shelter belt beyond, and a sundial designed by Mark Lennox-Boyd; a cheetah sculpted by Dylan Lewis slinks out of the bushes. A small orchard, canal garden and dovecote garden all add to the charm.

This is also a garden for arborealists, with magnificent and unusual trees. The arboretum is home to the national collection of *Juglans* (walnuts) and *Pterocarya*. Mown paths lead to a focal point formed by a labyrinth and a circle of twelve standing stones represent the apostles – and provide a suitable place to stand and contemplate the wonder and delight of this garden.

1 — The Canal Garden, which sits on a plateau beneath the house, was created by Anthony Archer-Wills.
2 — Weathered stone balls punctuate the strict formation of a row of Hidcote-inspired hornbeam trunks.
3 — The Emily Young Border is named after the leading British sculptor whose work provides its focus.
4 — Catmint (*Nepeta* 'Six Hills Giant') flowers along the path of the walled Upper Vegetable Garden.

# Old Rectory

· Gloucestershire, UK

| | |
|---|---|
| Dan Pearson | |
| 21st century | |
| 0.6 hectares / 1.5 acres | |
| Temperate Oceanic | |
| Formal / Naturalistic / Rooms / Water | |

An Arts and Crafts garden for the twenty-first century has been wrapped around this Cotswold house dating from the 1730s. There is a sensitivity to the rural setting with the deft use of vernacular honey-coloured stone combined with a fine plant palette that creates areas of quiet yet exuberant planting. Near the gate, in challenging conditions beneath an impressive beech tree, is a rich range of planting including *Ribes sanguineum* 'Tydeman's White' and a fine multi-stemmed katsura tree (*Cercidiphyllum japonicum*), which provides the candyfloss scent of its pastel yellow-pink foliage in autumn.

Walls divide the garden into distinct areas, each with their own character. Behind the house a canal forms the central axis of the garden, while a discreet cascade provides the gentle sound of water. At the far end of the canal, an enclosed seating area is covered by a trained wisteria. The borders are given height and winter interest by witch hazel (*Hamamelis*), which is underplanted by a succession of bulbs, including white tulips and alliums. A further summer display comes from flowering herbaceous perennials, including daylilies, the yellow *Hemerocallis citrina*, and the rich red *H*. 'Stafford'. The plants are given a sense of formality by dramatic spheres of box (*Buxus sempervirens*) that line the borders. The walls are pierced by windows in the style of traditional Cotswold barn slits, providing glimpses through to other parts of the garden.

Near the small vegetable garden a river supplies a circular pond that reflects the sky and the trees around it. On one side of the canal, panels of wild flowers and bulbs form a contrast with the mown turf; there is also a swimming pool. A thoughtfully curved path follows the perimeter, affording views back to the house and geometric squares of *Buxus*, some of which seem to provide plinths for delicate multi-stemmed *Amelanchier* trees. For contrast there are vertical clumps of *Calamagrostis* x *acutiflora* 'Karl Foerster', providing interest throughout the summer and winter. Indeed, this is a garden that delights the senses in every season.

1—The central canal uses local Cotswold stone to provide rich textural interest and a frame for the naturalistic planting of the borders.
2—Box plinths for delicate multi-stemmed *Amelanchier* trees contrast with vertical clumps of *Calamagrostis* x *acutiflora* 'Karl Foerster'.
3—Near the house, red *Hemerocallis* 'Stafford' and *Crocosmia* 'Lucifer' give a display of summer colour.
4—Water lilies fill the pond in a garden that is notable for its sensitive use of water.
5—Local materials are used to create seating areas from which to appreciate the different compartments of the garden.

# Hidcote Manor

Hidcote Bartrim,
Gloucestershire, UK

Lawrence Johnston

20th century

4 hectares / 10 acres

Temperate Oceanic

Arts & Crafts / Borders /
Plantsman / Rooms

Hidcote Manor, one of the most iconic and influential English gardens of the twentieth century, was created by an American. Lawrence Johnston, a naturalized British citizen, began his masterpiece in 1907 when his mother bought him a house with a view over the fields of the Gloucestershire countryside. Over the next forty-one years Johnston created what is now one of the most visited gardens in Britain.

A keen plantsman, Johnston was influenced by the Arts and Crafts gardens of Gertrude Jekyll and Edwin Lutyens in his colour-coordinated planting schemes and his division of the garden into compartments. He skilfully used the sloping site to create a seemingly haphazard yet rewarding succession of rooms that create an atmosphere of mystery and surprise – albeit lacking Lutyens' finesse.

Johnston's scheme uses two perpendicular axes aligned as a 'T', around which he grouped a complex of twenty garden 'rooms' – including the Stilt Garden, the Bathing Pool Garden and Mrs Winthrop's Garden (named for his mother) – divided by mixed hedges of holly, yew, beech, lime and hornbeam. But Johnston's triumph was the twin Red Borders: the reds of the flowers and foliage draw the eye and bring the foreground into sharp focus, while in the middle-distance gazebos frame the contrasting green of the Stilt Garden.

The character of the individual rooms comes from Johnston's artful planting, a skill that he developed in the 1920s with help from his friend Norah Lindsay. Vita Sackville-West described it as 'a kind of haphazard luxuriance, which of course comes neither by hap nor hazard at all'. Hidcote is unjustly less famous than Sissinghurst, and the characters of the respective creators could not have been more different. Vita was vivacious, stylish and charming; Johnston was described by the plant-hunter George Forrest as 'a right good old Spinster spoilt by being born male'. Johnston's own plant-hunting led him to discover two new mahonias (*M. lomariifolia* and *M. siamensis*), and in his garden he bred *Hypericum* 'Hidcote'.

1—Tulips in the Old Garden in May make a cheerful contrast to the honey-coloured stone of the Cotswold house.
2—Morning sun illuminates canna and dahlias in the Red Borders leading past the Pavilions to the Stilt Garden.
3—In the Bathing Pool Garden a cherub fountain stands before bird topiary.
4—The planting of Mrs Winthrop's Garden includes *Alchemilla mollis* and bronze cordylines in ornamental urns.
5—The Rock Bank is home to a Corsican pine and Mediterranean perennials.
6—Crambe cordifolia, lupins and foxgloves flourish in the Long Borders in June.

1

2

3

4

5

6

# Highgrove

Tetbury, Gloucestershire, UK

| |
| --- |
| Lady Salisbury, Rosemary Verey, Isabel and Julian Bannerman, and others |
| 20th century |
| 6 hectares / 15 acres |
| Temperate Oceanic |
| Edible / Formal / Informal / Meadow / Rooms / Woodland |

Royalty has given the world a rich legacy of gardens. At Highgrove, the Prince of Wales continues this tradition while demonstrating his belief that it is better to work with nature than against it. Highgrove is not a grand landscape garden but the creation of a keen gardener with organic principles. Prince Charles has been advised by key British gardeners, from Rosemary Verey, Lady Salisbury and Miriam Rothschild to Julian and Isabel Bannerman.

The gardens are mainly informal, but a formal axis from the Georgian house has been created by a stone-flagged path planted with thyme, which in summer buzzes with bees. Alongside the path are golden yew spheres pruned into fantastical shapes, while the design is delineated by pleached limes forming aerial rectangles of green. Beyond is a water feature, and the line continues into the wild-flower meadows as a lime (*Tilia*) avenue terminating in a dovecote.

The meadows are the epitome of summer, and a range of native species has created a rich matrix of wild flowers. These include summer-flowering ox-eye daisy (*Leucanthemum vulgare*), the semi-parasitic yellow rattle (*Rhinanthus minor*) and more exotic species such as late-spring-flowering *Camassia* and ornamental onions (*Allium*). The last are examples of the preference for blue and purple within the garden.

In contrast to the open meadows is the Woodland Garden, complete with a stumpery that provides a home for many ferns. Among the trees are green-oak classical temples and a fairytale tree house. *Acer* cultivars are used for their rich autumn colour, as is the purple-flowering *Hydrangea aspera* Villosa Group. The Walled Garden is home to a wealth of organic fruit and vegetables.

The Woodland Garden blends into a small arboretum that holds part of the Plant Heritage collection of beech (*Fagus*) trees, echoing the prince's commitment to conservation. The gardens at Highgrove are thus a testimony to one man's passion to live and garden sustainably with nature.

1—*Camassia*, buttercups and dandelions bloom in the Wild-Flower Meadow Garden in front of the house.
2—The Kitchen Garden includes rare and endangered varieties that are vital in terms of biodiversity.
3—The Sundial Garden was originally designed by Lady Salisbury as a rose garden.
4—Golden yew topiary adorns the Thyme Walk between hornbeam stilt hedges.
5—May blooms in the Cottage Garden designed by Prince Charles and the late Rosemary Verey.
6—In spring, daffodils welcome visitors to the thatched tree house 'Hollyrood House', in the Stumpery of the Woodland Garden, designed by Julian and Isabel Bannerman.

3

4

5

6

# Sezincote

Moreton-in-Marsh,
Gloucestershire, UK

| |
|---|
| Thomas Daniell, Graham Stuart Thomas, Lady Kleinwort |
| 19th & 20th century |
| 2 hectares / 5 acres |
| Temperate Oceanic |
| Historic / Islamic / Landscape / Water |

The surprise that is Sezincote (SEE-zin-cote, or 'the place of the oaks') is revealed at the final curve of the drive: an exotic-looking house that transports visitors to the foothills of northern India. A Cotswold hillside of oak woodland makes a backdrop to this small mansion in the Hindu–Mughal style, which was built around 1805 by the architect Samuel Pepys Cockerell for his brother Sir Charles Cockerell, an East India Company veteran who wanted a home to remind him of South Asia.

To carry this architectural style into the garden and the landscape beyond, Sir Charles employed the artist Thomas Daniell, who had also spent a decade in India. Daniell is credited with conceiving the Thornery and Water Garden north of the house, but in reality, the gardens were probably more of a collaboration. Sir Charles was involved in all aspects of the process, down to the placement of the Brahmin bulls on Daniell's Indian Bridge. Humphry Repton was also consulted, and the parkland at Sezincote has a similar feel to a Reptonian landscape.

A temple to Surya, the Hindu sun god, marks the start of the Water Garden at the top of the small valley, and the formal pool to the front continues the Indian style. From here, a stream flows along the valley, under the Indian Bridge to the Snake Pool, with its bronze serpent wrapped around a column, finishing downstream in two more naturalistic pools. The area was planted for year-round interest by the renowned plantsman Graham Stuart Thomas, who helped former owners Sir Cyril and Lady Kleinwort restore the run-down gardens from 1945 onwards.

Lady Kleinwort added the South Garden in 1965 after a visit to India. The design follows that of a traditional Islamic paradise garden, or *chahar bagh*, with four parts divided by paths or water that represent the four rivers of life. At Sezincote, two narrow canals are crossed by two paths of the same dimensions, with an octagonal pool and fountain as a focal point. Along each axis, Irish yews (*Taxus baccata* 'Fastigiata') are used in place of traditional cypresses, which are not reliably hardy in the Cotswold climate.

1 — Two elephants stand sentinel over the formal canals of the South Garden in front of the Mughal-inspired house.
2 — Ferns and *Lysichiton americanum*, the skunk cabbage, emerge each spring at the damp margins of the Stream Garden, along with other moisture-loving plants.
3 — Two Brahmin bull statues adorn Daniell's stone Indian Bridge above the stream and Snake Pool.
4 — A temple to the Hindu sun god Surya overlooks the Oriental Fountain Pool.

# Blenheim Palace

Woodstock, Oxfordshire, UK

Lancelot 'Capability' Brown,
Achille Duchêne

18th & 20th century

850 hectares / 2,100 acres

Temperate Oceanic

English Landscape / Formal / Historic

Lancelot 'Capability' Brown marked the zenith of the eighteenth-century English landscape garden tradition, and Blenheim is his masterpiece. But such was Brown's genius that his fingerprints are subtle. He called his work 'place-making', and aimed to create an entirely natural appearance. The English politician Horace Walpole wrote: 'When he was the happiest man he will be least remembered, so closely did he copy nature that his works will be mistaken.'

Brown did not invent the English landscape garden. Charles Bridgeman first broke the chains of the French-inspired formal garden, and he was followed by William Kent's picturesque compositions, steeped in classical imagery. But Brown took the naturalistic style to its logical conclusion. He eschewed classical inspiration, instead creating landscapes that were purely English in their character, and which themselves became an inspiration for poets and painters such as J M W Turner and John Constable.

Brown started working at Blenheim for George, the 4th Duke of Marlborough, in 1764 (the same year he was appointed royal gardener). Sweeping away the formal gardens behind the palace, Brown sowed grass and dug a ha-ha to introduce views of the 'borrowed landscape'. Elsewhere he gently sculpted contours, sowed more grass and planted trees – singly, in 'Brownian clumps' and as shelter-belt plantations – in order to control and manipulate vistas. In so doing Brown designed a landscape that begins at the door and disappears into the misty distance. His masterstroke was to dam the River Glyme to create the sinuous lake, which on a still day reflects the sky. The lake provides the perfect foil to Sir John Vanbrugh's celebrated bridge, although 10 metres (30 feet) of the structure are now underwater.

In the 1920s the 9th Duke reinstated a hint of formality to provide a transition between the architecture of the palace and the soft contours of the landscape. Both the Italian Garden and the French Baroque-inspired Water Terraces were designed by the French landscape architect Achille Duchêne; they are attached to either end of the palace.

1—An aerial view looking south shows 'Capability' Brown's famed lake in the foreground and the designed landscape beyond the palace.
2—Although much of Sir John Vanbrugh's bridge is now underwater, thanks to the damming of the river to create the lake, it still fits perfectly into the vista towards the palace.
3—The box and yew hedges in the Italian Garden, created in the early twentieth century, are trimmed precisely using spirit levels.
4—The Water Terraces are a twentieth-century echo of the great formal water gardens of the Baroque era, such as that at Versailles.

# Rousham House

Steeple Aston, Oxfordshire, UK

| |
|---|
| William Kent |
| 18th century |
| 12.1 hectares / 30 acres |
| Temperate Oceanic |
| Classical / English Landscape / Picturesque / Sculpture / Vistas |

Rousham is a surpassing expression of Britain's confidence during the eighteenth century, when military prowess was enlarging the Empire. Fittingly for a garden created for two army men involved in this process – Colonel James Dormer, followed by his brother General Robert Dormer – Rousham recalls the glories of ancient Rome and its empire.

At Rousham, as elsewhere, the work of Charles Bridgeman (the pioneer of the English Landscape movement) is overlaid by that of his successor, William Kent. Only the Long Walk remains of Bridgeman's design, since Kent swept away formality in order to evoke an emotional response to nature. Between 1737 and 1741 he created a picturesque landscape – specifically a landscape that looked like a painting by Claude Lorrain or Nicolas Poussin, rich in classical, allegorical and poetical ideas. At the terminus of the flat lawn behind the house and at the top of the slope down to the River Cherwell is a statue of a lion mauling a horse – an allegory of the British fighting the Spanish. Close by, a gladiator dies in restrained agony, and in a distant field is an 'eye-catcher', an ornamented barn placed to enhance the view. The visitor who enters the understorey of evergreen laurel in the woodland and follows the serpentine walks experiences a Stygian gloom and melancholy but is surprised by hidden statuary and a temple in a glade. Water flows along a sinuous rill in the middle of the path to the Cold Bath. Under the open sky again, one reaches the Venus Vale, with its statues of Pan, a faun and Venus, and a pair of (now dry) cascades. Back up the slope the colonnade overlooking the river is the Praeneste, named after an ancient temple complex outside Rome. Across the sloping lawn is the Pyramid House, built to provide views out over the borrowed landscape.

Although the landscape is the highlight of Rousham, the walled kitchen garden is now home to herbaceous borders and espaliered apple trees. Elsewhere is a small knot garden planted with roses, and a pigeon house.

1—At the end of the lawn behind the house, a statue of a horse being attacked by a lion stands at the top of the slope above the river. In a distant field is an 'eye catcher', a barn placed to enhance the view.
2, 3—William Kent's Temple of Echo and a statue of Apollo viewed along the Long Walk are typical of the classical references hidden throughout the garden.
4, 5—A rill snakes along the centre of a path to feed the Octagon Pond, which is overlooked by a statue of Pan.
6—The Praeneste contains seats designed by Kent, with views out over the Cherwell.
7—Like the other features, Kent's cascades in the Venus Vale were made from local stone rather than classical marble.

6

7

# Stowe

Stowe, Buckinghamshire, UK

| |
|---|
| Charles Bridgeman, Sir John Vanbrugh, William Kent, Lancelot 'Capability' Brown |
| 18th century |
| 101.2 hectares / 250 acres |
| Temperate Oceanic |
| Classical / English Landscape / Informal / Picturesque / Water |

Some gardens define an epoch: Villa d'Este for the High Renaissance in Italy (see page 302), say, or Versailles for the French Baroque (see page 246). Stowe defines the eighteenth-century English landscape garden. What the modern visitor sees at Stowe is a hybrid of the key designers who developed this highly influential garden style: Sir John Vanbrugh, Charles Bridgeman, William Kent and Lancelot 'Capability' Brown.

Funded by Richard Temple, later Lord Cobham, Vanbrugh and Kent worked at Stowe before Vanbrugh's death in 1726. Bridgeman and Kent then created a Baroque-inspired garden with innovative features such as the sunken fence or ha-ha, which is still in use. After Bridgeman's death in 1748, Kent made the garden less formal; he also erected many of its forty temples and monuments and created the allegorical programme that underlines it. The visitor is asked to repeat the Choice of Hercules by choosing between two gardens. The Eastern Garden stands for a severe but glorious life of virtue, where Cobham pins his political views to the mast in the Temple of British Worthies. The Western Garden represents a pleasurable but useless life of vice, symbolized by Kent's Temple of Venus, which had erotic murals and a 'pleasuring sofa'. From 1741 Kent worked closely with a new head gardener – then just plain Lancelot Brown – who cut his landscaping teeth at Stowe.

Stowe was the first British garden to have its own guidebook, and in its mid-eighteenth-century heyday visitors came from across Europe. They took home ideas, popularizing the English landscape garden – but Stowe's role came at a cost. After a few generations Cobham's family was bankrupt.

Today, to walk among Stowe's moulded contours, classical temples, sinuous lake, stately trees and views is to enjoy the best of designed nature. To experience the garden for itself is a simple pleasure, but being able to 'read' it makes the landscape that much richer – just as the designers intended.

1 — The view across the Octagon Lake rises to the Corinthian Arch, built in 1765.
2 — The Temple of Venus (1731), seen across the Eleven-Acre Lake, was the first garden building designed by Kent.
3 — The Temple of British Worthies is home to busts of Cobham's heroes and heroines.
4 — The Palladian Bridge was designed with gentle slopes for horse-drawn carriages.
5 — The sunken stone ha-ha (one of Bridgeman's original features) was intended to keep animals out of the garden without obstructing the sweeping views.
6 — Kent designed the Temple of Ancient Virtue as a memorial to Greek thinkers.

3

4

5

6

# Turn End

Townside, Haddenham,
Buckinghamshire, UK

| | |
|---|---|
| Peter Aldington, Margaret Aldington | |
| 20th–21st century | |
| 0.2 hectares / 0.6 acres | |
| Temperate Oceanic | |
| Courtyard / Modern / Rooms | |

Turn End feels much larger than it is, so successfully has the garden been designed and so much more expansive are its ideas than its size. The garden was created by the architect Peter Aldington as an extension to three houses he built in the mid-1960s to show how dwellings built from modern materials could be assimilated into a traditional English village. Although Aldington intended his family to live in one of the houses for only a short time, they still live there some forty years later, and the garden has meanwhile become internationally renowned as an example of a well-designed outdoor space.

Although the house fits into its English surroundings, parts of the garden feel more southern European. The large courtyard is subdivided into different areas, each with its own flavour or style. Throughout, a strong grid of sightlines and focal points divides the space so that visitors are encouraged to circulate as their eyes and feet are drawn towards large pots or specimen trees. Hedges delineate spaces, while walls extending outwards from buildings create smaller courtyards and outdoor rooms.

The garden's variations derive from contrasting combinations of hard landscaping and planting. Birches underplanted with spring bulbs combine with limestone paths to make a sylvan woodland area. A small lawn sets off curved borders of agapanthus, salvias and ornamental grasses augmented with summer annuals. Some paths and patios are paved with stable blocks and dark engineering bricks, while others have terracotta tiles, which enhance the sense of indoor–outdoor flow.

One intimate courtyard sums up the garden's combination of the traditional and the contemporary. It contains an archway built in traditional wychert (a pale clay mix) with a tile coping. A roughcast concrete wall forms another side of this courtyard, with a much taller house window just beyond it. A small pool fed by a suggestion of a stream, rocks, a specimen tree with gnarled bark and the textural contrast of herbaceous planting combine to make this a beautiful stand-alone garden. For the visitor, it is just one of Turn End's many delights.

1—Peter Aldington has used a wide range of plants in a relatively small area, but the results are coherent and every different variety adds to the whole.
2, 4—Doors fold back to allow an indoor area to spill out on to a terracotta patio beside the pond, which is swathed in lush greenery.
3—In the walled Mediterranean Garden, an armillary sphere is surrounded by beds of *Papaver orientale* 'Turkish Delight', *Rosa* 'White Pet', foxtail lilies, iris and others.
5—The Gravel Garden is full of alpines and dwarf conifers grown in different pots.
6—A large urn provides a focal point in a border of shade-tolerant planting, including *Hosta* 'Gold Standard' and *Persicaria* spp.

3

4

5

6

# Hatfield House

Hatfield, Hertfordshire, UK

| | |
|---|---|
| Salomon de Caus, 6th Marchioness of Salisbury | |
| 17th & 20th century | |
| 17 hectares / 42 acres | |
| Temperate Oceanic | |
| Formal / Historic / Renaissance / Tudor | |

Hatfield House has a place in English history: an oak tree in the park marks the spot where Elizabeth Tudor learned that she had become Queen Elizabeth I. The garden preserves not only parts of the Tudor original, but also a highlight of the English vogue for Mannerist gardens at the start of the seventeenth century. The greatest champion of the Italian Renaissance style in England was the French engineer Salomon de Caus, who designed gardens filled with complicated hydraulics and magical automata. At Hatfield, de Caus designed an elaborate garden for the new house built by Robert Cecil, 1st Earl of Salisbury, between 1607 and 1612.

The main formal garden is east of the house, where the land slopes down to the River Lea. The basic layout of 1609 – a terrace leading to an upper garden and thence to a lower one – was actually the work of Cecil's gardener, Mountain Jennings. By 1611, however, Jennings had been sacked in favour of the more fashionable de Caus. As far as possible, the current Marchioness has re-created de Caus's design.

The Upper Terrace Garden has an array of sixteen formal beds picked out in low, clipped box hedges that contain geometric yew topiary and informal plantings of perennials and roses. Lawns set with statuary and topiary lead between the beds, and the garden is flanked by rows of holm oak (*Quercus ilex*) clipped into lollipop shapes. Below, on the second level, is a maze and beyond is an informal pond, both echoes of the original layout. In 1610 Cecil sent his gardener, John Tradescant the Elder, to Europe to acquire unusual plants for the gardens, including cherries, quince, medlars and Provins roses.

Unusually for the time, Cecil left the old Tudor hall standing. In the 1970s the 6th Marchioness planted a period-correct knot garden in front of it and created a Scented Garden. West of the new house, enclosed by a pleached lime walk and a yew hedge, is the Privy Garden laid out by Lady Gwendolen, daughter of the 3rd Marquis. Beyond lies the Wilderness, a tree collection set within grass full of spring bulbs and wild flowers.

1 — A dusting of frost lends definition to the Parterre Garden and Hedge Maze in the lower part of the East Garden.
2 — Rows of clipped holm oak, *Quercus ilex*, surround the Parterre Garden.
3 — The intricate Palace Knot Garden was laid out in the early 1970s with three knots and a maze; the layout and planting were based on Tudor sources.
4 — A bowl acts as a focal point in the Herb Garden west of the house.
5 — Standard *Lonicera* grows around a sundial in a heavy hoarfrost.

3

4

5

# The Barn

Serge Hill,
Hertfordshire, UK

| | |
|---|---|
| Tom Stuart-Smith | |
| 20th century | |
| 2.4 hectares / 6 acres | |
| Temperate Oceanic | |
| Modern / Naturalistic / Rooms | |

Tom Stuart-Smith is one of the most intriguing contemporary garden designers, and The Barn is his private residence. Stuart-Smith's hallmark is a formal structure softened by exuberant planting, a formula that has characterized British horticulture from the sixteenth-century pleasance at Kenilworth to the twentieth-century garden 'rooms' at Sissinghurst (see page 174).

Stuart-Smith brings a contemporary touch to this traditional approach. Many of his gardens have an oriental air, with simple platforms, gravel paths and straight water channels; others follow the modern fashion for grasses and prairie planting. It is here in his own personal space that his work is displayed at its quirky best.

In the old farmyard surrounding the converted barn, Stuart-Smith has created a series of dramatic spaces. The cobbled courtyard in front is a combination of lime-green *Euphorbia seguieriana* and purple *Salvia nemorosa*, moderated with a wafty upper layer of yellow *Genista aetnensis*. Threaded through the space are a series of rusted rectangular troughs. These water-filled tanks pay witty homage to the former farmyard and mirror the sky, providing areas of calm in the dense planting.

Behind the barn an old wheat field has been given a framework of stone walls and hedges, creating distinct but interlocking spaces. Some are densely planted; some are left to self-seeding opportunists; others are kept as open lawns or grass paths; while the rest are flanked by deep flower borders. Over the years Stuart-Smith's plant palette has become increasingly naturalistic, as roses, pinks and peonies have given way to cardoons, thistles and mulleins. Texture and form take precedence over colour, and grasses prevail, with clumps of miscanthus, calamagrostis and stipa providing structure and rhythm while linking the garden to the wider agricultural landscape. Stuart-Smith is immensely tall, and the garden is laid out to his own personal scale: gigantic macleaya, hollyhocks, veronicastrum, veronica and fennel create an Alice-in-Wonderland atmosphere, and visitors delight in the anarchic spaces of his idiosyncratic garden.

1, 2—*Genista aetnensis* grows in the Courtyard Garden around one of the troughs left from Stuart-Smith's garden for the RHS Chelsea Flower Show in 2006.
3—Empty green rooms and a long, open lawn provide areas of rest amid the dense planting.
4, 5—The West Garden was a wheat field twenty years ago. Stuart-Smith has planted hornbeam hedges to create a series of interlinked rooms – some densely planted, others left empty – surrounded by an open meadow of trees and wild flowers.

1

2

3

4

5

# The Gibberd Garden

Harlow, Essex, UK

Sir Frederick Gibberd

20th century

2.8 hectares / 7 acres

Temperate Oceanic

Informal / Modern / Rooms / Sculpture

The architect, landscape architect and town planner Sir Frederick Gibberd only ever created one garden – the one beside his bungalow on the outskirts of Harlow New Town, for which he became master planner in 1946. Gibberd based the town layout on his ability to consult the *genius loci*, and the architect Dame Sylvia Crowe credited him with 'the idea of open space and landscape flowing between compact housing areas'.

On the fields that slope down to Pincey Brook, Gibberd began the garden that continued to evolve until his death in 1984. What he called his 'private pleasure' is highly individual. He wrote: 'The garden became a series of rooms each with its own character, from small intimate spaces to large enclosed prospects.' Such compartmentalization was not new, but Gibberd created a garden with a feeling of frictionless fluidity. The visitor moves through the series of interlocking spaces – they are too informal to be called 'rooms' – that are both unified and secretive, being filled with diversity, contrast, surprise and interesting plants that create a sense of drama and excitement. Paths lined with different styles of hedges define the vistas that link the series of individual experiences.

The compartments themselves are a mix of natural and semi-formal areas, each with its character enlivened with sculptures and *objets trouvés*. Moisture-loving plants such as *Rheum palmatum* flank the path of the sylvan walk beside the stream. In a grassy glade stands a pair of white, acanthus-motif Corinthian columns. A sensuous, naked female statue stretches on a circular, cobble-edge stage backed by an evergreen leylandii hedge. The bronze dogs rushing across the lawn look as if they will attack the unwelcome visitor. The twisted form of a cherry tree contrasts with the clean lines of a terracotta pot, but simultaneously the pot's swirling pattern melds with the shadows of the branches cast upon it. A Lime Tree Walk leads to a concrete gazebo, while the terrace boasts pots, sculptures and Heath Robinson-looking water features. Gibberd's genius is evident throughout in the contrast and diversity that never jar but only build interest.

1 — Bright yellow laburnum flowers harmonize with the rich green sward looking towards the Castle, a structure of chopped elm logs Gibberd designed as a plaything for his grandchildren.
2, 3 — The garden is full of *objets trouvés* and artworks, such as these Corinthian columns and the bronze dogs that lope across the grass.
4 — A statue named Lucinda, carved by the artist Gerda Rubinstein, forms a focal point at the end of a walk of coppiced nut trees.

# The Beth Chatto Gardens

Elmstead Market, Essex, UK

| |
|---|
| Beth Chatto |
| 20th century |
| 3 hectares / 7 acres |
| Temperate Oceanic |
| Dry / Informal / Nursery / Plantsman |

The sheltering coniferous hedge at Beth Chatto's garden hides a jewel box of plants brought together in striking and subtle associations. These combinations are informed by Chatto's ecological approach, guided by her husband's research into wild plants. Planting is the major feature of the garden, and there is little paving or statuary. Here, plants fulfil those roles: a striking white-barked birch (*Betula utilis* var. *jacquemontii*) forms a pivotal focal point, while the tracery of the Mount Etna broom (*Genista aetnensis*) appears lace-like against the sky.

The Gravel Garden is a triumph of sustainable gardening, using plants adapted to the area's poor gravel soil and dry climate. The paths flow like a dry riverbed, with plants pouring over the sweeping curves – there are no hard edges. The planting is based on foliage texture and contrast, such as bold bergenia set against fine-leaved *Stipa tenuissima*. Although flowers are valued, they are transient players, with seed heads such as those of ornamental onions (*Allium*) planted to best effect. Chatto often uses asymmetrical compositions derived from her study of Japanese flower arrangement. Punctuation is provided by vertical stalks of *Verbascum bombyciferum* and *Camassia*. From summer on, larger mounds are created by the translucent flowers of the giant oat grass (*Stipa gigantea*) and foamy white *Crambe cordifolia*. The plants almost crackle with summer heat and Mediterranean scents fill the air.

An ancient pollarded English oak (*Quercus robur*) – one of the only plants that predates the garden – welcomes visitors to the Water Garden, with its stream and cool green lawn. Here the foliage increases dramatically in size. *Gunnera tinctoria* thrives alongside the ponds created by Chatto, and there are dramatic combinations of irises and cultivated marsh marigolds (*Caltha*).

The Woodland Garden provides a different range of plants. Beneath a canopy of English oaks, the air has an earthy scent and the beds are rich with interest from early spring bulbs, varied hellebores and shade-tolerant shrubs. From here the visitor can see Chatto's nursery, for which the garden is an inspirational 'living catalogue'.

1 — The focal white-barked birch grows above a lawn bordered by bold-leaved hostas and finer *Hakonechloa macra* 'Alboaurea'.
2, 3 — In the Gravel Garden paths are edged by drought-tolerant plants such as phlomis and *Gladiolus communis* subsp. *byzantinus*.
4 — Cool greens from trees and marginal plants set off white arum lilies (*Zantedeschia aethiopica*) and foxgloves.
5 — Hostas, grasses and ferns spill over a wooden walkway.
6 — Early-morning sunlight illuminates spring bulbs in the Woodland Garden.

1

2

3

4

5

6

# Kensington Roof Gardens

London, UK

| |
|---|
| Ralph Hancock |
| 20th century |
| 0.6 hectares / 1.5 acres |
| Temperate Oceanic |
| Courtyard / Historic / Roof / Rooms / Urban / Water |

Some 30 metres (100 feet) above one of London's busiest streets, flamingos wade in a stream shaded by seventy-five-year-old trees. Commissioned in the late 1930s atop what was then the Derry & Toms Building, this is still one of Europe's largest roof gardens.

Much of the original design remains: the Spanish Garden, the Tudor Garden and the Woodland Garden surround the Babylon Restaurant, which has its own small roof garden. Diners admire meadow-like planting on the roof overhang – wild flowers, grasses and spring bulbs – where Virginia, a life-size painted cow, grazes. The gardens retain remarkable lushness given the constant stress of the wind and the heat generated by the building below.

The sunny Spanish Garden, modelled on the gardens at the Alhambra (see page 276), features a small canal animated by fountains, edged in purple iris and vertically accented by narrow Italian cypress trees. Flagstone walks are flanked by terracotta pots, mature palm, fig and olive trees, and flower beds that explode with orange dahlias, purple allium and red geraniums. Completing the Mediterranean ambience is a Spanish-style house facade, bell tower and flamingo-pink arched colonnade that creates a perfect shady retreat for drinks.

In the Tudor Gardens the visitor enters the sixteenth century beneath concrete arches festooned with wisteria and climbing roses, passing along brick paving laid out in a herringbone design. The garden's three courtyards – used for outdoor dining – are embellished by beds edged in box and filled with black-and-white plantings of peonies, tulips, foxgloves and elderflower.

A short stroll from these formal gardens and the visitor enters the English countryside. The Woodland Garden's meandering stream runs the entire southern length of the roof. Home to the four flamingos, this all-season garden is landscaped with hundreds of different species. The lawn is edged by trees – some date from the 1930s, including maple, oak and sycamore – and enhanced by informal plantings of Japanese maples, loosestrife, lilies, roses and ferns, among others. Iron benches invite the visitor to sit, listen to birdsong and leave the city behind.

1 — Inspired by the Alhambra in Granada, the formal Spanish Garden has fountains and vine-covered walkways centred on a sun pavilion designed by Bernard George. 2, 3 — The meandering Woodland Garden contains a remarkable variety of heritage trees, many protected by preservation orders. The stream and garden pond are home to pintail ducks and the famed flamingos: the venerable Bill and Ben, and the newcomers Splosh and Pecks.

# Garden in St John's Wood

London, UK

Christopher Bradley-Hole

21st century

Temperate Oceanic

Modern / Roof / Terraces / Urban

This garden succeeds on many levels. It is as if Christopher Bradley-Hole has managed to expand a 'typical' London garden beyond its boundaries. At the core of his work is the relationship of buildings to their surroundings, based on a philosophy of pure spaces and mathematically correct proportions. In his view, enclosing a garden space frames it and puts it in a showcase. The success of his designs is also due to crisp and careful construction details.

The roof above the large ground-floor extension forms a terrace that is effectively a huge balcony. An expansive deck is set with glass panels that reveal glimpses into the room below. A clear plate-glass parapet makes a low wall at the edge, which maintains the view of the garden but also gives a sense of enclosure. To the sides, yew hedges make a dark backdrop to simple, pale stone benches.

At ground floor level, the garden is entered via large sliding-glass walls. The terrace here is lower than the rest of the site. Retaining walls – one painted ferrous red, the other pale stone – have clean lines, a sharp finish and no decoration (a typical Bradley-Hole touch). The entire site is already enclosed, so these walls make a secondary layer of privacy, giving the terrace the feel of an intimate room. Detailing is crisp: joint lines in paving match those of the pale wall. Wide steps give access to the upper garden, and make built-in seats or shelves.

The view to the top of the garden is layered. A brick wall marks the boundary; in front of this, a red wall panel stops the eye. A single row of pleached hornbeam (*Carpinus betulus*) makes a hedge on stilts, adding a taller, organic layer and providing a vertical rhythm to the design. Clipped yew hedges (*Taxus baccata*) provide a dark backdrop to borders planted with drifts of ornamental grasses such as *Calamagrostis* and herbaceous perennials, including airy *Verbena bonariensis* and rich-toned sedum. The informal planting contrasts with both the clean-lined walls in front and the clipped yew enclosing it.

This London garden is a fine example of Bradley-Hole's work: a modern garden underpinned by a single system of proportion, with layers of enclosure and considered repetition of details, shapes and materials.

1—The clean geometry of the lower terrace is complemented by ornamental grasses and perennials in the upper level border.
2, 4, 5—The upper terrace has a clear glass balustrade looking over the lower garden, benches for sitting, areas of smooth pebbles and skylights looking into the room below.
3—A row of pleached hornbeam adds to the sense of enclosure, contributing height to the garden while also echoing the clean lines of the architecture.

# Royal Botanic Gardens, Kew

Richmond, London, UK

| |
|---|
| William Kent, Lancelot 'Capability' Brown and others |
| 18th century |
| 121.5 hectares / 300 acres |
| Temperate Oceanic |
| Arboretum / Botanical / Conservatory / English Landscape / Historic |

Kew is not the world's first botanic garden: that is at the University of Pisa. Nor is it England's oldest: that title belongs to the one at Oxford University (1621). It is, however, the world's premier botanic garden, a status it has held since its foundation as such in the last quarter of the eighteenth century. But the history of Kew, as the gardens are usually known, as a plant collection begins in the 1660s, when Sir Henry Capel established his botanical rarities and exotics around Kew House. In 1730 Frederick, Prince of Wales, leased the house and had William Kent lay out the grounds. Upon Frederick's death in 1751, his widow, Augusta, teamed up with the Earl of Bute and eight years later created a large Physic Garden.

In 1760 King George III acquired Kew House, and it became a refuge during his bouts of 'insanity' (he suffered from porphyria). The king also united the grounds with those of another royal residence, Richmond Lodge, and asked 'Capability' Brown to design the enlarged landscape. However, it was Sir Joseph Banks in the 1770s (lately returned from his circumnavigation of the world with Captain James Cook) who established Kew as a world centre for the study of botany. He sent plant-hunters around the world to develop the collections, organized the study of their discoveries and arranged to transport economically important plants between British colonies.

Kew's elegant grounds and plant collections are beautiful all year round. Highlights include William Chambers' Chinese-inspired pagoda; the Rhododendron Dell in spring (part of Brown's landscape); the Rock Garden; the arboretum; and the renowned glasshouse. Particular features are the Victorian Palm and Temperate houses, designed by Decimus Burton, and the Princess of Wales Conservatory (1987).

It is possible for the visitor to spend days at Kew wandering the grounds and soaking in all the history, beauty and botany. Yet Kew continues at heart to be a scientific institution at the very cutting edge of botany.

1—A vista leads to the ten-storey octagonal Pagoda built by William Chambers in 1762. At the far end a single Cedar of Lebanon (*Cedrus liban*) blocks the view –but it is such a fine specimen that it was left in place.
2—The famed Palm House was built in the mid-nineteenth century to house the many different types of palm being brought back from all parts of the British Empire.
3—The focus of the Woodland Garden, the Temple of Aeolus is framed in spring by the flowers of magnolias and camellias.
4—*Dicksonia antarctica*, native to Australia, thrives in the Temperate House, the largest Victorian glass structure in the world.

# Munstead Wood

Busbridge, Godalming, Surrey, UK

Gertrude Jekyll

19th–20th century

4 hectares / 10 acres

Temperate Oceanic

Arts & Crafts / Cottage / Plantsman

Gertrude Jekyll is arguably the most influential British garden designer of the twentieth century, and she used her own garden at Munstead Wood to develop her ideas. Jekyll's partnership with the architect Edwin Lutyens, who designed the house, created a whole new British garden style. This Arts and Crafts style was characterized by using local materials in local ways and by employing inventive geometry to define and link compartments and features in a garden filled with planting that was at once profuse and carefully ordered. Jekyll was a plantswoman *par excellence* and was the first to apply painterly colour theory to flower-bed design.

Jekyll bought the triangular plot in 1882 and began work on the garden while living across the road with her mother. Lutyens slotted the house into the space left; it was finished in 1897.

The outlying area is an ornamental woodland. Jekyll allowed five local heath species to regenerate: silver birch; holly; beeches; Scots pine; and Spanish chestnuts. Each was underplanted with different types of shrub and flower, of which arguably the most spectacular are the springtime displays of rhododendrons and azaleas.

North of the house Jekyll created a series of features. Linking the house and garden is the shady North Court, a paved area with steps leading past a water tank. From the court, the Nut Walk, flanked by shrubs and the Aster Garden, leads to a rose-covered pergola. At the west end of the Nut Walk is perhaps the garden's most famous feature. Backed by a wall covered with climbers and wall-trained shrubs is the long Main Border. Jekyll colour-choreographed this iconic border, with pale, cool-coloured flowers at each end building to hot reds and yellows at the centre. Through the arch in the wall are the Spring and Summer gardens, with displays including tulips, irises and peonies, and to the west of the house lies the sunken Rock Garden.

Munstead Wood was sold in 1948 and the plot divided, but it remains one of the most important twentieth-century British gardens. The current owners of the house and garden – the Clark family – have done much to restore the garden to its original form and planting.

1 — The Aster Garden is a mass of purples and pinks in front of the characteristic Lutyens house.
2 — An arched gate leads through the Main Border into the Spring Garden with a wall swathed in climbing roses.
3 — A paved area near the house features a water tank/pond and is planted with spheres of box (*Buxus*) and red pelargoniums.
4 — The hot-colour border features red-hot poker (*Kniphofia uvaria*) with cannas, dahlias and gladioli.

3

4

# Hampton Court Palace

East Molesey, Surrey, UK

Henry VIII, Claude Mollet, George London, Daniel Marot

16th–20th century

24.3 hectares / 60 acres

Temperate Oceanic

Baroque / Formal / Historic / Topiary

Hampton Court Palace was presented to Henry VIII by Cardinal Wolsey in 1529, in an unsuccessful attempt to regain royal favour. The king turned it into the last word in power gardening with a magnificent display of royal prestige that included a privy garden full of heraldic devices. Today the sunken Pond Gardens, which are filled in spring with tulips and in summer with bright bedding plants, are the sole survivor of Henry's original creation. However, part of Henry's Privy Garden has been re-created on the former Chapel Court Garden, with its 'King's beasts' – sculpted animals bearing coats of arms – and low wooden rails painted in the Tudor colours of green and white.

Between 1690 and 1702 William III and Mary II had Henry's Privy Garden overlaid by a larger Baroque garden designed by George London and Daniel Marot. This restored garden is ornate but simpler than, say, Versailles. The scrollwork lawns set within gravel paths are known as *parterres anglais*. With its terminus of ornate wrought-iron screens that allow a view of the River Thames, the Privy Garden is the perfect foil to the south front of the palace extension designed by Sir Christopher Wren. Against the east facade the layout of William and Mary's garden remains, with clipped yew trees lining the three avenues of the *patte d'oie* (goose's foot) that pierce a semicircular area at the centre of the building. This semicircle would once have featured ornate, Dutch-inspired *parterres de broderie*, but today is lawn studded with Victorian-inspired bedding displays. The main axis leads to the Long Water – a remnant of a French-inspired garden created for Charles II in the late seventeenth century. A third feature from the William and Mary era is the last vestige of the Wilderness Garden created in the Dutch style to the north of the palace.

The famous maze was planted in 1690 as a form of courtly entertainment. Meanwhile, near the Pond Gardens, a modern glasshouse has been erected over the Great Vine – *Vitis vinifera* 'Schiava Grossa' (also known as 'Black Hamburgh') – which was planted in 1768 by 'Capability' Brown when he was royal gardener to George III. The vine still bears fruit in early autumn.

1 — The Privy Garden has been restored to its appearance in 1702. The elaborate *parterres anglais* contain 33,000 box plants.
2 — Clipped yew (*Taxus baccata*) makes a strong geometric arrangement at the apex of a *patte d'oie* of avenues looking towards the Long Water and Home Park.
3 — In spring the Pond Garden brims with tulips. The garden once had citrus trees grown in tubs, but was filled with bedding plants in Victorian times.

# Sissinghurst Castle Garden

Sissinghurst, near Cranbrook, Kent, UK

| |
|---|
| Harold Nicolson, Vita Sackville-West |
| 20th century |
| 4 hectares / 10 acres |
| Temperate Oceanic |
| Artistic / Cottage / Romantic / Rooms |

Sissinghurst Castle has one of the most quintessentially English and influential gardens of the twentieth century. The configuration of interconnecting garden 'rooms', each with its own character, reflects the personalities of its creators – Harold Nicolson (the diplomat and author) and Vita Sackville-West (romantic poet and acolyte of the Bloomsbury set). As individuals the pair led fascinating lives; together they created a garden that is greater than the sum of their two characters.

Sackville-West made the garden famous through her writings, and often, though unfairly, receives all the credit. Certainly each room – of which there are nine, including the Nuttery, Orchard, Lime and Yew walks, Rondel Rose and Herb gardens and, most famous of all, the White Garden – is a stand-alone masterpiece demonstrating her skills as a plantswoman and designer. But the garden as a whole is a fusion of her romantic heart and Nicolson's classical mind. For it was Nicolson who gave the garden structure and form, carving out from the asymmetric plot a series of compartments divided by red-brick walls and tall hedges of clipped yew. Each of these is linked visually by vistas and physically by stone- or red-brick-flagged paths and often subdivided into beds by low, neat hedges of box.

Made in the decade before World War II, the garden nods respectfully to the work of another partnership – that of Gertrude Jekyll and Edwin Lutyens – in particular in the use of rooms and colour-themed planting schemes. Yet Sissinghurst is more personal and more romantic than a typical Jekyll and Lutyens garden. It is clothed with abundance and abandon, with choreographed colours that harmonize, contrast and blend, and it demonstrates a passion for roses. As Sackville-West noted, the garden has a 'profusion, even extravagance and exuberance, within confines of the utmost linear severity'. While it is a big garden by most standards, Sissinghurst has enduring appeal because each room is (relatively) small and intimate and there is always some small vignette or idea the visitor can take away and try at home.

1, 2—Views from the tower of the South Cottage and the Rondel Rose Garden reveal how Nicolson's structural framework melds with Sackville-West's exuberant plantings.
3—The tower rises behind daffodils in the orchard in early spring; the orchard also features a classical altar and a dovecot.
4—Yellow azaleas underplanted with bluebells and white *Wisteria floribunda* 'Alba' line the Moat Walk, crowned by a quartet of yews in the Cottage Garden beyond.
5, 6—The Cottage Garden is filled with red, orange and yellow flowers: tulips and wallflowers in spring; goldenrod and helenium in summer.

1

2

3

4

5

6

7— The Rose Garden in late spring,
with pink roses and neat box hedges.
8—Actinidia climbs a wall around a
doorway that offers a glimpse into the
Rose Garden. Such vistas from one 'room'
to another are characteristic of the garden.
9—In the Herb Garden, sedum and
houseleeks grow in a marble bowl in front of
cannas, roses and low-growing herbs. At the
back is yellow *Rudbeckia laciniata* 'Herbstsonne'.
10, 11, 12—The White Garden is at its
best in late June and July, when the *Rosa
mulliganii* flowers on the central iron trellis.
Masses of white or grey plants such as
*Crambe cordifolia*, variegated phlox and
artemesia are framed by dark box, while
a willow-leaved pear (*Pyrus salicifolia*
'Pendula') shades a statue by the sculptor
Toma Rosandic.

10

11

12

# Prospect Cottage

Dungeness, Kent, UK

| |
|---|
| Derek Jarman |
| 20th century |
| Temperate Oceanic |
| Artistic / Coastal / Rock / Sculpture |

Filmmaker Derek Jarman's garden is one of the smallest yet most magical in this book. Decades after his death, it remains a cult destination at his tiny fisherman's cottage on the bleak shingle headland at Dungeness. Created over eight years, it combines colourful planting with rusted metal 'sculptures' and arrangements of weathered driftwood and flint. Many of the plants are native to the unearthly landscape, so can tolerate the salt-laden winds, strong sunlight and low rainfall. There are stands of green broom, together with purple sea kale that grows wild among the boats pulled up on the beach, cotton lavender, sea pea and elder (traditionally planted as protection against witches). Jarman also introduced various species. Spring colours come from white pinks, red poppies, marigolds, irises and blue cornflower, while in autumn the palette is of the muted browns and skeletal greys of wood, lichens and mosses.

The front garden has a formal element, with two 1.2-metre (4-foot) circles of concentric flints and bricks, plus a similar oblong, all inspired by Jarman's interest in leylines. The planting at the back is more random, with scattered opium poppy, valerian, foxglove and viper's bugloss. There are no fences, so it is difficult to say where the garden begins and ends. Pillars of driftwood up to 1.2 metres (4 feet) tall rise above the vegetation like sentinels, and some stake dogrose or gorse, the honeyed scent of which surrounds the visitor. Jarman created sculptures from the rusted metal he found on the beach.

On the south wall of the cottage are written lines from John Donne's poem 'The Sunne Rising', whose words lend the garden a poignancy linked with Jarman's early death in 1994. Jarman created the garden in the shadow of the Dungeness nuclear reactor as therapy after being diagnosed as HIV positive. He took as his inspiration Gertrude Jekyll and his friends the gardeners Beth Chatto and Christopher Lloyd (see pages 164 and 200). In this, he succeeded so fully that, even now, the garden remains true to the magical and profoundly humane vision of its maker.

1 — In front of the cottage, clumps of poppies, marigolds and other spring flowers obscure Jarman's formal circles of flints and shingle.
2 — Among the columns of driftwood in the less formal back garden, the wind has fashioned tight clumps of artemisia, cotton lavender, cistus, roses, sage and *Crambe maritima* (sea kale).
3 — Sea kale grows next to a sculptural arrangement made from driftwood with flints and found pieces of iron.
4 — A circle of viper's bugloss surrounds a clump of lavender in one of the stone circles in the front garden.
5 — Californian poppies (*Eschscholzia californica*) bloom beside a circle of flints carefully sorted by colour.

1

2

3

4

5

# Barbara Hepworth Sculpture Garden

St Ives, Cornwall, UK

| | |
|---|---|
| Barbara Hepworth | |
| 20th century | |
| 0.1 hectares / 0.2 acres | |
| Temperate Oceanic | |
| Coastal / Informal / Modern / Sculpture | |

The British sculptor Barbara Hepworth conceived her Cornish garden as a creative and inspirational space in which she could think, as well as a display area for her increasingly large-scale works. She made a sculpture and then placed it where it would best fit into the garden, rather than producing site-specific pieces for particular locations. The result is an outdoor gallery that expresses the essence of her approach to her work.

Hepworth moved to Cornwall at the outbreak of World War II, in 1939, with her husband, the artist Ben Nicholson, and their young family. A decade later they purchased Trewyn Studio, a typical St Ives stone-built house with what Hepworth described as 'a studio, a yard and garden where I could work in open air and space'. She lived and worked there until her death in 1975, when she was killed in a fire that gutted the studio. Hepworth's will required that the studios and garden be opened to the public; the property has been managed by Tate since 1980.

When she designed the walled garden in the early 1950s, Hepworth was establishing herself as one of Britain's leading abstract sculptors. She was experimenting with large-scale bronze works well suited to outdoor display, and the garden would be a vital viewing area for these large works.

With her friend the composer Priaulx Rainier, Hepworth laid out a garden that works its way down the sloping site in a series of paths and flower beds. Many of the beds feature sculptural, evergreen plants in different shades of green. Bamboos, cordylines, phormiums and Chusan palms (*Trachycarpus fortunei*) give the garden something of a subtropical feel while simultaneously creating a stage on which Hepworth's sculptures are the main players. The changing shadows cast by the trees add dynamism and a sense of volume to the sculptures, while the sculptures in turn provide a still framework and visual punctuation to the naturalistic planting.

The topography, planting and artworks of the garden unite in a harmonious but varied whole that offers a unique insight into how the artist perceived and developed the relationship between two three-dimensional art forms – her abstract and motionless sculptures and the dynamic and organic garden.

1, 2, 3—Barbara Hepworth's garden of different levels, steps and profuse planting creates an outdoor gallery for her stone or bronze sculptures in which the natural shapes of the plants both echo and contrast with the smooth yet organic forms of the works of art. The pieces on display include Hepworth's *Corymb* (1, front left), *Sphere with Inner Form* (3, front) and *Four Square (Walk Through)* (3, back).

# The Lost Gardens of Heligan

Pentewan, St Austell, Cornwall, UK

| |
|---|
| Tremayne Family |
| 19th & 20th century |
| 32.4 hectares / 80 acres |
| Temperate Oceanic |
| Coastal / Edible / Naturalistic / Plantsman / Walled |

Heligan was one of the many large country-house gardens for which World War I sounded the death knell. Such gardens relied on ample labour, cheap fuel to warm the glasshouses and low taxes – all of which were absent after the conflict. On the south Cornish coast, Heligan was abandoned until the 1990s, when it was rediscovered, renamed – the 'Lost Gardens' – and restored.

The garden structure is rather eclectic. As with other gardens along the Cornish coast, the house stands at the head of a sheltered valley that here runs down to the fishing village of Mevagissey. Now named 'The Jungle', this part of the garden was developed in the later nineteenth century and boasted a collection of hardy and slightly tender perennials, shrubs and trees brought from all over the world by plant-hunters, which thrived in the valley's microclimate. Today the surviving specimens are mature, but the replanting aesthetic has been to maintain the romantic 'jungle' feel of the overgrown garden rather than restore the structured planting with its deliberate vistas and floral highlights.

Unusually, the Northern Gardens lie behind and separate from the house. Heligan also boasts two walled gardens with glasshouses and a famous pineapple pit, as well as an extensive 'open ground'. These are all gardened organically and planted with Heritage or Heirloom varieties. In high summer the serried ranks of vegetables and the glasshouses laden with fruits are a remarkable sight.

Surrounding the productive gardens are various ornamental areas: the Sundial Garden, with its herbaceous border and *Davidia involucrata*; Sikkim, with its collection of rhododendrons; the enclosed Italian Garden, with its pool; and the Ravine, with its rocky outcrops. Floras Green is a large lawn surrounded by rhododendrons with a perimeter walk that takes in views of the garden and offers vistas out of the rolling countryside to the sea.

1 — Rhododendrons flower amid tree ferns (*Dicksonia antarctica*) and other exotics (including Chusan palms, *Trachycarpus fortunei*) in the Jungle, thanks to the microclimate of the steep-sided valley.
2 — The *Mudmaid* was created by local artists Sue and Pete Hill as a version of Victorian garden 'ornamentation'.
3 — The Sundial Garden was the location of what *Gardener's Chronicle* in 1896 called the finest herbaceous border in England.
4 — A statue of *Pluto with a Dolphin* stands in the pond in the Italian Garden. Previously known as the Suntrap, this was the first garden at Heligan to be restored.
5 — The productive gardens grow over 200 old-fashioned varieties of fruit and vegetables using similar methods to those used by the Victorian gardeners at Heligan.

3

4

5

# Plaz Metaxu

Tiverton, Devon, UK

| |
|---|
| Alasdair Forbes |
| 20th–21st century |
| 13 hectares / 32 acres |
| Temperate Oceanic |
| Allegorical / Landscape / Rooms / Sculpture |

'Gardens of the mind' are rare today, but Alasdair Forbes's extraordinary garden landscape at Plaz Metaxu evokes the eighteenth century, not just in its spatial scope and concern with the classics, but also in its desire to express ideas and provoke thought. These ideas are not imposed, however – the garden can be enjoyed by anyone without engaging with any of its meaning.

The name Plaz Metaxu is Greek for 'the place between', expressing the idea of transition and a sense of tentative, searching space. A recurring theme in the garden is the transition from enclosed spaces to open vistas, in particular from parts of the landscape that are obviously gardened to those that look more like open countryside.

Visitors to Plaz Metaxu experience a feeling of ambiguity. Much of the garden appears to mirror the surrounding Devon countryside, and yet everywhere there are reminders that this is not so: standing stones, inscriptions, stone circles, hedged enclosures that are difficult to imagine any countryman making, and patterns in stone that resemble pictures cut into chalk downs.

Although there are many views down the valley, to Forbes Plaz Metaxu is more a book than a picture: 'You can read a valley like the pages of a book. The stream along the bottom is like the binding. There is a unifying, cradling aspect to valleys, and the sides are always in dialogue with each other.'

Plaz Metaxu can be enjoyed simply as a mysterious space, but visitors are provided with a plan, along with a list of Greek deities and mythological figures to which different parts of the garden are dedicated (the old farmyard is devoted to Hermes; the front garden to Artemis, goddess of the moon). The garden design also reflects Eastern philosophies, such as Taoism, and the influence of numerous poets.

Plaz Metaxu can be either a garden with a light touch or one that provides the opportunity to plumb philosophical depths – the choice is up to the visitor.

1—Beyond the small garden behind the house the pink berries of *Sorbus vilmorinii* show well against *Fagus sylvatica* 'Dawyck' and *Quercus ilex* (holm oak).
2—The old farm courtyard has been made into a sacred space, dedicated to Hermes, messenger of the gods.
3—This area is named Imbros after a site in ancient Greece. The stones represent man and boy.
4—Evergreen planting in the Hermes courtyard. A blacksmith's mendrel doubles as a magician's hat.
5—Spaces between parts of the garden are as important as the areas themselves
6—Sunset over the valley shows the close bond between the garden and the natural landscape.
7—On the Orexis mound, fillets of Delabole slate draw the visitor's eye to the skies.

5

6

7

# Hotel Endsleigh Gardens

Milton Abbot, Tavistock,
Devon, UK

| |
|---|
| Humphry Repton |
| 19th century |
| 43.7 hectares / 108 acres |
| Temperate Oceanic |
| Cottage / Formal / Plantsman / Water / Woodland |

If Lancelot Brown was nicknamed 'Capability', the last of the great eighteenth-century landscape gardeners – Humphry Repton – would perhaps be best known as 'Practicality'. His designs combined beauty and convenience with comfort, privacy and social use. Hotel Endsleigh, overlooking the River Tamar in Devon, was built as a *cottage orné* by Jeffry Wyattville for the extravagant 6th Duke of Bedford. Repton's garden is from 1811 and was one of his favourite commissions – and one of the last. Shortly afterwards his carriage overturned and he sustained spinal injuries that confined him to a wheelchair until his death in 1818.

The garden at Hotel Endsleigh, which has recently been restored, contains all Repton's signature features. Close to the house there are formal gardens, and beyond is the landscape. A grass terrace overlooks the Tamar, which the writer John Claudius Loudon described in 1842 as 'a clear and rapid river, passing through richly wooded banks', adding that he admired Endsleigh 'for its natural beauties, and for the very high keeping displayed in all that we saw'. The arboretum contains unusual trees from around the world, including ten 'Champion Trees', the largest of their type in England.

Repton began his career in 1788, five years after the death of Brown, to whom he considered himself a worthy successor, although his approach was somewhat different. In order to create an appropriate transition zone between house and park, Repton reintroduced a terrace, which was often balustraded and ornamented with a covered veranda of ornate ironwork. On the terrace or juxtaposed with it, Repton placed a formal flower garden, carefully screened from the park so that there was no jarring between artifice and nature. Repton's wooded and grassy landscapes were pierced by gravel drives and paths that followed the contours while keeping feet dry. Repton also used lakes with irregular outlines, and bays and promontories, rather than Brown's sinuous outlines, and he particularly enjoyed moving water in the form of rivers, streams and cascades.

1, 2—Formal beds on the terrace near the hotel are filled with *Salvia viridis*; the rill on top of the stone wall is testament to Repton's fascination with moving water.
3—A circular fountain provides the focal point of the semicircular parterre.
4—The Rose Walk, roofed over with iron arches, is bordered by black-eyed Susan and geraniums.
5—The Grass Terrace overlooking the Tamar is now used for relaxed games of croquet.
6—The view over the Rose Walk and the Grass Terrace shows how Repton incorporated the formal elements near the house into the wider landscape.

5

6

# Dartington Hall

Dartington, Totnes, Devon, UK

Leonard Elmhirst, Dorothy Elmhirst, Henry Avray Tipping, Beatrix Farrand, Percy Cane, Preben Jacobsen

20th century

10 hectares / 25 acres

Temperate Oceanic

Borders / Meadow / Modern / Sculpture / Woodland

An ongoing mystery at Dartington Hall is who regularly leaves flowers around the statue of Flora, the resting place of the ashes of Leonard and Dorothy Elmhirst, whose passion transformed the property after they bought it in 1925. The statue also marks the transition from the Woodland Walk, designed by US landscape architect Beatrix Farrand, to the High Meadow, created by British designer Percy Cane.

The Elmhirsts – he was English, she American – took an experimental approach to their gardens. After taking ownership of the run-down estate, they rebuilt the fourteenth-century hall and created some bold new buildings. The gardens looked forwards rather than backwards. The first designer, Henry Avray Tipping, made contributions in the Arts and Crafts style, including hedges around the house to delineate garden 'rooms' and broadening the garden out into the woodland valley.

Dorothy Elmhirst had worked with Beatrix Farrand in the United States, and she turned to her again. Farrand worked on Dartington Hall from 1933 to 1938; it was her only project outside her home country. She gave the fine Courtyard a collegiate atmosphere. Its wide York stone paving, with bands of limestone setts and cobbles from the river, echoes her work on American university campuses. Farrand's three Woodland Walks are also notable. She used 'backbone planting' to define certain areas with plant masses, and insisted on using natives such as beech, holly and Scots pine. Cedars were later additions, along with *Magnolia grandiflora*, wisteria and camellias.

After 1945 Percy Cane accentuated the garden's external views, such as those from High Meadow, and improved the Azalea Dell. He designed the Whispering Circle, the magnificent steps from the Glade to the Tiltyard and the Heath Bank steps. Preben Jacobsen later designed a herbaceous border. Meanwhile, an impressive series of site-specific sculptures has been created for the gardens. Thus Dartington Hall continues to evolve while respecting the place and its past.

1, 2—The Tiltyard gives a view over the garden to the house. Leonard Elmhirst named it after a jousting area, but in fact it had formerly been the site of a pond. The clipped yews on the lawn terrace are known as the 'Twelve Apostles'.
3, 4—The Swan Fountain, created by Willi Soukop in 1950, stands on the steps designed by Percy Crane to link the garden with the woodland above.
5—The Sunny Border in July has a fine show of nepeta, achillea, hemerocallis, agapanthus and echinops.

# Exbury Gardens

Exbury, Southampton,
Hampshire, UK

Lionel de Rothschild, Edmund de
Rothschild

20th century

101 hectares / 250 acres

Temperate Oceanic

Informal / Plant Collection / Woodland

Exbury is one of England's finest woodland gardens, and is best known for its important – and spectacular – collections of rhododendrons and azaleas. The woodland was planted largely to provide these collections with protection from salt-laden winds blowing up the Beaulieu River from the Solent. The garden was created by Lionel Nathan de Rothschild between 1919 and his death in 1942. He was a member of the famous banking family and was once described as 'a banker by hobby and a gardener by profession'. Rothschild's abiding passion was rhododendrons – the genus now includes azaleas – and he went to considerable lengths to populate his woodland garden.

As well as purchasing new cultivars from nurseries and breeding his own, including the Exbury hybrids, Rothschild was a major sponsor of plant-hunters who scoured the Himalayas and Burma for new species. Rothschild also had a strong influence on Ambrose Congreve and his garden at Mount Congreve in Ireland (see page 110).

After Rothschild's death, Exbury was expanded and developed by his son Edmund. Edmund repaired the damage suffered in World War II bombing raids – the garden is close to the port city of Southampton – and opened the gardens to the public in 1955. He also added a narrow-gauge railway, which transports visitors to the northeastern corner of the garden.

Today there is more to Exbury than rhododendrons. The season begins in early spring, when the Daffodil Meadow is a field of gold and the woodland is abloom with magnolias and camellias (there are more than 250 different types of the latter, including hybrids created by Lionel). In mid-spring, when the woodland is carpeted with bluebells and primroses, the show of ten thousand flowering rhododendrons and azaleas reaches its peak, particularly in the stunning Azalea Bowl. Summer is the season to enjoy both the Herbaceous and Grasses Garden and the Exotic Garden, while autumn brings a display of fiery foliage as the leaves of maple, deciduous azalea and dogwood turn colour. This is also a chance to enjoy Exbury's collection of nerine and the National Collections of tupelo (*Nyssa*) and sourwood (*Oxydendrum*) trees.

1, 2—Exbury is home to many remarkable specimens. In May the Spring Garden is a spectacular display of colourful maples (*Acer*) and azaleas.
3—Rhododendrons flower in early summer.
4, 5—Water is an integral part of the garden, with streams threading through the woodland past azaleas, maples, *Gunnera*, umbrella plants (*Darmera peltata*) and wild garlic.

# Hestercombe Gardens

Cheddon Fitzpaine, Taunton,
Somerset, UK

| Coplestone Warre Bampfylde, Gertrude Jekyll, Edwin Lutyens |
| 18th & 20th century |
| 20 hectares / 50 acres |
| Temperate Oceanic |
| Arts & Crafts / English Landscape / Formal / Romantic / Water |

Hestercombe has two temporally and physically distinct gardens. The older – recently restored – is the picturesque landscape garden in the valley rising behind the house. Created by Coplestone Warre Bampfylde between 1750 and 1786, it has a circular path that links a series of buildings and features, revealing contrived views. The path leads past the Pear Pond and up the side of the valley, where the sound of falling water heralds the dramatic 30-metre (100-foot) Great Cascade. At the top of the climb, the path passes through a tunnel of dark laurel to spectacular vistas from the Gothic Alcove and the Capriccio View. The path zigzags down to the mausoleum and back to the Pear Pond where, looking up, the full landscape is revealed and the Temple Arbour is reflected in the still waters.

A gate in the wall leads to the formal garden, one of the finest results of the partnership of Gertrude Jekyll and Edwin Lutyens. The ingenuity of Lutyens's tightly controlled yet bold, asymmetric geometry fits great beauty, variety and interest into a small space, while Jekyll provides a masterclass in planting design.

Beyond the gate are the Dutch Garden and the elegant Orangery, with its manicured lawn. Formal steps lead to the Rotunda, a circular water court that opens on to the terrace, below which lies the Great Plat, a sunken parterre divided diagonally by four grass paths edged with flagstones. In early summer the four beds are filled with bold groups of white lilies, blue delphiniums and peonies, which give way to red cannas, gladioli and dahlias, which reflect the heat of mid- and late summer. Defining the terminus of the garden – while also linking it with the borrowed landscape beyond – is the climber-clad pergola.

Raised above the Great Plat on either side are the East and West rills. In each, water spouts from a lion's-head fountain into a quarter-hemispherical pool recessed into the wall. From the pools, water flows along deep rills that run the length of the lawn before splashing down steps into water-lily tanks. The rills are planted with water forget-me-not, iris and arum, and their straight lines are broken up by whirlpools, which also help to control the water flow.

1 — The Great Cascade in the picturesque landscape garden crashes down a wooded cliff on to bare rock.
2 — The classical Temple Arbour stands on top of a small wooded rise above the Pear Pond, which reflects it on a still day.
3 — The path through the woodland leads past a hillside of foxgloves surrounding Pope's Urn, modelled on a design by William Kent for the poet Alexander Pope.

2

3

4—The formal walled Rotunda opens on to the terrace, which in turn gives on to the Great Plat below.

5— The Dutch Garden combines silver and grey planting in numerous flower beds surrounded by paving and decorative urns.

6—A pergola designed by Lutyens forms the backdrop to the Great Plat, a sunken parterre divided into four sections planted with evergreen begonia and changing annuals to provide colour interest.

7, 8—Figurehead fountains feed hemispherical pools that flow into rills along terraces on either side of the Great Plat. The rills are planted with various aquatic plants according to the varying depth of the water.

6

7

8

# East Lambrook Manor

East Lambrook, South Peverton, Somerset, UK

| |
|---|
| Margery Fish |
| 20th century |
| 0.5 hectares / 2 acres |
| Temperate Oceanic |
| Cottage / Historic / Naturalistic / Perennials / Plantsman |

Having been widowed in the 1940s, Margery Fish poured her energy into her garden at East Lambrook and in doing so reinvented the cottage garden for the twentieth century. Fish and her husband, Walter, had bought the manor house in 1937, a decade before Walter's death. Rather than create compartments, borders and colour-coordinated planting, Fish took a naturalistic, informal and loose approach, breaking with the Arts and Crafts tradition.

With a plantswoman's zeal and a designer's eye for arrangement, Fish developed a garden in which different areas flow seamlessly into one another and are interesting all year. She used the various microclimates in the garden and filled the different areas with those plants most suitable for the specific levels of sunlight, shade, moisture and so on. The word 'filled' is apposite: at any time the garden was crammed with about 2,000 different types of plant, with no soil left bare. The planting was so dense that it smothered most weeds, but if a weed appeared and looked good, Fish left it. The result was a weekend garden filled with diversity yet requiring minimal maintenance.

Fish disseminated her ideas in various books, most notably her influential *We Made a Garden* (1956). Michael Pollan, reviewing a belated first US edition of 1996, called her 'the most congenial of garden writers, possessed of a modest and deceptively simple voice that manages to delicately layer memoir with horticultural how-to.'

Fish was passionate about perennials and after World War II, when planting fashions began to shift towards shrubs, she recognized that many former favourites were in jeopardy. She set about collecting, propagating and, through her books, repopularizing them, and ensured their survival. Many of these perennials are again in vogue, and a number are named for her garden, including *Artemisia absinthium* 'Lambrook Silver', *Euphorbia characias* subsp. *wulfenii* 'Lambrook Gold', *Santolina chamaecyparissus* 'Lambrook Silver' and *Primula* 'Lambrook Mauve'.

When Fish died in 1969 her garden went into decline, but new owners have now restored it. Once again it is a beautiful and inspirational showcase of perennial planting at the highest level of the gardener's art.

1 — In the Cottage Garden, flowers include *Elaeagnus* 'Quicksilver', euphorbia, roses, phlomis, stachys and centaurea.
2 — Moisture-loving plants flourish in The Ditch, including hellebores and *Scilla bithynica*.
3 — Snowdrops flower along a small stream; Fish favoured forms of hardy and adaptable native perennials.
4 — *Achillea*, *Thalictrum delavayi* and *Eschscholzia californica* in a border.

# Stourhead

Stourton, Wiltshire, UK

| | |
|---|---|
| Henry Hoare II, Henry Flitcroft | |
| 18th century | |
| 40 hectares / 100 acres | |
| Temperate Oceanic | |
| Allegorical / English Landscape / Naturalistic / Shrubs / Vistas / Water | |

In an age when most of the famous English landscapes were made by professional designers – William Kent, Lancelot 'Capability' Brown and latterly Humphry Repton – there were nonetheless a few notable gardens made by gifted amateurs. Arguably the finest is at Stourhead, which Henry Hoare inherited from his banker father in 1724. In 1738 Hoare set off on a three-year Grand Tour to absorb the world of European culture. On his return he began to create (with help from Henry Flitcroft) an Arcadian idyll with strong Claudian overtones. The project was funded by the interest paid on loans the Hoare bank was making to the landed gentry busy improving their own estates.

Hoare's Stourhead took almost thirty years to complete. The design takes the form of a circuitous walk from the house in an anticlockwise route around the lake, with 'incidents' along the way. Carefully positioned, these incidents provide focal points and vistas and encourage movement along the route; more importantly, their form and type define the garden's programme: the journey of Aeneas after he fled Troy but before he founded Rome. Aeneas would have identified with the classical temples, but the Grotto and the Pantheon – and perhaps also the Hermitage – may have flummoxed him because of their not-so-classical neighbours: the Chinese Bridge (now lost), the Turkish Tent, the Gothic Cottage, the Bristol High Cross, the Turf Bridge and the picturesque village of Stourton.

Today's visitor will notice another odd juxtaposition. One of the highlights of Stourhead is the collection of trees and shrubs added in the nineteenth century. These beautiful interlopers meld successfully with the classically inspired and naturalistic setting. They put on spectacular seasonal shows: rhododendrons in spring and fiery tints of leaves in autumn offer ample photographic opportunities. They grab the attention of horticulturists because many are unusual, and they add another layer of interest to the garden. But they are not authentic, a fact that raises a dilemma about whether Hoare's original garden should eventually be restored.

1—The classical architecture at Stourhead includes the decorative Turf Bridge across the lake and the domed white Pantheon, based on the temple in Rome. The Grotto is on the far right.
2—Rhododendrons flower beside the path around the lake.
3—A view through the arches of the stone Grotto reveals a statue of the River God.
4—More rhododendrons cluster at the foot of the hill topped by the Temple of Apollo, dedicated to the sun god, which has fine views over the lake.

193

# Shute House

Donhead St Mary, Wiltshire, UK

Geoffrey Jellicoe

20th century

0.78 hectares / 2 acres

Temperate Oceanic

Historic / Modern / Perennials / Water

Shute House is one of the finest gardens created by one of the most influential landscape architects and garden designers of the twentieth century, Geoffrey Jellicoe. It bears all the hallmarks of his design approach: structured geometry, vistas, water, human scale and respect for the *genius loci*. Trained as an architect, Jellicoe first worked at Shute House for Michael and Lady Anne Tree in the late 1960s, but the Water Garden for which the property is most famous dates from 1978. Even then the project was not complete, and Jellicoe was employed again to finish the gardens when new owners arrived in 1994.

To the south of the house a grassy terrace terminates in a ha-ha, giving views over the borrowed landscape. To the west is a 'green bedroom', beyond which is a formal garden: a rectangle of six themed square beds of shrubs and flowers each enclosed by box hedges. The Camellia Walk, with more than a hundred varieties, has a spectacular flowering display in spring. Around the western perimeter is a romantic woodland garden, where a path winds past statues and through glades. Throughout the garden are carefully manipulated vistas.

Jellicoe's garden is really about water. A spring feeds the informal pools in the woodland before becoming the River Nadder. The largest pool has a formal, rectangular arm, which Jellicoe modified to create the Canal Garden, which he enclosed with lofty hedges, headed by three herms and with twin grottoes. This continues the classical landscape feel introduced by the romantic woodland. The famous Water Garden is set within a lawn but surrounded by dense plantings of perennials and trees that introduce a feeling of intimacy. A rill trips musically straight down the hillside over copper waterfalls into one square and two octagonal basins where gravity-fed, Kashmiri-inspired bubble fountains murmur. The composition has strong Islamic overtones and contrasts with the Western classical echoes elsewhere, but the Water Garden is nothing less than wholly modern in its execution and enchanting in its effect.

1—The rill flows through square and octagonal pools with burbling bubble fountains towards a statue and a view of the landscape.
2—An arch supports a spectacular display of wisteria against a background of yew (*Taxus baccata*).
3—The rill falls over musical waterfalls whose pitch reflects the number of small copper V-shaped chutes that make up each fall.
4—The classically inspired Canal Garden is enclosed by tall beech hedges. Arum lilies (*Zantedeschia aethiopica*) thrive in the water.
5—Topiary creates the 'green bedroom' garden at the west side of the house.

4

5

# The Peto Garden

Iford Manor, Bradford-on-Avon,
Wiltshire, UK

| |
|---|
| Harold Peto |
| 20th century |
| 1 hectare / 2.5 acres |
| Temperate Oceanic |
| Arts & Crafts / Formal / Italianate / Terraces |

Harold Ainsworth Peto was one of a group of British architects who found wealth designing country houses in the late nineteenth century. But, having designed houses such as Ilnacullin (see page 109), Peto became disillusioned. In 1899 he moved into Iford Manor, with its elegant eighteenth-century classical facade. He lived there until his death, in 1933.

Peto greatly admired the terraced gardens of the Italian Renaissance, and the steep slope behind and to one side of his new home was ideally suited for the construction of a series of terraces, augmented by pools and connected by flights of steps. Peto used local stone, ornamenting the broad gravel walks on the terraces with original Italian statuary and artefacts he had collected on his travels. He displayed more treasures in the arcaded courtyard he called his Haunt of Ancient Peace.

The highest Great Terrace is colonnaded, with a stone seat at the western end and an open-fronted *casita* at the eastern. In less skilled hands such a copyist approach might have been no more than *ersatz*, but Peto deftly re-created an Italian scene within the Wiltshire countryside. He also combined the architectural frame with an Arts and Crafts approach to planting. Dominant cypress and juniper inject an Italian ambience, but Peto's use of hardy plants received approval from as high an authority as Gertrude Jekyll herself. In late spring the blooming *Wisteria sinensis* enhancing the flights of steps that link the garden's terraces is particularly spectacular.

The garden is not entirely Italianate. Hidden in the woods above the terraces, where box (*Buxus sempervirens*) grows wild, is a small Japanese Garden. It may feel incongruous, but such gardens were all the rage at the turn of the twentieth century. To the east of the terraces, the garden takes on a medieval feel. A lawn in which *Lilium martagon* (the Turk's cap lily) has naturalized, echoing a floral mead, takes visitors to the Italian Cloister. To enter this airy structure is to enter another world and age. It is the perfect spot to reflect on Peto's masterful blurring of time and place to create his unique garden.

1—The colonnaded Great Terrace is lined with Peto's classical statues.
2—Peto melded an Italian Renaissance-inspired framework of terraces with an Arts and Crafts planting scheme that softens its structure.
3—Near the Great Terrace some of Peto's original planting still survives, including box (*Buxus sempervirens*), which also grows wild in the woods above.
4—The Italian Cloister is one of the largest buildings in the garden and today makes an atmospheric setting for concerts.

# Denmans

Fontwell, Arundel,
West Sussex, UK

John Brookes, Joyce Robinson

20th century

1.6 hectares / 4 acres

Temperate Oceanic

Gravel / Informal / Mediterranean /
Modern / Rooms / Walled

Denmans is an outstanding example of modern garden design. Although larger than average, the space feels domestic in scale, and there are plenty of design principles and planting ideas to absorb.

Joyce Robinson, who started gardening here in 1946, was a keen plantswoman and an innovative gardener. A visit to Greece in 1969 inspired her to use gravel as a ground surface and as a mulch around plants. In 1980 John Brookes brought his School of Garden Design to Denmans, and the garden continues to evolve as a workshop for his design philosophy. Through his books and teaching, Brookes has become one of Britain's most influential landscape designers.

There are no straight lines at Denmans, no formal axes leading to focal points and few traditional paths. Curving lawns appear to blend into large areas of planting and swathes of gravel paths. Spatial layout is achieved through the placement of plant masses – of trees and larger shrubs – balanced with void areas of lawn, gravel and low planting. Plant shape, foliage form, texture and colour make as big an impact as more transient flower colour. Brookes acknowledges the influence of Thomas Church, the Modernist Californian landscape architect, on his approach. Seeing the garden as an outdoor room is another concept Brookes originally championed in his influential book *Room Outside* (1969).

Denmans is a garden to be enjoyed. Seats are placed in sunny positions; areas of grass are left longer, with low-maintenance paths mown through. Expanses of lawn encourage visitors to explore; a gravel 'stream' flows under a large stone bridge into a real pond; while planting looks natural, offset by the surrounding space. Large empty pots are placed as focal points or as accents on the edge of plant groups.

The garden can be enjoyed following a range of routes, each of which reveals different discoveries. For plant-lovers, the make-up of taller plant groups and lower-growing plant associations are noteworthy. Brookes's choice and use of materials is an invaluable lesson for designers and gardeners alike.

1—Expanses of lawn are balanced by large areas of mixed planting that are anchored by trees and larger shrubs.
2— *Astelia chathamica* and *Eryngium* grow around a large urn in a circle of gravel.
3—In the Walled Garden, *Rheum palmatum* grows in a mixed border with different coloured tulips and euphorbia.
4—Wide gravel and railway sleeper steps have space for people and plants, including *Verbascum olympicum*, *Sisyrinchium striatum* and foxgloves.
5—The gravel 'river' of the Dry Stream Garden flows beneath a stone 'bridge' past graceful silver birches and *Euphorbia*.

# Gravetye Manor

East Grinstead, West Sussex, UK

| |
|---|
| William Robinson |
| 19th century |
| 12.1 hectares / 30 acres |
| Temperate Oceanic |
| Borders / Formal / Historic / Informal / Meadow / Naturalistic |

Gravetye Manor was the garden of William Robinson, a leading garden writer of the late nineteenth century and one of the protagonists of what became known as the 'Battle of Styles', an acrimonious debate about the future of British gardening. Robinson, who acquired the sixteenth-century manor in 1884, wanted to move Victorian fashions away from the formal Italianate garden towards a more naturalistic style of garden filled with hardy plants. He used Gravetye to put his ideas into practice. Following two decades of neglect after his death in 1935, the house became a hotel and the gardens were restored.

Robinson's dogmatic approach upset many, notably the architect Reginald Blomfield (see Mellerstain, page 122). Blomfield also wanted to see a new form of garden, but he preferred a return to Renaissance formality. Their broadsides led to the evolution of a new style created by the gardener Gertrude Jekyll and the architect Edwin Lutyens.

Gravetye's Wild Garden provides a good display of the Robinsonian method. Grass paths wind through meadows where ornamental bulbs, annuals and perennials have naturalized. There are ornamental shrubs and trees, including Corsican pines and a handkerchief tree (*Davidia involucrata*), which appear natural rather than deliberately planted.

Robinson was not shy of hypocrisy: he laid out the existing terrace garden as a formal flower garden. Today it is a four-square lawn flanked by mixed borders with views over the Wildflower Meadow. There the seasonal show begins with snowdrops and crocuses, which give way to blue *Scilla siberica* and soft yellow wild daffodils. Bluebells and lilac-hued *Anemone nemorosa* 'Robinsoniana' flower next, and in early summer come native wild flowers, including thousands of common spotted orchids. After it has been mowed, the meadow has a last flourish of autumn crocuses. In contrast, the Flower Garden's rustic terraces are informally planted with deciduous azaleas that provide glorious flowers in late spring and striking foliage in autumn.

1—Naturalistic planting softens the straight lines of the paths and the house's walls.
2—Flowers flourishing in the Wildflower Meadow include ox-eye daisies (*Leucanthemum vulgare*) and foxgloves (*Digitalis purpurea*).
3—In another border an unusual planting mixes tulips, forget-me-nots and rhubarb (*Rheum palmatum* 'Atrosanguineum').
4—The Flower Garden, a series of stone terraces, was home to the first modern mixed border, planted by Robinson in 1884.
5—Native wild daffodils (*Narcissus pseudonarcissus*) flourish in the meadow.

4

5

# Great Dixter

Northiam, Rye, East Sussex, UK

| Nathaniel Lloyd, Christopher Lloyd |
| 20th & 21st century |
| 2 hectares / 5 acres |
| Temperate Oceanic |
| Borders / Plantsman / Rooms |

Although Great Dixter is associated with the *enfant terrible* of twentieth-century horticulture, Christopher Lloyd, the bones of the garden were created a century ago by his parents around the family home, a medieval manor restored by the architect Edwin Lutyens. Over fifty years the younger Lloyd – known as Christo – transformed his parents' Arts and Crafts garden into a cutting-edge palette for contemporary ideas.

Lloyd's father, Nathaniel, created a series of hedged enclosures around the old farmyard, incorporating a barn and an oast house as boundaries, using drinking troughs as decorative pools and the cow shed as a loggia. He also created a series of topiary birds – which all gradually came to resemble abstract peacocks – and the Sunk Garden, created from an old croquet lawn.

Aged thirty-three, having studied for a horticultural degree, Christo Lloyd returned to Great Dixter to live with his widowed mother. Over the following years, he softened his father's design with luxuriant planting. Extending the 40-metre (130-foot) Long Border by a third, he replaced the tasteful Jekyllesque colour blending with striking combinations such as red tulips and lime-green euphorbia. Fascinated by form and texture, he incorporated such unusual plants as cannas, yuccas, miscanthus and eryngium. One of the first gardeners in England to adopt the loose 'perennial' style, Lloyd also promoted meadow gardens and pioneered succession planting to ensure interest from the earliest spring bulbs to the last winter seed heads. Late in life, Lloyd outraged the horticultural community by replacing the old Rose Garden with an exotic garden of dramatic plants such as Japanese banana (*Musa basjoo*), giant-leaved Polynesian elephant ear (*Colocasia*) and the tall grass *Arundo donax*.

A true plantsman, Lloyd shared his prodigious knowledge in lectures, books and newspaper columns, helping to make Great Dixter one of the most famous, most visited and most loved of England's modern gardens.

1 — The artfully planted Long Border, the most famous part of the garden, is a striking contrast to the meadow beside it.
2 — An elevated view shows how yew hedges give structure to the High Garden; in the foreground are the topiary peacocks created by Christopher Lloyd's father, Nathaniel.
3 — In spring the Orchard Garden is bright with *Tulipa* 'West Point' and forget-me-nots (*Myosotis* 'Blue Ball').
A border in the Barn Garden reflects Lloyd's fascination with dramatic plants, including *Verbena bonariensis*, canna and Abyssinian banana (*Ensete ventricosum*).
5, 6 — The garden retains its sculptural form even in the winter: seen here are the yew topiary of the Peacock Garden and the octagonal pool of the Sunk Garden.

1

# Tresco Abbey Gardens

Tresco, Isles of Scilly, UK

| |
|---|
| Augustus Smith, Dorrien Smith Family |
| 19th & 20th century |
| 7 hectares / 17 acres |
| Temperate Oceanic |
| Coastal / Exotic / Plant Collection / Plantsman / Terraces |

On the private island of Tresco, some 50 kilometres (30 miles) south of the most southerly point of mainland Britain, in the Isles of Scilly, five generations of dedicated garden-makers have used the warming effect of the Gulf Stream to create a remarkable garden. The garden is displayed over three terraces (upper, middle and lower), with the Lighthouse Walk and Neptune Steps providing vertical access between. Paths wind up and down the sloping site, amid richly planted beds filled with exotic planting.

Tresco has more than 20,000 exotic plants, which thrive in the Mediterranean climate. The plants come from more than eighty countries, as reflected in named garden areas such as Mexico, South Africa Cliff, and both Higher and Lower Australia. Within the garden, microclimates better suit plants from specific regions. At the foot of the terraces, for example, the shade suits New Zealand and South American plants, such as tree ferns of the *Cyathea* genus and Norfolk Island pine (*Araucaria heterophylla*). The partly protected middle terrace nurtures plants from the Canary Islands and South Africa (including passion flowers) and agave and puya from South America. The sunny top terrace is home to plants from dry regions of Australia and South Africa, such as banksia, callistemon, protea, aloe and Cape heaths.

Augustus Smith, a banker, began making the garden in 1834 around the ruins of a twelfth-century priory. An avid plant-collector, Smith soon ran out of space and created the steep, south-facing terraces the garden occupies today. In 1872 Tresco passed to his nephew Thomas Algernon Dorrien Smith, who planted extensive shelter belts of trees on the garden perimeter in order to protect the plants from winter gales. The next owner, Major Arthur Dorrien Smith, added to the collection, not least with plants from collecting trips to New Zealand and the Chatham Islands. From 1955 Commander Tom Dorrien Smith focused his collecting activities on plants from South Africa and Australia, in particular the family Proteaceae. Under the current owners, Robert and Lucy Dorrien Smith, much restoration was required after hurricanes in 1987 and 1990, but the garden continues to develop and to justify its worldwide reputation.

1—The dry and sunny Upper Terrace is home to succulents and proteas that originate mainly in Australasia and South Africa.
2—The Middle Terrace is sheltered, and thus suitable for plants from a range of climate zones.
3—A young Canary Island palm (*Phoenix canariensis*) grows next to an arch from the twelfth-century Benedictine priory.

4—Mixed planting on the Middle
Terrace includes agave, cordyline,
echium, *Geranium maderense* and palms.
5, 6—Drought-tolerant plantings of
herbaceous species and succulents include
a bank of *Lampranthus spectabilis* 'Tresco
Fire', *Amaryllis belladonna* and *Aeonium
arboreum* 'Atropurpureum'.
7—The rays of the early-morning
sun illuminate the Shell House in the
Mediterranean Garden.
8—The statue of 'Neptune' at the top of
the Neptune Steps is in fact a figurehead
salvaged from the SS *Thames*.

4

5

6

7

8

# Arboretum Kalmthout

Kalmthout, Antwerp, Belgium

Charles Van Geert, Antoine Kort, Georges De Belder, Robert De Belder

19th & 20th century

12.5 hectares / 31 acres

Temperate Oceanic

Arboretum / Botanical / Informal

This tangled woodland garden on the edge of Antwerp claims to be a 'garden for all seasons', yet the true glory of Kalmthout is revealed in winter, when the remarkable colours of its renowned collection of witch hazels (Hamamelis) give the lie to any idea that winter gardens lack life or interest. There are other winter-flowering plants among the apparently random plantings – the epitome of what may be called the gardenesque style – but witch hazels are so dominant that the gardens hold an annual Hamamelis Festival.

When the witch hazels fade at the start of spring, the interest for visitors barely drops. Groundcover blooms beneath flowering Japanese maples and hundreds of rhododendrons. Summer is a more subdued period, with the trees casting shade over hydrangeas, roses, agapanthus and dahlias, and the Butterfly Garden alive with butterflies and other insects. In autumn, trees such as apples and cherries are laden with fruit, while striking foliage creates a warm palette of browns, yellows, oranges and reds.

The nursery begun at Kalmthout in 1856 by Charles Van Geert was originally intended as a test bed for his nursery in Antwerp. Van Geert was interested in the suitability of species that plant-hunters were bringing to Europe from America and Asia – particularly newly discovered conifers from China and Japan – for northern Europe. He introduced many species to Belgium, including witch hazel, hydrangea, hosta and iris. But Van Geert had broader ambitions, too, boasting that the garden would provide employment, attract visitors and provide useful research. He established his arboretum within the garden to house his finest specimens, including Chinese conifers, gold-coloured maples, Japanese umbrella pines (Pinus pinea) and American snowdrop trees (Halesia diptera); having reached maturity, these specimens remain at the heart of the garden.

After Van Geert's death, Kalmthout was further developed by Antoine Kort. In 1952 it was bought by the De Belder brothers, Georges and Robert, and transformed into a private botanical garden that eventually included more than 6,000 species from around the world. It now belongs to the local authority in Antwerp.

1—Ling heather (Calluna vulgaris) blooms in the open, sandy soil.
2—The garden is renowned for its witch hazels (Hamamelis), which add fresh colours in winter and early spring.
3—Leaves begin to turn near a pavilion as autumn reaches the garden.
4—The leaves of a Japanese maple (Acer palmatum 'Tatsuta Gawa') make a striking display of yellow and brown.

# Rubenshuis

Antwerp, Belgium

| |
|---|
| Peter Paul Rubens |
| 17th century |
| 0.23 hectares / 0.5 acres |
| Temperate Oceanic |
| Baroque / Courtyard / Edible |

In 1610 Peter Paul Rubens, the most famous of all the Antwerp painters, purchased a house and a plot of land in his home city, where he lived until his death in 1640. Rubens had the house expanded to his own design to create a palazzo that combined the old Flemish dwelling with a lavish Baroque studio by means of a grandiose portico and a courtyard garden.

Today, the house has been restored by the city, based on a series of engravings made between 1684 and 1692, and opened as a museum. The courtyard is a re-creation of a Baroque garden typical of its time. It is assumed that Rubens designed the garden himself, but exactly how it was laid out is not known. The reconstruction made use of visual sources, including Rubens' paintings and contemporary horticultural and botanical sources.

Facing the balustraded, paved patio in front of the studio, the most dominant feature of the garden was and is the ornate pavilion with its statues. It survived almost intact, and is aligned on the cobbled main axis. The garden space itself is relatively plain and uncomplicated. The courtyard is divided into four compartments by low yew hedges and a cross axis path. Additional ornament is provided by means of clipped evergreens in wooden tubs and clay pots, placed along the main paths. Along one side of the garden is a wooden gallery over which are trained honeysuckle, roses and vines. Here too is a raised circular stone pool, which contains a fountain.

Within the four quarters of the garden, entered by means of little wooden gates, are a series of low, stone-edged rectangular raised beds separated by paths of dark grey gravel. The planting is correct in terms of both what plants would have been known to Rubens and how they would have been planted. No doubt this wealthy, highly respected and well-informed artist would have grown the latest plants to have arrived in Europe from distant lands, such as tulips, sunflowers and fritillaries, and even potatoes and tomatoes. Such prize specimens would have been displayed as individual plants within the beds in a haphazard but charming arrangement of varying heights, textures, forms and colours.

1 — The garden behind the house was laid out in Baroque style, with four compartments with their own gates.
2 — The ornate pavilion that formed the centrepiece of the garden has remained virtually intact.
3, 4 — The beds are planted with period-correct plants, including potatoes from the New World (then grown as an ornamental plant), and orange, fig and other fruit trees. Some plant choices are based on those shown in Rubens' own paintings.

# Garden in Schoten

Antwerp, Belgium

| | |
|---|---|
| Jacques Wirtz, Wirtz International | |
| 20th–21st century | |
| 1.6 hectares / 4 acres | |
| Temperate Oceanic | |
| Formal / Modern / Topiary / Walled | |

Timelessness and tranquillity typify the work of renowned designer Jacques Wirtz. His gardens are based on structural planting: plants are used in a highly sculptural, artistic way – almost as building materials – in an approach Wirtz says is about 'the expressive strength of plant material'. Wirtz's use of clipped hedges to define spaces and focus views recalls great landscape designers such as André Le Nôtre. It has become widely recognized as his trademark and is made more contemporary by being combined with perfectly proportioned mown lawns, reflective pools, gravel paths and borders full of massed planting. Wirtz gardens are constant: they work as well in winter months as they do in summer.

Although his approach and plant pakette is constant, each Wirtz garden is unique. His own garden at Schoten is fascinating. In 1970 the family moved into the former gardener's house of a large estate. The walled plot was derelict, with no plants apart from fruit trees and box hedging. The now cloud-pruned box hedges – the result of rehabilitating the old hedges – are a widely-recognized feature of the garden.

The large rectangular plot is divided into four by gravel paths flanked by roly-poly-shaped box hedges; in places fruit trees emerge above these green cumulus clouds. Their organic shapes contrast with straight-clipped hedges and topiary shapes, and foliage creates a diversity of textures and form.

Near the house, the garden is more traditional: a mown lawn; a formal pool, its strong lines blurred by masses of water plants at one end and water lilies at its centre; and borders, which may be filled with masses of the same plant. Further into the garden, the atmosphere shifts and borders are filled with nursery stock. Taller hedges of clipped hornbeam (*Carpinus betulus*) with a crenellated top make green walls that add to the air of enchantment.

Wirtz is inspired by music and art. His garden is a place of experimentation, a place where garden-making is pursued as rigorously as an art form. Textural contrasts, light and shade, and sculptural plant shapes all play their part in creating a special atmosphere.

1—Box spheres and crenellated hornbeam create a series of geometric patterns.
2—The formal lines of the pond are softened by dense planting of horsetail (*Equisetum*) and irises.
3—Near the house, patches of lawn and beds of perennials are the closest the garden comes to a conventional approach.
4—Pear trees grow among the garden's characteristic clouds of box (*Buxus*), which Wirtz created by trimming the neglected box hedges he inherited on the site.
5—Solid shapes of yew (*Taxus baccata*) form a backdrop to roses and weeping cherry (*Prunus pendula*).

# Hortus Botanicus Leiden

Leiden, South Holland, Netherlands

Carolus Clusius, Daniel Marot, Nathan de Rothschild

16th–17th, 20th & 21st century

2.5 hectares / 6.5 acres

Temperate Oceanic

Botanical / Bulbs / Informal

Located in the centre of Leiden, the Hortus Botanicus was established in 1590 by the city's university, making it the oldest botanical garden in the Netherlands. Four years later Carolus Clusius – famous for introducing the tulip to Holland – was appointed prefect and charged with researching the medicinal properties of plants and imparting his knowledge to medical students. Clusius's garden was small, but his botanical knowledge, reputation and international contacts enabled him to fill the beds with more than 1,000 different types of plant. Clusius's garden was reconstructed in 2009 in what is now the Front Garden (the oldest part of the Hortus). The rectangular raised beds are planted with the same plants that Clusius grew, including examples of very early tulip hybrids.

Today the Hortus Botanicus contains more than 10,000 types of plant, with especially fine collections of species native to East and Southeast Asia, Southern Europe and South Africa. The garden also remains an active institution for research, education and exhibitions. The new Winter Garden is filled with tropical plants and is noted for its large collection of cycads, Araceae (including the giant Titan arum, *Amorphophallus titanum*), *hoya* spp., carnivorous pitcher plants (*Nepenthes* spp.) and one of the world's largest collections of Asian orchids. Beyond is the renovated Orangery (1744) with its collection of subtropical plants, while the tallest greenhouse, the Victoria Glasshouse, contains specimens of the giant water lily (*Victoria amazonica*).

The wider grounds feature a fern garden, a rosarium, a herb garden and the Japanese Garden. Opened in 1990, the last honours the German physician Philipp Franz von Siebold, who worked for the Dutch East India Company in the 1820s, and who introduced hundreds of plant species from Japan to Europe. The garden also contains a number of venerable trees, including a golden chain (*Laburnum anagyroides*) planted in 1601, a tulip tree (*Liriodendron tulipifera*) from 1682 and a ginkgo (*Ginkgo biloba*) from 1785.

1 — Contrasting with the ultra-modern Winter Garden behind, Carolus Clusius's original garden has been faithfully re-created near the entrance to the garden.
2 — Eye-catching modern stone sculptures add contemporary interest to the garden beneath a blooming magnolia.
3 — In spring the riot of blooms and shades of green in the Wild Garden provides a naturalistic contrast with the more formal areas of the garden.
4 — Clusius introduced the tulip to the Netherlands, and the garden preserves some species and early cultivars.

# Paleis Het Loo

Apeldoorn, Gelderland,
Netherlands

| |
|---|
| Jacob Roman, Daniel Marot |
| 17th & 20th–21st century |
| 10,000 hectares / 24,710 acres |
| Temperate Oceanic |
| Baroque / Bulbs / Formal / Naturalistic / Parterre / Water |

Like much of Europe, the Netherlands fell under the influence of Versailles, the most grandiose of all seventeenth-century gardens, but at Het Loo – 'The Wood's Palace' – the version of the Baroque created by the French Protestant refugee Daniel Marot is intrinsically Dutch. It combines a small, intimate scale with a highly intricate design and the lavish use of flowers, particularly tulips in spring. Unlike Versailles, the palace and garden at Het Loo do not dominate nature; rather, they nestle within it. Indeed, the palace was originally built as a hunting lodge for William of Orange and his English wife, Mary, between 1684 and 1686. It became their favourite retreat, and the garden later influenced the design of their garden at Hampton Court near London.

Beside the palace is the *berceau*, a network of secret arbours and pathways roofed with clipped hornbeam, while behind it is the Lower Garden, which is arranged on an axis with a number of fountains. Arranged symmetrically on either side is a four-square of *parterres de broderie* with a fountain at the intersection of the perpendicular gravel paths. Along either perimeter, raised walkways look over the patterns of clipped box hedges set within expanses of gravel and grass. Orange trees in tubs symbolize the Prince of Orange and statuary throughout evokes Hercules: William, a new Hercules, had defended his country and his faith against the French Apollo, Louis XIV.

An avenue of trees marks the boundary between the Lower and Upper gardens. The latter contains *parterres anglais*, with patterns picked out in grass sward set within expanses of gravel around a large octagonal pool with fountains. Behind a smaller circular pool, colonnades form a visual boundary for the whole garden.

The Baroque garden was destroyed in the eighteenth century to make an English-inspired landscape, but the garden was fully restored for its 300th anniversary in 1984. Great attention was given to the layout, although far less care was taken with authentic reconstruction and planting details; nevertheless, the result is impressive.

1 — The view from the Colonnade sweeps over the Lower Garden, which included the highest-spouting fountain in Europe at the time it was built.
2 — An aerial view of the garden behind the house shows the symmetry characteristic of the Baroque style.
3 — The Fountain of Venus aligns directly with the fountains of the Lower Garden.
4 — Coloured gravel and clipped box hedges define the decorative scrolls of the parterres.
5 — The Gallery of Carpinus in the Queen's Garden is a palisade made of oak trelliswork clothed in hornbeam (*Carpinus betulus*).

3

4

5

# Tuinen Mien Ruys

Dedemsvaart, Overijssel,
Netherlands

| | |
|---|---|
| Mien Ruys | |
| 20th century | |
| 0.8 hectares / 2 acres | |
| Temperate Oceanic | |
| Borders / Plantsman / Rooms | |

Wilhelmina Jacoba Moussault-Ruys – known as Mien Ruys – was one of the most influential twentieth-century European garden designers. She studied in Berlin in the 1920s, and visited Gertrude Jekyll, a friend of her father, Bonne Ruys, owner of a nursery specializing in perennials and bog plants. In 1925 Mien began making small display gardens in the nursery, and she quickly became interested in materials and hard landscaping. Recycled railway sleepers deployed in different ways became her signature feature. Thus began what is now Tuinen Mien Ruys – Mien Ruys's Gardens – which comprise thirty experimental gardens.

The Dutch have a history of making intimate yet interesting gardens. Ruys followed the tradition, but was also influenced by the composition of small but detailed Japanese gardens. She combined artistry with a geometric formality and a profuse but controlled approach to the use of plants. The essence of Ruys's clean and direct style is her use of space, often expressed by a functional arrangement of features and horizontal surfaces combined with loose but choreographed planting.

After her first creation – the Wilderness Garden (1925) – Ruys designed the Old Experimental Garden (1927), with a 30-metre-long (98-foot) herbaceous border in which Jekyll's influence is clear. Here, too, she introduced what became another fashion: exposed aggregate paving slabs. In the Water Garden (1954) Ruys banished the lawn and instead introduced changes in level to devise a planting scheme of both moisture-loving and drought-tolerant plants. These three gardens were declared national monuments in 2004.

As a whole, Tuinen Mien Ruys give an overview of twentieth-century garden design as interpreted by one of its most skilful practitioners. It is constantly inspiring in its diverse use of materials and plants, and its subtle ways of defining and linking different garden compartments, so that the visitor is able to take away ideas to try at home.

1—A bench in the centre of the garden allows visitors to contemplate what Ruys called 'wild planting in a strong design'.
2—Asters, *Persicaria* and goldenrod bloom in the Autumn Garden.
3—In the Clipped Garden, purple *Berberis thunbergii* f. *atropurpurea* contrasts with *Geranium macrorrhizum* and sedum.
4—Triangular fountains and clipped yew (*Taxus baccata*) add geometrical precision to the pond in the Clipped Garden.
5—Stepping stones made from wooden decking give access to the Water Garden.
6—Exuberant bulbs including anemones, hyacinths and glory of the snow are planted in bands in the lawn, separated by neatly mown grass.

# Keukenhof

Lisse, South Holland,
Netherlands

| | |
|---|---|
| Princess Jacqueline of Hainault, Jan David Zocher, Zocher Family | |
| 15th, 19th & 20th century | |
| 32 hectares / 79 acres | |
| Temperate Oceanic | |
| Bulbs / Festival / Informal / Landscape / Woodland | |

Although it translates as 'kitchen garden', Keukenhof is not, today, about edibles. Rather it is a celebration of spring-flowering bulbs, for the cultivation of which Holland has been famous for centuries. Every year the gardens are planted with some seven million bulbs; they are open for just two months each year from mid-March, with the best show of tulips usually coming around the middle of April.

The history of the Keukenhof garden began in the fifteenth century, when the land was a hunting park owned by Princess Jacqueline of Hainault. She began a Herb Garden there, which supplied the castle and gave the garden its name. The more naturalistic Woodland Garden designed by Jan David Zocher in the 1850s – now home to the many beds of bulbs – has winding paths, groves of trees and curvaceous pools and streams.

The renowned festival of bulbs at Keukenhof is more recent in origin. It was first held only in 1949, in order to boost the Dutch bulb industry by enabling growers to exhibit their latest hybrids on a grand scale.

Even the approach to Keukenhof through the bold colours of the Dutch bulb fields is no preparation for the diversity and surprising beauty of massed displays of bulbs in large beds at Keukenhof itself. Were they not handled so well, they would risk being brash and gauche. In addition to drifts of bulbs in the informal woodland, there are seven inspirational gardens including a Historic Garden, which showcases herbs with historic tulip species and cultivars; a Nature Garden, which combines wild species of bulbs with perennials and shrubs; and a Japanese-inspired Country Garden.

Although Keukenhof is always thronged with visitors during its short season, one of the great delights of the design is its 15 kilometres (9.3 miles) of sinuous paths. These lead past changing vistas and generate a continual succession of variety, surprise and beauty. Occasionally, too, the visitor can enjoy a fleeting moment of solitude in which to reflect on the magnificence of the floral show and the enormous amount of work required to create this annual extravaganza.

1, 2—Visitors who wander along the miles of paths discover treats such as the Woodland Lake and a wooden bridge, all surrounded by massed plantings of brightly flowering bulbs.
3, 4—The bands and patches of colour carpeting the grounds are provided by a wide variety not only of the tulips for which the Netherlands are famed, but also of hyacinths, daffodils, fritillaries and grape hyacinth.

1

2

3

4

# Heerenhof

Maastricht, Netherlands

| |
|---|
| Jan van Opstal, Jo Willems |
| 21st century |
| 0.3 hectares / 0.7 acres |
| Temperate Oceanic |
| Bulbs / Modern / Topiary / Urban |

The Dutch gardening tradition has always tended to emphasize the modest over the expansive, the domestic over the vast, the intimate over the impersonal. This garden in Maastricht is a remarkable expression of how such a tradition can be made contemporary within a relatively small area.

Key to its success is a perfection of scale that allows a wide variation in a small area – *multum in parvo*. The garden is divided into compact areas, including the Peacock Garden (complete with white peacocks), the French Garden with its Baroque pergola, the Theatre Garden – named for its resemblance to rows of seats – and the Round Terrace. Apple and pear trees are carefully pruned to keep their shapes and to remain at the right size for the garden, despite the apparently naturalistic appearance of areas such as the pond. Yew is clipped into upright exclamation marks that echo Italian cypresses and give vertical interest – but at the same time the garden remains generally low, so that the scale never becomes overwhelming and it is always possible to see beyond the boundaries to surrounding trees.

Another underlying principle in the garden is the contrast between the formal and the informal. There are numerous formal areas, including a raised rectangular canal and a steel pergola that fits in well despite its space-age feel. More naturalistic features include the large pond edged with wild-looking planting including *Darmera peltata*, *Lysimachia ciliata* 'Firecracker', tulips and roses. Straight lines and geometric shapes are softened by drifts and billows of flowers and shrubs. Tulips are a particular characteristic of the garden. They appear in brick-edged, terraced beds, in planters and containers, in dense beds and in sinuous waves that wind among the more formal hedges. Even when the bulb season has passed, the box and yew topiary and the knotted fruit trees provide considerable winter interest.

1—The Peacock Garden is based on a contrast between the formal low hedges and raised canal and the meandering river of white tulips and other spring bulbs and billowy mounds of box.
2—A willow-leaved pear tree, *Pyrus salicifolia* 'Pendula', provides a focal point for the view across the pond.
3—The French Garden contrasts formal box hedging with fountains of *Paeonia lactiflora* 'Jan van Leeuwen' and *Cornus kousa* var. *chinensis*.
4—The Theatre Garden features tulips and other spring bulbs in a framework of red bricks and cobbles, like a city garden from the Dutch golden age.
5—In the Round Terrace, parallel low hedges of yew are planted with tulips.

3

4

5

# Hummelo

Gelderland, Netherlands

| |
|---|
| Piet Oudolf, Anja Oudolf |
| 20th & 21st century |
| 1 hectare / 2.5 acres |
| Temperate Oceanic |
| Modern / Naturalistic / New Perennial |

Although the garden at Hummelo has become something of a shrine for lovers of contemporary naturalistic planting, it began in the early 1980s as a nursery for a garden design business. Since then, Piet and Anja Oudolf's garden has become a key location in a growing worldwide gardening movement.

The garden is on either side of a traditional farmhouse. Dominated by perennials and grasses, whose main season of interest is from early summer until late winter, it exemplifies the potential for a palette characteristic of what is often termed the New Perennial Movement. Early summer is colourful but relatively low-key: the main interest is the beauty of plant form and structure, which develops through the summer to peak in autumn. The impact of seed heads and dead foliage remains important for several months afterwards.

The garden started with a strongly architectural feel, heavily influenced by the Dutch Modernist garden designer Mien Ruys (see page 214). Over time, however, the Modernist proportions of clipped foliage, lawn and graphic structure have been displaced by perennials and, latterly, ornamental grasses. For many years, layered yew hedges formed a much-photographed backdrop to the front garden.

Behind the property, Anja Oudolf's nursery has been replaced by an experimental combination of perennials and a meadow of native species. This has matured to form a distinctive and innovative feature – a rare example of northern European native grasses in apparent coexistence with non-native perennials. The front garden is also almost totally dominated by perennials, although the distinctive style of the enclosing hedges still has a strong impact. There has been very little replanting, which says much about the longevity of the species chosen.

The Hummelo garden has become a key source of images for contemporary, perennial-focused planting design. The social function of the garden has also been very important, as the Oudolfs for many years organized events there for fellow garden enthusiasts, thereby establishing an influential network.

1 — The front garden ended in pruned yew hedges that helped to soften and disguise the boundaries of the property. These hedges have now sadly been lost to flooding.
2, 3 — Undulating clipped and unclipped yew hedges create geometric forms among beds of perennials. Over time the clipped shapes have been replaced by perennials.
4, 5 — Oudolf's characteristically dense and innovative planting finds echoes and contrasts of colour and shape from alliums, *Eryngium giganteum*, *Salvia* x *sylvestris* 'Mainacht', *Monarda* 'Cherokee' and *Persicaria amplexicaulis*.

# Priona Tuinen

Schuinesloot, Overijssel,
Netherlands

| | |
|---|---|
| Anton Schlepers, Henk Gerritsen | |
| 20th–21st century | |
| 1.5 hectares / 3.5 acres | |
| Temperate Oceanic | |
| Informal / Meadow / Natives / Naturalistic / New Perennial | |

The garden at Priona was at the centre of the 'Dutch Wave' of contemporary planting design, marked by a focus on naturalistic aesthetics and the use of native species and perennials. Priona's creators spent their youth in the counter-culture of Amsterdam in the 1960s and 1970s before moving to the Dutch hinterland. Anton Schlepers and Henk Gerritsen found gardening a key part of the process of reconnecting with nature. They also travelled, mostly in central Europe, and found inspiration in wild plant communities. Schlepers and Gerritsen created Priona together until Schlepers died, in 1993, after which Gerritsen continued until his death in 2008. The garden's new owners are committed to maintaining it.

Although in basic form the garden has many conventional elements – borders, hedges, lawn, topiary – it also contains others that at the time of its making were more radical: areas of wildflower lawn; vegetable and annual gardens allowed to go to seed; wayward, rank-growing perennials; and abstract topiary shapes that look like something out of a sculptor's studio. Its creators, particularly Gerritsen, wanted to embrace the wild even in a small space, to encourage as much biodiversity as possible and, above all, to find beauty where it had not been seen before.

While some visitors find the garden untidy, others find it inspirational. A series of photographs of seed heads taken by Marijke Heuff made a big impact on the garden world in the 1990s, while a friendship with the designer Piet Oudolf led to joint book projects about garden perennials. Oudolf credits Gerritsen with opening his eyes to new ways of looking at plants, in particular outside their conventional decorative season. The appearance of perennials after flowering, almost in their autumn death-throes, particularly appealed to Gerritsen, although by the mid-2000s he was eager that Priona no longer be known as 'the death garden'. The garden also includes several sculptural elements that are distinctly humorous, such as the topiary chickens on the main lawn. Thus Priona is a garden with an important message, but also one that does its best to entertain.

1 — A bright red sculpture by Henk Gerritsen provides vertical punctuation in the Woodland Garden; the sculpture was intended to be temporary, and is gradually deteriorating from the top down.
2 — The Wildflower Meadow reflects the inspiration Gerritsen and Schlepers found in the flower meadows of central and southern Europe.
3 — Exuberant topiary reflects the sense of humour that runs through the garden.
4 — An autumn border includes *Euonymus*, *Callicarpa* and *Liriope*.

# Herrenhausen

Hannover, Lower Saxony, Germany

| |
|---|
| Electress Sophia of Hanover, Martin Charbonnier |
| 17th & 18th century |
| 501 hectares / 125 acres |
| Temperate Oceanic |
| Baroque / Formal / Historic / Parterre |

Herrenhausen's Great Garden is one of Europe's finest Baroque masterpieces, but it is only one of three different and contrasting gardens that make up the complex. Being formal and symmetrical along either side of its main axis, the moated garden gives an overriding impression of nature ordered and controlled by man. Immediately in front of the castle are the most intricate elements of the design – four *parterres de broderie*. With their swirling patterns picked out in neatly clipped, low box hedges and ornamented with white sculptures, they are guarded by a club-swinging statue of Hercules. Beside them to the west is a maze, and to the east the Grand Cascade. Beyond are more hedge-enclosed squares laid out in geometric patterns, which in summer are a riot of colour from 30,000 flowering plants. The garden's focal point is the Great Fountain, which sends up a jet 82 metres (270 feet) high. Surrounding the fountain is a 'Wilderness' of square compartments divided into triangles, enclosed by beech hedges and planted with trees.

Although the Great Garden was first laid out in 1666, its current form was created between 1696 and 1714 by the Electress Sophie of Hanover (mother of the British king, George I), who called Herrenhausen her life's work. Sophie also added Germany's first garden theatre – and the only one in Germany still used for performances. In the northwest corner of the garden is the Grotto. Built in 1676, it was redesigned by the artist Niki de Saint Phalle between 2001 and 2003 and now adds colourful modern elements to the mix.

Abutting the Great Garden to the east, and in striking contrast to it, is the George Garden on either side of the Herrenhäuser Allée. It is laid out in the informal, naturalistic English landscape style, with winding paths, a sinuous lake and woody glades. The third garden is to the north, behind the castle. Known as the Berggarten, it was originally the castle's vegetable garden but is now a botanic garden featuring some fine specimens, including a cucumber tree (*Magnolia acuminata*) from 1794, as well as a range of glasshouses, together with areas of specific habitat including a prairie and heathland.

1, 3—The parterre of the Great Garden combines some 30,000 summer flowers and ornamental box trees with snow-white sandstone sculptures, including Hercules with a club and Venus and Cupid. The Great Fountain at the heart of the garden is one of the tallest in Europe, sending a jet 82 metres (270 feet) into the air.
2—The Garden Theatre is still used for performances. Hedges form the wings, either side of a stage lined with gilt figures.

1

2

3

# Branitzer Park

Cottbus, Brandenburg, Germany

| |
|---|
| Prince Hermann Ludwig Heinrich von Pückler-Muskau |
| 19th century |
| 600 hectares / 1,483 acres |
| Humid Continental |
| English Landscape / Romantic / Vistas / Water |

Prince Hermann von Pückler-Muskau had many passions – women, poetry, travel – but his love of landscape design surpassed them all. The dashing nineteenth-century man of action and letters spent nearly thirty years creating the Bad Muskau landscape in northeastern Germany, a process that left him nearly penniless. To pay his debts, he sold the property and moved 12 kilometres (8 miles) away to his smaller estate, Branitz Park, in 1845.

Von Pückler set about transforming this featureless landscape with a dedication bordering on mania. His inspiration was the popular English Landscape style, which he had experienced while searching for a rich wife in England and about which he wrote a classic book. Von Pückler introduced the typical features of this style in Branitz Park: rolling meadows interspersed with tree and shrub groupings and water features. He moved farmsteads, built hills, diverted rivers, planted thousands of red maple, chestnut, spruce, ash and oak trees, laid out drives and paths, and created the lakes and streams that snake through the park. The result was a serene and natural-looking landscape, which could be explored on horseback or in a carriage by the nineteenth-century visitors, rather than on foot.

By using the interplay of light and shadow, form and colour, von Pückler created sightlines of beautiful pictures including a lake sited deliberately to reflect the Baroque castle. Each vista entices the visitor deeper into the landscape, to discover delights such as the two earthen pyramids that von Pückler built, inspired by his travels. The larger of the two is the Lake Pyramid, where von Pückler and his wife are buried, and it seems to float on the water. It measures 13 metres (42 feet) high and 32 metres (105 feet) wide, and is sheathed in false Virginia creeper (*Parthenocissus vitacea*) and grapevines. In autumn, the pyramid slowly changes colour as the creepers turn from green to red. The sight is truly spectacular.

1 — The view from the pyramid over a pond towards the castle is a major vista von Pückler carefully created on well-proportioned axes over the undulating scenery.
2 — The Lake Pyramid, where von Pückler is buried, is topped by a quotation from the Qur'an: 'Graves are the mountain-peaks of a distant new world.'
3 — A bronze griffin looks west from the castle terrace, which was added in the mid-nineteenth century.

# Liebermann Villa

Wannsee, Berlin, Germany

Max Liebermann, Albert Brodersen, Alfred Lichtwark

20th century

2.6 hectares / 6.5 acres

Humid Continental

Cottage / Plantsman / Rooms

There is a great poignancy about visiting the Liebermann Garden on Berlin's Wannsee Lake. Only a few minutes' walk away stands the villa that hosted the Wannsee Conference of January 1942, where the Holocaust was conceived. The garden owner, Max Liebermann, a well-known artist who died in 1935, was himself Jewish; his widow died in Theresienstadt concentration camp in 1943.

In summer the visitor is greeted by colourful perennials, annuals and dahlias in narrow borders on each side of the path. Nearby, perennials and vegetables grow in a style inspired by north German cottage gardens. At the rear, a terrace with box-edged beds filled with scarlet pelargoniums fronts a lawn that leads down to the lake. Hornbeam hedges and pleached limes define three formal 'rooms'. A gravel path leads through a grove of birches to the lake – but one tree grows out of the middle of the path, a masterstroke of 'nature over design' that featured in one of Liebermann's paintings.

Liebermann laid out the garden in conjunction with Albert Brodersen, director of Berlin city parks from 1910 until 1926. He also took advice from Alfred Lichtwark, director of the art museum in Hamburg and a prominent leader of a reforming movement in garden-making. Liebermann's garden is an excellent example of this style, which can be seen as a parallel to the Arts and Crafts movement in Britain. Lichtwark's involvement underlines the high status gardening enjoyed in Germany. More than anywhere else, planting design was seen as a true art form, and the use of shape and colour was the subject of intense debate. This lively garden culture survived the economic and political crises of the interwar years in a weakened form, with the focus very much on public rather than private gardens and on ecology rather than aesthetics.

Wartime saw the destruction of the garden. After German reunification in 1990, the house became a museum, and the garden was restored in the early 2000s. It is now a peaceful location to appreciate an important period of garden history – and to reflect on the terrible decisions made nearby.

1—A view from a lakeside gazebo towards the villa demonstrates Lichtwark's idea that the garden should have clear lines of sight.
2—At the front of the house the colourful flower garden is based on the cottage gardens of northern Germany.
3—Behind the flower garden are box-edged beds of pelargoniums, from where the lawn stretches down to the lake.
4—Lichtwark intended the hornbeam walls of the three Hedge Gardens to make the visitor curious about what lay within.

# Karl-Foerster-Garten

Potsdam-Bornim,
Brandenburg, Germany

| |
| --- |
| Karl Foerster |
| 20th century |
| 0.5 hectares / 1.2 acres |
| Humid Continental |
| Informal / Perennials / Plantsman |

Karl Foerster's garden was central to the life of a man who was not only immensely influential in the twentieth-century German garden, but also, given the growing respect for German planting design, possibly the most influential gardener ever. Nurseryman and plant-breeder, as well as writer and broadcaster, Foerster started the garden in 1912 as a trial ground for his nursery business, a test bed for plants and a place to entertain visitors. It was inspired by historical English sunken gardens, with a series of terraces that provide micro-habitats for perennials and shrubs centred on an oval pool. Today, the secret and reflective character of the space is reinforced by a partial surrounding of mature trees.

Originally the garden was filled with phlox and delphinium, both of which Foerster bred. Later his interests turned to a wilder plant palette, including ferns and grasses, as reflected in today's planting. As his prominence grew in the 1920s and 1930s, Foerster became the centre of the so-called *Bornimer Kreis* (Bornim circle), mainly of garden and landscape designers but also including architects, writers, artists and musicians. This reflected the fact that in pre-World War II Germany gardening was an activity that was taken seriously by the cultural elite, alongside painting, philosophy, music and nature.

Foerster remained in Potsdam-Bornim during the war, helping Jewish and dissident friends by employing them in the nursery. After the war, he found himself in the Soviet-ruled part of Germany. Honoured by the communist regime of East Germany, he continued to be involved in running the nursery, although it became effectively a state-run enterprise. Even in retirement he continued to write.

After Foerster's death in 1970 the garden became run-down. With the reunification of Germany in 1990, its restoration became a priority for the German-speaking garden world. Overseen by Foerster's daughter, Marianne, the Karl Foerster Foundation reopened the garden for the Federal Garden Show in Potsdam in 2001. Much was replanted, mostly with plants that Foerster would have grown, although a new autumn bed was added. Today the garden has become a shrine for plant-lovers, and an essential part of any garden tour of the Berlin area.

1, 2, 3—Foerster's garden is renowned for its influential combination of architectural and naturalistic garden styles, and particularly for its Sunken Garden.
4, 5—Details from the purple- and mauve-planted Sunken Garden show *Chrysanthemum* 'Cinderella', asters, a *Miscanthus* hybrid and *Sedum telephium*, together with a ceramic sculpture by Dorothea Nerlich.

# Schloss Sanssouci

Potsdam, Brandenburg, Germany

| Frederick II of Prussia, Georg Wenzeslaus von Knobelsdorff |
| --- |
| 18th century |
| 299 hectares / 740 acres (park) |
| Humid Continental |
| Baroque / Edible / Park / Terraces |

'True riches consist only of what comes out of the earth', wrote the Prussian king, Frederick II in a letter to the French philosopher Voltaire. 'Whoever improves the soil, cultivates land lying waste and drains swamps is making conquest from barbarism.'

The land on which Frederick II built his summer palace and garden, Sanssouci, had been wooded until his father cleared it to make way for the expansion of Potsdam. In 1744 Frederick II outlined his plans to transform the hillside into a retreat, drawing up a design with the architect Georg Wenzeslaus von Knobelsdorff for what would be a Prussian Versailles.

Frederick intended Sanssouci not as a gaudy symbol of monarchical prowess but rather as a haven from the concerns of office. It takes its name from the French words for 'without worries', and the palace was constructed essentially as a kind of rustic villa reimagined in rococo style.

The main gardens consist of six concave vineyard terraces that lead from the simple, single-storey palace to the formal gardens below. Figs grow in glazed niches between the vines, benefiting from the terrace's curve, which maximizes their exposure to sunlight. The vines themselves were sourced from German, French, Italian and Portuguese stocks – an apt reminder that Sanssouci is a confection of different European styles and influences, created by a monarch with an enthusiasm for the arts and the sciences. A fountain at the centre of the formal garden is surrounded by box hedges and Neo-classical statues.

Beyond the formal garden lies an ornamental lake, a kitchen garden and the Sanssouci Park, also decorated with Greek- and Roman-style follies. The park was planted with fruit and vegetables under Frederick II's direction.

Frederick was not the only eighteenth-century monarch to seek refuge in ornamental agriculture, and like his peers he may have seen in careful husbandry a metaphor for responsible monarchy. But few of his peers reached the heights of productive gardening that Frederick achieved at Sanssouci.

1—The glazed niches that are interspersed with the vines on the palace's concave terraces house fig trees.
2—The Chinese House, one of a number of pavilions in the garden, was built in the mid-eighteenth century, during a vogue in Europe for *chinoiserie*.
3—Neo-classical sculptures are dotted throughout the larger park at Sanssouci.

# Bergpark Wilhelmshöhe

Kassel, Germany

Giovanni Guerniero, Heinrich Christoph Jussow

17th & 19th century

240 hectares / 593 acres

Humid Continental

Baroque / Formal / Landscape / Park

Described by the art historian Georg Dehio as 'possibly the most grandiose combination of landscape and architecture that the Baroque dared anywhere', Bergpark Wilhelmshöhe is Europe's largest landscape park created on a mountain slope (and the world's second largest). It was proclaimed a UNESCO World Heritage Site in 2013.

Created by the Italian architect Giovanni Guerniero from 1689 for Landgrave Carl von Hesse-Kassel – inspired by the Villa Aldobrandini in Italy – Wilhelmshöhe is a statement of man's dominion over nature and an expression of the ideals of absolute monarchy. Only the upper third of Guerniero's grandiose scheme was built; it is aligned on an east–west axis that runs through the castle and stretches 5 kilometres (3.1 miles) to the city of Kassel. The other terminus of the axis is the eye-catching high point of the design, the octagonal Hercules Monument (or Wasserschloss, as it houses the water tank) on the summit of Karlsberg Mountain, 526.2 metres (1,726 feet) above sea level.

From the peak, the monument's giant bronze statue – a copy of the Farnese Hercules – looks over the Grand Cascade, which in full flow is highly dramatic, especially when lit at night. The water rushes, tumbles and falls via the Vexing Grotto and Artichoke Basin – with hydro-pneumatic sound effects – the Felsensturz Waterfall and Giant's Head Basin down to Neptune's Basin to the final climax, the Grand Fountain. When the fountain was created in 1767, its 50-metre (164-foot) jet was the tallest in the world.

Following the Seven Years' War in the mid-eighteenth century, the lower part of the park around the Cascade axis was redesigned for Carl's great-grandson Elector Wilhelm I by Heinrich Christoph Jussow, who created an idealized, romantic natural landscape. The reservoirs that feed the Cascade also supply the water courses that wind across the axis, flowing over a series of dramatic waterfalls and cataracts. Towards the end of the century the eighteenth Mulang – a Chinese village with a pagoda – was added, and in the early nineteenth century Landgrave Wilhelm IX added the final heroic, romantic landscape flourishes in the form of the Aqueduct and the Lowenburg, a medieval-style castle.

1 — From the Hercules Monument there is a spectacular view down the 350-metre (1,150-foot) Grand Cascade.
2, 3, 4 — For the romantic refashioning of the gardens around 1800, the German architect Heinrich Christoph Jussow created a series of follies and other structures, including the Roman Aqueduct and the Devil's Bridge.

# Sichtungsgarten Hermannshof

Weinheim, Baden-Württemberg,
Germany

| |
|---|
| Urs Walser, Cassian Schmidt |
| 20th century |
| 2.2 hectares / 5.5 acres |
| Temperate Oceanic |
| Informal / Naturalistic / New Perennial |

For anyone interested in planting, Sichtungsgarten Hermannshof is one of the most exciting gardens in Europe. There has been a garden here since the eighteenth century, so it contains many heritage trees, including a myrtle, because Weinheim has one of the warmest climates in Germany. In the 1920s, Heinrich Wiepking-Jürgensmann redesigned the garden for the local Freudenberg family – industrialists who still own and fund it – in collaboration with the town.

In 1979 a plan was developed to turn the site into a trial garden based on the principles of planting design developed largely by Professor Richard Hansen, from the trial garden in Weihenstephan, Bavaria. A design was created by the landscape architect Hans Luz with planting by Urs Walser, who became the first director when the garden opened in 1983. The planting was based on the concept of creating communities, mostly of perennials, which would function as artificial ecosystems with a naturalistic feel but with a long period of visual interest: inspiration habitats included prairie, steppe and wetland. The visitor could explore decorative plant combinations grouped around two central lawns, looking out past old trees to the wooded hills of the landscape.

After Cassian Schmidt became director in 1998, one lawn was replaced with a prairie-style planting, divided into habitats that reflect the wide diversity of prairie conditions. Schmidt used North American species in his quest to evaluate plants and combinations for larger-scale plantings. He also introduced planting based on northwest Asian monsoon climates. The maintenance required by plant combinations is analysed and informs the production of commercial plant combinations and research.

Sichtungsgarten Hermannshof contains a huge range of plants, with many that are new or rare in cultivation. Styles vary from the subtle to the colourful, reflecting the varied types of planting developed for public or private situations, and for different levels of light and soil moisture. In spring, there are several weeks of colourful tulips, while winter can be attractive, too – at least until snow flattens the seed heads of the perennials.

1 — In spring, the conference hall looks over beds of massed tulips and flowering trees.
2 — In early summer, Chinese wisteria (*W. sinensis*) showers a path with pastel flowers.
3 — Seed heads of grasses and perennial planting in the Prairie Garden include *Miscanthus* spp. and *Veronicastrum* spp.
4 — Perennial borders feature *Achillea* 'Coronation Gold', *Lychnis coronaria*, *Lavandula* spp. and *Salvia* spp.

# Pomeranzengarten

Leonberg, Baden-Württemberg,
Germany

| |
|---|
| Heinrich Schickhardt |
| 17th & 20th century |
| 0.16 hectares / 0.4 acres |
| Temperate Oceanic |
| Formal / Historic / Terraces |

Pomeranzengarten is Germany's only courtly terraced garden from the High Renaissance. The structure seen today derives largely from soon after 1600, when Duke Johann Friedrich asked the court architect Heinrich Schickhardt to create a garden for his mother, the Dowager Duchess Sibylla. In 1609 she moved into the palace, which had been converted from a medieval castle, in the historic town of Leonberg.

On a steep slope to the southwest of the palace, Schickhardt created a terraced garden with a fountain and a Pomeranzengarten – a *Pomeranzen* being a type of bitter orange. Despite his concern for his mother, the duke also worried about his purse, for what was constructed was less ornate than Schickhardt's initial plan. In 1742 the terrace was converted to a fruit and vegetable garden, but in 1980 it was restored to its original layout.

Rectangular and compact – but with no architectural relationship to the palace – the terrace is laid out with its corners marked by four small pavilions with pyramidal roofs. Aligned on the central walk is a large octagonal pool featuring an ornate obelisk fountain and wooden balustrades, and either side of the walk are two rectangular areas enclosed by simpler balustrades. The rectangles are subdivided into quarters by perpendicular gravel paths, which intersect at a central stone-bowl fountain; meanwhile the quarters are repeatedly divided geometrically and symmetrically into patterns of small raised beds edged with low box hedges and stone.

As in the Renaissance, the beds are once again planted with an ornamental mix of period-correct aromatic and medicinal herbs, together with flowering plants. The eponymous oranges were grown in pots along the central axis of the garden in summer, and in colder weather were moved to a proto-greenhouse. A double staircase with a fountain grotto led from the terrace to an orchard on the slope below, and next to the terrace was a kitchen garden. These areas were not part of the 1980s' restoration, but there are plans to bring them back into cultivation.

1 — The view across the terrace, with the castle to the right, shows how the garden lies below and southwest of the building. The bitter Seville oranges that gave the garden its name were exotic and highly valued at the time of its creation, both as a food and as a source of medicinal extracts. They were also a symbol of the golden apples of the Hesperides, suggesting a link between the garden and those of antiquity.
2 — A fountain stands amid the dozens of rectangular raised beds created by the perpendicular paths that crisscross the terrace.

1

2

# Schloss Schwetzingen

Schwetzingen,
Baden-Württemberg, Germany

| |
|---|
| Johann Ludwig Petri, Nicolas ce Pigage, Friedrich Ludwig von Sckell |
| 18th & 19th century |
| 72 hectares / 178 acres |
| Temperate Oceanic |
| Baroque / English Landscape / Formal / Rococo / Sculpture |

The garden of this eighteenth-century palace, a residence of the rulers of the Palatinate, is a tour de force. Restored in the 1990s, it is an enjoyable lesson in garden history that covers both the Baroque and Rococo styles and the reaction against them, in the shape of the informal English garden around the formal core. Classical formality here comes across as playful and inventive, and rich in the symbolism of the Enlightenment and classica learning. Although contemporary planting is not absent, one of the great pleasures of the garden is the fact that it has changed little since the eighteenth century.

The electors Carl Philipp and Carl Theodor employed Johann Ludwig Petri and Nicolas de Pigage to lay out the formal garden and later Friedrich Ludwig von Sckell to create the English landscape garden (one of the first in Germany). The contrast between the styles is not readily noticed today, but must have had a considerab e impact at the time.

The garden next to the palace is in a French Baroque style, with fountains, parterres, allées and pleached lime trees, together with a pergola-type covered walkway. Buildings and statuary play a major role, often employing the imagery and allegory seen in many other gardens of this period. Exceptional, however, is the *moschee* (mosque) and its accompanying Turkish Garden. This is by far the largest of the false mosques that were not uncommon in European gardens of the time. Another interesting survival is the 'End of the World', a piece of perspective trickery that forms part of a complex of pleasure buildings.

Part of the garden experience is the constant chiaroscuro (darkness and light) effect. This is part of the garden's central message, which is a celebration of the Enlightenment raising humanity out of darkness into a golden age of light and wisdom, as represented by the god of art and culture, Apollo, who has a temple here. Ruins symbolize the past, particularly a mock Roman aqueduct. Various classical-style structures include a Temple of Botany. For anyone wanting to understand the world view of the eighteenth century, this is an exceptionally good place to discover.

1, 2, 5—The formal garden near the palace is laid out with flower-filled parterres and walks of pleached lime trees dotted with statuary and water features, such as fountains in the shape of stags.
3—The Temple of Apollo represents the triumph of culture over ignorance.
4—The mosque in the Turkish Garden is entirely ornamental.
6—The 'End of the World' is a series of gazebos with a *trompe-l'oeil* painting at the end.

3

4

5

6

# Insel Mainau

Lake Constance,
Baden-Württemberg, Germany

| |
|---|
| Grand Duke Frederick I, Lennart Bernadotte |
| 19th & 20th century |
| 45 hectares / 111 acres |
| Temperate Oceanic |
| Arboretum / Bedding / Rooms / Water |

The first garden at Insel Mainau was created by Grand Duke Frederick I of Baden after he acquired the island and its eighteenth-century Baroque palace in 1853. Frederick landscaped the grounds and planted the arboretum, which now contains 500 taxa and provides a contrasting backdrop to the various flower gardens. He also designed the Italian Rose Garden and the Orangery. But it was Count Lennart Bernadotte who reshaped the gardens and put them on the horticultural map. He was a member of the Swedish royal family who gave up his right to the succession and moved to the island in 1932. In 1974 Bernadotte transferred ownership of Insel Mainau to the foundation that bears his name, to ensure the garden's long-term survival.

Today the garden comprises a series of contrasting events and 'rooms' that provide variety and interest within a unified whole. The different rooms offer a mix of exuberant floral shows, which – thanks to the local climate – include both tropical and subtropical plants. It is little wonder that Insel Mainau is known as the 'Garden Island'. In the spring the great drifts of tulips and the show of rhododendrons are spectacular. In summer the grounds are ablaze with bedding plants inspired by nineteenth-century British gardens; they lend the garden a sense of fun. Summer is also the time for the display of dahlias, and the formal Italian Rose Garden, near the palace, is as perfumed as it is vivid, the tones of the blooms contrasting with the verdant lawns. Below the Rose Garden, the Mediterranean Terrace features plants from various regions that enjoy a Mediterranean climate.

Water is never far away in this garden, and one of its most attractive features is the Italian Water Stairs. Flanked by slender cypress trees and massed, bright bedding plants, water cascades down a long slope over a series of stone steps into a rectangular pool. Other attractions in this varied garden include the Palm House, the Butterfly, Herb and Scented gardens, and the five experimental Seasonal Gardens. The last, which are changed every year, are built to the winning designs of a student competition.

1—Some of the 100,000 tulips planted each year in the Meadow provide a spectacular foreground to a view of Lake Constance.
2, 5—Sculptures – of flowers or more permanent materials – contribute to the gardens' overriding sense of fun.
3—The Water Stairs are built from precious Swiss granite and bordered with wide beds of flowers and pillar-shaped conifers.
4—The formal Italian Rose Garden is today used mainly for growing hybrid tea roses.

1

## France, Spain and Portugal

### France



### Spain



### Portugal

# Château de Brécy

Brécy, Lower Normandy, France

Didier Wirth, Barbara Wirth

17th & 20th century

1 hectare / 2.5 acres

Temperate Oceanic

Baroque / Formal / Parterre / Terraces

Château de Brécy is a gem waiting to be discovered – an exquisite but little-known modern garden created within the tradition of Italian and French formal gardens. Proportion and order have been retained so that the late twentieth-century garden complements a house built in the 1620s.

The house – attributed to François Mansart – lies in a dip, while the garden rises behind in a series of terraces that have their horizontal lines accentuated by flights of steps, clipped hedging and stone balustrades. The horizontals reinforce the horizon where turf meets the sky, seen through the wrought-iron Gates of Paradise at the top of the garden. The design is anchored by a strong central axis, evident from the entrance along a beech (*Fagus sylvatica*) allée cut through woodland to a lawn bounded by pleached limes (*Tilia*).

Behind the house the terraces unfold along the central axis. A visitor is greeted by the triumphant parterre, with arabesques of box (*Buxus sempervirens*) that pattern the gravelled area next to the house. The focal point of the garden – the Gates of Paradise and the horizon – are immediately visible, and the perspective is increased by formal cones of evergreen topiary along the central path. The first turfed terrace is dominated by four triangular divisions of lawn on each side surrounded by pleached hedges of hornbeam, while the next is formed of a quartered square lawn dominated by clipped domes of hornbeam, giving structure even in winter, when the brown leaves contrast with the green lawn. Within the lawn are two matching stone fountains carved into pyramids of artichokes, an allusion to the emblem of the property.

The garden has a refined palette – green, white and blue – which complements the stonework of the house and the walls. The formality is softened by plantings of white-flowered *Romneya coulteri*, *Perovskia* 'Blue Spire', globe artichokes and topiary specimens. Despite the formality, this is a garden full of delight and charm. Although modern, it clearly speaks of Renaissance symmetry, planting and sculpture while making reference to the grand tradition of French garden design – but without being overwhelming.

1 —An aerial view shows the Gates of Paradise at the top of the terraces that rise behind the house.
2, 3—Fountains of artichokes – the symbol of the estate – balustrades and staircases are typical of the carved stonework that is a feature of the garden.
4—The skilfully clipped box parterre forms arabesques in front of blue Versailles planters that contrast with the pale stonework of the wall behind.
5—Box hedges and lime trees form an arch above a path in the Formal Garden.

# Jardins de Kerdalo

Trédarzec, Brittany, France

| | |
|---|---|
| Peter Volkonsky | |
| 20th century | |
| 18 hectares / 44.5 acres | |
| Temperate Oceanic | |
| Arboretum / Coastal / Formal / Naturalistic / Perennials | |

Kerdalo, close to the mouth of the Jaudy River on Brittany's northern coast, is not simply a French confection. The garden was conceived and planted by the Russian aristocrat Peter Volkonsky in 1965. Having adored gardening throughout his adult life, he began work on Kerdalo while in his mid-sixties, and turned this garden into his final great achievement. It is filled with exotic varieties and serves as testament to a gardener who appreciated both horticultural order and commotion.

The initial terraced, formal stages are set beside an old country house, which Volkonsky also bought and restored. Beds of agapanthus separate the southern edge of the house from the garden's large lawn. This area then leads down to an equally formal rectangular garden, divided into four squares and planted with geraniums, alchemilla and other flowers. Below these beds is a more impressive, informal area, planted with exotic trees and shrubs. As the soil is acidic, Volkonsky favoured ericaceous plants, such as rhododendrons, camellias and magnolias, as well as more exotic species, such as the Chilean evergreen *Maytenus boaria*. From here, the garden descends to the very edge of the estuary, and breaks into a wilder, more forest-like region: a stream runs through this part of the garden, which is planted with Gunnera and arum lilies as a contrast to the more formal planting above.

Such singular creations as Kerdalo are difficult to maintain after their progenitor's demise, and, when Volkonsky died in 1997, some thought the garden would soon fade with him. But Volkonsky's daughter the RHS-trained gardener Isabelle Vaughan and her husband, Timothy, took on Kerdalo and continue to maintain it. Today Kerdalo has been designated a *Jardin remarquable* (remarkable garden); France's Ministry of Culture bestows such an honour on only 300 or so gardens nationally in recognition of their outstanding beauty, botanical interest and exemplary maintenance.

1—The formal garden beside the house is planted with alchemilla, geraniums and other flowering plants, while large rhododendrons and camellias thrive in the acidic soil.
2, 4—Beyond the formal garden, the nearby Jaudy estuary allowed Volkonsky to introduce many water features, from formal pools to naturalistic ponds with fountains.
3—Volkonsky was not only interested in rarer trees and shrubs; he also planted many popular French plants, such as lavender.
5—Volkonsky's daughter Isabelle maintains the original features of the garden, such as this grid of cobbled and grassy squares.

237

# Le Vasterival

Sainte-Marguerite-sur-Mer,
Upper Normandy, France

| |
|---|
| Princess Greta Sturdza |
| 20th century |
| 12 hectares / 30 acres |
| Temperate Oceanic |
| Botanical / Coastal / Plant Collection / Rhododendrons / Wood and |

At Le Vasterival one of the twentieth-century's most remarkable gardeners created what many enthusiasts believe is the finest private garden in France. The gardener was the Norwegian-born Princess Greta Sturdza, who in 1995 moved to Normandy with her Romanian husband to live in what had previously been the home of the celebrated composer Albert Roussel. There she began to assemble botanical collections that are the envy of many official or national botanical gardens.

Although she was entirely self-taught, the princess had previously created gardens in Norway and Romania. Therefore, when she began clearing the swampy forest on the cliff-top site, she was already an experienced botanist who placed great emphasis on developing young plants. She was also a great advocate of mulching, which protected and nourished the soil, did away with the need for weeding and meant that no watering was required during dry seasons. Another of the princess's gardening skills was pruning; despite the naturalistic look of the woodland gardens, all the shrubs and trees have been pruned in order to open up vistas through the garden that highlight fascinating combinations, colours and shapes of plants.

Being set in a sheltered valley, the sloping garden at Le Vasterival has colour all year around, from delicate spring blossoms to the golds and reds of autumn foliage, and from the bright perennials and roses of summer to the warm palette of leaves even in the depths of winter. One of the stars of winter, the coppery *Hamamelis* 'Le Vasterival', was raised by the princess to provide colour. In all she acclimatized more than 10,000 species as she transformed the wild undergrowth into a managed garden with a hand so light that the human interference is barely noticeable. Among the highlights of Le Vasterival's collections are hellebores, magnolias and rhododendrons, and a huge range of hydrangeas.

Princess Greta died in 2009 – at the age of ninety-six – but the upkeep of the garden has been taken over by her son Prince Eric and his wife, Irène Sturdza.

1—In autumn the Grande Allée is a show of shapes and colours from varieties of Japanese maple (*Acer palmatum*) and *Clethra*.
2—*Actinidia kolomikta* climbs the wall of an outbuilding surrounded by *Rhododendron* 'Halopeanum', *Choisya* x *dewitteana* 'Aztec Pearl' and *Helleborus argutifolius*.
3—Sweeping lawns provide open vistas and add a sense of scale to the shrubs and trees.
4—*Acer palmatum* 'Bloodgood' provides a display of rich brown foliage next to hellebore and viburnum.
5—Cultivars of Japanese maple are planted close together to form an autumnal tapestry.

3

4

5

# Giverny

Upper Normandy, France

| | |
|---|---|
| Claude Monet | |
| 19th century | |
| 2 hectare / 5 acres | |
| Temperate Oceanic | |
| Artistic / Cottage / Japanese / Water | |

Claude Monet's renowned garden at Giverny is actually two very different gardens. Of course there is his famous lily pond, but on the other side of the road, next to the house that was his home from 1883 until his death in 1926, is his first garden: the Clos Normand. This formal pattern of flower beds was influenced by Monet's visit to the Dutch tulip fields, and is full of perspective, symmetry and colour. In spring, for example, it is filled with irises, peonies, tulips and forget-me-nots.

The wide central allée leading down from the house towards the road is arched over with iron rocs, covered in climbing roses in early summer. By autumn the path is smothered in self-seeded nasturtiums. As beautiful as the flower displays are, Monet also used them as a laboratory to experiment with colour combinations, letting the plants grow freely. It is little surprise that Monet had a huge influence on another painter-turned-gardener, Gertrude Jekyll, who applied painterly colour theory to her planting designs.

Monet's second garden, which he made in 1893, was the Japanese-inspired Water Garden. With its informal pool covered with water-lily pads, fringes of weeping willow and a wisteria-clad Japanese bridge, it is instantly recognizable from Monet's famous water-lily paintings, which dominated the last thirty years of his life. Yet there remains something almost surreal about passing beneath the road to emerge into a living painting. Visitors experience Monet's two-dimensional art as a three-dimensional garden, and gain a new insight into his skill as both artist and garden designer. As the visitor moves around the lake, the vistas and light change, and the water reflects the sky or is rippled by the wind. There is a clear sense of how Monet found this garden forever intriguing and inspiring.

Monet purchased his water lilies from the nursery firm Latour-Marliac, which is still in business. The varieties he used – including *Nymphaea mexicana*, *N.* 'Laydekeri Rosea' and *N.* 'Odorata Sulphurea Grandiflora' – are still in cultivation for those who want to grow a little of Monet's garden at home.

1, 4—From the house, the Grande Allée passes beneath a rose-arch tunnel past a flower garden with up to seventy flower beds to the celebrated Water Garden on the other side of the road (foreground).
2—The house is covered with climbing roses in early summer. Monet's wife, Camille, made the painter keep the two yews nearest the house from the trees that formerly flanked the path.
3—Red, yellow and orange sunflowers (*Helianthus annuus*) interspersed with asters and pink cleomes create a painterly colour combination near the house.

2

3

4

5—Monet's famed Water Garden was inspired by his interest in Japanese woodcuts, and was particularly inspired by Oriental images of plants and water. In 1883 he planned a pond, which involved regrouping plants such as water lilies, irises and willows that grew naturally near the Epte River, as well as planting other flowers.
6—The iconic Japanese Bridge (the subject of many of Monet's paintings) has a canopy of wisteria (*W. sinensis*), while weeping willows and bamboos grow nearby – some planted merely to discourage visitors from approaching the water's edge.
7, 8—Familiar from the series of paintings to which Monet devoted the last thirty years of his life, the water lilies (*Nymphaea* spp.) and foliage of the Water Garden often resemble an Impressionist masterpiece.

5

6

7

8

# Le Jardin Plume

Auzouville sur Ry,
Upper Normandy, France

Patrick Quibel, Sylvie Quibel

20th–21st century

2.8 hectares / 7 acres

Temperate Oceanic

Edible / Formal / Grasses / Parterre

Le Jardin Plume takes its name from the tall, feathery plumes of grasses that are illuminated by the setting sun. Dusk gives the garden a luminous quality that highlights the seductive mixture of grasses and wild-seeming perennials with a more traditional, formal French framework of box parterres.

When the Quibels bought the property in 1996, it was an orchard. Pasture and apple trees still form the backdrop to this modern formal garden. The pair designed a garden that drew on ideas from both the old gardens of France and England and the new perennial gardens of Holland and Germany. Le Jardin Plume reflects these twin inspirations: the south-facing terrace has squares of ruler-straight box hedges – protection against the sweeping winds – that barely contain the early-flowering oriental poppies and later dahlias and sunflowers. Beyond, the echoes of formality are underlined by a simple mirror pool reminiscent of a grand Renaissance water feature.

Other parts of the garden have distinct atmospheres. In the Barn Garden the reddish buildings and clipped hedges form the backdrop to coloured swaths of meadow grasses. The Vegetable Garden is busy not only with rows of marigolds and arches of sweet peas, but also with self-seeding poppies and nasturtiums. Next door, the profusion is countered by a pool surrounded by miscanthus.

The Autumn Garden has an old well as its focus. It again combines clipped hedges and feathery grasses with perennials such as mingled asters, anemones and fleabane (*Erigeron annuus*). After the garden's final flowering, grasses and any seed heads are left to be enjoyed through the winter.

The Quibels do not plant in large blocks, although the Orchard has paths mown through blocks of miscanthus. Instead they use different combinations of the same plants. The result of this limited palette, however, is a garden of great variety – and true originality.

1—Morning sun bathes mixed nasturtiums trailing over parterres in the South Garden in early October, punctuated by clumps of stripy zebra grass (*Miscanthus sinensis* 'Zebrinus').
2—Late in summer, the square pool of the Miscanthus Cloister is hidden behind the tall grass.
3—Grasses, Japanese anemones (*Anemone* x *hybrida*) and Michaelmas daisies create an autumnal palette in the Nursery.
4—Grasses, sedum and wild flowers crowd the path towards an old barn.
5—*Crocosmia* 'Lucifer' blooms in the South Garden in summer.
6—In May, the Flower Garden is full of blue black iris and poppy 'Mother of Pearl' in front of box and young chestnut trees.

1

2

3

4

5

6

# Château de Versailles

Versailles, Ile-de-France, France

| | |
|---|---|
| André Le Nôtre, Louis Le Vau, Charles Le Brun | |
| 17th century | |
| 3,019 hectares / 7,400 acres | |
| Temperate Oceanic | |
| Baroque / Formal / Water | |

The garden that André Le Nôtre created in the 1660s for Louis XIV, the Sun King, was the most magnificent in Europe, and the most politically charged. It was a display of humanity's triumph over nature. It was also the final word in 'power gardening', sending a clear message to the monarchs of Europe about the political superiority of France, and of Louis himself. Although the garden today is half the size it once was, the core remains an intact expression of the extravagance of Louis's vision.

A garden that matched the splendour of Louis's palace threatened to become overpowering, but Le Nôtre drew on a style he had successfully developed at Vaux-le-Vicomte (see page 252). He retained a sense of proportion by controlling the gently sloping site through the use of formal symmetry. He hung the garden on a main axis aligned on Louis's west-facing bedroom; it is variously a terrace, a grassy slope and a 1.9-kilometre-long (1.2-mile) lake. He created changes in level and planted long allées to impose regularity. Le Nôtre also devised a series of events and compartments, which feature statues, surprises, architecture and – above all – water. The 1,400 fountains used six times as much water each day as the whole of Paris.

On the terrace closest to the house, the *parterre de l'eau* reflects the facade on a still day, uniting the garden and the palace. On either side are the *parterres de broderie* – flower beds inspired by embroidered fabrics, with their patterns picked out in clipped, low hedges and turf, and filled with flowers. Steps lead down to the Latona Fountain (Latona was the mother of the sun god, Apollo, a reference to Louis shared by many of the garden's sculptures). Beyond the fountain the *tapis vert* (grass walk) slopes gently down to the extravagant Bassin d'Apollon at the head of the canal. On either side of the *tapis vert* are *bosquets* (geometrical, wooded compartments) linked by tree-lined allées and filled with fountains, statues and buildings.

Other highlights of the garden are the Bassin de Neptune to the north of the top terrace and the vast Orangerie to its south. Further out in the landscape are the Menagerie, Le Grand Trianon and Le Potager du Roi. Le Petit Trianon was added in 1762 and Le Hameau (the hamlet where Marie-Antoinette played at being a dairy maid) was built in 1783.

1, 2—The main axis of the garden extends from the palace past the Latona Fountain, down a grassy slope to the long lake.
3—The Neptune Fountain was created by Le Nôtre in 1679–81, but its sculptures date from 1740. Its ninety-nine water features aroused great admiration.
4—The Apollo Fountain features a gilded lead sculpture of the sun god driving his chariot.

3

4

5

5—The Orangerie Parterre was used to grow orange, lemon and pomegranate trees in pots in summer before they were moved into the vast Orangerie for the winter. It was originally ornamented with sculptures.
6—Elaborate iron pergolas surround a dramatic fountain.
7—King Louis XV built this pavilion as part of the French Garden, so named because it was more formal than the English landscape garden.
8—Among the *bosquets* off the main allée, at the meeting point of several groves, are the gilded Four Seasons fountains, of which this represents Flora (Roman goddess of spring), resting on a bed of sculpted flowers.

248

6

# Villa Savoye

Poissy, Ile-de-France, France

| |
|---|
| Le Corbusier, Pierre Jeanneret |
| 20th century |
| Temperate Oceanic |
| Courtyard / Minimalist / Modern / Roof |

The trees that enclose and isolate the Modernist Villa Savoye make it resemble a white liner floating on a sea of green sward – but that appearance comes at a cost. In the spring of 1928 Pierre and Emilie Savoye approached the Swiss architect Le Corbusier to design them a new country home on a site with a magnificent view to the northwest towards the Seine Valley; but the trees have now been allowed to obscure that view. Working with his cousin Pierre Jeanneret, Le Corbusier deliberately kept the natural setting and placed the stilted house – one of what he called his 'machines for living' – on the high point of the plot. The iconic, revolutionary and highly influential house narrowly avoided demolition in the 1960s, when much of the wider garden was hived off to construct a school. Added to the French register of historical monuments in 1965, the house underwent major restoration in the 1980s and 1990s.

Today the trees screen the house from visual intrusion and from the school. In front is a rectangle of lawn and, somewhat surprisingly, a pair of long flower beds planted very traditionally with shrub roses. The garden spaces are integrated into a house that encapsulates Le Corbusier's 'Five Points of Architecture': pilotis or slender columns, a facade free of structural members, an open plan, ribbon windows and a flat roof garden. The outdoor space is on two levels. Surrounded by the living spaces and accessed through sliding glass doors that blur the boundary between inside and outside is a 'hanging' paved courtyard, ornamented with a couple of raised planters and a concrete table. Here, too, the architecture frames views out over the wider landscape. A returning ramp leads up to the rooftop garden or solarium, with its paving and gravel, planters, 'windows' and arrangement of rectilinear and sinuous tall walls that define the space and create shelter.

Villa Savoye, like other Modernist gardens (such as Villa Mairea in Finland and El Novillero in California; see pages 97 and 364), was iconoclastic, but only one element of their design ethos entered the mainstream. Such properties pioneered the notion of removing the barrier between indoors and outdoors, and of using the garden as a living space rather than simply a location in which to grow plants.

1—Lavender and other small shrubs fill concrete planters in the roof garden. 2—A 'window' in the wall of the solarium frames the outside view, helping to unite the building and the landscape beyond. 3, 4—Ribbon windows blur the boundaries between interior and exterior, a pioneering idea that entered the architectural mainstream; the sloping ramp leads up to the roof garden, creating a smooth flow between the levels.

1

2

3

4

# La Roseraie du Val-de-Marne

L'Haÿ-les-Roses,
Ile-de-France, France

Jules Gravereaux, Edouard André

20th century

1.5 hectares / 4 acres

Temperate Oceanic

Botanical / Formal / Plantsman / Roses

At its best for only one month a year – June – La Roseraie was the first single-species garden dedicated to showing off all aspects of roses, from climbers and shrub roses to standards and roses on frames, arches and rope swags. The garden was started by Jules Gravereaux, who retired to the area in 1892. Gravereaux was beguiled by roses and began sourcing and growing them, contacting growers around the world in order to gather as complete a collection as possible. In 1899 he commissioned the landscape architect Edouard André to create a garden setting in which roses of all types could be grown.

The popularity of La Roseraie led in 1914 to the municipality changing its name from L'Haÿ to L'Haÿ-les-Roses. After Gravereaux's death in 1916, the gardens declined until the Department of the Seine bought them in 1937. Since the late 1960s the gardens have been preserved and managed by the local council of Val-de-Marne.

André's design of beds and supports such as trellises, arches and pergolas around a central fountain pool housed the original collection of some 1,600 roses. Today the collection has expanded. The garden is perfumed and coloured in the summer by thousands of rose bushes of around 3,500 varieties.

La Roseraie has a value that goes far beyond its ornamental appeal. It serves as a gene bank of old rose material and a history of the uses of roses. One area of the garden showcases the history of the rose, with a special avenue displaying all the roses grown by Napoleon's empress, Josephine.

The largest of the thirteen distinct collections is the Old Horticultural Rose Garden, which holds several hundred varieties created by breeders before 1945. These include Gallicas, Bourbons, Noisettes and Polyantha roses. The Rugosa Rose Alley includes many roses that Gravereaux used to breed his own highly perfumed roses, including 'Rose à Parfum de l'Haÿ'. As one of the leading authorities on roses, Gravereaux contributed roses to the public rose gardens at Château de Bagatelle in Paris, and to the historic re-creation of Empress Josephine's rose collection at Malmaison.

1—An aerial view looking east shows the symmetry of André's design around the central Fountain Pool.
2—Arches support a tunnel of climbing roses, including the pink 'Alexandre Girault' on the second arch.
3—The roses growing on a trellis next to one of the flower beds are 'Léontine Gervais' (pale pink at top), 'Veilchenblau' (pink, bottom left) and 'Record' (red, bottom right).
4—The rose bush 'Jean Girin Palissé' grows on a column in the Temple Amour garden.
5—A statue of Cupid dances in a small rose-filled bower.

# Château de Vaux-le-Vicomte

Maincy, Ile-de-France, France

André Le Nôtre, Louis Le Vau,
Charles Le Brun

17th century

40 hectares / 100 acres

Temperate Oceanic

Baroque / Formal / Parterre / Water

Versailles (see page 246) is the grandest European garden of the seventeenth century, but for all its magnificence it is deliberately impersonal, designed to reflect the power of both the king and France. The inspiration for Vaux-le-Vicomte, on the other hand, is very different. It was built in 1650 by Nicolas Fouquet, finance minister to King Louis XIV. Fouquet engaged the architect Louis Le Vau to build an opulent château decorated by the painter Charles Le Brun. To design the garden, Le Brun recommended his young friend André Le Nôtre, who complemented the château with the most elegantly proportioned, balanced and geometrically harmonious of all High Baroque gardens.

The view from the roof of the château reveals how Le Nôtre organized the garden around a 3-kilometre-long (1.8-mile) central axis. This passes between the *parterre de broderie* and terraces ornamented with fountains and pools before cutting a swath through a forested hillside and terminating at a statue of Hercules. The patterns in the *parterre de broderie* are picked out in clipped box hedging and the spaces between filled with terracotta and black gravel. From on high, the central axis appears to flow in one unbroken sweep, but this is deceptive. The axis has numerous changes in level that are not visible from the château. For example, just beyond the circular pool that marks the end of the *parterre de broderie*, the first principal cross axis is emphasized by a pair of previously unseen pools. Even more dramatic is the wide canal that forms the second main cross axis, which is hidden by a substantial drop, the retaining wall for which becomes a water feature, the Grandes Cascades. Le Nôtre also used what is termed decelerated perspective: for example, the reflecting pools are narrower closer to the château, which makes them appear nearer the viewer.

At Vaux-le-Vicomte, Le Nôtre first showed his ability to design on a grand scale, marrying architecture, formal gardens and natural topography. His skill was recognized by Louis XIV, who took the team of architect, painter and garden designer to Versailles and told them to get on with the job.

1—An aerial view from the north shows the château and the axis of the garden beyond.
2—From the house, the view stretches past a *parterre de broderie* to a cross axis formed by a canal that Le Nôtre placed to conceal it from view until the visitor is almost upon it.
3—The eastern Triton Fountain gives a view up the wooded hill to the statue of Hercules, the terminus of the garden.
4—Statuary and clipped yews mark the sunken canal that divides the formal garden from the hillside beyond.

1

2

3

4

# Oasis d'Aboukir

Paris, France

| |
|---|
| Patrick Blanc |
| 21st century |
| 25 metres / 82 feet (height) |
| Temperate Oceanic |
| Modern / Urban / Vertical |

What kind of garden is opened to coincide with Design Week in Paris, one of Europe's most stylish cities? The answer is a stylish one – L'Oasis d'Aboukir, one of French botanist Patrick Blanc's renowned *murs végétaux* (vertical gardens). Blanc has been making vertical creations, fitted to the sides of buildings, for more than three decades, combining his deep botanical knowledge with a near-evangelical urge to bring gardens into the most inaccessible parts of the city. For example, L'Oasis d'Aboukir was installed on a southwest-facing wall on the intersection of rue des Petits Carreaux and rue d'Aboukir in the French capital's second arrondissement in 2013.

Like many of Blanc's gardens, L'Oasis d'Aboukir is held in position by a wall-mounted frame. This in turn holds a series of dedicated pipes, which feed water and nutrients to the garden via an artificial felt substrate, into which the plants take root.

Blanc designs each of the gardens by hand, creating a series of interlocking, leaf-shaped beds, which give each garden a natural look. This one contains about 7,600 plants, drawn from 237 carefully selected species. This particular *mur végétal* features herbaceous varieties such as *Begonia grandis* and heucheras, as well as elliptical-leaved *Pilea plataniflora* and flowering evergreens such as *Aeschynanthus buxifolius*. Thus, while L'Oasis d'Aboukir blooms in various seasons throughout the year, it is also carefully planned so as not to look bare in winter. It took about seven months for the vegetation to cover the wall completely after it was planted.

Aesthetics aside, Blanc believes his *murs végétaux* have significant ecological benefits, arguing that the plants' exposed roots purify the city air and that the garden's irrigation system harvests rainwater that would otherwise drain into the sewage system. The psychological effects are also considerable, he claims. And, with ever more people choosing to live in cities, the botanist believes that ever more gardeners will choose surfaces such as the ones he favours to cultivate their own small oases.

1 — A combination of plants from a total of 237 different species forms a series of diagonal waves that seem to sweep up what was previously a plain concrete facade on a busy Parisian street corner.

# Promenade Plantée

Paris, France

| | |
|---|---|
| Jacques Vergely, Philippe Mathieu | |
| 20th century | |
| 4.7 kilometres / 3 miles (length) | |
| Temperate Oceanic | |
| Park / Perennials / Urban | |

The city of Paris set a global precedent in the late 1980s when it cancelled plans to demolish a long-abandoned, crumbling railway line in its less-touristy Twelfth Arrondissement. Instead the old Vincennes line was transformed into the world's first elevated park between 1988 and 1993, a long *promenade plantée* ('planted walkway'), also known as the *coulée verte* ('greenway'). The idea was later repeated in similar sites in other cities, most famously with the High Line in Manhattan (see page 404). To be on the raised promenade is to experience simultaneously both immersion in and retreat from the city. It is not only a chance to sightsee on a human scale – 9 metres/30 feet above the pavement – but also a vernal respite from congestion and grit.

The linear greenway starts in the city's Bastille section, with a wide set of stairs edged by a planted wall. The staircase opens on to a footpath supported by an old viaduct, a series of sixty-four soaring red-brick arches that have since been enclosed and turned into artisan workshops. Here pedestrians stroll past beds and trellises filled with roses, lavender and other aromatic perennials, as well as cherry and lime trees. Some areas of wild vegetation that sprang up after the railway's decommissioning in 1969 have been left to blend into the highly cultivated copses of Canadian maples, a bamboo forest, swathes of wild flowers and stands of oaks, beeches and hazels. Designers Jacques Vergely and Philippe Mathieux incorporated water in channels and children's pools, and old tunnels have been transformed into mossy caves. Hardscaping includes sundials, mazes and all manner of iron latticework, trellises and pergolas, which are repeated along the path.

As the Promenade Plantée heads towards its end at the Bois de Vincennes (the city's largest park), it rises and descends, abutting the small Jardin Hector-Malot and intersecting not only the large circular lawn of the Jardin de Reuilly but also a modern building that rises six storeys above the walkway.

1—The Promenade Plantée begins with wide stairs rising between walls planted in a series of terraces.
2—The walkway passes a section known as the Viaduc des Arts, where the old arches have been turned into galleries and studios.
3, 4—The walkway is bordered by a changing variety of flower beds and trees.
5—The viaduct is carried over another green space, the Jardin de Reuilly, on a graceful bridge.

# Garden of Peace

UNESCO Headquarters,
Paris, France

| |
|---|
| Isamu Noguchi |
| 20th century |
| 0.2 hectares / 0.5 acre |
| Temperate Oceanic |
| Formal / Japanese / Modern / Rock / Sculpture |

The Noguchi Peace Garden blends Eastern and Western horticulture. Its creator, the Japanese–American sculptor Isamu Noguchi, claimed it was not a Japanese garden, yet its oblique approach and asymmetrical layout; the prominence of rock, cobbles and sand; and the use of plants such as magnolia, pine, maple and cherry trees, bamboo, grass and lotus flowers give it an oriental air. In a distinctly un-Japanese feature, however, the garden has an upper platform from which the whole layout can be viewed. It also has clearly defined spaces and a straight, linking axis – another deviation from the oriental approach, in which boundaries are usually blurred and paths obscured.

The Upper Terrace is abstract and austere, with a few squares of low bamboo emerging from the stone paving and groups of cube-shaped, concrete seats. The central element is a Peace Fountain created from a slab of rock etched with a stylized version of the Japanese character for 'peace'. Water trickles down the rock face into a rectangular pool, then empties into a channel, which descends via a stepped cascade to the Lower Garden, where it becomes a meandering stream. The Lower Garden is a more verdant and sensual space, with sculptures, a gravel garden, a lake with stepping stones, a ceremonial plaza and a floral path beside the stream. The planting clearly emphasizes the passing of seasons with spring blossom, autumn leaf colour and evergreen boughs in winter.

Noguchi's first large-scale landscape design harmoniously links two large buildings on the UNESCO site, creating a space for both contemplation and discovery, for sitting and strolling. A poignant later addition is the Nagasaki Angel on the Upper Terrace. Donated in 1976 by the city of Nagasaki, this part of an angel's head was salvaged from the rubble of a cathedral after the atomic bomb explosion. Another reference to that apocalyptic event is found in the Meditation Space on the Upper Terrace. This cylindrical concrete pavilion, created by the contemporary Japanese architect Tadao Ando, sits in a pool paved with granite stones that were irradiated by the atom bomb and which are now washed by a constant flow of water over their surface.

1, 3—A straight path bisects the garden linking the upper and lower terraces. Stones in Japanese garden pools often symbolize moored boats; in the informal Lower Garden they are meant to be used as stepping stones.
2—Plants such as bamboo, plum and willow evoke the natural landscape of Japan and emphasize the passing seasons.
4—Water lilies are cut to form the Japanese ideogram – or picture symbol – for a pure heart.

# Château du Rivau

Lémeré, Indre-et-Loire, France

Patricia Laigneau

20th–21st century

6 hectares / 15 acres

Temperate Oceanic

Modern / Potager / Sculpture

Château du Rivau was built in the fifteenth century, but the garden is the late twentieth-century creation of Patricia Laigneau, whose lavish restoration of the neglected castle has made its towers and turrets the backdrop to a garden with fourteen distinct areas that echo a childhood world of fairytales and fantasy, as in Gargantua's Kitchen Garden, the giant, four-square potager, which greets visitors as they enter. In autumn pumpkin and squash fit for Cinderella's coach fill the potager, celebrated every September by Rivau's Festival of the Pumpkin. Other giant vegetables, such as leeks and colourful cabbages, star in this larger-than-life kitchen garden.

In the other gardens around the château, Laigneau weaves more children's fairytales. Underlining the 'larger than life' theme are many huge sculptures, including two Wellington boots made of polyester resin – two left feet, in fact – and a large watering can created by Lilian Bourgeat. Also complementing the scale of the château buildings are bright red cement flowers in cement pots, the work of the artist Jean-Pierre Raynaud. These and other sculptures at Rivau are the result of Laigneau's commissions for the ongoing collection of Art in the Garden.

Although the gardens have plenty of interest for visitors in all seasons, summer is a highlight. The lavender spiral outside the gates is a spectacular welcoming feature, while the roses that hug the property's grey stone walls and romp into trees offer up their fragrance and colour. There are more than 450 roses in the collection, including a climbing rose, 'Rivau Castle', bred by the French rose nursery André Eve.

In late summer large clumps of tall, dramatic perennials fill the borders. Laigneau uses grasses and herbaceous perennials to great effect in many areas of the gardens, in particular in the red-hot borders, which are lined with grasses and filled with dahlias, polygonum and roses.

1 — In the Gargantua Garden, plaited chestnut hurdles enclose the flowers and giant produce displayed during the Festival of the Pumpkin.
2 — Grasses and drumstick alliums fill one of the borders beyond the moat.
3 — Visitors can rest on benches beneath an iron pergola covered in climbing roses.
4 — The tall *Eremurus* among the ornamental herbs in the Tom Thumb Garden remind visitors of how plants towered over them in childhood; beyond is the sculpture of two Wellington boots.
5 — The Lavender Knot Garden combines lavender with a framework of iris, whose blooms herald the spring.

# Jardins du Prieuré d'Orsan

Maisonnais, Centre, France

Sonia Lesot, Patrice Taravella

20th–21st century

3 hectares / 7.5 acres (gardens);
15 hectares / 37 acres (grounds)

Temperate Oceanic

Modern / Parterre / Potager

Monks grew fruit and vegetables at Prieuré Notre-Dame d'Orsan for more than 900 years after Robert d'Arbrissel founded the priory here. In acknowledgement of its history, Patrice Taravella (the current owner) has created a garden that echoes those productive gardens, albeit with added ornamentation. With head gardener Gilles Guillot, Taravella has produced a garden where fruit trees, hedging plants, vines and climbers are trained over elegant structures and – by much tying in and pruning for shape – become architectural features.

At the heart of the new gardens is the enclosed Cloister Garden – a space to encourage meditation, like the original cloisters. It is edged with hornbeam arches that echo the shapes of the old stonework. The garden is divided into quadrants filled with vines and edged by grass paths that meet at a central stone fountain. At the corners of the central vineyard and around the fountain, trained quince trees form arbours.

In the raised beds of the Kitchen Garden, Taravella grows tomatoes, beans and peppers. Carrots are cultivated in terracotta-tile clamps which encourage straight, long roots. Produce from the gardens is harvested for use in the kitchen when the hotel and restaurant are open; otherwise it is made into preserves for sale. Elsewhere among the outbuildings is a parterre with a difference: instead of creating patterns with flowers or herbs (or gravel), wheat and chard, leeks and cabbages are used here.

To support and train plants or to provide focal points, seats and other structures, Taravella uses willow, hazel and other wood. Everywhere, natural materials blend with the plants and the stone of the buildings. A floral meadow, an orchard and a Maze Garden are among the many enclosed spaces. The Berry Path is flanked by borders where soft-fruit bushes and fruit trees are trained into various shapes. This triumph of horticultural expertise, like the whole garden, recalls the labours of the early monks to produce food to sustain themselves.

1 — The heart shape made by training ivy around a window honours the priory's founder, Robert d'Arbrissel, whose heart was kept as a relic after his death.
2 — The pink *Rosa* 'Eden Rose' covers the wall of one of the priory buildings.
3 — A window in a hornbeam hedge (*Carpinus betulus*) gives a view to a bed of cabbages.
4 — Hornbeam hedges guide the eye to an elegant gate panel and the meadow beyond.
5 — Vegetables are trained on wooden frames to make them easier to harvest.
6 — Along the Berry Path fruit trees are trained on various wooden frames to create architectural effects.

4

5

6

# Château de Villandry

Loire Valley, Centre, France

| | |
|---|---|
| Dr Joachim Carvallo | |
| 16th & 20th century | |
| 5 hectares / 12 acres | |
| Temperate Oceanic | |
| Formal / Historic / Potager / Terraces | |

Although there has been a garden at the Château de Villandry in the Loire valley since the sixteenth century, what visitors today see is a faithful early twentieth-century re-creation of the original. At its heart is the large formal Potager, or ornamental Kitchen Garden, which features a remarkable range of ornamental vegetables, including the iconic purple cabbage.

When Dr Joachim Carvallo bought Villandry in 1906, he began replacing the eighteenth-century landscape garden with a series of parterre terraces best seen from the château's tower. (Many other Loire châteaux had also lost their original gardens by then.) Immediately to the south of the château is the Jardin de l'Amour, where the patterns of the four parterres are picked out in clipped box filled with bedding plants symbolizing 'fickle love', 'passionate love', 'tender love' and 'tragic love'. To the west is the formal Potager, with nine equally sized square compartments defined by low trellis fences. Within each compartment, low box hedges and narrow gravel paths define unique geometric patterns of smaller beds filled with striking masses of colourful vegetables and aromatic herbs complemented with bright annuals and standard roses.

Fruit trees are trained against the retaining walls, and on the terrace above the Potager are three flower-filled parterres and a gallery covered with vines. On the highest terrace directly to the south of the château is a formal pool surrounded by geometrical lawns and viewed from above from the shade-giving allées of pleached lime trees. Water from the pool runs into the canal separating the Potager and the château. Adjacent to the Pool Garden is the Sun Garden, opened in 2008. Inspired by the New Perennial Movement, the planting of the Sun Chamber beds in hot tones of reds, oranges and yellows contrasts with the cool blues and whites of the roses and other shrubs in the adjacent Cloud Chamber.

1—An aerial view looking west over the château shows the Potager with the water garden beyond.
2—The Water Garden is bordered with grassy banks. Its central ornamental pond is in the shape of a Louis XV mirror, and is surrounded by square parterres of lawn, perpendicular avenues and four secondary ornamental ponds.
3—The Music Garden uses triangles of topiary to represent lyres, lit by clipped yew 'candelabra' at the edges.
4—In the Sun Garden, the Cloud Chamber's grassy paths wind between beds filled with cool purple and white plantings, including Michaelmas daisies, airy purple *Verbena bonariensis* and silver-leaved *Lychnis coronaria*.

3

4

5

5—A bed in the Ornamental Garden takes
the form of the Maltese Cross; other designs
include the Cross of Languedoc, the Basque
Cross and highly stylized fleurs-de-lys.
6—'Passionate Love', a maze of box hedges
in the Ornamental Garden, represents hearts
broken by the whirlwind of passion.
7, 8, 9—The ornamental Potager includes
nine equal-sized beds, each with a different
geometric motif of vegetables and flowers.
The beds are planted with vegetables in
unusual colours – blue leek, red cabbage
and beetroot – as well as lush green carrot
tops, lettuces and kale. Fruit trees mark
the corners of the larger sections.

6

7

8

9

# Festival International des Jardins

Chaumont-sur-Loire, Centre, France

Jacques Wirtz
and various show designers

20th & 21st century

3 hectares / 7.5 acres (show gardens);
21 hectares / 52 acres (estate)

Temperate Oceanic

Artistic / Festival / Sculpture

Since 1992 Château de Chaumont – perched above the river in the heart of the historic Loire Valley – has hosted an annual International Garden Festival that brings together contemporary and inspirational garden designs from all over the world. Each year thirty gardens, awarded by competition and all designed to a specific theme – such as 'Gardens of the Seven Deadly Sins', 'Gardens of Sensations' and 'Gardens of Delight, Gardens of Delirium' – showcase new plants and planting design, new materials and ornaments, new ideas and new approaches.

The festival site was itself designed by renowned landscape architect Jacques Wirtz, who took his inspiration from a nearby tulip tree (*Liriodendron tulipifera*). Each garden is made within a leaf-shaped compartment defined by hedges of beech or hornbeam. Unlike at other shows, the display gardens at Chaumont must look fresh and exciting for the duration of the festival, which lasts from late April until early November. The gardens must not only exhibit high levels of ingenuity and innovation in layout, materials and construction, but also take account of the fact that the planting will mature and change over three seasons. The resulting display gardens offer the visitor 'realistic' inspiration – but inspiration that is at the cutting edge of contemporary garden design.

The quality and range of the gardens – from straightforward to complex, astonishing to incredible – have given the festival an international reputation that attracts the world's finest garden designers. In addition to the festival gardens, the surrounding site also features the Valley of the Mists (*Vallon des Brumes*), an ornamental vegetable garden, a children's garden and several permanent experimental gardens. The most recent addition (since 2008) is the Centre of Arts and Nature, the first of its kind to examine the relationship between artistic creation and nature. Each year the centre exhibits works by invited visual artists and photographers inspired by the Domaine de Chaumont-sur-Loire.

1 — Bamboo canes edge paths and enclose a sculpture at the festival in 2010, in a garden called *Hortithérapie sensorielle*.
2 — *Earthly Paradise* was created for the 2012 Festival, 'Gardens of Delight, Gardens of Delirium'.
3 — Also in 2012, *Foxes in the Garden* used a straight path through sparse planting with bright red cut-out foxes.
4 — The Islamic inspired *Locus Genii* from 2012 included flooring made from broken tiles.
5 — An army of golden garden gnomes hold their rakes ready for action in the garden *Liberté, Egalité, Fraternité* in 2012.

# Les Jardins de l'Imaginaire

Terrasson-Lavilledieu,
Aquitaine, France

| |
|---|
| Kathryn Gustafson |
| 20th–21st century |
| 5.6 hectares / 14 acres |
| Temperate Oceanic |
| Modern / Park / Terraces / Water |

The Dordogne in southwest France has numerous historic towns, so in the late 1990s, when the mayor of Terrasson-Lavilledieu held a competition to design a new park to give the town its own tourist attraction, the challenge was considerable. The winner, US landscape architect Kathryn Gustafson, has reinterpreted fragments of garden history in a highly contemporary way.

Visitors to historic gardens will recognize many compositional elements of Gustafson's garden, including the use of axes and perspective, water as a feature and the garden's relationship to the topography of the site. Gustafson has brought these elements up to date and expanded on them to create a series of gardens that trace the community's relationship with the landscape from its natural state through agriculture and horticulture to urban life.

The terraces on the steep slope above the town were once covered with vines, and natural springs provided water. Gustafson used these elements to develop the site's potential. The path from the Sacred Wood runs through a clearing of wild flowers to the Plant Tunnel, which leads to an area that echoes the gardens of medieval monasteries. As the path winds through woodland, the visitor's gaze shifts upwards to a metallic ribbon (the *Fil d'Or*) snaking through the canopy, signifying the unpredictable twists of life. Further along, pylons support weather vanes with hanging bells that catch the wind. An amphitheatre fits naturally into the contours of the hill. Each step houses a metal bench looking over the town below. On one side the vista is framed by the roof of a conservatory by the British architect Ian Ritchie; on the other, a metal pergola resembles a giant plant-entwined net.

Gustafson uses water in a series of imaginative features. Fountains shoot up from pavements, while streams cascade down concrete steps, in some places babbling over undulating forms, and in others flowing more gently. A single jet erupts from a grid set in a lawn, while a raised canal defines an axis that elongates perspective.

The new gardens' critical success was reinforced when they won a European Award for twentieth-century heritage. It is easy to understand why they have also captured the public imagination.

1—The *Fil d'Or*, a golden metal ribbon, threads its way through the trees along the main path.
2—Metallic benches curve around the bowl of the Theatre of Greenery.
3—The Rose Garden has 1,600 shrub roses and 360 climbing roses tied to frames.
4, 5—Water is a central feature of the garden, in a rill surrounded by jets that rise from cobblestones or tumbling down chutes that resemble Islamic *chadar*.

# Villa Noailles

Hyères, Provence, France

| |
|---|
| Gabriel Guevrekian, Charles de Noailles |
| 20th century |
| 1.8 hectares / 4.5 acres |
| Temperate Mediterranean |
| Artistic / Mediterranean / Minimalist Modern / Walled |

Visiting the garden at Villa Noailles is like stepping into an abstract painting. That is exactly the effect Charles and Marie-Laure de Noailles wanted to achieve when they set out to create a garden for their new, Modernist villa on the hillside above Hyères in Provence. They appointed Gabriel Guevrekian to create a garden to complement Robert Mallet-Stevens's villa. In response, Guevrekian designed one of the first Cubist gardens.

By chance, the triangular plot close to the house resembled the shape of the Jardin d'Eau et de Lumière (Garden of Light and Water) created by Guevrekian at the groundbreaking Exposition Internationale des Arts Décoratifs held in Paris in 1925. Guevrekian's show garden had made an impact, and its innovative celebration of artificial materials rather than plants chimed with the Modernist spirit of the Jazz Age in its approach to living and garden-making.

The tight plot at Villa Noailles was the basis for a purely geometric, abstract garden with a thread of Japanese influence: Guevrekian designed it to be viewed from the outside – looked down on from above – rather than experienced from within.

White walls mark an isosceles triangle, the base of which is against the house. The ground rises towards the apex, beyond which tall trees provide a green backdrop. The plot is divided into a grid of rectangular beds and terraces of different levels or heights. Some of these compartments were originally painted different colours and are now tiled; others are planted with carpeting plants. There is a simple rectangular pool near the highest point of the site.

In such an abstract arrangement, plants are no more than a material used to give texture and colour, rather than cultivated as living specimens. Purity of form is paramount. Beyond the triangular area, the rest of the garden is terraced in a more conventional way and planted with Mediterranean plants suitable for the conditions.

The Villa Noailles garden is small in size yet has been hugely influential. At the time of its creation, it represented a new way of thinking about gardens and their design.

1, 2—In the beds of the triangular garden are box balls and succulents. At Villa Noailles colour and texture have always been more important than individual plants.
3, 4—The more conventional parts of the garden have white walls with window openings framing views from the terraces. The planting includes many highly perfumed species, such as tea olive tree (*Osmanthus fragrans* var. *aurantiacus*), jasmine and roses.

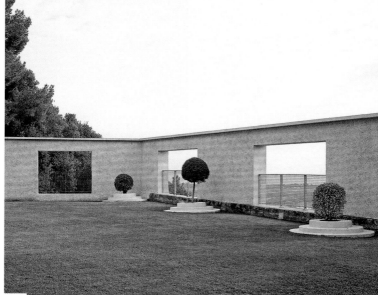

# Jardin de la Noria

Saint-Quentin-la-Poterie,
Gard, France

| |
|---|
| Arnaud Maurières, Eric Ossart |
| 21st century |
| Temperate Mediterranean |
| Historic / Islamic / Meadow |

The original idea behind the Jardin de la Noria ('The Garden of the Waterwheel') was to create an Islamic-style Paradise Garden inspired by that created in 1998 for the Garden Festival of Chaumont-sur-Loire by Arnaud Maurières and Eric Ossart, in collaboration with the artist Rachid Koraïchi. The original request of the proprietors of Mas de Licon, as it was originally known, at Saint-Quentin-la-Poterie was simply to move the show garden to the new site. But Koraïchi's sculptures had been promised to an English collector – and without them the garden lost all its meaning.

A visit to the site convinced Maurières and Ossart to propose a garden totally independent of the buildings, in the form of a vast prairie around a centrepiece formed by an old waterwheel with its associated stone structures: a terrace where donkeys walked to turn the wheel, a canal and two basins. Such waterwheels were once common throughout the area but disappeared completely during the twentieth century. They are still in use in southern Morocco, however, and it was there, in the town of Taroudant, that ironsmiths created the wheel for the garden. The ancient irrigation system was reconstructed, not in stone but in ochre-tinted concrete, which was laid so that it created a unified form that would both channel the water and provide paths for the viewer.

Visitors to the Jardin de la Noria are greeted by two walls separated by a narrow opening; their positioning reflects a traditional local use of such omnipresent walls. Two wooden buildings dominate the site. One is at the entrance to the garden, behind the entry walls, while the other is at the end of the path, set in the middle of an orchard. The concrete furniture was created by the sculptor Pierre Baye.

The Jardin de la Noria offers a contemporary version of the Arab–Andalucian gardens of the past, with a planting scheme that is faithful to those originals. Its cypress, figs, pomegranate trees and scented roses are symbolic of the original Paradise Gardens and remain perfectly suited to the Mediterranean climate.

1 — In the Jardin des Grenadiers, an Islamic-style pool fed by a rill is ornamented with architectural agapanthus in large pots.
2 — The *noria*, or traditional waterwheel, had to be commissioned from ironsmiths in southern Morocco.
3 — The sunken pool in the Cloître des Micocouliers (Hackberry Cloister) is surrounded by the trees that give the cloister its name.
4 — The garden makes innovative use of concrete, including in the novel garden furniture designed by Pierre Baye.

# Jardin des Colombières

Menton, Alpes-Maritimes, France

| | |
|---|---|
| Arnaud Maurières, Eric Ossart | |
| 20th & 21st century | |
| 3 hectares / 7.4 acres | |
| Temperate Mediterranean | |
| Classical / Coastal / Natives / Sculpture | |

The Jardin des Colombières was created by Ferdinand Bac between 1920 and 1930. Previously a cartoonist and novelist, Bac became a gardener at the age of fifty. He first designed a garden at Villa Croisset, which no longer exists, before dedicating himself to Colombières for his friends and patrons, the Ladan-Bockairys. Bac himself lived in the house until World War II, when it was requisitioned by the Italian army.

Colombières is a unified and complex work, where Bac was at one and the same time architect and stonemason, decorator and gardener. Sited on cliffs overlooking the sea, it is a hymn to the ancient values of the Mediterranean, a creation that went against the vogue for the exotic that was dominant at the time on the Côte d'Azur. Bac preferred native plants to foreign introductions, and rustic olive jars to Medici vases. Straight and winding paths invite the visitor to move from feature to feature, some of which recollect the voyages of Ulysses, while others are ancient temples, each offering a different view of the sea: framed between two cypresses, hidden behind the branches of an olive tree or underlined by a hedge of *Pistacia lentiscus*.

In 1952 the heirs of the Ladan-Bockairys developed the house as a hotel, but its garden remained abandoned and the immediate surroundings were built on, with new construction replacing the ancient olive grove. Recognition of the site as a historic monument at the end of the 1980s did not stop the garden's decay.

It took the courage – and fortune – of Michael and Margaret Likierman to save Colombières. They bought the property in 1995 and threw themselves into five years of restoration work overseen by the architects Camous & Kriegel and the landscape designers Maurières & Ossart (see Jardin de la Noria, page 267). In addition to Bac's own writings about Colombières and his vision for the garden, the restoration was also inspired by the work of the Mexican architect Luis Barragán, particularly because it was a visit to the Jardin des Colombières in 1931 that first inspired him to become an architect.

1 — Echium flowers on a terrace above a flat-roofed *ombrière*.
2, 5 — The garden references classical literature, such as Homer's *Odyssey*, with features including Nausicaa's fountain and a head of Medusa.
3 — The garden has transformed a series of olive terraces.
4 — At the centre of an avenue of large olive jars is a 600-year-old carob tree, said to be the oldest in France
6 — *Geranium maderense* flowers near a footbridge among the garden terraces.

# La Louve

Bonnieux, Luberon,
Provence, France

| |
|---|
| Nicole de Vésian |
| 20th century |
| 0.3 hectares / 0.75 acre |
| Temperate Mediterranean |
| Dry / Landscape / Mediterranean / Sculpture / Terraces / Vistas |

La Louve, a sunstruck garden built on narrow terraces in Provence, has inspired designers and home gardeners since its creation in 1986 by the retiring fashion designer Nicole de Vésian who, at seventy, fell in love with a narrow valley at the edge of a medieval hill town. Until her death ten years later, Vésian worked in her garden every day, inspired by her changing vision rather than a set plan. She distilled and stylized the Lubéron landscapes of wild woodland and small fields, rocky outcrops and drystone walls. Interiors and exteriors connect and flow from house to garden to hillside. Vésian grouped tough Mediterranean subshrubs – sometimes pruned, sometimes naturally mounding – to echo the curves of the horizon. She chose mainly local species: box, *Viburnum tinus*, laurel, rosemary, arbutus and iris, to which she added silver-leafed plants such as dorychnium, lavender and *Teucrium fruticans*.

Vésian's 180-degree panorama is too vast to be called 'borrowed' in the Japanese manner, nor is it a succession of framed pictures. Instead, a constant link between garden and landscape evolves through a series of planes – shapes, volumes, colours and textures – arranged from near by to far away. Vésian's clipping is sculptural rather than architectural: each plant keeps its individual character, the pruning being directed by its natural growth. Groupings are asymmetrical, fanciful, tactile, but never abstract.

Vésian's sensuous simplicity depends more on foliage than on flower, mixing scents and textures in a subtle blending of greys, greens and beige. But she also encouraged self-seeding hollyhocks, gaillardia, borage and wild poppies. This essentially dry garden is also very mineral, intermingling paving, walls, rough rock and – instead of formal sculpture – recycled stones. Everything at La Louve pays homage to layers of human dialogue with the land. The US designer Garrett Finney later added to the Lower Garden a discreet swimming pool, adhering to what he calls Vésian's gift for 'integrating the exceptional within the vernacular'.

1—Vésian drew on her experience with fabric design to create plant tapestries that could be enjoyed from the house as well as from the garden.
2—Clipped shapes and tones of green and grey lead the eye from plane to plane through the garden to the wild hillside in the distance.
3—On the East Terrace, a pebbled path is a deliberate echo of the cobblestone street outside, linking village, garden and larger landscape in a seamless progression.
4—Cardoons, grown as a vegetable in Provence, provide a brilliant silver fountain in spring but die back in summer; Vésian planned the garden's planting for all seasons.

1

# Real Jardín Botánico

Madrid, Spain

| |
|---|
| José Quer y Martínez, Francesco Sabatini, Juan de Villanueva |
| 18th century |
| 8 hectares / 20 acres |
| Temperate Mediterranean |
| Botanical / Historic / Terraces |

Today a refuge from the heat of the city, Madrid's Royal Botanical Gardens were designed to be at the cutting edge of botanical sciences. Originally installed with 2,000 specimens in an orchard to the north of the old city in 1755 (an area now subsumed by government buildings), the botanical garden was transferred by royal command to a more central location in 1774.

The architects, Francesco Sabatini and Juan de Villanueva, were tasked with creating both a pleasant garden and a facility for research and education. At the time Spanish botanists were exploring an enlarging world, and the specimens with which they returned needed a place where they could be properly studied. In 1794 alone, 10,000 specimens were donated by the Italian nobleman Alessandro Malaspina following a five-year voyage around the Pacific Rim.

The design solution was to create a garden in three sections, or terraces, each with beds arranged using the Linnaean system of classification, then still in its infancy. The scheme survives today, with a few modern additions: the garden today contains 30,000 specimens, including 1,500 trees.

The main gate leads to the Terraza de los Cuadros, named after its framed beds. This area contains medicinal and aromatic plants, some ornamentals, a rose garden and a small orchard. Across a central avenue is the Terraza de las Escuelas Botánicas, which contains an evolutionary display of the plant kingdom arranged around twelve small fountains. The third section is the Terraza del Plano de la Flor, a densely planted pleasure garden in the nineteenth-century romantic English style, a place more for strolling than for studying. This area contains the Villanueva Pavilion and a pond with a bust of Carl Linnaeus, the inspiration for the garden's design, in the middle.

There have been additions to the park since the 1780s. Behind the villa is an upper terrace with a display of bonsai. To the west is an olive grove, and to the east are the hothouses: a nineteenth-century palm house and a newer building that re-creates exotic climate zones. The herbarium has about 1 million specimens, and scientific work still goes on behind the public facade of the royal garden.

1 — A bust of Carl Linnaeus stands on a column in the pond in front of the Vilanueva Pavilion, named after the garden's architect.
2 — Mature trees, such as ash, provide pools of shade in the heart of the city.
3, 4 — The square 'framed' gardens that give the Terrraza de los Cuadros its name hold ornamental plants – including tulips – plus medicinal, aromatic and endemic plants.

# Los Jardines del Real Alcázar

Seville, Andalucia

| | |
|---|---|
| Peter I, Charles V | |
| 13th–20th century | |
| 16.2 hectares / 40 acres | |
| Temperate Mediterranean | |
| Courtyard / Formal / Historic / Water | |

A serene refuge in the heart of Seville, the Alcázar is a remarkable showcase of garden cultures and styles – including Moorish, Mudéjar (a Spanish fusion of Gothic and Islamic influences), Renaissance and Neo-classical – reflecting a history that stretches back to the eighth century. The nucleus of the complex we see today was constructed in the twelfth century for the Moorish Almohad governor of Al-Andalus. A century after the Catholic reconquest of Seville in 1248, the palace was remodelled by Peter I. It has remained a royal residence ever since, as both its architecture and its gardens have been blown by the winds of fashion.

The gardens stand as testament to eight centuries of Iberian garden-making. An example of this fusion is the rectangular Patio de las Doncellas (Courtyard of the Maidens) within the palace complex. Its sunken garden, with a long, narrow pool flanked by flower beds, reflects a Moorish aesthetic, yet it was constructed by Peter the Cruel, as Peter I was nicknamed.

Outside the palace, in the extensive formal pleasure grounds, the various styles and garden areas blend unexpectedly well, with clipped hedges, glittering fountains and softly babbling streams. In total they contain 170 plant species, with extensive use of architectural evergreens such as palms, cypress, myrtle, magnolia, jasmine and citrus, which add to the structure of the gardens and fill them with perfume.

Among the many highlights are the Galera and Gruta gardens, which date from the Moorish period. At that time the flower beds would have been sunken and plants grown so that blooms were at ground level, creating a carpet of flowers. The Jardín del Estanque (Garden of the Pond) built into the Almohad wall consists of a large pond presided over by the god Mercury, while the Jardín de la Danza (Garden of the Dance) with its cypress trees and palms is graced by decorative benches faced with brightly painted tiles. The Patio del Crucero (Courtyard of the Cross) has palm trees towering over four square compartments, each defined by clipped hedges. Here too are *burladores* (joke fountains that squirt water at the visitor when they are not expecting it). Last but by no means least is the New Garden; made in the early twentieth century, its plan resembles a glazed tile.

1 — The Courtyard of the Maidens is an Islamic style sunken garden planted with citrus trees.
2, 3, 5 — The Garden of the Dance is a sunny haven of low-clipped hedges, Seville orange trees (*Citrus* x *aurantium*) and fountains.
4 — A square tiled fountain in the Garden of Troy.

# La Concepción Jardín Botánico-Histórico

Málaga, Andalucia, Spain

| | |
|---|---|
| Amalia Livermore, Jorge Loring Oyarzábal, Jacint Chamousset | |
| 19th century | |
| Temperate Mediterranean | |
| 25 hectares / 61 acres | |
| Botanical / Plant Collection / Tropical | |

The gardens at La Concepción form one of Spain's most important botanical collections, yet they retain the individual touch of Amalia Livermore and her husband, Jorge Loring Oyarzábal, first Marquis of Casa Loring. They created the private pleasure gardens in the 1850s in the grounds of the house belonging to Livermore's grandfather, a former British consul in Malaga. Amalia and Jorge were pioneering plant-hunters, travelling widely around the world and bringing back plants from wherever they visited. They commissioned a French gardener, Jacint Chamousset, to design the tropical garden to hold their vast collection of plants. In 1943 the Spanish declared La Concepción 'a garden of historical–artistic importance', and it was bought by the municipality of Malaga in 1990 and opened to the public a few years later.

The garden covers a lush hillside, threaded by sandy paths lined with stone irrigation channels. There are many water features, including a waterfall and pools, and an avenue lined with palms from the Canary Islands and shade-giving London plane (*Platanus x hispanica*), which eventually climbs to a viewpoint marked by a classical gazebo. In autumn the plane trees suffuse the garden with a coppery glow.

Among the more than 2,000 species of plant, trees predominate, some of them of great age. Bamboo groves, stands of shell ginger (*Alpinia zerumbet*) and huge specimens of Indian laurel (*Ficus microcarpa*) are among the many plants that thrive in the hillside's microclimate. The palm collection is considered one of the best in Europe, with more than 500 individual palms given space in a tree-lover's paradise.

Two species of bird of paradise (*Strelitzia*), the small and brightly coloured crane flower (*S. reginae*) and the giant *S. nicolai*, make strong architectural statements, whether in flower or not. Clivias, hibiscus and dombeya are among other prominent flowering plants. Much of the garden is perfumed by the fragrance of *Pittosporum tobira*, and near the elegant Georgian house wisteria and jasmine have leapt from their iron pergolas to sweep through the mature trees.

1 — A view over a bed of aloes shows the hilly nature of the garden.
2 — Dense subtropical woodland surrounds a simple bridge over a small stream.
3 — An open rotunda stands at the end of a mirror pool edged with clipped box.
4 — Chinese wisteria (*Wisteria sinensis*) flowers among the many palm trees.
5 — Green-tip bush lily (*Clivia nobilis*) adds spectacular bursts of orange to the woodland floor.
6 — Aloes flower in the Cactus and Succulents Garden.

3

4

5

6

# Alhambra & Generalife

Granada, Andalucia, Spain

| |
|---|
| Various |
| 14th century |
| 12.9 hectares / 32 acres (total complex) |
| Temperate Mediterranean |
| Courtyard / Formal / Historic / Islamic / Terraces / Water |

From the outside, the Alhambra (Red Fort) is appropriately forbidding for its fourteenth-century role as the fortified seat of Nasrid power in Granada. Inside, however, its succession of planted courtyards and pools are a testament to the creativity, imagination and sophistication of this Moorish dynasty (1232–1492), which created it as a local capital. The complex's structure, including the celebrated Generalife, has remained relatively intact since the late fourteenth century.

As in other Islamic structures, the Alhambra seamlessly integrates gardens and buildings. Such a blurring of internal and external space reflects philosophical ideals that join humankind with nature. When wandering through stuccoed rooms, the visitor is frequently surprised by coming across a courtyard as tranquil as the Patio de los Arrayanes (Court of the Myrtles), with its mirror-like pool, or as stimulating as the Patio de los Leones (Court of the Lions), with its central fountain, shaded gallery and rills of bubbling water.

Originally linked to the Alhambra by a covered walkway and now incorporated into the complex, the Generalife (one translation means 'Garden of the Architect') was the Nasrids' summer retreat. Dating from the early fourteenth century, this rectangular complex is far simpler than the Alhambra, and the decoration plainer. The central courtyard garden is defined by facing pavilions at each short end linked by a colonnade and a wall on the uphill side.

The Generalife is approached through an Islamic-inspired twentieth-century garden of terraces, tall, clipped cypress hedges, paved walks, fountains and flowing rills. Yet such elegance is no preparation for the courtyard itself. The garden remains hidden until the visitor passes through the dim pavilion and arcade and out into the sunlight of the Patio de la Acequia (Court of the Water Channel). The flower beds either side of the central rill are a riot of colour. Tucked behind the northern pavilion is the Jardín de la Sultana (Sultana's Garden) – another water garden, but square, small, enclosed and intimate.

1—The Patio de los Arrayanes (Court of the Myrtles) takes its name from the myrtle hedges that surround the central pond, whose green colour contrasts with the white marble of the paving.
2—The Patio de los Leones (Court of the Lions) is laid out as an Islamic *chahar bagh*, quartered by rills, with a central fountain supported by stone lions.
3, 4—The Patio de la Acequia (Court of the Water Channel) in the Generalife has striking views towards the Alhambra.
5—The Jardín de la Sultana (Sultana's Garden) is a courtyard with fountains, pools and box hedges. The planting includes roses, *Nerium oleander* and orange trees.

1

2

# Jardines de Alfàbia

### Buñola, Mallorca, Spain

| |
|---|
| Benihabet (attrib), Don José Calvet |
| 15th & 17th century |
| 4 hectares / 10 acres |
| Temperate Mediterranean |
| Formal / Islamic / Water |

Alfàbia – the name derives from the Arabic *al fabi*, meaning 'jar of olives' – is a complex of a house, gardens and orchards set on a hillside below the Coll de Sóller Pass in the heart of the Tramuntana mountains near Mallorca's northwest coast. Alfàbia reflects the island's Hispano–Moorish heritage. Its origins as a farm dated to the Muslim occupation of Mallorca in the tenth and eleventh centuries, when the land was arranged in terraces for the cultivation of citrus and other fruit. After the Reconquista in 1229, the estate passed into the hands of the nobility, and it was made more luxurious.

The current house was built in the fifteenth century, with an extra wing and Baroque facade added later. The house encloses a cobbled courtyard, shaded by a large plane tree (*Platanus orientalis*) with a canopy over 20 metres (65.6 feet) in diameter. Here, an octagonal pool holds a stone fountain in the form of a boy and a fish.

The gardens predate the house. This was once the estate of the Moorish governor Benihabet, who may have laid out the gardens. The most delightful feature, the Water Pergola, has all the hallmarks of the ingenious and artistic ways in which the Moors used water in their gardens. The wisteria-covered pergola is fed by water stored in a barrel-vaulted cistern at the highest point of the garden. A patterned cobblestone path runs between two lines of seventy-two stone columns supported by low walls, from where twenty-four stone fountains spray fine arches of water over the path. Emerging from the refreshing shower, the visitor's eye is drawn to the mountains of the borrowed landscape beyond; meanwhile the water flows down the slope to irrigate an orange grove.

The garden was expanded in the nineteenth century, when a romantic, English-inspired landscape was added. An informal lake filled with water lilies is surrounded by a collection of palm trees and bamboos. The whole is a delightfully tranquil yet structured garden, in which formality and informality rub shoulders gracefully while mature palms, carobs, bamboo, olives and citrus provide welcome verdant shade.

1 — A large pool shaded by palm trees helps to cool the house.
2 — Terracotta pots with bright orange clivia decorate the cobbled courtyard in front of the house, shaded by a plane tree.
3 — Parallel hedges of clipped box are softened by cascades of magenta bougainvillea.
4 — In the celebrated Water Pergola, twenty-four low fountains spray fine arcs of water over a path that leads to an eye-catching fountain bowl.

1

2

4

3

# Mas de les Voltes

Castell d'Empordà,
Catalonia, Spain

| |
| --- |
| Fernando Caruncho |
| 20th century |
| 10 hectares / 25 acres |
| Temperate Mediterranean |
| Formal / Landscape / Parterre / Water |

At first sight, the garden at Mas de les Voltes (sometimes known as 'The Wheat Garden') appears to be a formal, controlled space, but on exploration it becomes more fluid. Each shift in viewpoint yields more surprises. Fernando Caruncho studied philosophy, and it was his realization that the ancient Greeks studied the nature of the world and philosophy in gardens that inspired him to become a gardener.

Cypresses make a traditional screen on one side of the estate, and a winding drive leads to the old farmhouse that looks over the sloping site. Paths follow an invisible grid over the garden, and mark out different areas. The underlying geometry is fused with a palette of olives, cypresses and grass, plus ornamental plantings of vines and wheat. The design simultaneously looks forwards and reflects the traditions of Catalonia.

In front of the house, three narrow terraces linked by wide brick steps control the gradient. Ivy-covered retaining walls make green bands behind lines of trained vines. The spacing of dark, columnar cypresses sets up a rhythm across the garden; they alternate with silver-leaved olive trees on the long paths running down the slope. Below the terraces and a line of cypresses, a modern parterre of four dark, rectangular, brick-edged reflecting pools recall the layouts of classical Moorish gardens. Wide, green lawn paths surround the pools, which appear like four huge mirrors reflecting the sky and the cypress sentinels.

Beyond the pools lies the garden's most renowned feature, the expansive wheat parterre. Olives alternating with cypresses edge each section. The grid appears regular, but in reality sections become uneven in size as they near the estate's boundaries. The unique use of wheat and vines for ornamental planting highlights the annual seasonal cycle and the transformation of the garden's appearance: from fresh green shafts of new wheat and vine leaves in spring to bales of golden wheat and swollen grapes in summer; and from the grape harvest in autumn to the skeletal forms of the vines in winter, when the wheat is ploughed under.

Mas de les Voltes is a celebration of the harvest, not a garden of species-rich plantings of colourful blooms. And ultimately, it pays homage to the ancient landscape of Catalonia.

1, 2—Caruncho's gardens have a lyrical quality that gently contrasts with their underlying geometry. Rows of vines play a role in the design, in addition to the placements of cypresses and olives beyond. The parterres of wheat are the garden's signature feature.
3—The four pools of the water parterre reference the *chahar bagh* of Islamic design and its influence on Spain's historic gardens, particularly in Granada and Córdoba.

# Ariante

near Pollença, Mallorca, Spain

| | |
|---|---|
| Heidi Gildemeister | |
| 20th–21st century | |
| 4 hectares / 10 acres | |
| Temperate Mediterranean | |
| Bulbs / Dry / Mediterranean / Plantsman / Vistas | |

Ariante sits high on the north coast of Mallorca, with both northern and southern exposure. Over decades, while her husband farmed sheep and planted trees here, Heidi Gildemeister experimented with drought-tolerant plantings adapted to Mediterranean landscapes. She began by making the most of what she had: bare rock and thin soil, drifts of lentisk (*Pistacia lentiscus*) and buckthorn (*Rhamnus alaternus*), ancient holm oaks (*Quercus ilex*) and majestic olive trees. The whole flows harmoniously into the woodland and dramatic mountains among which it is set.

Ariante is both a collector's and a landscape garden. Shrubs and trees, boulders and rocks shelter carpets of mixed groundcover, hundreds of bulbs and rhizomes, and rare taxa from orchids to cacti, while cultivars of passion flower and bignone emerge throughout. The many microclimates allow specialized groupings of Australian and South African plants. Each season has its own treasures, so the garden is an ever-changing display.

The garden has evolved as a series of concentric rings moving outwards from the house. Gildemeister first laid out the paths, connecting the best flat spaces with curved walkways and making decisions moment by moment with no overall plan. Her main contribution, besides planting, is pruning – 'creative shaping' – to establish or maintain harmony among neighbouring plants. She accentuates natural growth habits, letting the plants be her guide (the opposite of topiary). Self-seeded plants are kept whenever possible. Gildemeister's most recent addition is her Sheep Park, where she experiments with plants that grazing animals leave alone, such as *Euphorbia dendroides*.

Gildemeister's approach has always been about partnership: 'I got to know the available plants more intimately and learned about their likes and dislikes. I cherish those plants that have proved their worth over the years.' Ariante is a garden of patience and of deep respect for the landscape, the diversity of species and the natural growth of plants.

1—Plantings at Ariante settle among existing landscape features, from stone outcrops to olive and oak groves leading up to the surrounding mountains.
2—Species originate from various continents: *Coronilla glauca*, an orange aloe, *Agave attenuatea*, Aeonium and white-flowering *Eriocephalus africanus*.
3—Sheltered by a rock, silver cineraria sets off red *Crocosmia* x *crocosmiiflora* behind.
4—Under ancient olive trees in the Sheep Garden, wild grass is cropped by grazing animals amidst mounds of euphorbia.

# El Jardín de Cactus

Guatiza, Lanzarote,
Canary Islands, Spain

| | |
|---|---|
| Cèsar Manrique | |
| 20th century | |
| 24 hectares / 59 acres | |
| Temperate Humid Subtropical | |
| Artistic / Cactus / Dry / Terraces | |

Lanzarote's Jardín de Cactus may have been conceived as a horticultural project, yet the site for this incredible garden had actually been carved out of the Canary Island landscape long before by local agriculturalists. Guatiza, in the northeast of the island, is known for its cactus farms, where locals cultivate prickly pears in order to harvest the cochineal insect from the plant's fruit: the insect is used to produce a deep red food dye. It was the agricultural demand for *lapilli* (gravel-like volcanic ash), which is used to aid water retention, that resulted in the quarrying of rock at Guatiza. When the local artist and architect César Manrique discovered the site in the early 1970s, the circular, amphitheatre-shaped space had already been formed, thereby protecting the area from the worst of the Atlantic's winds.

By the time he began work on the garden, Manrique was an established painter and sculptor. Although his home has been turned into an art gallery, it is his garden that best demonstrates his eye for aesthetic pleasures, as well as a highly practical appreciation of cacti and other succulents. Manrique worked with the botanist Estanislao González Ferrer, planting the cacti into stepped terraces, and grouping them together by genus. There are about 1,400 varieties in the garden, and around 10,000 cacti and succulents in total. These vary from little-known Canary Island cacti through to more familiar types from Africa and Latin America.

Paths wind among the gravelled beds, and are interspersed with fish ponds, fountains and water features. A restored chalk-white windmill gives visitors an overview of the garden. The plants ensure a colourful display against the black setting all year round, but many of them flower in late summer and early autumn – the former being the most spectacular season at the Jardín de Cactus. A remarkable turnaround has transformed a formerly neglected area into a botanical wonderland.

1—The garden's amphitheatre contains a wide range of cacti and succulents that come from locations as varied as Peru, Mexico, Chile, the United States, Kenya, Tanzania, Madagascar, Morocco and the Canary Islands themselves. The garden is dominated by a restored windmill, which serves as a viewing point.
2, 3—The sculptural quality of monoliths of compacted volcanic ash echo the upwards-reaching spires of the taller cacti and succulents. Contrast is provided by the squat lumps of *Echinocactus grusonii*.
4—The sun creates halos as it catches the spines of *Echinopsis huascha*.

# Parque de Serralves

Porto, Portugal

Jacques Gréber

20th century

18 hectares / 44.5 acres

Temperate Mediterranean

Formal / Modern / Roses / Topiary / Water

The formal parkland that surrounds the clean lines of the 1930s' pink facade of the Serralves villa comprises a number of distinct areas that seem to flow naturally into one another. The Art Deco villa dominates the upper area of the Park, which descends through a couple of terraces to the canal and water features. The central axis is provided by a canal that runs perpendicular to the villa through the different levels, its geometric lines contrasting with the curved central bay of the villa. The terraces feature sweeping lawns, fountains, reservoir pools and the long, straight water channel itself. This channel, flanked by yellow granite-edged paths of gravel that match the colour of the villa, gleams in blue-green tones. Each terrace descent is faced with turquoise tiles that match the canal, and shapely topiary casts its shadows, offering another architectural layer to the view.

At the end of this formal garden, a stair leads down to the Romantic Lake, which interrupts the central axis as it leads down towards the fields and the herb garden. At the far end of the park are the stables. On the way back up to the villa, bearing north, are the orchards and the new gardens of the Museum of Contemporary Art.

Parque de Serralves is the work of the French architect Jacques Gréber, who was the main designer of the Paris Exhibition of 1937. The style of the garden is as clear-cut and sharply architectural as that of the villa and, although they do not share precisely the same aesthetic, they do fit well together. Close to the villa are formal areas with good examples of topiary in box, teucrium and euonymus. Further away are two long avenues of horse chestnut and sweet gum (*Liquidambar styraciflua*), the latter setting the site ablaze in autumn with its burnished leaves. Both avenues accentuate the open aspect of the central garden.

Other attractive areas include a formal Rose Garden; a Sundial Garden; and the pink gravel tennis court. Showers of white and mauve 'rain' from the established wisteria pergola offer a breathtaking spectacle in spring.

1—The straight pink-gravel paths and the turquoise water channel contrast with ball topiary in the heart of the geometric Central Parterre.
2—Petals add touches of red to the Horse Chestnut Avenue in late spring.
3—The Sundial Garden – the sundial itself has been removed – is planted with *Helichrysum petiolare* inside low clipped box hedges.
4, 5—The lake and its grove from the original garden were retained in order to provide a more romantic counterpoint to the more formal modern gardens.

# Quinta da Regaleira

Sintra, Portugal

| |
|---|
| Luigi Manini, António de Carvalho Monteiro |
| 19th century |
| 4.5 hectares / 11 acres |
| Temperate Mediterranean |
| Grotto / Romantic / Terraces / Water |

The journey through Quinta da Regaleira is governed by a succession of mystic allusions evoking a quest for paradise: references and allusions to Greek gods, epics of ancient Rome and the Middle Ages, rituals of the Knights Templar and the works of John Milton and Luís de Camões all abound. For lovers of the occult and esoterica, the garden is richly symbolic; for the casual visitor, its iconography enhances Regaleira's wild romanticism.

The garden, known in the eighteenth century as Quinta da Torre, was bought in 1840 by Baroness da Regaleira, who transformed it into a summer retreat befitting its situation in Sintra, an elevated hilly region within easy reach of Lisbon, famed for its Moorish castle and royal palace. The purchase in 1893 of the garden and additional land by the Brazilian-born entomologist and millionaire António de Carvalho Monteiro presaged construction of the current residence and garden, with key design input by Luigi Manini, architect, painter and set designer, then fresh from working in Italian and Portuguese opera houses.

The Portuguese word *quinta* means 'country estate', but Regaleira is no farmhouse. Rather, it is a fantastic and sophisticated ensemble of buildings, water features and mature plantings. The main residence sits at the foot of the site, near the palace, on the road leading to another of Sintra's great romantic gardens, Monserrate. A rooftop terrace and turret give panoramic views over the Sintra Hills and west towards the Atlantic Ocean. By extensive use of terracing, the garden ascends the steep, north-facing slope. Frequent vantage points afford views within and beyond the garden, while subterranean passages make unexpected links (most notably from a deep well with spiral stairs to a grotto and waterfall). Alongside European favourites, an equable climate permits a vast range of other plants to grow, such as massive Australasian conifers and tree ferns, cycads and North American conifers. The resulting ensemble – here and in nearby properties, such as the Palácio Nacional da Pena – combines to form a privileged botanical and horticultural enclave.

1 — The lush gardens crowd right up to the buildings of the romantic retreat, helping protect it from the Portuguese sun.
2 — Stepping stones and a rope bridge offer alternative ways across the Waterfall Lake.
3 — At the top of the garden, away from the house, the woodland becomes wilder, reflecting Carvalho Monteiro's interest in primitivist beliefs.
4 — A spiral staircase winds down the inside of a well leading to the entrance to the grotto.

# Jardim do Palácio dos Marqueses de Fronteira

Benfica, Lisbon, Portugal

| |
|---|
| Marquis of Fronteira |
| 17th century |
| 0.4 hectares / 1 acre |
| Temperate Mediterranean |
| Formal / Parterre / Renaissance / Water |

The uniquely Portuguese approach to garden design – comfortable and intimate yet grand, boldly coloured and revelling in displays of *azulejo* (traditional glazed tiles) – reaches a peak in this beautiful seventeenth-century garden. Although strongly influenced by Italian Renaissance gardens, the gardens at Palácio Fronteira are also imbued with indigenous Indo-Portuguese and Moorish influences.

In front of the building, below a small terrace, the first Marquis of Fronteira, Dom João de Mascarenhas, for whom the palace had been built as a hunting lodge in 1670, laid out the Jardim Grande. Covering some 3,700 square metres (39,712 square feet) are four parterres, each of which is subdivided into four. Their complex geometric shapes are defined by tightly clipped box hedges, and each quarter represents one of the four seasons. The beds within the parterres are planted with roses, with additional height and interest from large bowl fountains, a dozen lead statues of classical figures and varied topiary. The walls enclosing the garden on two sides are ornamented with *azulejo* depicting an eclectic mix of subjects, including mythological events, fairytales and everyday activities.

Fronting the parterre, perpendicular to the house, a large rectangular water tank reflects the sky and its surroundings and provides a contrast with the dark green of the parterres. Behind the tank is the ornate Galeria dos Reis (Gallery of the Kings), a balustraded raised terrace walk reached by a flight of steps at either end. These ascend to a small pavilion with a pyramid roof and thence out on to the terrace, which offers a picturesque view over the parterres. The entire Galeria dos Reis is decorated with *azulejo* used in several ways: as large panels depicting various scenes; as ornamental motifs; and *en masse* in blocks of brilliant colour, especially cerulean blue. Niches in the walls hold busts of Portuguese kings. From the Galeria dos Reis the Gallery Walk leads to the chapel, which is also decorated with tile panels and fronted by an ornamental pool. From there, the Chapel Terrace, which is ornamented with tiles painted with allegories of the arts and sciences, leads back to the palace.

1 — The parterres of the Jardim Grande are fronted by a water tank and the Galeria dos Reis (Gallery of the Kings), with its spectacular *azulejo* tiling.
2 — A detail of the tank and the Galeria dos Reis reveals the remarkable variety of effects the craftsmen achieved with the traditional cerulean blue-glazed tiles.
3 — A statue adds height and interest to the intricate box parterres of the Jardim Grande in front of the palace.
4 — Beautiful scrolls form the edge of the ornamental pond outside the chapel.

# Terra Nostra

São Miguel,
Azores, Portugal

Thomas Hickling, Visconde da Praia,
Marquis da Praia, David Sayers

18th, 19th & 20th century

12.5 hectares / 31 acres

Temperate Mediterranean

Plant Collection / Water / Woodland

Terra Nostra lies in the crater of an extinct volcano that in the late eighteenth century was popular for its mineral springs, which were used to treat health problems. Today, ample water helps maintain the fertility of the gardens created here more than 200 years ago. Around 1775 Thomas Hickling, a wealthy Bostonian merchant and honorary American consul, built a small wooden summerhouse here and planted North American trees nearby as a reminder of his homeland.

In 1848 the property was bought by the Visconde da Praia, who replaced the house and extended the garden. Today's gardens are largely the result of the developments undertaken by the Visconde and his successor, the Marquis da Praia. Between them they introduced water gardens, a grotto, formal parterres and less formal areas of woodland that were planted with new species from around the world. A monument to the pair surrounded by Canary Islands date palms (*Phoenix canariensis*) is approached via an avenue of bangalow palms (*Archontophoenix cunninghamiana*) as well as species imported from North America, New Zealand, China and South Africa, taking advantage of the Azores' benign climate. In the second half of the nineteenth century the islands became something of a plant acclimatization centre, with thousands of trees nurtured there that originated in distant regions.

By the 1920s the gardens had fallen into disrepair, but the opening of the Terra Nostra Hotel in 1935, and its subsequent purchase of the gardens, began a process of modernization. More land was added, the pond and canal were restored and new flower beds were planted. In the late 1980s and early 1990s the horticulturalist David Sayers oversaw the renovation of the garden, introducing more than 3,000 species of trees and shrubs. The garden now houses collections of major historical value, such as those of ferns – including evocative tree ferns – cycadales and camellias. The Azorean Endemic and Native Flora Garden nurtures plants endemic to São Miguel, while the Vireya Garden is filled with Malaysia rhododendrons, which provide a colourful display all year round.

1 — Red cannas add a startling note of colour to a lake bordered by tree ferns.
2 — Surrounded by sheltering hedges, the Cycas Garden features Cycodophytes, which resemble tree ferns and palms but are old enough to be classed as 'living fossils'.
3 — Blue hydrangeas flower in the park.
4 — The mineral waters on which the region's reputation as a resort was based still flow through the park's many streams.

# Quinta do Palheiro

## Funchal, Madeira, Portugal

| | |
|---|---|
| Conde de Carvalhal, John and Mildred Blandy | |
| 19th & 20th century | |
| 12 hectares / 30 acres | |
| Mediterranean | |
| Coastal / Landscape / Plant Collection / Woodland | |

Far out in the Atlantic, cliff-fringed Madeira is so fertile that it is known as the Garden Isle: almost anything can grow in its rich volcanic soil. At Quinta do Palheiro, the speciality is a world-class display of camellias. The centrepiece of the garden, the Avenue of Camellias begun by its founder, the Conde de Carvalhal, is at its best between November and April, when some 1,500 species sourced from all over the world come into bloom.

The gardens (the name 'Palheiro' means 'haystack' in Portuguese) are set in the hills 500 metres (1,640 feet) above the southern coast of Madeira, with views of the island's capital, Funchal. When the breeze is blowing off the sea, the air fills with the scent of flowers as the visitor explores the varied gardens. There is a rugged mountain brook and a lily pond, a rose garden, a sunken garden, an ornamental teahouse and box topiary depicting a family of chickens and other more gnomic designs.

The gardens have been maintained and developed since 1801, when the Conde de Carvalhal began the camellia collection and also planted an avenue of 200 trees – mainly plane, but also a few more exotic types such as jacaranda and fountain trees (*Spathodea*) – along the track to his newly built hunting lodge on the hillside. Many of those original plantings are still in place.

In 1885, the house and gardens passed to the Blandy family, and during the twentieth century the collection was extended first by Mildred and later by Christina Blandy. They introduced many more exotic plants, including proteas from South Africa, Brazilian *Araucaria*, *Metrosideros* from New Zealand, and *Erythrina* and *Bauhinia* from Asia.

In the late 1990s the gardens became part of a hotel and resort, but they remain open to the public. In recent years it has become apparent that the laurel and holm oak trees in the gardens and the surrounding hills are offering a refuge for the Trocaz pigeon, a relative of the wood pigeon found only on Madeira.

1—Many of the original trees planted by the Conde de Carvalhal survive, making an impressive setting for the current garden.
2—The Sunken Garden is home to many colourful flowers, including tangerine-coloured *Gazania* and multicoloured *Lampranthus*.
3, 6—Throughout the garden there are glimpses of gnomic topiary, including a family of chickens.
4— A path lined with box hedges winds through colourful beds
5—The Blandys Garden was created by the garden's new owners in the twentieth century.

# Isola Bella

Lake Maggiore, Piedmont, Italy

| |
|---|
| Angelo Crivelli, Carlo Fontana |
| 17th century |
| 1.8 hectares / 4.5 acres |
| Temperate Mediterranean |
| Baroque / Formal / Historic / Parterre / Terraces / Water |

If the grandest of all European Baroque gardens is Versailles, perhaps the most unusual is this small island in Lake Maggiore. The rocky crag was home only to a fishing village in 1632, when Angelo Crivelli designed an opulent palace and garden that Carlo III of the ruling Borromeo family dedicated to his wife, Isabella d'Adda. Her name was shortened to give the garden its name, Isola Bella, or 'beautiful island'.

After a break in construction caused by an outbreak of plague, Carlo Fontana reworked the design for Carlo III's sons, who developed the notion that Isola Bella should appear as a ship sailing across the lake, an idea that took full advantage of the dramatic alpine backdrop. The gardens were inaugurated by Carlo IV in 1671, but finishing touches continued to be added until the twentieth century.

The Baroque began in Italy about 1600, at the end of the Renaissance, and Isola Bella captures the essence of the style: exaggerated motion, easily interpreted detail, drama, exuberance and grandeur. From the palazzo at the 'prow' of the ship, the visitor enters the gardens via the Atrio di Diana, with a statue of the goddess in a niche. Flights of steps lead to the Piano della Canfora at the 'waist' of the ship: a long terrace with six geometric lawns with flower beds and two enormous camphor trees (*Cinnamomum camphora*) planted in the 1820s. Terraces descend to the east, and the Azalea Garden.

But the main feature is to the south, where the ship's 'stern' rises in a series of terraces to form a truncated pyramid that reaches a height of 37 metres (120 feet). Set into the terraces is a three-tiered, shell-shaped Water Theatre crowned with a large statue of a unicorn (the Borromeo heraldic symbol) flanked by statues representing Nature and Art. At the southernmost point is the Giardino del Amore, a terrace of four small *parterres de broderie* and large citrus trees around a circular pool. The garden is planted with exotic flowers and shrubs that thrive in the mild microclimate. These plantings are not part of the original design, however, and tend to detract from the garden as it was intended to be appreciated.

1, 2—The terraces of the 'poop deck' are now planted with roses, hydrangeas, bedding plants and espaliered citrus.
3—The shell-shaped Water Theatre is topped with a unicorn, the heraldic symbol of Borromeo power and wealth.
4—The upper terraces offer a range of views over Lake Maggiore.
5—A peach tree (*Prunus persica*) blossoms above potted box and perennials.
6—The Giardino del Amore ('Garden of Love') has geometrical box parterres and citrus trees.

1

2

3

4

5

6

# La Mortola

(Giardini Botanici Hanbury)

Ventimiglia, Liguria, Italy

| |
|---|
| Sir Thomas Hanbury |
| 19th & 20th century |
| 18 hectares / 44 acres |
| Temperate Mediterranean |
| Botanical / Coastal / Informal / Mediterranean / Terraces |

This beautiful landscape of natural terraces that cascade down the hillside forms a promontory jutting out into the Mediterranean. It is sheltered from the wind on the other three sides by mountains. This gives La Mortola an especially mild microclimate, even for the Côte d'Azur, and made it the perfect place for Sir Thomas Hanbury to develop his botanic garden after retiring at the age of thirty-five, having made a fortune in China as a tea and silk merchant. Hanbury's family had been London pharmacists at a time when most medicine was made from plants, and as a child Hanbury had developed a love of horticulture that would become his passion for the rest of his life.

Around the house at La Mortola, Hanbury added a formal terrace, beyond which a series of paths and flights of steps wind along and between terraces ornamented with pools, fountains, belvederes and pergolas. These complement and enhance the natural landscape of the site. With help from his brother and a number of British and German botanists, Hanbury developed an experimental garden where he would test plants from regions with Mediterranean climates all over the world, which he hoped would be suitable for the conditions at La Mortola. Today plants from all around the Mediterranean rub shoulders with those from Australasia, South Africa and Central and South America. Hanbury was so adept at cultivating new introductions that *Hortus Mortolensis*, a catalogue of the plants grown in the garden published in 1912, listed approximately 6,000 taxa.

Yet this botanical collection – primarily of herbaceous plants, succulents, shrubs and trees – is also a true garden. The plants are not gathered according to botanic classification but are planted as individual specimens so that their beauty can be admired. This gives the garden rich interest not only for aficionados of Mediterranean gardening (a warm climate all year round with dry summers and wetter winters), but also for those who come to admire the combination of the beauty of the plants and their setting.

1—Towering cypress trees and flowering agaves frame a view to the Mediterranean.
2—Hanbury retained the olive terraces that were already in place to add structure to the garden, augmenting them with plants from his collection.
3—Plants came from the nurseries of Huber at Hyères and Nabonnand at Golfe-Juan, and from fellow plantsmen such as Gustave Thuret at Antibes.
4—Spectacular *Agave americana* and *Aloe* spp. revel in the Mediterranean conditions, in some spots growing on nearly bare rocky slopes.

# Giardino Giusti

Verona, Veneto, Italy

Agostino Giusti

16th century

1.8 hectares / 4.5 acres

Temperate Humid Subtropical

Formal / Renaissance / Topiary

For centuries the Giardino Giusti has delighted intellectuals and thrill-seekers with its oblique iconography and its physical delights. The garden's two distinct sections are very different. The lower level, which is divided by gravel paths and cypress-lined allées, consists of box-edged quadrants of scrollwork topiary, green lawn, fountains and classical statuary. Looming over this formal garden is a gigantic, grotesque tufa mask, cut from the cliff-edge behind and accessed via a wild and vertiginous Woodland Garden. In contrast to the light, open and rational horizontality of the lower garden, the dark woodland and its twisting paths remind visitors of the darker side of human nature. Indeed, with its dominant position, presiding over the garden, the mask suggests the triumph of passion over reason, of the natural over the human, of savagery over civilization.

The mask is, in fact, a large grotto ornamented with mirrors, shells and coral. At its heart sits a faun fountain that proclaims this as a pagan realm, a place of unbridled lust and mysterious transformations. In the past, during evening theatricals, the mask would breathe fire and emit music over the torchlit garden below. Today, even among the avenues of the Lower Garden, the visitor remains uncannily aware of the mask's brooding presence.

The garden was created in the sixteenth century by Agostino Giusti, a nobleman whose family came from Tuscany. A great patron and collector, Giusti littered his garden with classical statuary and Roman epigrams – objects proclaiming his wealth and taste. Over the centuries the early gravel parterres have been replaced variously with topiary, flowers and mazes; the backing line of cypresses have been cut down to open up the views, then replanted; a collection of Mannerist dwarfs has been added to the base of the woodland path; and lemon trees from the eighteenth century have been recently reinstated.

In the eighteenth century the garden was so celebrated that the family incorporated it into their surname, becoming the 'Giusti del Giardino'. Today the garden remains a perplexing but enchanting space, an oasis of greenery in the centre of the busy city.

1—An aerial view looking north over the Renaissance gardens shows parterres and scrollwork topiary in the Lower Garden.
2, 3—The lower garden originally consisted of two square parterres and topiary mazes on either side of the Cypress Way; more parterres were added some years later.
4—A staircase leads up the slope to a grotto that was once magnificently decorated to evoke the elements, with coral for fire, mother-of-pearl and shells for water and tiny painted alpine flowers.

295

# Villa Gamberaia

Settignano, Florence,
Tuscany, Italy

| | |
|---|---|
| Unknown | |
| 16th, 17th & 18th century | |
| 1.4 hectares / 3.5 acres | |
| Temperate Mediterranean | |
| Baroque / Formal / Parterre / Water | |

Villa Gamberaia is probably the best-loved garden in Italy, even though its history boasts no great plantsmen or designers. The garden has evolved over 400 years, and today the modest grounds offer the richness and variety of a much larger property. The villa, set into a rural hillside, may have been named after the freshwater crayfish that once flourished in its ponds. It is typically Tuscan: low and austere, with a deep overhanging roof, irregular windows and open loggias. The key to Gamberaia's enduring appeal is its layout: a cruciform shape consisting of a long central axis bisected by a shorter cross axis, with the villa itself at the heart of the design, anchoring the garden to the hillside.

Spread out around the villa is a spectacular range of spaces. The tall, cypress-lined entrance *allée* is balanced by a horizontal water parterre. The sensuous, enclosed *nymphaeum* at the back is offset by the open terrace in front, with its spectacular 180-degree views over farmland, villages and olive groves that reach up to the garden walls. A long lawn runs parallel to the main axis, linking a woodland grotto at one end to an exedra framing views of Florence at the other, while a formal Lemon Garden above is matched by a woodland *bosco* (sacred grove).

The main garden is encircled by a balustraded stone wall, embellished with urns and statuary, but the garden's most famous feature is the water terrace, created in the early twentieth century by the Serbian Princess Ghika and her American companion Miss Blood. While restoring the original eighteenth-century scrollwork parterres, they filled the spaces with water rather than gravel or plants, and creating a dazzling horizontal mirror animated by simple jet fountains and embellished with an Edwardian froth of water lilies, rose swags, oleander shrubs and cascading geraniums.

Gamberaia offers a masterful blend of variety, harmony and contrast; of wide, open plazas and dense, dark enclosures; of magnificent panoramas and tightly framed views; of billowing greenery and smoothly carved stone. By integrating natural and artificial into a single harmonious whole, it epitomizes the best of the Italian horticultural tradition.

1—The Water Terrace was created in the early twentieth century, with water replacing gravel or plants within the low box hedges.
2—Potted geraniums are displayed on the balustraded Upper Terrace.
3—The formal Lemon Garden has a collection of lemon trees in terracotta pots, which can be moved indoors in winter.
4—Shaded by cypresses, the Nymphaeum at the end of the Bowling Green echoes both the Renaissance and ancient Rome, with its statue of Dionysus; it once ran with water.
5—Looking north along the Bowling Green lawn, the view ends in the Nymphaeum.

1

2

3

4

5

# Villa Il Roseto

Florence, Tuscany, Italy

| |
|---|
| Pietro Porcinai |
| 20th century |
| 0.02 hectares / 0.4 acres |
| Temperate Mediterranean |
| Architectural / Formal / Modern |

Although it is little known outside the garden design profession, Il Roseto is one of Europe's most exciting and unusual gardens. Created by Italy's foremost landscape designer, Pietro Porcinai, it combines the boldness and abstraction of 1960s Pop art with the swirling grandeur of the local Baroque style. Il Roseto is also an engineering tour de force in which Porcinai took a tall but undistinguished three-storey villa and reconfigured its relationship with the surrounding countryside. Raising the main entrance level to the first floor *piano nobile*, he created a hanging garden around it, 4 metres (13 feet) above the original level of the ground.

Porcinai had been brought up at the famed Villa Gamberaia, where his father was head gardener, and this formative experience of one of Italy's oustanding seventeenth-century gardens gave him a visceral appreciation of classical horticulture. Updating traditional motifs and materials, at Il Roseto he created a dramatic garden of circular lawns, meandering stone paths and curved box hedges, which sweep round the skylights illuminating the space below. Views are framed by two plane trees, while the spherical crown of an ancient holm oak rises from the level below and a fountain jet at the end of the garden provides a further vertical element. In true Italian style, this is a monochrome garden, where flowers have little place amid the water, evergreens and stone.

The raised garden offers spectacular views of the olive groves to the south and the Florence skyline to the north. Meanwhile the ground-level plaza has been transformed into a remarkable grotto-like carport. Its domed, vaulted ceiling is supported by concrete columns, which resemble tree trunks, while a swirling pebble-mosaic floor recalls the terraces of grand Baroque villas. The space can be emptied to create an open ballroom. The lower floor of the villa, now effectively underground, has been turned over to services such as laundry, storage and staff quarters. A small door leads from the garage to the villa, but the main entrance is from the garden above, accessed by a spiral stone-and-steel staircase curtained by vines and winding round a small fountain jet. Porcinai has transformed even this gloomy level into a horticultural space.

1, 2—Porcinai constructed massive retaining walls to support a series of 'hanging gardens'; from each terrace, views framed by plane trees open to the wider landscape in accordance with the perspectival principles of the Renaissance theorist Leon Battista Alberti.
3, 4—Beneath a terrace with an oculus, circles of grass and sweeping curves of box, a room of imposing proportions serves as the main entrance and an underground car park.

# Villa Medici

Fiesole, Tuscany, Italy

| |
|---|
| Leon Battista Alberti, Cecil Pinsent, Geoffrey Scott |
| 15th & 20th century |
| 3 hectares / 7.5 acres |
| Temperate Mediterranean |
| Historic / Renaissance / Terraces |

The renowned Medici family were serial villa- and garden-makers, but even for them the villa built at Fiesole for Giovanni de' Medici in the 1450s was especially significant. It was one of the first Renaissance gardens in Italy, and a prototype of the domestic *villa suburbana* rather than the earlier villa-castle. Research suggests that it was designed not by Michelozzi Michelozzo, as once thought, but by the celebrated architect Leon Battista Alberti.

As Alberti recommended, the terraces made on the rocky hillside were not axially aligned with the villa, as would become the fashion in High Renaissance gardens. The villa and garden were deliberately outward-looking, in an analogy of the new Renaissance spirit of inquiry. The Upper Terrace (sometimes called the Lemon Garden) was accessed from the *piano nobile* (the first floor of the villa) and was a public extension of the villa.

Villa Medici was inherited by Lorenzo de' Medici (Il Magnifico) in 1469, and it became a gathering place for artists and men of letters. In 1772 the property was bought by Lady Orford, who added the drive by which the visitor now reaches the house via the Upper Terrace.

The original design for the garden is not known, and today the layout has three square and rectangular expanses of lawn shaded by two large foxglove trees (*Paulownia tomentosa*) and surrounded by gravel paths. In the warmer months the terrace is decorated with lemon trees in large terracotta pots. On the western side of the villa is a small *giardino segreto* (secret garden) reached by an indoor staircase. This, the least altered part of the garden, is trapezoid in shape and has four flower beds edged with box hedges set around a large oval fountain. The magnolia trees are later additions.

The third terrace was redesigned between 1911 and 1923 by Cecil Pinsent and Geoffrey Scott. It is aligned longitudinally below the first terrace and has a long pergola positioned midway between the two levels. It has a central pool, on either side of which are square grass plats, with large magnolias, and a square bed divided into a geometric pattern. The pergola also leads to the *giardino segreto*.

1, 2—The terrace was originally laid out for Giovanni de' Medici in the fifteenth century; it has panoramic views over the River Arno and Florence.
3—In summer, the lawns on the Upper Terrace are shaded by paulownias and the paths are lined with lemon trees and geraniums in terracotta pots.
4— The third terrace was built in the Italian style about 12 metres (39 feet) below the first. A long pergola leading to the *giardino segreto* is positioned midway between the two levels.

# Sacro Bosco

(Villa Orsini)

Bomarzo, Lazio, Italy

| |
|---|
| Pirro Ligorio |
| 16th century |
| 50 hectares / 123.5 acres |
| Temperate Mediterranean |
| Allegorical / Informal / Renaissance / Sculpture / Woodland |

At the entrance to this native woodland inhabited by bizarre buildings and fantastical sculptures is carved: 'You who go wandering about the world in search of sublime and awesome wonders, come here where horrendous faces, elephants, lions, bears, ogres and dragons are to be seen.' The motto is as true now as when the gardens were made for Count Vicino Orsini from 1552 by the architect Pirro Ligorio, who was also then creating the formal terraces of the Villa d'Este. Although both have allegorical programmes, as do many Renaissance gardens, the contrast between the two could not be stronger.

Orsini's Sacro Bosco is like no other garden. The woodland conceals a surreal dream world of mythology and fantasy. Whether walking the paths or scrambling over the rocky, gently sloping site among cedars and stands of oak, it soon becomes clear that the landscape is populated with a seemingly casual array of unusual buildings and larger-than-life statues and boulders, many hewn from the bedrock. The Leaning House, for example, was deliberately built at an angle. Inside the Orcus Mouth – carved with the inscription 'Abandon all reason, you who here enter' – visitors sit around a table formed from Orcus' tongue. There is a pair of wrestling colossi, the grotesque Mask of Madness and a war elephant with a soldier in its trunk. No wonder Sacro Bosco made such an impression on later Surrealists, such as Jean Cocteau and Salvador Dalí.

Yet there is method in the seeming madness. Orsini seems to have made the garden as a memorial to his wife. Its iconography is highly allegorical, and the enlightened Renaissance visitor with enough Latin to read the classical quotations could understand the gardens as a philosophical journey through themes such as love, death, loss and memory. For example, the carved acorns and pine cones at the perimeter of the Hippodrome Garden are emblems of both the Golden Age and death. Even for visitors who lack such knowledge, Sacro Bosco is still an enthralling garden where mystery rules and the imagination can roam free.

1 — The Leaning House is intended to illustrate the corrupt state of the world.
2 — This sculpture represents the 'Mother of all Monsters', Echidna, the half-woman, half-snake who in Greek tradition gave birth to the enemies of Hercules.
3 — A war elephant picks up a soldier, but is it rescuing the man or attacking him?
4 — A lion fights a dragon in an ambivalent fight in which either could represent positive or negative qualities.
5 — 'Lasciate ogni pensiero voi ch'entrate' ('Abandon all reason, you who enter here') is inscribed on the Orcus Mouth.

# Castello Ruspoli

Vignanello, Lazio, Italy

| |
|---|
| Ottavia Orsini Marescotti, Claudia Ruspoli |
| 17th & 20th century |
| 0.5 hectares / 1.2 acres |
| Temperate Mediterranean |
| Formal / Parterre / Renaissance / Terraces / Topiary |

Castello Ruspoli, in the Cimini Hills north of Rome, has a more tangled history than might be apparent from its restoration by its current owner, Claudia Ruspoli, as one of the most authentic Renaissance gardens in Italy. The first castle was built here in 847 and became a convent in the Middle Ages, when it became the focus of a dispute between the Catholic Church and the Aldobrandini, Orsini and Borgia families – all great garden-makers – that lasted from the twelfth to the sixteenth century. The property was converted into a palace in 1574 by Marcantonio Marescotti, the 3rd Count of Vignanello and Parrano, and the garden was added around 1612 by his widow, Ottavia. She, too, had a garden-making pedigree: her father was Vincino Orsini, who created the allegorical Sacro Bosco at Bomarzo (see page 300).

The main garden at what is now Castello Ruspoli is detached from the palace and is reached by a raised walkway over the former moat. It comprises three elements: a main terrace with twelve rectangular compartments; a *giardino segreto* (secret garden); and a *bosco* (a small, enclosed woodland). On the main terrace the compartments around the central pool and fountain are defined by clipped hedges of box, cherry, bay, laurel and myrtle. Within each compartment, hedges of dwarf box pick out geometric patterns, including the hidden initials of Ottavia and her two sons, Galeazzo and Sforza. The terrace, with its citrus trees in ornamental terracotta pots, was designed to be viewed from the *salotto* (sitting room) on the first floor of the palace, from where the patterns could be fully appreciated.

The *bosco* lies beyond the main garden, while the *giardino segreto* is below it to the south. Compared with the very public main garden, this small enclosure hidden away on a narrow terrace was a place where the owners could enjoy privacy. A simple geometric pattern of triangles, circles, diamonds and crescents is picked out with low, clipped box hedges that define beds full of plants for colour and scent. Here, Claudia Ruspoli has preserved the red roses planted by her grandmother and added white ones of her own.

1—The focus of the main terrace is a large balustraded fountain around which are twelve rectangular compartments with patterns of dwarf box, designed to be seen from the family's living quarters on the first floor of the castle.
2—The restored gardens in different shades of green once more provide the perfect foil for the Renaissance villa that replaced that replaced the 9th-century Benedictine Monastery and subsequent castle.

# Villa d'Este
Tivoli, Lazio, Italy

Pirro Ligorio

16th century

4 hectares / 10 acres

Temperate Mediterranean

Allegorical / Formal / Renaissance / Sculpture / Terraces / Water

Designed from 1550 by Pirro Ligorio (who also made the Sacro Bosco; see page 300) and named for its creator, Cardinal Ippolito (II) d'Este, Villa d'Este is the most magnificent and elaborate example of the Italian High Renaissance garden. It influenced garden design across Europe in the seventeenth century and continues to inspire today.

The garden was designed so that the full revelation of the owner's demesne was the *pièce de résistance* of an experience that began at the bottom of the garden and increased in intensity as one ascended the terraces. Today visitors enter from the villa at the top of the hill and immediately see the vista over the garden and the countryside beyond. Their first impressions are of a steep slope conquered by a central axis and a series of terraces, tall evergreen trees (oaks and cypress dominate) and, above all, the sight and sound of moving water. The engineering feat that diverted the Aniene River to feed the 500 or so jets is the garden's unseen marvel (the original system is still in use), while the fountains, cascades and pools are its most dramatic element. Highlights include the iconic third terrace, on which the Walk of the Hundred Fountains connects the Oval Fountain at one end to the Fountains of Rometta (a model of ancient Rome) at the other. Below, on what was the entrance level, are three rectangular fish ponds into which falls the Fountain of the Cascade, itself crowned by the Water Organ, which, powered by water pressure, plays music.

The terraces are also the stage for a display of statuary and sculptures. This being a Renaissance garden, both the fountains and the statuary deliver an allegorical narrative. The main theme celebrates the d'Este family's lineage, which claimed descent from Hercules himself. Some elements of the original garden have disappeared: the *boschi*, labyrinths, trelliswork tunnels and flower beds filled with exotic specimens. Today the planting is dominated by clipped hedges, lawns and trees. But, as many of the fountains have been, the lost features will be restored and replanted in due course.

1, 4—At the bottom of the garden – previously the entrance level – the water fills three large fish ponds. Today visitors enter the gardens at the top, by the Water Organ, with a view over the Fountain of the Cascade to the terraces and fish ponds beyond.
2—One feature of the Fountain of Rometta is a grotto now covered in mosses and ferns and home to a statue of a reclining river god.
3—A curtain of water falls from the Oval Fountain above a pool with a balustraded arcade topped by the Tiburtine Sybil.
5, 6—On the Walk of the Hundred Fountains, water falls from three tiers of moss and fern-covered jets.

1

2

# Giardino di Ninfa

Cisterna di Latina,
Lazio, Italy

| Caetani Family |
| 20th century |
| 8 hectares / 20 acres |
| Temperate Mediterranean |
| English / Informal / Plantsman / Romantic / Water |

The spring-fed river and the ancient town that is home to this garden both take their name – Ninfa – from a little Roman temple dedicated to nymphs. And it is the combination of the ruins of the medieval castle and town, the crystal-clear pools and streams and the artlessly arranged diversity of plants that defines this most romantic of gardens. Roses scramble over abandoned archways, climbers twine over ruined walls and flowering shrubs provide a foreground to a vista of the ruins.

Ninfa grew rich thanks to its location on the Appian Way, the ancient route between Rome and Brindisi. However, in 1382 the castle was sacked during one of Italy's interminable power struggles between rival factions. Apart from a brief revival in the seventeenth century, Ninfa never recovered, and its ruins became entombed in ivy.

Then, in the 1920s, Prince Gelasio Caetani undertook a restoration project and together with his English mother, Ada Wilbraham, set about creating a garden. Inspired by the evocative and mysterious ruins, they made fullest use of the natural water source to lay out an informal network of sinuous paths set within lawns, and imported and planted thousands of ornamental trees and shrubs. Highlights among the more than 1,300 different plant types that thrive in the garden's advantageous microclimate include collections of ornamental cherries, deciduous magnolias, roses and Japanese maples, which give Ninfa a long and varied season of horticultural interest.

The garden was successively developed by Ada's American-born daughter-in-law Marguerite Chapin. Marguerite's daughter Lelia Caetani applied her painterly talent to planting, and this gave the gardens their current romantic character.

As well as the flower- and ruin-filled informal garden, Ninfa also has a *hortus conclusus*. In strong contrast to the whimsical naturalistic garden, this small, formal garden dating from the seventeenth century is enclosed behind walls at the foot of the castle.

1, 4—With its reservoir, rivers and medieval ruins smothered in climbing flowers, Ninfa is the epitome of the romantic garden. Among its highlights are nineteen varieties of deciduous magnolia, along with birch, Japanese maples and early-flowering ornamental cherries.
2, 5, 6—Ninfa sits where the alluvial Pontine plain and the limestone Lepini hills meet, helping to create its abundant fresh water; the river is home to rare brown trout.
3—The particularly mild climate allows the cultivation of tropical plants such as aquatic iris, avocado, South American *Gunnera* and banana.

1

2

# Villa Lante

Bagnaia, Lazio, Italy

Giacomo Barozzi da Vignola

16th & 17th century

1.5 hectares / 3.5 acres

Temperate Mediterranean

Allegorical / Formal / Parterre / Renaissance / Water

Built in 1568 for Cardinal Gianfrancesco Gambara, Villa Lante is relatively small by Italian Renaissance standards, but its garden is one of the best preserved and least altered of its period. The celebrated architect Vignola used the garden to create an allegory of the rise of civilization, from the primeval grotto at the top of the garden to a terrace of cultured *parterres de broderie* (embroidery-like patterns) at its foot.

The villa itself takes the form of two square casini on the lowest of the four terraces, where the visitor enters the garden. In front of the casini is a *quadrato* (square parterre) bordered by three tall box hedges. In the centre of the *quadrato* is the Islamic-inspired Fountain of the Moors, which appears to float within a quadripartite pool crossed by four bridges. Around the fountain are twelve *parterres de broderie*, their patterns defined by low, clipped box hedges and terracotta-coloured gravel. Dating from the seventeenth century, these parterres replaced the original *compartmenti*, which would have been filled with flowers.

The sloping garden is arranged symmetrically in a series of terraces. Steps lead to the narrow second terrace, dominated by the circular, tiered Fountain of Candles, so named because the 160 small jets glint in the sunlight. On the third terrace, aligned on the central axis, is a water table that was used to cool wine and fruit. Its simplicity contrasts with the ornate massiveness of the Fountain of the River Gods, which rears up behind it. The fountain is fed by the celebrated *catena d'aqua*, or water chain, a raised stream with edges carved with the legs of *gamberi* (crayfish), the symbol of the cardinal.

Surrounded by a *bosco* (sacred grove) of shade-giving plane trees, the centrepiece of the fourth, and upper, terrace is the Fountain of the Dolphins. At the end of the garden, two Houses of the Muses flank the grotto of the Fountain of the Deluge. Carved from the living rock, the grotto is now thickly encrusted with mosses and ferns, whose rich greens only enhance its primeval atmosphere. Outside the walls beyond the grotto is the remnant of the *barco* (wooded hunting park).

1—The Fountain of the Moors, which dominates the *quadrato* was a seventeenth-century addition, like the French-style *parterres de broderie.*
2—The water table, fed by the Fountain of the River Gods behind it, was used by diners to keep food cool by floating it on the water.
3—The famous water chain carries water from the fourth to the third terraces.
4—Two small loggias on the highest terrace provided the Cardinal's guests with a place not only to relax but also to recapture the feeling of living in the classical world.
5—In the Fountain of Candles, tiers of tiny fountains shaped like Roman oil lamps spout jets of water that glint in the sunlight.

306

3

4

5

# Giardini
# La Mortella

Ischia, Italy

Susana, Lady Walton, Russell Page

20th century

2 hectares / 5 acres

Temperate Mediterranean

Coastal / Informal / Mediterranean / Naturalistic / Plantsman / Water

La Mortella ('place of myrtles') – named after the purple myrtle that grows wild on the island of Ischia – was the home of the English composer Sir William Walton and his wife, Susana, from 1956 until 2010. Early on, the couple engaged the English garden designer Russell Page to transform a disused stone quarry on a rocky promontory overlooking the Tyrrhenian Sea. The garden became the life work of the charismatic Lady Walton. She not only filled Page's garden with a fine array of rare and exotic plants, but also expanded it to include the Hill Garden.

The Valley Garden (designed by Page in 1956) is shaped like a letter 'L': its long axis is formed by a rill running down the path between the circular pool and fountain (surrounded by the Bog Garden) and the octagonal pool and fountain, which combine to give the area an Islamic feel. The sense of a luxurious paradise is enhanced by dense planting, while the atmosphere is enveloping, intimate and humid. Beyond the octagonal pool is the focus of Page's garden, the large, egg-shaped Main Pool from which a path takes one to Villa Walton (built in 1962). The short axis of the 'L' is a shallow flight of steps up to the Palm Court, which is home to the Victoria House, with its specimens of Amazon water lily (*Victoria amazonica*).

In strong contrast to the lushness of the Valley Garden, the atmosphere of the Hill Garden, designed by Lady Walton from 1983 – the year of her husband's death – is of openness and sunlight, with views out over the island and the azure sea. The planting is mostly of Mediterranean species, many selected for their strong architectural form. Here, too, water plays an important part. An informal stream flows from the Lotus Pool and its associated structure, the Thai sala, down to the Crocodile Pool with its lifelike sculptures. At the top of the garden stand twin monuments: Sir William's Rock and Lady Walton's Nymphaeum, a concave water basin in polished stainless steel that reflects the sky. This 'Mirror of the Soul' pool is surrounded with an inscription that reads: 'This green arbour is dedicated to Susana, who loved tenderly, worked with passion and believed in immortality.'

1—This fountain in the Valley Garden was designed by Russell Page surrounded by a Bog Garden of four semicircular flower beds planted with marsh plants.
2—*Victoria amazonica*, the largest of all water lilies, grows in a pond overlooked by *The Mouth*, a sculpture by Simon Verity.
3—A fountain plays in the large, egg-shaped main pool that forms the focus of Page's garden.

1

4—At the top of the site, overlooking
the sea, is Sir William's Rock, which holds
the ashes of the composer.
5—A path climbs through dense planting
in the Valley Garden.
6—Near the top of the garden is the
Crocodile Pool, surrounded by *Agapanthus
campanulatus* and has *Encephalartos
manikensis* growing on its bank.
7—The fountain in Lady Walton's
Nymphaeum is made of polished stainless
steel that reflects the sky above.
8—Near the highest point of the garden
is an Oriental Garden, with a Thai pavilion
and a pond filled with lotus plants (*Nelumbo
nucifera*), around which grow white-flowered
*Hedychium coronarium*, Japanese maple
and trees of the tropical Rhododendron
group *Vireya*.

6

7

8

# Mediterranean Garden Society Garden

Peania, near Athens, Greece

Derek Toms, Mary Jacqueline Tyrwhitt

20th century

Temperate Mediterranean

Drought Tolerant / Mediterranean / Plantsman / Terraces

The site of this garden in Attica is demanding for plants, with hot, rainless summers, poor soils and strong winds. So Jaqueline Tyrwhitt, the British town planner who created the garden in 1960s, put an emphasis on plants that were compatible with the climate. Her pioneering work with native plants is continued by the Mediterranean Garden Society, which now manages the site.

The garden includes plants from other Mediterranean-climate regions, but they must be able to withstand four or five rainless summer months with temperatures reaching 40˚C (104˚F), with the scant annual rainfall concentrated in the winter. They must also be able to cope with stony, alkaline soil and strong, dry north winds.

Only some parts of the garden are irrigated. To the east of the house lie three long terraces, which are home to a great variety of plants, including salvia and teucriums. Bulbs include the black-flowered Greek *Fritillaria obliqua* and the South African *Haemanthus coccineus*. These terraces receive some water in summer, as does the border on the west side of the house, which includes roses.

In many ways the unirrigated parts of the garden, where plants are left to follow their natural cycle of summer dormancy, are even more interesting. The raised bed at the northern end of the Upper Terrace is home to the Cretan endemics *Ebenus cretica* and *Origanum dictamnus*, as well as the summer-deciduous *Euphorbia acanthothamnos*. A circular area southwest of the house is managed as a dry meadow, with partial shade provided by a carob (*Ceratonia siliqua*), a Judas tree (*Cercis siliquastrum*) and tall *Yucca elephantipes*. The meadow is surrounded by a border containing drought-tolerant species, such as rosemary and santolinas, as well as the summer-deciduous *Euphorbia dendroides*.

To the south, a cactus and succulent area leads into an area of phrygana to whose natural flora other species have been selectively added, such as *Amaryllis belladonna*, *Iris* x *germanica* and aloes. In the same way, selective additions to the natural flora have been made to the hillside to the north, reflecting the garden's ongoing role as an experimental place where new plants are constantly being tested for their ability to withstand drought.

1—On the edge of the phrygana in spring, a multi-stemmed olive is underplanted with *Clematis cirrhosa*, *Iris* x *germanica* and *Acanthus mollis*.
2—Fragrant chamomile forms a carpet in front of blooming *Euphorbia characias* and *Yucca elephantipes* (left) and a *Cercis siliquastrum* waiting to come into leaf.
3—On one of the top terraces, a *Cereus* cactus is planted amid a patch of *Oxalis purpurea*, with pots of the red-flowered succulent *Kleinia fulgens*.

# John Stefanidis Garden

Patmos, Greece

| |
|---|
| John Stefanidis |
| 20th century |
| Temperate Mediterranean |
| Dry / Mediterranean / Terraces |

John Stefanidis might be well known as an interior designer today, overseeing projects across the globe, yet when he first arrived at this house and garden on the slopes of the Greek island of Patmos, his working life had barely begun. Born to Greek and Jewish parents in Alexandria, Egypt, Stefanidis was educated at Oxford and worked in the advertising industry until a work-permit complication brought on an early sabbatical. In 1963 he and a university friend, Teddy Millington-Drake, travelled to this island in the Dodecanese, north of Kos in the southern Aegean. Stefanidis bought the property in Chora, the island's capital, on a hillside just below the Monastery of Saint John the Theologian, for £1,000.

Built in the sixteenth century, the house and its grounds had lain derelict for a couple of decades. It was while renovating the house that Stefanidis found he had a talent for both garden and interior design, which he later developed into a career. On Patmos, Stefanidis's skills converged, as a series of shady terraces bring the inside outdoors, with furniture and furnishings spilling out into the gardens. It is little wonder that certain parts of the grounds have been dubbed the Garden Room and the Breakfast Terrace.

Stefanidis has combined local eastern Mediterranean traditions, such as using washes of lime to protect tree trunks from being scalded by the sun, with more exotic introductions, including tubs of bougainvillea, beds of African lily and the beautiful elliptical blue blooms of *Echium candicans*, as well as numerous non-flowering species such as maidenhair ferns and potted palms. There are humorous additions, too, such as a couple of sun parasols set into the vine-covered pergola.

Despite such innovations, Mediterranean cypress trees continue to dot the hillside and an antique dovecote still welcomes birds to Stefanidis's steep garden. It is all unmistakably Greek, but not in a clichéd or picture-postcard sort of way. Stefanidis points out that what might be called Mediterranean style is a conceit in any case, given the numerous layers of civilizations and histories that have contributed to it; yet someone as cultured and patient as he is has nevertheless managed to create a beautifully conceived garden in Patmos.

1—The terraces around the house are an extension of the living areas, brightened by bougainvillea, and with ample seating and areas of sunlight and shade thrown by mature trees.
2—Their trunks painted with lime to protect them from sunlight, olive trees grow in beds of rosemary around a traditional shrine.
3—Succulents grow among pebbles, which are a traditional Mediterranean way of conserving water in dry gardens.

# Chalet Garden

Gstaad, Switzerland

Louis Benech

21st century

0.75 hectares / 1.8 acres

Alpine

Cottage / Natives / Rooms

The Swiss resort town of Gstaad is a contradiction: stunning wild scenery combined with all the sophistication and wealth of Europe's most glamorous socialites. It is a contradiction the French landscape designer Louis Benech sums up in this chalet garden. It is natural yet controlled, homely yet imposing, local in its planting yet international in its plan.

Benech is one of the leaders of a new generation of garden creators who use the – not inconsiderable – wealth of their clients to create gardens of a beauty that perfectly complements their setting. In Gstaad the immediate problem was of coming up with a design that could hold its own with the spectacular alpine scenery. Benech incorporated elements of hardscaping, such as paving and paths, together with planted retaining walls, to give the garden structure and delineate areas within. He also deliberately kept the planting relatively low – despite his great love of trees – and placed a large, flat lawn in front of the chalet, incorporating the views into the garden. At its front edge, the lawn slopes down into a hillside of lush, uncut grass that laps at it like surf.

As in all his more than 300 projects to date, Benech here incorporates dozens of native plants, including many colourful wild flowers from alpine meadows. He prefers such hardy species that can look after themselves even in crowded planting, in which he typically combines flowers and colours with great panache. Here the wild, naturalistic planting is selected to ensure a long flowering season, starting as soon as the winter snow melts. But Benech also introduces an element of formality, such as the use of box and yew to create a series of small, low compartments for planting at one end of the lawn. Like the dense planting of shrubs and grasses at the other end of the lawn, however, even these formal elements have a romantic, slightly unkempt feel, rather than being tightly clipped. It is as if there is a constant reminder that this garden is part of the wider natural landscape.

1—A view from the top of the garden shows a combination of species-rich planting and hardscaping with a fence and flowers reminiscent of an alpine cottage.
2, 4—Benech's signature use of cottage-style plants creates an apparently wild profusion that spills over a stone path and threatens to engulf an old stone press.
3—At one end of the lawn, stone paths, low hedges and topiary create small compartments for flowers, including roses. Wooden frames support climbing plants to add an element of vertical interest without obscuring the breathtaking alpine scenery beyond.

3

4

# Schloss Schönbrunn

## Vienna, Austria

Jean Trehet, Nikolas Pacassi,
Jean-Nicolas Jadot, Louis Gervais

17th & 18th century

185 hectares / 457 acres

Humid Continental

Baroque / Formal / Landscape

The word *schönbrunn* ('beautiful spring')
derives from the well that supplied the
sixteenth-century palace built by the
Emperor Maximilian II in this former
hunting park. A glance, however, reveals
that the garden belongs to the eighteenth
century – and above all to the influence of
Versailles (see page 246). The view from
the terrace across the Great Parterre
– enclosed by avenues of lofty trees –
was designed as an impressive symbol
of the imperial power of the Habsburgs.

After Schönbrunn was devastated
in the Ottoman siege of Vienna in
1683, Leopold I built a new palace
with a Baroque garden designed by
Jean Trehet, a pupil of André Le Nôtre.
Under Empress Maria Theresa in the
eighteenth century, Schönbrunn became
the centre of Habsburg court life, and
architect Nikolaus Pacassi made it
a perfect example of *Gesamtkunstwerk*
– the masterly fusion of many art forms.

Trehet's Baroque garden – with its
single main axis and *parterres de broderie*
– was extended. Jean-Nicolas Jadot
and Louis Gervais added radiating
avenues and walks, together with two
diagonal axes that emanate in a *patte
d'oie* (goosefoot pattern). Between the
avenues and paths, ornamental *bosquets*
(groves of trees and hedges) enclosed
glades and events. More ornamentation
was added in the 1770s, when the
*parterres de broderie* was lined with
classical sculptures. The largest, the
Neptune Fountain, nestles at the foot
of the Schönbrunn Hill, from where the
colonnaded Gloriette offers a sweeping
vista down over the gardens to Vienna.
A Roman ruin is a monument to
recovery after disaster.

The garden is famous for its zoo,
which was founded as a menagerie
in 1752 by Maria Theresa's husband,
Emperor Francis Stephen. A year later
he added a Dutch Botanical Garden
in the western part of the garden. In
the 1820s this was transformed into an
English landscape garden, in which an
iron-framed Palm House was erected
in the 1880s. East of the palace is the
Orangery, which at 186 metres (610 feet)
is the longest in the world. Like these
additions, the original Baroque gardens
have survived more or less intact today.

1—The main axis of the garden extends
over the vast Great Parterre to the
60-metre-high (197-foot) Schönbrunn Hill
in the distance, topped by the Gloriette.
2—A tree-lined bosquet takes the form
of a circle of raised flower beds set in
grass surrounding statues of Alexander
and Olympia.
3—The Gloriette takes the form of a
triumphal arch – it was glazed in 1780
– with arcaded wings.
4—Flowers pick out scrollwork patterns
in a bosquet alongside the Great Parterre.

3

4

# Łazienki Park

Warsaw, Poland

| |
|---|
| Tylman van Gameren, Domenico Merlini |
| 17th & 18th century |
| 76 hectares / 188 acres |
| Humid Continental |
| Baroque / Neo-classical / Royal / Sculpture |

Many of the world's finest city parks allow a public appreciation of horticulture alongside other arts, such as music, theatre and architecture. Łazienki Park, best known as the summer residence of the last king of Poland, is no exception.

This park in the heart of the Polish capital was first laid out as a hunting ground in the late seventeenth century by the Dutch-born architect Tylman van Gameren for the Polish nobleman Stanisław Herakliusz Lubomirski. It takes its name from a bathing pavilion that once stood beside the lake. Stanisław August Poniatowski, Poland's last monarch, acquired Łazienki in 1764 and, with the Italian-born architect Domenico Merlini, set about re-creating the park as a romantic pleasure garden. Poniatowski was a renowned patron of the arts, as reflected in Łazienki's Neo-classical palace, Orangery, hermitage, cylindrical water tower and Roman-style theatre; the park's buildings also house and display the royal art collection.

Yet Łazienki's true treasures lie outdoors. The formal gardens are arranged around two bodies of water, and are planted with purple lilac and rhododendrons, as well as beds of tulips, forget-me-not and asters. Łazienki was part of a forested area before it was enclosed, and the park's beeches, willows, chestnuts, maples, black poplars and limes recall this earlier time, while also bearing some more recent scars. When restoring the park after the fall of the Soviet Union, horticulturalists reported finding fragments from World War II fighting embedded in the Łazienki's trees. Locals claim that the park's trees are among the oldest in Poland.

The trees are at their most colourful in early autumn, while the floral displays are best in summer. Łazienki also boasts lively fauna, including peacocks and red squirrels. The park is a perfect setting for free, open-air piano recitals throughout the summer, of the best-loved works of Frédéric Chopin, beside a beautiful Rose Garden and a monument dedicated to Poland's national composer. It is a tradition that would have pleased King Stanisław himself.

1—The imposing Neo-classical palace is reflected in one of the park's two large lakes.
2—The Chopin Monument was sculpted by Wacław Szymanowski and installed in 1926.
3, 5—Neo-classical statuary is dotted among the allées and paths throughout the park's extensive woodlands.
4—The Long Lake was traditionally a popular place for the inhabitants of Warsaw to swim on warm summer days.

# Valdštejnský Palác
## (Wallenstein Palace)

Prague, Czech Republic

| | |
|---|---|
| Giovanni Pieroni, Andrea Spezza, Nicolo Sebregondi | |
| 17th century | |
| 2 hectares / 5 acres | |
| Humid Continental | |
| Baroque / Formal / Parterre | |

Wallenstein Palace was created for the powerful general Duke Albrecht of Wallenstein. Inspired by the Mannerist style of the imperial court in Prague, Wallenstein commissioned Italian architects to build the most magnificent palace in the country: Giovanni Pieroni and Nicolo Sebregondi. Shortly before work began, a catalogue of the great palaces of Genoa had been published, created by Peter Paul Rubens for the Duke Vincenzo Gonzaga. The Gonzagas, the Habsburgs and Duke Albrecht had many connections and shared similar cultural inspirations.

As in great Italian palaces of the period, the Wallenstein palace and its garden were closely connected, in this case mainly by a loggia that echoes a similar one created in Livorno, Italy, by Pieroni's father, Alessandro. In its original form, the basic grass parterre was arranged as a cross, with a fountain of Venus and Cupid in the middle, and linked to the loggia by mythological bronze statues created by the Flemish sculptor Adriaen de Vries (they were looted by Swedish soldiers during the Thirty Years' War and taken to Sweden). The statues now in the garden are copies arranged along the newly created main axes. The whole garden is visually linked by a series of blind arcades on the tall wall, which includes a stucco grotto and aviary for birds of prey beneath canopies of chestnut trees.

The second part of the garden was originally formed by hedges of box and hornbeam *bosquets*, behind which Sebregondi created a large open space with a rectangular pool in front of the former stables (now an exhibition hall). In the pool's centre is a later island with a bronze statue of Hercules. The 1950s' reconstruction of the garden opened up the long central vista between both parts of the garden and changed the grass parterre in front of the loggia into a concert stage. This change was retained in a further reconstruction after 2000, when the hornbeam *bosquets* were reduced and the large grass area opened up for safety reasons, as the garden now belongs to the Senate of the Czech parliament. During the reconstruction all the old chestnut trees and hornbeam hedges were removed and replaced, while the gravel paths were excavated to allow engineering work beneath.

1 — The imposing three-arched loggia links the inside of the palace with the garden, with its formal clipped hedges planted with tulips in spring.
2, 4 — Fountains and pools reflect the garden's inspiration from the Italian Renaissance.
3 — By contrast with the graceful loggia, a wall covered in stalactites and grotesque carvings covers the aviary.

# Peterhof

St Petersburg, Russia

| Peter the Great, Jean-Baptiste Alexandre Le Blond |
| --- |
| 18th century |
| 120 hectares / 297 acres |
| Humid Continental |
| Baroque / Formal / Water |

Early in the eighteenth century Peter the Great began to plan a summer palace and gardens on the Gulf of Finland to rival the famed water gardens at Versailles in France (see page 246). With the Great Cascade, however, he did not simply rival Versailles: he eclipsed it – and all Europe's other contemporary gardens – by creating what remains probably the outstanding water garden in the world. Peterhof remains an important tourist destination, not least for its gardens of different styles and eras.

The formal Upper Gardens consist of parterres and basins with closely planted trees and plant-covered tunnels or walkways. An equally formal Lower Park again reflects the European styles of the period, with allées and fountains. But it is the north facade of the palace that holds the real drama: the gilded extravagance of the Great Cascade, with its sixty-four or so fountains and attendant jets of water, gilded statues of deities and mythical figures, double cascades, canals and pools. The centrepiece – the Samson Fountain – and the other statuary are intended to symbolize Peter the Great's restoration of Russia's Baltic lands and the country's international importance. The most dramatic view of the Great Cascade is that enjoyed from the quay by visitors arriving by boat. Dramatic views are also offered from the terrace above the Samson Fountain.

The Great Cascade was designed by the French architect Jean-Baptiste Alexandre Le Blond – a pupil of André Le Nôtre, who designed the gardens at Versailles. Its creation was overseen by a young hydraulics engineer, Vasily Tuvolkov, who devised a system to bring in water from some 22.5 kilometres (14 miles) away. After flowing down the cascade, the water eventually reaches the Marine Canal and thence the sea.

Although much of the work was completed in Peter the Great's lifetime, additions and remodelling continued under his successors. In World War II the hydraulic system was destroyed and many of the buildings were badly damaged. Nevertheless, restoration was so successful that by 1946 the fountains at Peterhof played once more.

1—The Great Cascade is one of the world's largest water features; the water eventually flows along the Marine Canal to the sea.
2—An aerial view shows the formal Upper and Lower Gardens to the south of the palace.
3, 5—In the Samson Fountain, Samson tears open the jaws of a lion, symbolizing Russia's defeat of Sweden in the Great Northern War in 1721; the lion's mouth shoots a jet of water 20 metres (65 feet) high, the tallest in Peterhof.
4—On the Lion Cascade, water gushes from the mouths of classical masks.

3

4

5

6, 7—The Upper Gardens were originally
used as the kitchen garden but by the second
quarter of the eighteenth century they had
become more formal, with lawns, avenues
of clipped trees and ornate fountains.
8—In the middle of the eighteenth century
new parterres were added to the Upper
Garden and bordered in various materials;
the parterres were restored in 1953.
9—Peter the Great ordered the building
of the Peter and Paul Cathedral not in the
usual Orthodox style, but in a Gothic form
borrowed from Protestant churches.
10–An arched tunnel clothed in Virginia
creeper covers a path through the
Upper Garden.

# Tsarskoye Selo

St Petersburg, Russia

| |
|---|
| Jan Roosen, Johan Busch, Vasiley Neyelov |
| 18th century |
| 102 hectares / 252 acres (Catherine Park) |
| Humid Continental |
| English Landscape / Formal / French |

Tsarskoye Selo ('tsar's village') lies in the town of Pushkin, which is now more or less a suburb of St Petersburg, some 20 kilometres (12 miles) away. It includes two parks of historical importance: Catherine Park, the extensive grounds of Catherine Palace (named for Catherine I, the second wife of Peter the Great); and Alexander Park, which was carved out of Catherine Park when Alexander Palace was built in the last decade of the eighteenth century.

The Catherine Park gardens surround Catherine I's small house, in the Dutch formal style, and were created by Jan Roosen in the early eighteenth century. Later in the century Catherine II – Catherine the Great – used the wider park to give expression to her admiration of the English Landscape style. She therefore called a halt to the formal clipping and topiary work of trees. At first her enthusiasm for the Landscape style was not reciprocated by many of her gardeners, but in 1771 Johan (or John) Busch came to work for her. (He later became the father-in-law of Charles Cameron, Catherine's architect and creator of many notable buildings and rooms at the palace.) Busch had helped to establish a renowned nursery in London, and was a plantsman and designer of great note. He had been introduced to Catherine by the architect Vasiley Neyelov, who the previous year had been sent with his son to England by Catherine, to visit all the notable gardens, with a view to re-creating their features.

In order to design at Tsarskoye Selo a landscape that looked as if it had been made by nature, Busch and Neyelov first had to reshape the land. They planted trees, adapted the lake to an irregular shape and worked into this 'natural' terrain numerous architectural features. These included a range of buildings – follies, bridges, pavilions and temples – to echo the English landscape that Catherine so admired. Thus, there are particular echoes of Stowe (see page 156) and Wilton at Tsarskoye Selo.

Like many estates and buildings in Russia, the parks at Tsarskoye Selo were damaged during World War II and have since been restored.

1, 2—Scrollwork parterres adorn the formal garden directly in front of the distinctive blue-and-white facade of Catherine Palace.
3—A small pagoda adorns an oriental bridge in the Chinese Village in Alexander Park.
4—The Grotto Pavilion in Catherine Park, decorated inside with seashells and tufa (porous limestone), was based on Western European grottos of the eighteenth century.
5—Autumn turns the trees and topiary and many groundcover plants into a rich tapestry of browns, yellows and reds.

# La Mamounia

Marrakech, Morocco

| |
|---|
| Pasha Mamoun, Jacques Garcia |
| 21st century |
| 8 hectares / 20 acres |
| Dry Semiarid |
| Cactus / Exotic / Potager / Romantic |

The British prime minister Winston Churchill once called the garden of the renowned Hotel La Mamounia 'the most lovely spot in the whole world'. The gardens existed long before the hotel opened its doors, having formerly been a traditional *arsat* (orchard garden) given to Pasha Mamoun by his father as a wedding gift in the middle of the eighteenth century. Today, following a refurbishment by the French architect, interior and garden designer Jacques Garcia, palm trees, hundred-year-old olive trees, orange and lemon trees, roses, Madagascar periwinkles (*Catharanthus*) and amaranthus offer treats to eye and nose alike.

Although the modern garden holds true to the tradition of the former productive orchard – with its olive and citrus trees, date palms and a vegetable garden – it does have some additional embellishments. Garcia widened the main avenue of crushed pink stone, so that it is more in proportion with the width of the doors that lead out into the garden from the hotel. The avenue was lined with olive trees and underplanted mainly with white-flowered plants, including basil and cosmos. Garcia also added a new Cactus Garden, which holds some twenty-one species of succulent, and he extended the Potager, at the far end of the garden. The hotel's chefs pick the produce from the Potager every day; they particularly favour salad leaves, tomatoes, coriander and basil, as well as citrus fruit, which features very highly in Moroccan cuisine.

Enclosed on the west side by the pink rampart walls of the old Medina and on the other side by modern walls wreathed with magenta bougainvillea, the garden of La Mamounia continues to be a place of tranquillity and productivity in the heart of a bustling city. Its central avenue has many lateral paths lined with roses, ginger, jacaranda, delphinium, cosmos and canna, leading to different parts of the garden. Lawns, well manicured and watered, are the cooling green foil for the rows of citrus trees, each of which is planted within a circle of rich red soil.

1—A path of crushed stone runs between borders of calendula, antirrhinum and orange trees.
2—One of Garcia's innovations was to use underplanting of white flowers that are set off by the pale pink crushed stone of the main avenue.
3—The richly planted borders feature hot-coloured annuals: mixed with the purple-blue Larkspur 'Consolida' are the reds and golds of calendula, petunia and antirrhinum.

# El Bahia Palace Garden

Marrakech, Morocco

| |
|---|
| El Haj Mohammed El Mekki |
| 19th century |
| 0.8 hectares / 2 acres |
| Dry Semiarid |
| Courtyards / Formal / Islamic |

The sprawling complex of El Bahia Palace – courtyards, private apartments and public audience halls – is a wonderful example of the Islamic integration of interior and exterior space. Although it appears haphazard, in fact it was created as a piece by the architect El Haj Mohammed El Mekki for the sultan's vizier, Ba Ahmed. The vizier's palace was so luxurious that when the French protectorate began in the early twentieth century, the governor claimed it as his residence.

The labyrinthine layout reflects the Islamic demand for the separation of public and private life, with separate accommodation for wives and concubines. Each of the vizier's four wives had her own apartment opening into a private garden, while the harem surrounded a large tiled courtyard with rooms leading off it for his twenty-four concubines. The Grand Courtyard – 30 by 40 metres (98 by 131 feet) – was for the family. Bisected into rectangular plots with three fountains, decorative pavilions and an ornate entrance, this large but intimate, cloister-like space reflects the importance of domestic life.

The Great Marble Courtyard is even larger. It was designed for public audiences; the surrounding gallery provided shade for waiting petitioners, and the marble pavement reflects the sun in the daytime while retaining heat for the cold nights. Although its vast empty spaces seem austere by today's taste, the dense planting in many of the palace's courtyards is a European import. Traditionally such spaces would have contained few plants – a scented jasmine, an evergreen cypress, a few palms, citrus or banana trees and some potted herbs.

In the dry heat of Morocco, courtyard gardens often used architectural features to simulate horticultural effect: green roof tiles link to trees beyond, blue zigzag paving suggests cool streams, deep galleries and cut plaster or stonework give dappled shade, and a central fountain humidifies the air to make a pleasant atmosphere in a space where plants would struggle to survive. Despite its size and grandeur, the Bahia Palace Garden offers a calm retreat from the chaos of city life.

1 — In the Petit Riad, made in 1898 and planted with orange trees, a complex pattern of blue tiles covers the floor of a courtyard surrounding a fountain, reflecting the Moroccan technique of using architecture to simulate the elements of a garden, such as cooling water.
2 — The Great Marble Courtyard is notably austere for modern tastes, but the green tiles high on the wall link the courtyard visually with the trees beyond.
3 — An orange tree grows in a quiet courtyard.

# Le Jardin Majorelle

Marrakech, Morocco

Jacques Majorelle

20th century

0.4 hectares / 1 acre

Dry Semiarid

Artistic / Cactus / Exotic / Islamic / Modern / Subtropical / Water

If there is one word to describe La Majorelle's fusion of Art Deco and Islamic inspiration, it is 'blue'. Behind its high walls, this garden of quietly burbling water provides a striking contrast with the chaos of the surrounding 'Ochre City'. Begun in 1924, the garden occupied the painter Jacques Majorelle for forty years. If truth be told, the garden, rather than his art, was his masterpiece.

Majorelle composed the garden like a painting, with a series of formal features including a pergola; raised pools and rills filled with lotus and water lilies; tiled pathways; and calm courtyards. As with design, so was colour approached with a painterly eye. The dominant colour, inspired by Moroccan tiles and Berber *burnouses*, is an intense shade of cobalt blue that Majorelle trademarked with his own name. The blue contrasts with rich red tiles, chrome-yellow pots and softer terracotta tones.

The house and garden are the perfect foil for the plant collection. Majorelle was a plantaholic and filled his garden with an eclectic mix of exotic and architectural plants, many from North and South Africa, the Americas and Asia. The planting design relies heavily on species with bold forms, so the botanical element works with the architectural one to provide overall balance in the composition. Tints of green underscore the Majorelle Blue, while the ebullient foliage contrasts with the clear lines of concrete and tiled features as when, for example, a domed mound of bougainvillea draped over a pavilion contrasts with the architectural shapes of prickly pear and agave.

The Gravel Garden next to the house is home to bizarrely shaped cacti and other plants such as euphorbias, set in red gravel. Throughout the garden, lofty bamboos, banana trees and coconut palms add a sculptural quality while casting welcome shade. Visitors who move away from the dense planting near the house discover a collection of trees – an arboretum with a different yet complementary character.

1

2

3

4

5

6

# Aïn Kassimou

Palmeraie, Morocco

| |
|---|
| Madison Cox, Marella Agnelli |
| 21st century |
| 18 hectares / 45 acres |
| Dry Semiarid |
| Exotic / Informal / Romantic / Rooms / Roses / Water |

Originally built by descendants of the famous Russian writer Leo Tolstoy, Aïn Kassimou was redeveloped in the 1980s before being acquired in the early 2000s by Marella Agnelli, the Italian garden photographer, art collector and widow of former Fiat chairman Gianni Agnelli.

Agnelli brought in the US garden designer Madison Cox – he has a home near Tangiers – who spent a decade evolving the modern garden. Cox's design style is difficult to categorize, for all his gardens are unique. But they all exhibit both designed complexity and refined simplicity, and an understanding of the *genius loci*, the 'spirit of the place'. Cox also pays careful heed to the wishes of his clients – in this case 'simplicity, simplicity, simplicity' and an evocation of Agnelli's beloved Corsican estate at the Convent of Alziprato.

The gardens have the ambience of a *jardin clos* or *hortus conclusus* – the kind of enclosed, private space engrained in Islamic and medieval European garden traditions. Cox turned barren paddocks and polo fields into a rustic, pastoral setting reminiscent of that made by the Tolstoy family. Between the groves – the trees are mostly aligned in rows – he laid out a somewhat rectilinear network of plant-lined or pergola-covered paths, with billows of nasturtiums and cotton lavender. He also brought in many plants from neighbouring farms being redeveloped for housing: more than 3,000 venerable olive trees, 50-year-old citrus trees and mature grapevines, together with many indigenous Moroccan species and 5,000 rose bushes of 3,000 cultivars.

The garden's romantic and bucolic periphery gives way to lawns and greater formality near the house, such as a yellow-and-white garden and a walk of espaliered lemon trees underplanted with New Holland daisies (*Vittadinia* spp.). Here, too, is a striking *Crinum*-edged pool with its aquatic planting of papyrus and water lilies, and a poolside pavilion inspired by Le Jardin Majorelle (see page 332), where Cox also worked. Around the pool the planting includes *Agapanthus* and *Amaryllis*, climbing roses, jasmine and Port St John's creeper (*Podranea ricasoliana*) and pomegranate trees.

1—The gardens are based on the Islamic tradition of enclosed gardens: a private space in which formal planting near the house becomes more natural further away.
2—The pool pavilion, designed by Bill Willis, was based on the one at Le Jardin Majorelle. Yellow water lilies and papyrus, carefully kept, grow in the pool.
3—A split bamboo pergola planted with bougainvillea provides shade on the terrace outside the master bedroom.
4—A drift of poppies flower in meadow-like planting beneath palm trees.

1

2

3

4

# Al-Azhar Park

Cairo, Egypt

Sites International, Cairo

21st century

30 hectares / 74 acres

Dry Arid

Formal / Islamic / Park / Urban / Water

In this most historic of cities, the Al-Azhar Park has come full circle. The park – the brainchild of the Aga Khan – was created in 2005 on the site of a 500-year-old rubbish dump (the old soil was removed, cleaned and returned), which itself overlaid a garden made in the late tenth century.

The park's dominant visual spine of terraces linked by water is surrounded by a series of gentle walks winding through the contoured site, with expanses of sward studded with shade-giving palms and other trees, and flower beds filled with informal plantings that showcase 325 different plant taxa, the vast majority of which are Egyptian natives. The green areas provide a recreational space for families and children, but they are also home to a series of interconnected garden spaces arranged around a central spine. While it is not an Islamic garden in the sense of a *chahar bagh* – although there is an example in the Lakeside Cafe – the park's design reflects a range of influences, styles and gardens from all over the Islamic world.

The spinal axis of the garden begins at a high point that commands a view of the distant citadel and, closer to hand, the necropolis, or ancient cemetery. In Islamic fashion, the terraces are linked by water that cascades between the twin flights of steps by means of *chadar* (chutes) with an uneven surface that makes the water jump and glitter in the sunlight. The main walk follows the Palm Promenade past water jets that squirt up through the paving. At the fountain the path doglegs right towards the Lakeside Cafe, flanked by twin Sunken Gardens set within an orchard. The elegant cafe pavilion seems to float over the informally shaped lake, from where water is pumped to a mirror pool in a grove of trees on the hillside above, cascading back into the lake by means of a rocky stream.

Despite its beauty, the park adds more to the city than mere green space. The Aga Khan Trust for Culture, which oversaw the project, designed the park to stimulate socio-economic rehabilitation projects – such as health and education or microcredit schemes – in neighbouring Darb al-Ahmar, one of Cairo's poorest areas.

1—The view from the highest point of the park – marked by a restaurant – looks out over formal water terraces to the citadel in the distance.
2—A rocky stream carries water from the circular mirror pool into the lake.
3—The elegant cafe pavilion appears to float over the informally shaped lake.
4—Water tumbles down the terraces by means of corrugated *chadar* that break its flow and make it sparkle.
5—The fountain plays at the end of the Palm Promenade, where cooling jets of water squirt up through the paving.

# Babylonstoren
## Cape Town, South Africa

| |
|---|
| Patrice Taravella, Karen Roos |
| 17th & 20th century |
| 3.2 hectares / 8 acres (garden); 202 hectares / 500 acres (estate) |
| Temperate Mediterranean |
| Edible / Modern / Rooms / Roses |

The garden and estate at Babylonstoren in the heart of the Cape wine lands echo the historic Cape Dutch homestead created there in the seventeenth century. The early Dutch settlers established gardens to supply ships with fruit and vegetables en route to and from the Dutch East Indies via the newly discovered Cape.

The modern garden, designed by Patrice Taravella for owner Karen Roos, harks back to these productive traditions yet transcends them in the beauty of his layout and the use of natural wooden supports and plants trained into architectural shapes. There are more than 350 varieties of edible or medicinal vegetables, herbs, fruits and flowers. Daily harvests provide ingredients for the restaurant and tearoom on the site.

The garden is laid out in a grid system, with two long main walkways running east to west, and another north to south. In all there are some fifteen clusters of gardens within gardens. These include a citrus and subtropical fruit orchard, an almond plantation with beehives, an olive plantation and a prickly pear maze. There is also an avenue of eighty-year-old guavas, while near the garden's entrance a planting of thymes and other shrubby herbs that wreathe and writhe into a labyrinth and scent the air in the heat of the day.

Fruit and vegetables are grown in rows in formal beds. Many, such as lettuces, alternate in colour in each row. Fruit trees and bushes are trained into shapes, and the beds and borders are crisscrossed by pathways.

Babylonstoren is full of fragrance, thanks to the forty-eight pergolas hung with climbing roses, which thrive in the Cape climate. One of the most pleasing features is a snake-like latticed-timber tunnel called the Puff Adder (complete with a bulge to represent an ingested mouse), which houses a collection of 7,000 indigenous clivias, which need protection from direct summer sun. The open slats offer sun protection and allow a current of cooling air to flow through. The Puff Adder also provides welcome shade to visitors walking towards the woodland along the stream that is the garden's main water source.

1 — The garden is arranged on three main axes, two running north–south and one east–west.
2 — *Tulbaghia*, South African wild garlic, is planted round the edge of the garden as a snake repellent. Citrus trees grow in front of apricots trained over a wooden framework.
3 — Formal beds of vegetables and herbs are bordered by espaliered fruit trees.
4 — The Babylonstoren Hill rises behind a walled reservoir used to grow various indigenous water plants.

3

4

# Bridle Road Residence

Cape Town, South Africa

Rees Roberts + Partners LLC

21st century

0.45 hectares / 1 acre

Temperate Mediterranean

Grasses / Naturalistic / Shrubs / Sustainable / Terraces

South Africa's Western Cape is home to a unique vegetation of light shrubs and heath-like plants that thrive in the Mediterranean-style climate. Locals call this vegetation fynbos, and despite its hardy appearance it is highly endangered. In 2004 UNESCO designated the Cape Floral Region Protected Areas, including the Table Mountain National Park in which the Bridle Road Residence is situated. Planting in this area has to be carefully managed. The introduction of foreign species there could result in the disappearance of native ones.

The Bridle Road Residence is a beautiful modern house, and its garden is built into a verdant ravine surrounded by parkland, with views over Cape Town and the sea. When the New York-based landscape design practice Rees Roberts + Partners was asked to come up with a garden to accompany a house, the designers knew they had to tread carefully. However, rather than see the restricted planting as a difficulty, they chose to make it a feature. They designed and planted a fynbos garden, placing endangered plantings at the heart of their creation. Thus there are dense grasses such as *Chondropetalum tectorum*, frond-like bunches of *Restio subverticillata*, delicate flowering shrubs such as *Leucadendron cordifolium*, and fragrant, herb-like plants such as *Penaea mucronata*. Many of the rarer species were supplied by Kirstenbosch National Botanical Garden (see page 342).

The careful ecological considerations extend to the swimming pool. There is no chlorination: a combination of gravel filtration, mechanical skimming and botanical water-cleansing techniques keeps the water fresh. Water passes through a water garden – planted with Cape pondweed (*Aponogeton distachyos*), dwarf papyrus (*Cyperus papyrus*), water lilies and rush species – which removes impurities before the water is pumped into the pool and out over a waterfall.

The Bridle Road Residence was heralded at the American Society of Landscape Architect Professional Awards of 2010 as 'very thoughtful'. More than being thoughtful, however, it is also exceedingly beautiful – and it is proof that modern landscaping need not disturb prehistoric biodiversity.

1 — The house, garden and pool nestle into a ravine with views across the Table Mountain vegetation to Cape Town and the Atlantic Ocean.
2 — The view from the pool towards the house shows the garden's use of fynbos, the fine shrubs native to the region.
3 — Amid the local vegetation, the design makes maximum use of typical local building materials, such as concrete steps and balau wood.

# Vergelegen

Somerset West, Western Cape,
South Africa

Willem Adriaan van der Stel,
Lady Florence Phillips, Cynthia Barlow,
Ian Ford, Margaret Roberts

18th, 20th & 21st century

10 hectares / 24.5 acres

Temperate Mediterranean

Edible / Formal / Modern / Plant
Collection / Rooms / Roses

Originally owned by the Dutch East India Company and begun as a farm and vineyard in 1700 by Willem Adriaan van der Stel, one of the young Cape Colony's earliest administrators, Vergelegen is now a renowned wine estate. Among the features dating from its original period are some historic trees, including five huge camphor trees, an ancient yellowwood (*Cladrastis kentukea*), a venerable mulberry and what is claimed to be the oldest oak in Africa. Van der Stel also laid out the Octagon Garden, now restored as the site of the Rose Garden.

The twentieth-century garden was created by a series of custodians. From 1917 to 1940 Lady Florence Phillips owned the garden. Her English gardener, William Hanson, helped to establish thriving shrubs, trees and herbaceous plantings. Lady Florence was followed by Cynthia Barlow, who developed the garden for nearly fifty years. She founded a camellia collection, which was augmented in the 1990s to create a dedicated camellia show garden with some 1,000 plants covering 550 cultivars. In 2010 the collection was recognized by the International Camellia Society as a Garden of Excellence. The camellias, which offer a floral show from mid-spring to late summer, depending on species, are in three main areas; the most dramatic is accessed across a swing bridge over the Lourens River, which runs through the estate.

In 1987 the Vergelegen estate was sold to the company Anglo American, for which the landscape architect Ian Ford designed a series of enclosed gardens, now numbering eighteen. The Octagon Garden was restored and is now home to the David Austin Rose Garden, a collection of fragrant Old English rose varieties, enclosed by a rosemary hedge. There is also a formal Hybrid Tea Rose Garden of 1,200 rose plants arranged in eighteen formal beds.

Other massed plantings include white arums in the restored wetland, and clivias and agapanthus growing in the shade of established trees. The doyenne of South African herb growers, Margaret Roberts, designed a Herb and Vegetable Garden in 1993.

1 — The borders of the front garden are filled with agapanthus.
2 — Vergelegen is home to a series of huge trees that date back to the founding of the original estate.
3 — The Rose Garden holds some 1,200 rose plants arranged in eighteen formal beds.
4 — The light of sunset falls on the distant mountains behind the stables – now home to a restaurant – and the Herb Garden.

# Kirstenbosch National Botanical Garden

Cape Town, South Africa

| |
|---|
| Harold Pearson |
| 20th century |
| 36 hectares / 89 acres (garden); 528 hectares / 1,305 acres (park) |
| Temperate Mediterranean |
| Botanical / Informal / Naturalistic |

Kirstenbosch is one of the world's great botanic gardens, not only for its setting on the eastern slopes of Table Mountain, but also for its history. Founded in 1913, it was the world's first garden set up for the express purpose of preserving and displaying a regional flora. Today more than 7,000 taxa, or types of plant, are cultivated at Kirstenbosch, one of South Africa's nine national botanic gardens.

Kirstenbosch owes its creation to two men: Cecil Rhodes and Professor Harold Pearson. The imperialist Rhodes bequeathed what was formerly a run-down farm to the nation in 1902. Pearson established the garden in the following decade, taking an unpaid position as the garden's first director.

With occasional exceptions, the garden is still planted entirely with species from the Cape floral kingdom, a shrubland vegetation known as fynbos. The outdoor flora is complemented, within a conservatory, by collections from other regions, including the Karoo and the Namib Desert, featuring that strangest of plants, *Welwitschia mirabilis* – the sole member of its genus.

Snaking paths lead the visitor past highlights, including the spectacular Protea Garden on the Fynbos Walk and the 'living fossils' in the Cycad Garden in the Dell, the oldest part of the garden. The Peninsula Garden is a reminder that the Cape Peninsula alone is home to in excess of 2,500 plant species, more than the whole of Great Britain. Noteworthy among the non-indigenous species are the remnants of a hedge of wild almonds planted in the 1660s to mark the perimeter of the Dutch Cape Colony, and the avenue of camphor trees planted in the nineteenth century in honour of Queen Victoria.

Beyond the cultivated garden, the scenery of the park is more natural but no less dramatic. A trail ascends the Skeleton Gorge ravine to the summit of Table Mountain, and a path leads through forests to Constantia Nek, a low pass leading to Hout Bay.

1—Table Mountain rises behind the gardens, which are home to 450 species of tree and renowned collections of succulents.
2—Robinson pincushion (*Leucospermum pluridens*), a near-threatened species, blooms vigorously in the garden.
3, 4—Kirstenbosch has rich collections of aloe; the succulents are native to Africa and occur in numerous species.
5—Yellow parachute daisy, *Ursinia calenduliflora*, blue *Centaurea cyanus* and white *Osteospermum* bring splashes of colour to the characteristic fynbos vegetation.
6—The cycads of the Dell are 'living fossils'; cycads have changed little since the Jurassic period.
7—The avenue of camphor trees planted by Cecil Rhodes shades herbaceous perennials and ferns.

# The Rock Garden, Magaliesberg

Gauteng, South Africa

| |
|---|
| Geoffrey Armstrong, Wendy Vincent |
| 21st century |
| 0.8 hectares / 2 acres |
| Humid Subtropical |
| Artistic / Dry / Rock / Sculpture |

Land art, or the large-scale sculpting of earth as popularized in the 1970s by such art-school trained practitioners as Richard Long and Robert Smithson, has had little effect on horticulture. But here in Magaliesberg, a small town about an hour's drive from Johannesburg, the artist couple Geoffrey Armstrong and Wendy Vincent have created a wooded, watery, sculpted garden that spans horticulture, landscaping and the kind of work Long and Smithson pioneered forty years ago.

The garden at Magaliesberg has no formal name and is not officially open to visitors. Vincent, a painter, and Armstrong, a sculptor, live here for about eight months of each year, and it is difficult to say where their house ends and the grounds begin. The couple say they began work here, in a humid ravine, around the turn of the century, and have continued to cultivate it ever since, as an aside from their formal artistic practice. 'Cultivate' is perhaps the wrong word, however, since they have cut river courses, piled up stones into beguiling forms, worked in concrete and added wooden sculptures in strange, vernacular forms. Vincent has painted out a garden plan, yet this plan evolves as the garden changes.

Despite the apparent exoticism, most of the species here are indigenous. Plants have been donated to the couple, and they also take part in Operation Wildflower, a countrywide association of plant-lovers who save rare species threatened by development, and replant them in their own properties. There are acacia trees, haemanthus, eucomis, and stapelias, although the most striking plants are the charismatic giant aloes.

Yet the Magaliesberg rock garden is no fantasy land or idle folly. In botanical and artistic terms, it is a product both of the environment and of lives lived around the land. As the architecture critic Pattabi G Raman put it, 'This type of work cannot be executed anywhere else, not because of any technical concerns but quite simply on the grounds of appropriateness and authenticity.' It is a distinctly African garden, though a unique one, even within the continent.

1, 2—On the way to the main terrace, is a display of rocks and succulents, including numerous *Aloe peglerae*. Beyond is the 'Stairway to Paradise', cut from a bluegum trunk and leading to a viewing platform, surrounded by various succulents including *Aloe castanea* (2, left).
3, 4—The natural sculptural shapes of many of the plants are echoed by artfully arranged structures of rocks collected from the garden and wooden sculptures created by Armstrong.
5—The garden is a great attraction for wildlife, such as this vervet monkey.
6—The pond is surrounded by an area of sculpted cairns, constantly modified by Armstrong and native animals.

# Abkhazi Garden

Victoria, British Columbia, Canada

Prince Nicholas Abkhazi, Princess Peggy Abkhazi, John Wade

20th century

0.6 hectares / 1.4 acres

Temperate Oceanic

Alpines / Rhododendrons / Rock / Rooms / Woodland

Like all great gardens, Abkhazi has mystery in abundance. Its entrance gives nothing away – the garden is hidden from the road by a hornbeam hedge.

Garden creator Marjorie (Peggy) Pemberton-Carter met exiled Georgian Prince Nicholas Abkhazi in Paris in the 1920s, beginning a relationship that survived a long separation during World War II. When Peggy bought the land in 1946, she was determined to celebrate its large rocky outcrops and mature trees when she created her garden. Later that year the couple were reunited and married, and thereafter they devoted forty years to turning the land into the garden they called their 'child'.

The first building on the site was the summerhouse, designed and positioned by the architect John Wade, who also advised on garden layout. The building perfectly suited its location, providing a focal point. From its porch are the best views of the garden and the wider landscape of the Strait of San Juan de Fuca and the Olympic Mountains.

Peggy Abkhazi, who grew up in Shanghai, saw this garden as being like a Chinese scroll: as it is unrolled, its contents are revealed in a series of views within and beyond the garden that lure visitors on to discover new areas, with different moods and character. Guests started their tour in the Rhododendron Woodland Garden, just as visitors today begin their visit. Native Oregon oaks (*Quercus garryana*) shade a collection of species and hybrid rhododendrons, some of which were fifty years old when they were planted; their trunks now resemble living sculptures. Flowering of this upper canopy begins in midwinter and continues to early summer. Swathes of bulbs and woodland flowers make a rich carpet of spring colour, including wood anemones, cyclamen and erythronium. In summer, ferns, hostas and the giant Himalayan lily (*Cardiocrinum giganteum*) take over.

Paths play a key role in the garden, and its design also ensured that long views were framed to best advantage. As a result, the site appears much larger than it actually is.

1—This memorable view of lawn and a heather-lined path at the base of a rocky outcrop is known as the Yangtze River because it reminded Peggy Abkhazi of the landscape near her former home in China.
2—A view from the highest point of the garden shows how pockets in the rock have been dammed to create pools.
3—An old oak tree towers over a lower part of the garden. A stunning, low-growing Japanese maple provides rich colour in the foreground.
4—Rhododendrons line a path leading to the summerhouse, a focal point of the garden.
5—Ferns and hostas thrive in the moist, shady conditions in a secluded walk of azaleas and rhododendrons.

# Butchart Gardens

Victoria, British Columbia, Canada

| | |
|---|---|
| Jennie Butchart | |
| 20th century | |
| 22 hectares / 55 acres | |
| Temperate Oceanic | |
| Alpines / Bedding / Rock / Rooms | |

The remarkable Butchart Gardens – designated a National Historic Site by the Canadian government in 2004 – had their origins in the impulse of a non-gardener, Jennie Butchart, who was moved to act when her husband's cement company abandoned a rubble-filled limestone quarry. Butchart is said to have told him: 'We've made it ugly. Now let's make it beautiful again. Let's put some flowers in there.' Over a period of two years, the 2-hectare (5-acre), 23-metre-deep (75-foot) quarry was cleared, topsoil brought in and plants chosen. As the quarry floor started to bloom, Butchart realized that the bare walls needed softening. Soon she was dangling over the quarry edge on a bosun's chair, planting ivy and dribbling seeds of alpine plants into crevices.

The Quarry Garden was only the beginning. Between 1906 and 1939, Butchart laid out four more areas as a series of 'rooms' following the popular pre-World War I landscape style. A formal Rose Garden with pergolas smothered in climbing and rambling roses was joined by a sunken Italian Garden, filled with statuary and dominated by a pool and fountain. At the foot of that garden, the twelve-pointed Star Pond was interplanted with annuals. Beyond that, a traditional Japanese Garden features paths leading through terrain dominated by moss, bamboo and Japanese maple. Today these speciality 'rooms' have been joined by a Bog Garden and a Mediterranean Garden, which features drought-resistant plants from all over the world.

A million bedding plants – showcasing more than 900 common and rare varieties – provide a stunning floral display from early spring until mid-autumn. Deep red camellias, towering, sky-blue delphiniums, baskets of pink fuchsias and yellow tuberous begonias all thrive in the moderate climate. One of the most popular rarities, the fussy Himalayan blue poppy (*Meconopsis baileyi*), is a feature in the Japanese Garden. Butchart was one of the first North American gardeners to grow it successfully.

The gardens have been passed down through the Butchart family, who have maintained the original exuberant plantings, keeping alive Jennie Butchart's horticultural joie de vivre.

1, 4—The Sunken Garden was laid out in a former quarry; the stairs from the top give fine views over the floral display.
2—The Italian Garden features a fountain with a Florentine sculpture, reflecting the formal nature of this part of the garden.
3—Autumn foliage of Japanese maples in all colours makes a stunning backdrop for a stone lantern by a pond in the Japanese Garden.

# Jardins de Métis/ Reford Gardens

Grand-Métis, Québec, Canada

| |
|---|
| Elsie Reford |
| 20th century |
| 16.1 hectares / 40 acres |
| Humid Continental |
| Borders / Festival / Naturalistic / Plant Collection / Sculpture / Vistas |

Imagine creating a garden hundreds of kilometres from the nearest nursery. That is what Elsie Reford did at her summer retreat on the Gaspé Peninsula, where she designed a garden from scratch in 1926 at the age of fifty-four. Today it is both a beautiful garden and an international centre for garden design and art.

Reford laid out the gardens over a decade, and devoted the rest of her life to honing her skill in plant propagation and cultivation. The stream running through the site provided the basis for the design, and Reford used local stone to build walls to stabilize the steep slopes. She learned through trial and error which plants were best suited to specific microclimates.

The gardens are revealed naturally as the visitor strolls along the paths. An avenue of dwarf mountain pine (*Pinus mugo*) frames vistas down to the water, and tantalizing glimpses of the rivers shine through mature shelter-belt planting in other areas. The gardens appear to have been carved out of the surrounding forests.

Reford acquired exotic plants from all over the globe, and her collections of natives and exotics were among the largest in North America. Himalayan blue poppy (*Meconopsis baileyi*) was at that time a rarity there, but Reford discovered that it thrived in the humidity and cold night air of the lower St Lawrence region. Now, Blue Poppy Glade is a haze of blooms in June and July. Reford's Long Walk is a very personal version of a traditional herbaceous border. Its mounded soil and straight path made from unusual paving slabs lure visitors towards a distant focal point with a view through the trees to the St Lawrence River.

Since 2000, the garden has been the venue of an international garden festival, based on that held at Chaumont in France (see page 264). The Canadian version is different, however, in that its show gardens or installations are integrated into the woodland, which helps to establish a synergy between the permanent garden and the transient displays. The combination of a range of garden styles with contemporary garden art is truly inspirational.

1, 2—Elsie Reford transformed the former fishing camp by creating terraced beds and paths along the stream and through the woodland, so that the garden blends into the natural topography of the site and plants are suited to the microclimates within it.
3—Distinctive concrete slabs make a die-straight path through mounded borders on the Long Walk.
4—Native forest rises behind a wild-flower meadow at the edge of what is now the site of the international garden festival.

3

4

5—Peter and Alissa North filled a grid
of Plexiglas tubes with organic and
non-organic material to create a garden
based on the idea of core samples, used
by the mining industry to determine the
geology of an area.
6—The US company Stoss Landscape
Urbanism, led by Chris Reed, used recycled
materials to create *Safe Zone*, a safe playing
environment for children.
7—Canadian designers Angela Iarocci,
Claire Ironside and David K Ross created
*Pomme de Parterre* around a sunken wooden
building using old potato varieties in beds
lined with nasturtiums and marigolds.
8—In *Réflexions colorées*, Hal Ingberg
enclosed part of the forest in a triangle
of semi-reflective glass that subtly alters
viewers' perception of the environment.

6

7

8

# Les Quatre Vents

Québec, Canada

Francis Cabot

20th century

15 hectares / 37 acres

Humid Continental

Formal / Landscape / Rooms

Northern Québec is an unexpected place to find one of Canada's largest and most glorious gardens. Snow can begin here in mid-autumn and last until late spring, and temperatures vary from lows of -30°C (-22°F) to highs of 30°C (86°F). Yet Les Quatre Vents is a world-class garden of striking variety.

In 1965 the New York financier Francis Cabot inherited an estate overlooking the tidal reaches of the St Lawrence River. Gradually he began to expand the existing Arts and Crafts garden with a series of remarkable additions: a Chinese moon bridge, an Indian gate, a Swedish music pavilion, a French *pigeonnier*, a Japanese garden with authentic teahouse, a bridge inspired by the Greek Temple of the Four Winds, a Rose Garden, a White Garden, a Potager, a Stream Garden, a ravine traversed by rope bridges, formal allées, deep herbaceous borders and glorious primula glades. The features are stitched together and anchored to the landscape with hedges of native thuja, avenues of paper birch and cedar log fences that zigzag in the local style.

This is a garden of wit as well as sophistication: the Guest Garden contains topiary sofas of thuja, while the kitchen opens on to the Baker's Garden, where topiary loaves of bread sit around a bread oven. Deeper into the garden visitors entering the *pigeonnier* are magically serenaded by French crooner Charles Trenet's song 'Un Jardin Extraordinaire' (1957). From the Mosaic Terrace beyond, visitors who turn left are engulfed with excerpts from Schubert's 'Trout' quintet played by a quartet of life-sized copper frogs, while those moving to the right trip the sounds of a Dixieland jazz band. The swans on the nearby lake are trained to hover within the framework of trees, while the picturesque Highland cattle that graze in a field beyond the garden often pose beside an ancient stone, which rises like a prehistoric lingam.

Despite its formal glories, one of the delights of this incomparable garden is the meadow, which, as the snow recedes, fills with wild flowers before becoming a midsummer sea of lupins.

1—Swans glide on the dark waters of the lake, which reflect the French-styled *pigeonnier* at the back of the garden.
2—Cabot designed the Moon Bridge to create an elegant oval with its reflection in the water.
3—Cedars clipped into the shapes of loaves of bread flank the outdoor oven in the Baker's Garden.
4—Poppies and lupins fill a meadow in front of one of the garden buildings.
5—A tall wooden arch frames a view of a standing stone outside the garden.
6—A frog quartet plays Dixieland jazz, with an accompanying soundtrack for visitors.

3

4

5

6

# Annapolis Royal Historic Gardens

Annapolis Royal,
Nova Scotia, Canada

| | |
|---|---|
| Community gardeners | |
| 20th century | |
| 6.9 hectares / 17 acres | |
| Humid Continental | |
| Bedding / Historic / Informal / Roses | |

These gardens are not just a masterclass in horticultural techniques: they have a more complex message. Annapolis Royal was the first permanent European settlement in North America (1605), and the gardens were designed to celebrate the rich heritage of the town by representing the region's different eras and influences.

Although the gardens are relatively modest in scale, their setting above a tidal river valley provides considerable character. Early European settlement is reflected in an atmospheric re-creation of a seventeenth-century Acadian house set within a productive garden of vegetables and orchard tree cultivars selected through archival research. From the house the view reveals the pattern of dykes in the fertile salt marshes beyond, which reflect the reclamation of the lowland by early settlers for their crops. The dykes allow the visitor to walk beyond the ornamental gardens into the wilder, riverine environment. Behind the re-created settlement, mature trees form an excellent foil and lead the visitor into a richly planted Woodland Garden.

Elsewhere, the Governor's Garden represents eighteenth-century influences and is filled with a wide range of herbs and herbaceous plants, while the Victorian Garden references the plant and technological discoveries of the nineteenth century, with seasonal bedding designs of brightly coloured annuals and other exotic introductions. In late spring visitors are greeted by an eye-catching cascade of yellow laburnum flowers hanging down from a pergola. Azaleas provide a blazing display in the Woodland Garden, where a rich mix of aquatic and moisture-loving plants with architectural foliage thrive around a series of ponds. The Rose Garden houses an extensive collection, with more than 270 different varieties growing in informal beds linked by winding paths.

The gardens do not only look back. In the Innovative Garden visitors learn about sustainable approaches for their own gardens, and how to grow food crops in limited spaces. The whole garden thus looks to the future as well as reflecting the richness of the past.

1—The symmetrical beds and vibrant colours of the Victorian Garden reflect the tastes of the nineteenth century.
2—The potager outside the replica Acadian Cottage is based on seventeenth-century diaries.
3—The spectacular Rose Collection has more than 270 cultivars, ranging from the historic to modern hybrids.
4—In autumn, the foliage makes a spectacular display of colours.
5, 6—Rhododendron, laburnum and daylilies (*Hemerocallis*) all add colour to the gardens in the spring and summer.

356

# Tangled Garden

Grand-Pré, Nova Scotia, Canada

Beverly McClare, George Walford, Nina Newington

20th century

1.9 hectares / 5 acres

Humid Continental

Edible / Naturalistic / Sculpture

The Tangled Garden is a magical place that allows the visitor to experience both an artistic vision and a productive landscape. Beverly McClare, the driving force behind the garden, was inspired to purchase the site by its venerable quince (*Cydonia oblonga*), a tree that offered both character and fruit. This combination of the aesthetic and productive is the key element of the garden's philosophy. Fresh herbs and fruits are transformed into jellies, liqueurs and cordials in a building that is integrated into the garden's design.

The entrance to the garden is defined by an elegantly weeping beech (*Fagus sylvatica* 'Pendula'). Visitors pass under a pergola draped with a wisteria and flanked by the old quince tree, which forms its own grove. Inside the garden, a potting shed welcomes visitors to see work in progress, while small garden spaces run seamlessly together, full of incident and diverse plants. The veranda of the house offers a chance to enjoy the atmosphere while providing vistas through the garden.

Following the garden paths reveals plant associations and contemporary sculptures that are incorporated so that they both complement the planting and are enhanced by it. What appears to be a dry riverbed, banked on either side by bold groupings of towering herbaceous perennials and statuesque grasses, acts as a path leading to a pond. Woven among such features are areas of herbs and soft and stone fruit, blurring the line between the productive and ornamental gardens. Rows of bronze fennel (*Foeniculum vulgare* 'Purpureum') form a transparent curtain for the plants beyond, offering a sense of mystery.

At the highest point of the garden, the terrain has been sculpted into tiers, on top of which a labyrinth provides a meditative walk while offering views of the Minas Basin. On an earthwork bank, sea buckthorn (*Hippophae rhamnoides*) has been established both as a screen and to produce fruit for the kitchen. A personal vision has created a strong sense of identity for a garden with a distinctive character, which reminds the visitor of the productive nature of the land: slow food in a soul-filled garden.

1—A path in the form of a dry riverbed leads past striking plant associations and contemporary sculptures.
2—There are constant reminders that there is a productive garden woven into the more ornamental features.
3—Formality and relaxed planting are mixed in this varied garden. Clipped hedges and timber-edged raised beds combine with abundant herbs.
4—The potting shed with its cool verandah is a welcome source of shade and a central feature of the garden.

# Lawa'i Kai

(Allerton Garden)

Lawai Bay, Kauai,
Hawaii, USA

| | |
|---|---|
| Robert Allerton, John Gregg Allerton | |
| 20th century | |
| 32.5 hectares / 80 acres | |
| US Zones 12a–12b | |
| Coastal / Naturalistic / Rooms / Water | |

Allerton Gardens combine a royal pedigree with dramatic mid-twentieth-century garden design. Created in the later nineteenth century, the gardens, which are traditionally known as Lawa'i Kai, were created as a retreat overlooking Lawai Bay by Emma, queen consort to King Kamehameha IV of Hawaii. The building thought to have been the queen's residence has been moved to the valley floor and renovated.

The current garden was the creation and passion of Robert Allerton and his long-time partner – and, thanks to a loophole in Illinois law, his adopted son – the architect John Gregg Allerton. Robert Allerton purchased the property in 1938 and the pair began to develop a garden when they moved permanently to Kauai in the 1940s. They exploited the dramatic possibilities offered by the topography of the rising valley walls, and created a series of rooms and habitats that include open meadows, moist, shady ravines and rugged cliff faces. Water is also a dominant theme, not just in the shape of the natural stream but also in elegant pools and burbling waterfalls and fountains. The most noteworthy of all the water features is the long, narrow, sinuous water chain headed by a mermaid sculpture.

The gardens showcase a broad range of tropical species, incorporating Hawaiian plants and those from other Pacific islands and tropical Asia. While the planting is mainly ornamental, the garden also features a number of distinct collections, including members of the order Zingiberales, which includes heliconias, calatheas, spiral gingers and torch gingers. The Palmetum exhibits species of native and exotic palms, and elsewhere groves of golden bamboos rub shoulders with tropical fruit trees, cordylines, ferns and plumerias, while the cutting garden is a riot of blooms. Perhaps the most famous residents of the garden are the 'Jurassic trees', Moreton Bay figs (*Ficus macrophylla*) with huge buttress roots that featured in the film *Jurassic Park* (1993).

Despite its European overtones, this is very much a Hawaiian garden, as reflected in the respect for – and careful manipulation of – the natural beauty of the site, which melds with an effervescence of tropical planting typical of the islands.

1—Coconut palms shade the lawn looking out over the Pacific Ocean and private beach in front of the house.
2—A latticed pavilion overlooks the Diana Fountain: most of the garden's statuary comes from the Allertons' trips to Europe.
3—Giant anthuriums border a stream that cascades down a hillside; the sound of running water is audible almost everywhere.
4—The Mermaid Fountain empties into a wavy water chain against a tropical backdrop of massed Lady palms (*Rhapis excelsa*).

# Bloedel Reserve

Bainbridge Island,
Washington State, USA

Prentice Bloedel, Virginia Bloedel,
Thomas Church, Richard Haag,
Fujitaro Kubota

20th century

60.7 hectares / 150 acres

US Zone 8b

Informal / Japanese / Landscape /
Naturalistic / Rooms / Woodland

In one sense, Bloedel Reserve is just a
small step from wilderness. In another,
it is a highly refined garden. Whatever
one's view, this is a garden where art
and nature have been fused to produce
a strong emotional response.

Prentice Bloedel and his wife, Virginia,
bought the property on Bainbridge Island
in 1951 and added areas of wilderness
over the following decades. They set out
to blend the natural with the artificial
using as light a hand as possible, while
also capturing the essence of the
Japanese garden.

Visitors enter Bloedel via paths that
curve through meadows before moving
on into marsh and woodlands. Raised
boardwalks allow visitors to hover above
lush groundcover while appreciating the
upper canopy of shade-making trees
and shrubs. The woodland undergrowth
is species-rich – the plant communities
provide a habitat for wildlife and birds
– but is so lightly managed that it
appears totally natural.

There is a more formal landscape
around the house, where the renowned
Californian landscape architect Thomas
Church designed terraces, steps and
patios scored with diagonal lines and
geometric patterns. A fabulous view
over Puget Sound is framed by perfectly
placed groups of trees, while mown
lawn sweeps towards the water with
longer, meadow-style grass at the
margins shaping it into a river of green.

Conditions in the Glen are perfect
for masses of rhododendrons to thrive;
in spring, they are accompanied by
thousands of bulbs and wild flowers.
Fujitaro Kubota designed the main part
of the Japanese Garden. Its stone-and-
gravel area holds the eye inside the
space, but the design also highlights
the views beyond. The Guest House is a
fusion of a Japanese teahouse with a
Pacific Northwest Native American
longhouse. All the essential elements of
garden-making – sky, earth, grass, trees
and water – are combined in perfect
proportions to make the Reflection
Garden, a place for quiet contemplation
of the sublime surrounding gardens.

1—A boardwalk zigzags above the wetland
vegetation while also allowing visitors to
view the tree canopy overhead.
2—A trail leads past the white-trunked
Himalayan birches into the Birch Garden
and the Glen.
3—Clipped English yews (*Taxus baccata*)
create a green room in the Reflection
Garden, where the pool was designed to
hold groundwater at its natural level.
4, 5—The Japanese Garden, designed by
Fujitaro Kubota, has meandering stroll
paths, a traditional rock and gravel garden,
with conifers and Japanese maples that
display bold colours in the autumn.

1

# Chase Garden

Orting, Washington State, USA

Ione Chase, Emmott Chase,
Rex Zumwalt

20th century

1.8 hectares / 4.5 acres

US Zones 8a–8b

Japanese / Meadow / Naturalistic /
Rock / Woodland

Chase Garden is situated in a spectacular location on a high bluff overlooking the Puyallup River valley and has stunning views of the snow-covered peak of Mount Rainier. The garden and house – now managed by The Garden Conservancy – were the creation of the long-time owners, Emmott and Ione Chase, who devoted more than forty years of their lives to transforming land that had once been a logging area into one of the finest examples of a mid-twentieth-century garden in the Pacific Northwest.

The Japanese-inspired ponds and bridges that surround the house display characteristic attention to detail, such as meandering pebble pathways, thoughtfully placed rocks, reflecting ponds and dwarf conifers that hug the wooden benches and walkways. A *lanai* (roofed patio) at one end of the house marks the Chases' favourite spot from which to view the garden. Sheltered from the sun, the viewer can contemplate red-flowering bergenia and moss-covered rocks.

Moving away from the house, the design becomes looser, taking its cues from the native terrain. A sweeping Rock Garden, inspired by walks on Mount Rainier, is filled with a colourful display of plants such as *Aquilegia vulgaris*, *Armeria maritima* and dwarf wallflower (*Erysimum*). A naturalistic Woodland Garden extends under the old Douglas firs and has been cleared of bracken, ferns and blackberries to encourage early native spring ephemerals such as large drifts of trilliums, erythroniums and vanilla leaf (*Achlys triphylla*) – a hard-to-grow but delightful native groundcover plant. A 900-kilogram (2,000-pound), locally quarried sandstone bench installed by Emmott Chase is surrounded by *Maianthemum racemosum*, a herbaceous perennial whose blooms smell like lily-of-the-valley. The garden is also home to an impressive collection of Japanese maples, rhododendrons and a variety of conifers, including Douglas firs – a particular favourite of Emmott and Ione Chase.

1—Reflecting pools, gravel and rocks from the Cascade Range give a Japanese character to the Entrance Garden, designed by Rex Zumwalt in the 1960s and planted with low-growing thyme and penstemons.
2—The garden has an impressive collection of rhododendron and Japanese maple; thrift (*Armeria maritima*) has naturalized in the grass in the foreground.
3—One of the garden's few geometrical shapes, the Badminton Lawn is surrounded by junipers and rhododendron, with white *Maianthemum racemosum* flowering behind the bench.
4—A path leads past a colourful display of *Aquilegia* spp., thrift and yellow sedum.

# Sustainability Garden at Turtle Bay

Redding, California, USA

| |
|---|
| Lutsko Associates, Trilogy Architects |
| 21st century |
| 4 hectares / 10 acres |
| US Zone 7b |
| Grasses / Native / Sustainable / Water |

For those behind the garden at Turtle Bay the key word is, as the name suggests, sustainability. But other words are just as important: elegance, simplicity and power. The simple architecture – sinuous walls and wide terraces – echoes the broad plantings. A pyramid with a water staircase provides a focal point, and the rills and spills punctuating the stone paths underline the garden's soft power.

Part of the much larger environment of Turtle Bay, the Sustainability Garden is largely – but not exclusively – filled with native Californian plants, mainly ornamental grasses. There are, in essence, three habitats: the streamside plantings, an oak savanna grassland and a chaparral (heathland) mound.

The pyramidal mound is planted with the beautiful blue grass *Festuca idahoensis* 'Siskiyou Blue' and whiteleaf manzanita (*Arctostaphylos viscida*). It is a simple yet dramatic design where the blue of the grasses contrasts with and complements the red stems and white flowers of the manzanita against the golden stone and grey-blue concrete. The grasses soften the hard stone and walls, and their fluid motion continues and echoes the flow of water in the cascade that flows down the mound.

Three species of Californian oak – canyon oak (*Quercus chrysolepis*), blue oak (*Q. douglasii*) and valley oak (*Q. lobata*) – create the garden's acclaimed oak savanna. The trees dance in golden grassland comprising a mix of grasses, annuals and perennials. The sweet blue-and-white lupin (*Lupinus nanus*) brightens the three species of needle grass (*Nassella*) and the lovely California onion grass (*Melica californica*). A Californian garden would not be complete without the Californian poppy (*Eschscholzia californica*), with its orange flowers in late winter and spring, and yellow mariposa lily (*Calochortus luteus*) with its soft golden tones, and both grow abundantly here.

The Sustainability Garden has the power of restrained planting and striking architecture. It is a place in which a gardener can bend to focus on the small flowers growing in a modern meadow and, at the same time, stand up, look at the sky and breathe. It is a striking twenty-first-century garden.

1, 3—The rill meanders like a natural stream through paving surrounded by tussocks of grass that soften the effect of the hardscaping.
2—Water tumbles down the staircase in the middle of the pyramid mound, planted with blueish *Festuca idahoensis* 'Siskiyou Blue'.
4—Grass tussocks rise in regular curved rows up the bank above the stream, creating an impression of formality in contrast with the chaparral beyond.
5—Blue-and-white lupins bloom in the meadow at the foot of the pyramidal mound.

# Pool Garden at El Novillero

Sonoma County, California, USA

| |
|---|
| Thomas Church |
| 20th century |
| 0.2 hectares / 0.5 acre |
| US Zone 9b |
| Minimalist / Sculpture / Water |

The garden that Thomas Church created for Dewey Donnell in 1947 is one of the most influential of the mid-twentieth century. Unashamedly abstract, it is also deeply rooted in the landscape. Church is credited with pioneering the California style, designing gardens that suited the lifestyles of his cosmopolitan West Coast clients. Rather than emulating conventional European-style gardens with lawns, clipped hedges and deep flower beds, Church provided basketball hoops, barbecue pits and swimming pools. At El Novillero he raised this functionalist formula to perfection. Set in the middle of a cattle ranch, out of sight of the house below, the garden sits on top of a ridge, with views of dry, rolling hills and the Sonoma River snaking in the distance.

At the heart of the design is a free-form pool whose shape was inspired by the meandering salt marshes of the river beyond. The pool is set into a concrete terrace, tinted earth-like ochre and etched with a grid pattern – a favourite of the Modernist movement – which anchors the pool to its setting. In the middle of the pool is a concrete sculpture by the artist Adaline Kent. Part-lounger, part-diving board, its anthropomorphic form humanizes the simple space. An island of lawn is also incorporated into the terrace, ornamented with three boulders from the site. These strange forms enhance the garden's abstract quality while further integrating it with the landscape. Church kept some old live oaks to lend an imprimatur of age, incorporating them into the terrace by using a chequerboard of wooden slats that blends with the grid pattern while allowing the trunks to expand. The oaks provide the only vertical element in the horizontal design; the shadow of their waving canopies animates the ground while echoing the form of lawn, boulders, sculpture and pool.

While some commentators see the influence of Cubism in El Novillero's intersecting, overlapping, curvilinear forms, the design might also have been inspired by camouflage motifs from World War II, then recently ended. One of the most significant designed landscapes of the twentieth century, El Novillero is frequently photographed and often described, but neither images nor words can convey the extraordinary stillness, serenity and sheer beauty of this seminal garden.

1—Thomas Church's signature curvilinear pool sits in a terrace of ochre concrete; the sculpture by San Francisco artist Adaline Kent is both a lounger and a diving board.
2, 3—Live oak grows through removable decking on the terrace and surrounds the garden. Church's quintessential Californian garden integrated places to barbeque, entertain, relax and swim, with easy transitions between indoors and outdoors.

# Cornerstone

Sonoma County, California, USA

| |
|---|
| Chris Hougie and others |
| 21st century |
| 3.6 hectares / 9 acres |
| US Zone 8b |
| Festival / Modern / Sculpture |

Cornerstone Gardens is an ever-changing gallery of gardens by the world's leading designers, but the man behind it all is Chris Hougie, who was inspired by the Chaumont International Garden Festival (see page 264) to inaugurate in 2004 the first gallery-style exhibition of gardens in the United States. With individual gardens or installations lasting anything from a season to several years, the process of natural growth and decay is the same as in any 'traditional' garden, and offers the opportunity for revivification and evolution. What makes Cornerstone different is that the changing series of walk-through gardens showcase designs from the world's finest landscape architects and designers, including Pamela Burton, Andy Cao, Xavier Perrot, James van Sweden and Sheila A Brady. Visitors enjoy unique visions of modern, conceptual landscape that draw on global influences to surprise and entertain but also to inspire reflection.

Martha Schwartz's 'Usual Suspects' was a profession in-joke, with an industry leader symbolized by each hole on a crazy-golf course. A moving garden is 'Small Tribute to Immigrant Workers' by Mario Schjetnan, which is inspired by Mexicans who leave home to find work. In a similar vein, 'Red Lantern' by Andy Cao and Xavier Perrot references the history of Chinese immigrants. Both gardens share themes of migration, diaspora and assimilation.

Topher Delaney's allegorical 'Garden Play' poses the question, 'What is a garden?' Its whiteness nods to Sissinghurst (see page 174), yet it questions whether a garden can be a commodity. A barcode sculpture suggests consumerism, while the garden's beauty and performance challenge a garden's function.

Cornerstone lies only 5 kilometres (3 miles) from the renowned garden at El Novillero (see opposite). Both that garden and its designer, Thomas Church – who first decreed that 'Gardens are for People' – have had an enormous influence on Cornerstone and the function its gardens fulfil.

1 — 'Garden Play' by Topher Delaney challenges perceptions of just what constitutes a garden.
2 — 'Red Lantern' by Andy Cao and Xavier Perrot commemorates the role of Chinese migrants in building the railways in the nineteenth century.
3 — Ron Lutsko, who helped to design the whole site, also created this dramatic courtyard garden with its olive trees.
4 — Suzanne Biaggi created 'Ecology of Place' to link the region's former wetlands with modern California's vineyards.
5 — In 'Small Tribute to Immigrant Workers' by Mario Schjetnan, a path of terracotta shards makes walking difficult, an echo of the immigrants' hard journey.

# Sea Ranch

Sonoma County, California, USA

| |
|---|
| Lawrence Halprin |
| 20th century |
| 1,820 hectares / 4,500 acres |
| US Zone 8b |
| Coastal / Landscape / Naturalistic |

In a groundbreaking example of collaboration between landscape design and the built environment, the 17.8-kilometre-long (11-mile) resort community of Sea Ranch was created beginning in the 1960s with close attention to preserving the site's natural beauty. A former sheep ranch on the bluffs of the Pacific Ocean, the site was a perfect getaway for residents of San Francisco, with its dramatic cliffs, beaches and hiking terrain. It would attract all manner of wildlife, from sea lions to cormorants and mountain lions, especially when it was encouraged to return to its pre-livestock state.

The landscape designer Lawrence Halprin had been an apprentice with Thomas Church (author of the classic *Gardens Are for People*), and credited his penchant for environmental concerns and human-scale design to the three years he spent on a kibbutz. Through restrictive covenants and a design manual that uses the word 'suburban' as wholly negative, Sea Ranch's nature-first aesthetic dictated that houses be clustered against cypress windbreaks, leaving meadows and the shoreline available for common use and giving every resident ocean views. The unassuming residences were built with slanting roofs and sidings made of redwood or cedar, while the owners' association discouraged details that would distract from the surroundings, such as contrasting window frames or reflective metal flashing, tall fencing and – most suburban of all – mown lawns. Design constraints for landscape were equally specific. The approved plant list favours indigenous plant material and discourages the use of massing, geometric patterns, and eye-catching or overly fragrant plants. Common native accent plants throughout Sea Ranch include hairy manzanita, coyote bush, lupin and – inevitably – the coastal California poppy (*Eschscholzia californica*).

Cul-de-sacs and mini-palazzos have found their way into the community after fifty years, but the southern portion of the property has largely adhered to the original plan. Visitors are at one with the wind-sculpted pines and are part of something as inspiring as it is austere. In a later essay, Halprin tellingly admitted: 'Our most difficult task was to find a way for people to inhabit this magnificent and natural system in numbers without destroying the very reason for people to come here.'

1, 2, 3—The whole concept of Sea Ranch embodies Halprin's philosophy of 'living lightly on the land', incorporating local vegetation, limiting the nature of plants that could be introduced to gardens and using building regulations to forbid all but unassuming residences constructed in local materials.

# Ruth Bancroft Garden

Walnut Creek, California, USA

| |
|---|
| Ruth Bancroft, Lester Hawkins |
| 20th century |
| 1.2 hectares / 3 acres |
| US Zones 9b–10a |
| Cactus / Drought Tolerant / Informal / Succulents |

From the road, there is little sign of the vibrant showcase of drought-tolerant planting on the other side of the Ruth Bancroft Garden fence. Ruth and Philip Bancroft, Jnr, moved there in the 1940s. but it was not until 1971 that Ruth took over part of the adjacent former fruit farm. She created a new garden for her large collection of succulents, which were outgrowing the lath houses and greenhouses where they were tended.

Ruth had established a garden around the house from 1950 onwards, planting bearded irises, roses, herbs, alpines and perennials. But the discovery of *Aeonium* 'Glenn Davidson' in the same decade fired her enthusiasm for succulents and cacti. Today the garden is a fine example of a gardener's garden, a collector's collection.

The garden design is informal. Lester Hawkins, a local landscape designer and plantsman, helped to lay out the beds, where soil was mounded to ensure good growing conditions and drainage. Hawkins also designed a simple modern structure that casts shade in the hot summers. Philip Bancroft built the distinctive traditional timber structure at the garden entrance.

Apart from these features, planting takes centre stage. Winding paths invite visitors to explore the diversity of plant shape and form, with space left to allow the appreciation of plants with a strong architectural shape. The upper canopy includes majestic native 300-year-old valley oaks (*Quercus lobata*), with trees and shrubs from regions with similar dry climates, such as mesquite or palo verde. Mid and lower planting layers add a range of foliage colour and texture all year round, but these are thrown into different relief by flower colour and by changes in light and shade.

Splashes of colourful blooms add drama. Aloes, gasterias and haworthias bear flowers at the hot end of the spectrum in late winter and early spring. Many drought-tolerant plants are dormant in summer: here, yuccas and agaves produce a later burst of colour.

The garden is a powerful example of the beauty of drought-tolerant planting. From a single succulent, it has evolved through the passion of its creator. Bancroft's vision will be preserved: the garden was the first site to be sponsored by The Garden Conservancy, which was set up to preserve significant private gardens.

1, 2—Many of the aloes with orange and red flowers bloom in the winter, keeping hummingbirds in the garden.
3, 4—Shape, texture and colour are artfully blended in mixed borders of cacti and succulents.

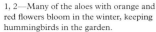

# Filoli

Woodside, California, USA

| |
|---|
| William Bowers Bourn, Bruce Porter, Isabella Worn, Lurline B Roth |
| 20th century |
| 6.5 hectares / 16 acres |
| US Zones 9b–10a |
| Bulbs / Formal / Italianate / Rooms / Walled |

Filoli takes its name from combining the first letters of each clause of its creator William Bowers Bourn's credo: 'Fight for a just cause; Love your fellow man; Live a good life.' Bourn created the garden as part of the surrounding landscape, retaining and framing natural features. The view north to Crystal Springs Lake reminded him of a family home in Ireland. To the west rise the foothills of the Santa Cruz Mountains, covered in native vegetation including oaks.

Filoli is a rich centrepiece to the landscape, with its blend of Italianate terraces and Sunken Garden, combined with the English overtones of the Walled and Woodland gardens. Seclusion and privacy were priorities in the garden's design. The long narrow site is divided into rooms by clipped hedges and walls.

The garden is organized around two long axes. One starts at the High Place, a classical yew theatre that once gave views to the lake. It leads down an avenue of Irish yews (*Taxus baccata* 'Fastigiata') to a brick path that crosses the Walled Garden. The other axis links the dining-room terrace along a brick path to the Walled, Rose and Cutting gardens. A network of secondary paths allows visitors to explore without retracing their steps.

Some of Filoli's many rooms were designed for horticultural display; others for leisure and recreation. Traditional and modern elements combine: a Knot Garden is given a contemporary twist; swirling low hedges and domes of box are neatly trimmed; olive trees are a reminder that the garden enjoys a Mediterranean climate. The terraces and Sunken Garden have colour-themed seasonal displays. Permanent plants include camellias, magnolias, rhododendrons and roses.

A marble plaque carved with the words *Festina lente* (Make haste slowly) hangs above an archway in a brick wall. (Its usual translation is 'more haste, less speed'.) The relaxed elegance of this immaculately maintained garden is a world away from the frenetic pace of life in nearby Silicon Valley.

1, 2—Different views of the Sundial Garden, with potted pink, purple and white petunias and daffodils encircling the sundial. The face of the dial is inscribed with the words 'Life began in a garden'.
3—Violas flower in the Chartres Cathedral Garden; 'Jersey Jem', a strain developed at Filoli from the heirloom *Viola cornuta* 'Jersey Gem', is a small-flowered purple or blue viola.
4—The High Place is a classical yew theatre. Dark, evergreen Irish yews enclose the rear of this space; it is the perfect viewing point down to the rest of the garden.
5—A clipped yew hedge surrounds the Sunken Garden, the first of the four main garden rooms: the pool at its centre houses hardy and tropical water lilies.

4

5

# Ackley Residence

Atherton, California, USA

| |
|---|
| Andrea Cochran |
| 21st century |
| 0.4 hectares / 1 acre |
| US Zone 9b–10a |
| Formal / Minimalist / Modern / Water |

The Ackley garden exemplifies Andrea Cochran's approach to garden design: spare geometry and a controlled palette of materials combined with vibrant planting. Cochran's major influences are Dan Kiley, Garrett Eckbo and James Rose, but the range of new materials and plant hybrids at her disposal reflects contemporary times. Blurring the boundaries is important to Cochran in every sense, both those of her gardens and the point where architecture and horticulture meet.

The entry garden at the Ackley Residence sets a tone of crisp detail: an avenue of lime trees ends at a dark monolithic wall, the whole surface of which is a fountain. The straight-trunked trees are planted in square planting holes with a mulch of dark stones to match the fountain wall.

In the rear garden, the view from the house is across a sleek terrace for dining and entertaining. Slim trees shade both house and seating area without obscuring views from inside the house. Ample space makes for sociable groupings of furniture and a slim fireplace built into a long wall.

In the sunken pool terrace, amid an L-shape of pale paving, the swimming pool doubles as a reflective surface. Five fountainheads pour streams from a low stone wall along one side; on the other is simple chaise seating. In this central area, a stately live oak spreads above the fountain wall and low mounds of box provide a single species groundcover.

Beyond, a backdrop of trees and taller shrubs might be the boundary or a foretaste of the next part of the garden – that line is blurred. Paths are highly directional – they make the garden appear 'endless' and focus on beautifully composed pictures or scenes within it. Although expansive, the garden exudes a sense of privacy and refuge. Planting is in tiers using just a few species. In some areas, linear planting reflects horizontal terrace walls. In others, loose domes of box add textural contrast as well as year-round greenery. Quality of materials and detailing are central to the success of this garden. Less is more, and yet the area is a real garden for real people.

1 — *Hydrangea paniculata* grows in box-edged beds that are a looser version of the formal hedged parterres of the past.
2 — An unobtrusive spa pool echoes the slim form of the swimming pool behind.
3 — Tiers of *Lavandula* spp. and *Lavandula angustifolia* 'Hidcote' maintain a subdued colour palette above a grey retaining wall.
4 — The allée of lime trees in front of the house ends in a stacked quartz fountain.
5 — Rows of lavender and box alternate in characteristic linear planting.

# Beach and Marsh Garden

Santa Barbara, California, USA

Isabelle Greene

21st century

US Zone 9b

Coastal / Gravel / Naturalistic / Sustainable

The Beach and Marsh Garden is a seamless fusion of designed space with the surrounding landscape, inspired by the location on a finger of land between sea and marsh. Designer Isabelle Greene has always been inspired by landscape, both the area around her commissioned projects and the observed scenery she records in her photography and artworks. For Greene, designing gardens is also all about movement – through the garden, of plants in a breeze, and of time – and the way it affects the experience of being in a garden. This garden has a great sense of motion: it reaches out to meet visitors before they arrive at the property and flows out towards the ocean behind it, appearing to merge into the beach.

When the garden is approached from the marsh side, low-growing bands of groundcover plants in glaucous hues – from steely greys through to frothy white – resemble ocean waves. These waves reach up a 'shoreline' of curving gravel paths that echoes the results of tidal ebb and flow. Dome-shaped shrubby plants punctuate the space in the manner of water-worn rocks, and real boulders define edges and corners.

The house sits above the entrance area, its main living space hovering 3 metres (10 feet) above garden and sea level. A silver-grey boardwalk forms a wide path with a gentle gradient that is also highly attractive. From the entrance, the boardwalk loops around the house and slithers through the rest of the garden down towards the beach. It links all major elements – marsh, house, garden and beach – in a curvilinear route that resembles another swirling wave. On the seaward side, planting is again low, with salt-tolerant specimens kept down by coastal winds. It appears as though seed has been scattered around the rock-encrusted berms or landforms, resulting in natural communities of coastal plants.

This garden has been designed with a light hand and with great skill. It has a tough beauty, to match the prevailing conditions. And it fully reflects Greene's approach as a landscape architect: 'I try to bring my love affair with this land into the tiny patches of earth entrusted to my design.'

1 — On the marsh side, low groundcover of silver greys and sparkling whites grows among meandering gravel paths seemingly the results of tidal ebb and flow.
2 — The boardwalk rises gently from the beach, looping up through the garden to the house, echoing waves lapping on the shore.
3 — Gravel paths break up soft bands of planting that is rugged enough to withstand strong salt-laden coastal winds and sandy soil conditions.

371

# Casa del Herrero

Montecito, California, USA

Ralph Stevens, Lockwood de Forest

20th century

4 hectares / 11 acres

US Zones 9b–10a

Formal / Islamic / Italianate

The garden at Casa del Herrero ('House of the Blacksmith') glows with a style, often now long lost, of what garden historians call the Golden Age of American gardens, a period that lasted from about 1895 to 1940. As with many gardens in southern California, Casa del Herrero offers a juxtaposition of plantings and a confluence of influences, but in this instance these are set against a backdrop of one of the finest examples of Spanish Colonial Revival architecture in the USA.

The large, whitewashed house, designed by the architect George Washington Smith and completed in 1925, was the home of George Fox Steedman, an industrialist, engineer and amateur architect. Steedman was deeply involved in the design not only of the house but also of the gardens, in partnership with noted garden creators Ralph Stevens and Lockwood de Forest.

The formal garden, along the major axis extending from the house, has a Beaux Arts design, with Moorish overtones added by brightly tiled walkways and decorated walls, fountains and rills. A little Italianate styling is thrown in for good measure. Other rooms open up off the formal garden, including the Rose Garden. Horticulturally, the collection of plants is splendidly diverse, from large palm trees to 'Iceberg' roses, orange trees and large cacti. What makes the varied collection so pleasing is the order of the geometrical design and the unfolding of the garden as it flows away from the house towards the dry, wilder Arizona Garden, which features cacti and succulents growing in a mulch of gravel.

The blue of agapanthus and the white of roses surround a blue-and-white tiled seating area. Orange trees with their stiff branches, fragrant flowers and fruits – of course – are softened by the violet flowers of *Hardenbergia violacea*, a twining vine of great beauty. Even the wildness of the Arizona Garden has refinement, dominated as it is by enormous specimens of dragon tree (*Dracaena draco*), originally from the Canary Islands.

1—White climbing roses on an arbour and an orange tree frame a view of the house, which is a renowned example of a well-preserved Spanish Colonial Revival residence.
2—The lavish tiling used in this seating area is inspired by the use of decorative tiles in both Moorish Spain and, later, Spanish Mexico.
3—The Islamic theme continues in the Formal Garden, where a pool in the shape of an eight-pointed star is just one of a series of centrally aligned water features.
4—Standard roses grow in parterres of neatly clipped box in the Rose Garden, another reflection of the Islamic influence.

3

4

# Lotusland

Santa Barbara, California, USA

| |
|---|
| Madame Ganna Walska and others |
| 20th century |
| 14.9 hectares / 37 acres |
| US Zone 9b |
| Cactus / Exotic / Plantsman / Water |

Lotusland is one of those gardens that makes one grateful for eccentrics who combine plentiful money with a passion for eclectic garden-making. The key words are eccentric and eclectic – and they refer as much to the flamboyant Polish wannabe opera singer Ganna Walska, who created the garden, as to the garden itself. She worked her way through six wealthy husbands before she bought the isolated, sun-parched Cuesta Linda estate in 1941 – her sixth marriage and operatic aspirations over. Renaming the estate Lotusland after the flowers blooming in one of its ponds, Walska dedicated forty-three years to creating this truly bizarre garden.

The original landscape was partly wooded, with groves of oaks as well as large specimen cedars, pines and *Araucaria bidwillii* planted in the 1880s. Walska modified this framework and integrated into it her characteristically unlikely changes. She made a floral clock and constructed an outdoor theatre, complete with a cast of grotesque dwarf figures brought from her French château. She also developed planting to reflect her passion for succulents and tropical plants with a bold form, making collections of cacti and euphorbias as well as bromeliads, palms and cycads that she planted in big, bold, primeval groups.

The three most remarkable gardens here are the Blue Garden (1950s and 1960s), the Aloe Garden (remade 1975) and the Cycad Garden (1978–9). The shady Blue Garden is a grove of blue Atlas cedars (*Cedrus atlantica* Glauca Group), Colorado spruce (*Picea pungens*) and Mexican blue palms (*Brahea armata*) underplanted with blue fescue grass (*Festuca glauca*). Through it winds a path lined with big lumps of glass slag.

Within the Aloe Garden more than 170 different types are planted in bold groups in a gently rolling landscape punctuated with black volcanic rocks. The pool at the centre of the garden is edged with abalone shells and water drips from a fountain constructed from giant tridacna clam shells set on a coral column. Similarly the Cycad Garden is a large collection of these primitive plants, divided into beds and arranged geographically, from Africa, Asia, Australia and Mexico.

1—The Aloe Garden includes more than 120 types of aloe, including *Aloe speciosa* (centre) and a tall *Beaucarnea stricta* (right).
2—To create the Water Garden, Madame Walska planted an old swimming pool with Asian lotus (*Nelumbo nucifera*), in a tribute to Eastern philosophy.
3—A cascade made from giant clam shells falls into a pool edged with abalone shells in the heart of the Aloe Garden.
4—The floral clockface is surrounded by a topiary menagerie.

5—Weeping *Euphorbia ingens* forms a
dramatic welcome at the end of the drive.
6—The new Cactus Garden was designed
by Eric Nagelmann in 1999 and contains
about 300 different species of cacti, grouped
by their country of origin.
7—In the Blue Garden, blue atlas cedars
and Chilean wine palms (*Jubaea chilensis*)
grow above blue *Festuca glauca* and *Senecio
mandraliscae*. The paths are lined with
blue-green glass.
8—Bulbous ponytail palms give this grove
an otherworldly atmosphere.
9—In the Fern Garden – created in 1968
around Madame Walska's collection of
Australian tree ferns – shade-loving ferns
and plants grow beneath coast live oak and
other trees.

5

# Huntington Botanical Gardens

San Marino, California, USA

Henry Huntington, William Hertrich

20th century

4 hectares / 10 acres (desert garden); 83 hectares / 207 acres (park)

US Zone 10a

Botanical / Cactus / Drought Tolerant / Historic / Japanese / Rose

The Huntington Gardens are home to one of the most extensive cultivated collections of botanical exploration in the world. The ranch acquired by the railway magnate and art collector Henry Huntington in 1903 covered nearly 240 hectares (600 acres), but the gardens today are far smaller. Huntington and his superintendent, William Hertrich, began laying out what became a dozen main garden areas, including the renowned Japanese Garden and the Rose Garden. But the Desert Garden is perhaps the botanical highlight. It contains one of the most diverse collections of drought-tolerant plants in the world. The garden contains over 5,000 species of cactus and succulent, divided among sixty designed beds.

There are many plants of note, such as *Fouquieria columnaris*, or the Boojum tree. Native to Baja California, this oddity grows up to 18 metres (60 feet) tall and has right-angled branches, leaves that grow on the trunk and stems and creamy yellow flowers. The largest cactus is *Cereus xanthocarpus*, a treelike species native to South America. The lower part of the garden is dominated by 18-metre-high (60-foot) specimens of *Yucca filifera* from northeastern Mexico. The garden is softly scented by their white flowers.

The garden is also home to about two-thirds of the world's known species of aloe. *Aloe barberae*, which can grow 18 metres (60 feet) tall, is Africa's largest aloe. The aloes flower in golds, oranges and reds in southern California's mild winter. They are underplanted with masses of globelike golden barrel cactus (*Echinocactus grusonii*).

In addition to the outdoor displays, a conservatory protects delicate succulents. They include *Lithops*, living stones from South Africa; the bishop's cap (*Astrophytum ornatum*), an enormous specimen from the highlands of central Mexico; *Welwitschia* from Namibia, which grows only two leaves but can live up to a thousand years; and a *Pachypodium horombense* collected from Madagascar in 1928 and today the oldest plant in this remarkable collection.

1, 2—The whole complex contains many varied gardens, including the Rose Garden, with more than 1,200 cultivars, and the Japanese Garden, with its distinctive Japanese House and moon bridge.
3, 5—The golden barrel cacti of the Desert Garden were raised from seed planted a century ago. The plants' ribs expand and contract as they store and use water.
4—The Southwestern Desert Garden features *Agave*, Chusan palms (*Trachycarpus fortunei*) and ponytail palms (*Beaucarnea recurvata*).
6—*Aloe vera* provides a colourful foreground for a spectacular display of *Carnegiea gigantea* in the Desert Garden.

3

4

5

6

# Central Garden, Getty Center

Los Angeles, California, USA

| |
|---|
| Robert Irwin |
| 20th century |
| Less than 0.2 hectares / Less than 0.5 acre |
| US Zones 10a–10b |
| Formal / Modern / Terraces / Water |

In many ways the Lower Central Garden at the Getty Museum overlooking Los Angeles is a late twentieth-century version of Villa Lante, the famous sixteenth-century villa and garden in central Italy (see page 306). Both take the basic form of a series of terraces and fountains ending in a parterre surrounded by water. But four centuries have made a difference, and this dramatic Modernist garden twists architectural convention away from the decadence of the past towards a contemporary artist's interpretation of garden as sculpture.

Created by the artist Robert Irwin, the garden features an undulating stream bordered by London plane trees. This leads to a waterfall and then to the maze, a water parterre created by hot-pink Kurume azaleas planted and pruned into spiral circles, which appear to be floating in water. Surrounding the maze is ever-changing planting that has elicited criticism from some and praise from others. Because of its constantly varied palette of plants, it provides an ephemeral contrast to the palatial architecture of the museum and the rigidity of the maze. Key plants used are *Berberis thunbergii* 'Royal Cloak', coco-yam (*Colocasia esculenta* 'Fontanesii'), *Tulbaghia violacea* 'Silver Lace' – which smells awful despite its pretty name – and crepe myrtle (*Lagerstroemia indica* 'Muskogee').

The sinuous ravine, coated in river pebbles, is punctuated by a concrete path that angles across the water, often disturbing the soft rippling with its metal-edged, right-angled bends. The path leads to a plaza where tall rebar umbrellas support enormous bougainvilleas. Irwin's motto, 'Always changing, never twice the same', is carved into the plaza floor.

Irwin sums up his approach: 'A garden is an adventure, and nature is probably the closest thing you are going to get to that kind of moving in a world – push-pull, in-out, up-down, right and wrong. After a certain time, once the garden got going, it changed all the rules. It did things that were so much better than I had thought.'

1—Abundant mixed plantings fill the terraces around the lake, in which appears to float a water parterre of clipped azaleas.
2—Sculptures support bougainvilleas to form an arbour above the plaza, lending it a sense of scale and intimacy.
3, 4—The planting along the pathways is constantly changing as spaces are redesigned and new plants introduced, bringing to life Irwin's motto, 'Always changing, never twice the same.'
5—Water flows down a stone ravine interrupted by concrete walkways to end up in the central pool.

# Getty Villa
## Pacific Palisades, California, USA

Denis Kurutz, Matt Randolph, Amy Korn

20th century

26 hectares / 64 acres

US Zones 10a–10b

Courtyard / Edible / Historic / Water

Getty Villa and its gardens offer a unique insight into Roman life nearly 2,000 years ago. The villa is based on the excavation of the Villa of the Papyri at Herculaneum, which was buried by the eruption of Vesuvius in AD 79. This substantial complex outside the city was typical of the villas and gardens created by wealthy Romans as rural retreats and locations for *otium* – a withdrawal from daily affairs to engage in more enlightened activities, such as oratory, writing or philosophy.

There are four gardens at Getty Villa. West of the villa is a Kitchen Garden planted with fruit: cherries, damsons, apples, figs, lemons, pears, yellow and blue plums, pomegranates and peaches were all Roman favourites. There are also period-correct flowers, herbs and vegetables. The enclosed East Garden is enlivened by two water features: a central fountain and a colourful mosaic-and-shell *nymphaeum* (a shrine to the nymphs).

The two most important gardens are enclosed by peristyles (covered arcades), which provide shelter from the sun or rain. The Inner Peristyle is in the centre of the villa, and all the ground-floor rooms open on to it. This sunken, square garden has at its centre a narrow pool with small jets flanked by replicas of statues discovered at Herculaneum. The hedged beds have period-correct plants and feature herms (stone columns carved with genitalia and topped with a bust).

The villa's south doors lead to the larger Outer Peristyle. The peristyle wall is richly painted; in smaller gardens such walls were sometimes painted with *trompe l'oeil* nature scenes to help make the garden seem larger. This Outer Peristyle, which provides spectacular views of the Pacific, is laid out around a long reflecting pool. Gravel paths separate flower beds enclosed by low, clipped box hedges and planted with topiary bay laurel trees and other Roman favourites, including myrtle, ivy and oleander. Such evergreen plants were popular because they provided year-round colour. Other favourites were arbutus, date palm, *Viburnum*, citrus and ivy, as used in the Inner Peristyle groundcover.

1 — The Long Pool dominates the Outer Peristyle, where painted walls guide visitors to views over the Pacific Ocean.
2 — A water-lily pool is the focus of the Kitchen Garden, which produces fruit, herbs and vegetables the Romans used in cooking, medicine and religious ceremony.
3 — Around the narrow pool in the Inner Peristyle, the statues include the figures of women drawing water from the stream.
4 — The East Garden is shaded by sycamore and laurel trees; water plays in the central fountain and a mosaic fountain (left).

# Dawnridge

Beverly Hills, California, USA

| | |
|---|---|
| Tony and Elizabeth Duquette | |
| 20th century | |
| 0.2 hectares / 0.5 acre | |
| US Zones 10a–10b | |
| Exotic / Rainforest / Sculpture | |

On paper, it seems as though Dawnridge should not work – but it does. To visit is to enter a fantasy world, a theatrical experience completely unlike the surrounding homes of Beverly Hills. What else would one expect from a prominent Hollywood set decorator? Tony Duquette's talent had already led to a career designing idiosyncratic interiors for a widening circle of clients when Dawnridge was built in 1949 on a canyon site covered with native scrub, sagebrush, pine trees and eucalyptus. Garden-making began in earnest when Duquette bought the adjacent plot.

This is not a less-is-more garden. Duquette's motto was 'more is more'. He accumulated materials, using recycling on a grand scale long before sustainability became a byword in garden design. He rescued native plants that were being cleared to make way for construction, and added jade (*Crassula ovata*) and other succulents from his ranch at Malibu.

This is a garden of structures placed to best effect. Set in what resembles a Southeast Asian rainforest are seven buildings – but they are as much sculpture as they are specific types of structure. They embody the art of repurposing cast-off materials. The dome of a tree house came from a film, *The Gazebo* (1959), with wall panels fashioned out of World War II landing strips. Other buildings have an Eastern flavour, but are crafted from an eclectic range of materials: a roof from Thailand, window frames from an old Chinese house, decorative timber known as gingerbread from Victorian houses and resin models from a film set. Duquette set out to use objects and materials in new ways. Decorative grilles at the doorway to a Chinese-style house are made from panels used for underfloor computer wiring.

Duquette liked to repeat masses of the same plants in different places across a garden. Planting is hardy in the climate of Beverly Hills, yet the garden looks exotic and unusual. At night, lights cast a romantic glow: the dining terrace and the buildings take on a different atmosphere and appearance. Although the garden contains many different materials and styles, it is unified by Duquette's singular aesthetic. Everything looks as though it belongs in this fantasy world, full of mystery and allure.

1—The garden is filled with idiosyncratic 'pavilions', which Duquette called 'spirit houses', surrounded by more than two hundred plant species. The Little Thai House, deep inside the canyon, was created using architectural fragments from Thailand and Bali, together with Gothic spires and Victorian 'gingerbread' from Los Angeles' historic Bunker Hill area.

# Kaufmann House

Palm Springs, California, USA

Richard Neutra, Chester Moorten, Marmol Radziner, William Kopelk

20th century

1 hectare / 2.5 acres

US Zones 8–10

Cactus / Desert / Landscape / Modern

The Kaufmanns' main residence was the iconic Fallingwater, designed by Frank Lloyd Wright, and their vacation home is just as impressive. The house, built by the architect Richard Neutra in Palm Springs in 1946, has been widely acclaimed as an architectural masterpiece. Neutra brought the landscape into the house to fuse the interior and exterior by using plate glass to create 'invisible' walls and huge sliding doors.

Neutra's pinwheel design ensures views of the desert from all four wings of the house, which divide the garden into four areas. Neutra made no detailed drawings for the garden, but made extensive plant lists (including favourites such as roses and camellias that were unsustainable in the Palm Springs climate, so were never planted).

Chester 'Cactus Slim' Moorten – an early local plant preservationist and landscape designer – was hired to develop the landscape around the new house. Through plant-hunting expeditions, Moorten inspired the Kaufmanns to embrace desert plants in their garden. The early planting included staghorn cholla (*Opuntia versicolor*) – a gift from Frank Lloyd Wright – *Yucca schidigera* and ocotillo (*Fouquieria splendens*).

After changes in ownership of the property, the garden declined. From 1998, however, new owners restored it along its original lines. Sustainability was a watchword, and plant selections were extended to include types from Chihuahua in Mexico and the entire US Southwest. Rows of agaves were added; the lawn was reduced in size, the large boulders that used to punctuate it put back and a cactus garden created at its edge. An area west of the house was designed as a dry stream bed that comes alive in spring with yellow palo verde (*Parkinsonia florida*) contrasting vibrantly with pink Mexican evening primrose (*Oenothera berlandieri*) – proof that deserts can be colourful. Another area east of the house is a Desert Mediterranean Garden, an oasis with shade, water, grass and an orchard of pomegranates and citrus trees.

1 — The restoration of the house and garden – which was doubled in size – preserved the desert buffer Neutra envisioned, as typified by an arrangement of boulders interspersed with cactus, yucca and agave.
2 — Neutra used glass walls and doors to bring the interiors and exteriors together; the lawn (alien to the Palm Springs environment) was deliberately kept small and left strewn with boulders.
3 — Beyond the swimming pool – an essential element in the balance of Neutra's design – low-growing desert plants are backed by an orchard of pomegranates, citrus trees and palms.

# New Century Garden

(A Garden of Light and Water)

Palm Springs, California, USA

| |
|---|
| Steve Martino |
| 21st century |
| 0.6 hectares / 1.5 acres |
| US Zones 8–10 |
| Cactus / Drought Tolerant / Formal / Modern / Succulents / Water |

Like other Steve Martino landscapes, New Century Garden grabs visitors' attention before they enter. Martino wanted to add impact to the streetscape, creating a public show of how gardening with native desert plants can be both aesthetically appealing and eco-sensitive. His model for garden design comprises not just a new attitude to plant selection but also the use of new materials and technology.

The San Jacinto Mountains make a dramatic backdrop to the garden, where Martino was asked to create something 'groovy, cool and sexy'. In response he created a series of smaller intimate outdoor rooms and expansive dramatic spaces. The tennis court doubles as a terrace and is enclosed by a fence of fibreglass panels that overlap vertically and horizontally, adding privacy but allowing a breeze to flow through. The fence also creates interesting shadows – an important element of the garden.

An outer hedge and a variety of boundary treatments create privacy without cutting the garden off from its surroundings. Some walls and screens are quite close to the house, yet they do not create a feeling of claustrophobia. Wall colours link to those found in the natural landscape, and the ochre-coloured Domino Wall again casts interesting shadow patterns.

Martino reused all ninety-two existing palms on the property. A cactus 'hedge' on top of a low wall defines the intimate guest terrace, where the sound of water cascading from a fountainhead helps mask traffic noise. Native plants in the Entry Garden create a stylized version of local canyons in a boulder-strewn landscape. The space around the planting is given as much importance as the shape of the plants themselves.

Every room in the house has access to the garden through sliding glass doors. Views beyond the garden are acknowledged, while the arrangement of each area provides arresting internal vistas. Such a mastery of spatial design, combined with the innovative use of water and modern materials, makes New Century Garden an exciting space.

1—Martino reused all the palm trees on the site, including a striking group placed in an island planter in the reflecting pool.
2, 4—The geometric lines of fibreglass panels, concrete and water contrast with the irregular shapes of cacti and succulents.
3—The panels of the Domino Wall form a permeable boundary that acts as a screen and casts interesting shadows. Just beyond the corner the 'dominoes' are set at an angle, appearing to topple.
5—Sculptural agave and cacti are planted in relation to large rocks, walls and taller plants. Their natural appearance is complemented by rubble mulch: an apt finish for a desert garden of xeric plants.

# Dickenson Residence

Santa Fe, New Mexico, USA

| |
|---|
| Martha Schwartz |
| 20th century |
| 24.2 hectares / 60 acres (garden); 0.02 hectares / 0.05 acres (courtyard) |
| US Zone 6b |
| Courtyard / Modern / Vistas / Water |

The Dickenson Residence garden displays the high level of creativity and originality typical of its designer, Martha Schwartz. The garden combines two distinct areas around an adobe house: the first acknowledges the fantastic views to the horizon from its hilltop location; the second is the Entry Garden, an enclosed, intimate courtyard with strong internal views.

Visitors arrive at the house through a walled area. A line of poplar trees and a walled corridor resembling a colonnade lead to the Entry Garden, where gravel and brick set out a grid pattern centred on four raised brick fountains. Pattern definition is further emphasized by the grid of narrow rills that connect the four fountains. Nine crab apple trees are planted within the grid, the base of each tree being delineated by either a circle or a square of white rocks. The courtyard walls are colourful painted stucco, the metal well of each fountain is brightly coloured and the water channels are finished with small, brightly coloured tiles. At night, lighting gives the courtyard a different feel: interior lights turn the fountains into glowing columns and cast plant shadows dramatically against walls and on the ground.

Beyond this area, the garden looks outwards. An ornamental fence stretches from the front of the house out into the landscape. At the rear, this line is continued by a long row of plum trees, which contrast sharply with the landscape of this arid region. The swimming pool is set in a stone-paved terrace overlooked by a turfed roof terrace: both terraces enjoy views of the surrounding landscape. The terraces mark an open-sided boundary between the end of the designed, planted space and the start of the native scrub vegetation.

With its contrasting combination of wide-open views and enclosed, private space, the garden at the Dickenson Residence is an object lesson in design. It acknowledges the fantastic surrounding landscape and sets the house in an appropriate context, and yet it also creates a domestically scaled area with a more intimate atmosphere and a real sense of 'home'.

1 — The Entry Garden has something of the feel of a cloister, framing a matrix of low, square fountains linked by a grid of brightly coloured rills and interspersed with crab apple trees set in beds of white marble rocks.
2 — Below the house, block planting of Spanish green yuccas provides a spiky green counterpoint to the pink adobe walls.
3 — The turfed roof terrace overlooking the swimming pool has spectacular views over the New Mexico landscape.
4 — A long, wide stone stairway climbs through a copse of native pine and juniper trees.

# Garden on Turtle Creek

Dallas, Texas, USA

Michael van Valkenburgh Associates

20th century

0.2 hectares / 0.5 acres

US Zone 8a

Landscape / Minimalist / Modern / Natives / Sustainable

Steep slopes challenge garden-makers, but the Garden on Turtle Creek shows not only that it is possible to make a beautiful garden on a sloping site but also that it can be done in an environmentally sensitive way. Michael van Valkenburgh's low-impact design of 1999 creates a union between the mature trees and lush vegetation and his clients' contemporary home of glass and concrete. His clients were birdwatchers: their brief included the creation of a birdbath in scale with the house, site and nearby Turtle Creek.

Steps and paths are essential in any sloping garden. Here, they form the garden's backbone. Different surface materials and path layouts affect the rhythm as one walks around. Despite their angularity, the paths, steps and pool blend with the natural vegetation. A textured stainless-steel staircase appears to float above a predominantly native-planted understorey. In another area, a dark gravel path emerges into the light alongside a series of hefty, pale concrete blocks forming a loosely stacked retaining wall. The path leads to a large, cantilevered, concrete water basin, which is both a reflective pool and a giant birdbath. Long 'planks' of black granite float just above the water's surface, offering a path reminiscent of a Japanese garden bridge.

Elsewhere, topography and mature trees regulate the spacing of exposed aggregate steps. Huge concrete blocks and rectangular logs nestle in lush planting – these retain soil in case of flooding and stabilize the creek banks and water's edge.

A velvet-textured lawn forms a wide 'collar' around the house, edged on the outside by a low concrete wall. Textured stainless-steel planks installed on low sonotubes, which provide invisible structural stability, appear to hover slightly above the grass. They give the appearance of being randomly scattered, yet each is carefully positioned in terms of the path's route and possible damage to plant roots.

Sensitive pruning of mature trees has created a corridor of sunlight that traverses the slope, letting in more light for the lower planting layers. This garden is a sophisticated experience for the senses and the whole body.

1—The irregular paths and steps were dug by hand in order to minimize damage to the extensive root systems of the trees around the garden.
2—At the edge of the lawn, the chequerboard stainless-steel pavers appear to hover slightly above the ground, supported by sonotubes.
3—The water basin is both a reflecting pool and a birdbath; it is crossed by 'planks' of black granite that float just above the water.

# Bass Garden

Fort Worth, Texas, USA

Robert Zion, Russell Page

20th century

3.2 hectares / 8 acres

US Zone 8

Courtyard / Parterre / Plantsman

Scale, proportion and the relationship between the architecture of the house and the landscape are key to the design of the Bass Garden. In 1970 Anne and Sid Bass commissioned the architect Paul Rudolph to design their new home among the trees on this hillside. The building's overlapping horizontal planes are based on a complex grid with spaces of different volumes. It seems to levitate above the sloping site and its lines appear 'simple', with no superfluous decoration.

Anne Bass set about creating a landscape to match her home. She engaged Robert Zion and Russell Page to draw up a master plan to relate the house to the garden and the garden to the house. They came up with a layout based on a series of interlocking rectangles, including parterres and the lily pond. Within its four main storeys and twelve different living spaces, there is a semi-enclosed internal courtyard garden, which opens up to reveal views to the garden proper. The main living areas are cantilevered over the slope, providing panoramic views. White interior walls and huge windows frame the landscape.

Trees, shrubs, grass, water and stone are the constituent elements of the Bass Garden, but these common elements are combined in unique proportions to make an expansive 'natural' setting that underlines the connection of the house to the site. Scale is derived from the architecture; an overhang of the building covers the terrace. From this area, steps down into the garden wrap around the corner of the house. Their design is simple and comprises deep, mown grass treads and low, stone-edged risers. This makes them an expansive link between different garden levels rather a narrow access point. A single planting of evergreen shrubs covers the main slope from which the house projects; with the backdrop of mature specimen trees at the top, they appear to anchor the building into the slope. Further into the garden and looking back towards the house, a dark reflecting pool contrasts with the pale mass of the house.

1—Page built a Modernist pergola adjacent to a greenhouse designed by Paul Rudolph, and trained wisteria over the top. The rectangular lily pool is backed by a row of Italian cypresses.
2, 4—Page's design of rectangular parterres reflected the lines and shapes of the house interiors to the garden design.
3—The lawn in front of the house is edged by a striking allée of pleached evergreen oak.

# Peckerwood Garden

Hempstead, Texas, US

| |
|---|
| John Gaston Fairey |
| 20th–21st century |
| 16 hectares / 40 acres |
| US Zone 8b |
| Arboretum / Artistic / Botanical / Natives / Naturalistic / Sculpture |

In the often boiling-hot flatlands of Texas, between Houston and Austin, lies Peckerwood Garden. This remarkable oasis owes its existence to the vision of one man – the artist John Gaston Fairey – who used his understanding of colour, texture, shade and light to create a landscape of rare beauty and refined sensibility. The garden is also horticulturally invaluable: it is home to almost 3,000 plants, including native Texans and many from Mexico and parts of Asia. A number are rare, or even extinct in the wild. The highly personal, aesthetically based conservation plant collection works in harmony with Fairey's other passions – Mexican folk art and the furniture of George Nakashima. The house museum contains some of the best contemporary Mexican folk art in the United States.

Peckerwood is also a garden of living collections, notably of agave, yucca, cactus and oaks. The Dry Garden, built with mounds of gravel above the hard Texas clay, contains plants such as *Yucca rostrata*, *Nolina nelsonii* and *Daisylirion*, rain flowers (*Zephyranthes*) and many rare and beautiful species.

In the Woodland Garden trees and shrubs from Asia grow beneath canopies of ash, elm, magnolia, native oak, pine and sycamore. In the heat of the day, the visitor can cool off beneath bald cypresses (*Taxodium*) in the creek that runs through the property.

Rare trees abound throughout the garden. The beautiful Mexican hornbeam *Carpinus caroliniana* was rescued from extinction with seed collected and grown at Peckerwood. *Magnolia tamaulipana*, with its creamy white flowers similar to those of *M. grandiflora*, is a rare beauty. The large and impressive collection of Mexican and Texan evergreen oaks includes loquat leaf oak (*Quercus rysophylla*), with its large, rough and crinkled texture; Monterrey oak (*Q. polymorpha*) with its thick, leathery leaves that emerge pink in spring; the so-called graceful oak (*Q. gracilis*) with its blue-green leaves; and *Q. sartorii*, a vigorous semi-evergreen tree of substantial grace. A visit to Peckerwood Garden is an immersion in splendour and intelligence, grace and beauty.

1—The reflecting pool – flanked by a cycad (*Dioon edule*) and clipped Texas pistachio (*Pistacia texana*) – introduces a formal element to the garden's profuse planting.
2, 3, 4—Fairey scours Texas and northern Mexico for seeds from rare cacti, yuccas, agaves, nolinas and dasylirion – native to Mexico – some of which are highly endangered species.
5—Among the numerous modern sculptures is this novel arrangement of ceramic bamboo by Marcia Donahue.

# Missouri Botanical Garden

## St Louis, Missouri, USA

| | |
|---|---|
| Henry Shaw, George Engelmann, Peter Raven | |
| 19th & 20th centuries | |
| 20.8 hectares / 51.5 acres | |
| US Zones 5a–5b | |
| Botanical / Conservatory / Japanese | |

When the Englishman Henry Shaw discovered the site of the current Missouri Botanical Garden, it was a beautiful native prairie on the edge of a wilderness some distance west of St Louis. Almost forty years later, after Shaw had made his fortune from a hardware business and retired early, he bought the land for what became, through his philanthropy, passion and vision, one of America's first botanical gardens – and one of its finest.

On his retirement, Shaw travelled to Europe, where he saw the Great Exhibition of 1851 in London and visited the Royal Botanic Gardens at Kew (see page 168) as well as estates such as Chatsworth (see page 136). Initially he planned to use his land to build a weekend retreat with a park and gardens that would be open to the public. But consultations with Sir William Hooker, the director of Kew, and Dr George Engelmann, an amateur botanist, instead persuaded Shaw that the land should become a botanical garden, with research facilities and a herbarium for study in addition to areas for horticultural displays. The garden opened to the public in 1859 and, until his death thirty years later, Shaw remained the driving force behind it. The Missouri Botanical Garden was his passion; he never married, and referred to the garden's plants as his children.

The central Victorian District around Shaw's former home has been restored in a nineteenth-century garden style. The Linnean House dates from 1882; it is the oldest continuously operating greenhouse in the United States, and has a notable collection of camellias. The garden has survived periods of reduced budgets and enthusiasm. A marked decline in visitors in the 1950s encouraged a revamp that began with the construction of the Climatron in 1960. This striking geodesic dome houses a collection of 1,200 tropical species planted in a naturalistic setting.

Peter Raven was director from 1971 to 2010. Under him the garden's botanical research and horticultural displays attained levels not seen since Shaw's time. Of particular note from this period is the Japanese Garden, one of the largest stroll gardens in the West. Elsewhere there is an English Woodland Garden, also created in the mid-1970s.

1—The plant tapestries – 'carpet bedding' – of the Victorian Garden around the central statue of Juno are characteristic of Victorian planting.
2, 3—The main feature of the Japanese stroll garden is the lake, planted with irises, with an authentic Japanese teahouse on an island connected to the bank by bridges.
4—The Climatron, which opened in 1960, was the world's first Plexiglas geodesic dome housing an air-conditioned conservatory.

# Lurie Garden

Chicago Millennium Park,
Chicago, Illinois, USA

| | |
|---|---|
| Gustafson Guthrie Nichol, Piet Oudolf, Robert Israel | |
| 21st century | |
| 2 hectares / 5 acres | |
| US Zone 6a | |
| Modern / New Perennial / Park / Urban | |

A team selected by international competition designed Chicago's Lurie Garden as an urban oasis. It incorporates contemporary gardening ideals of environmental sensitivity, engagement with the user, symbolism and a naturalism that uses high-density interplanting of bulbs and perennials.

Lurie Garden lies in the northeast corner of the 10-hectare (24.5-acre) Millennium Park, a mixed-use public space that also hosts the gleaming *Cloud Gate* sculpture by Sir Anish Kapoor. The garden is bounded on two sides by a dramatically lit 4.5-metre (15-foot) hedge. This not only distinguishes the space from the rest of the park but also acts as a windbreak for the perennials within.

Two planting areas form the heart of the garden: the Light Plate and the Dark Plate. The former features full-sun perennials and is meant to represent the city's artistic control of nature. The Dark Plate uses plants that grow in the shade of flowering trees and recalls the site's early history as wild shoreline. The perennial list is especially long, with varieties of allium, echinacea, geranium and a river of mixed salvia. The Dutch plantsman Piet Oudolf was also involved in the planting schemes, and he chose fifteen varieties of tulip. In addition to six varieties of arborvitae, the garden's trees include hornbeam, bur oak, black locust, Kentucky coffee tree and two types of cherry. Bisecting the two plates is a diagonal seam formed by a wooden boardwalk that floats over a shallow water feature; it is accessible to pedestrians to cool their feet on hot days and is reminiscent of the city founders' earliest efforts to build out of marshland. Crushed stone walkways in each plate invite visitors to engage further with the landscape.

Lurie Garden prides itself on using no synthetic pesticides, and more than half of its plants are native to North America. True to Oudolf's penchant for close, non-geometric plantings, more than 100,000 bulbs have been planted since the garden opened. These share space with more than 35,000 perennials and 5,200 woody plants. Given the climate's harsh and windy winters, the design team chose wisely in its extensive list of grasses and perennials that bear stalks and seed heads to offer considerable winter interest.

1 — Skyscrapers rise beyond the hedges and trees of the park, which pays tribute to Chicago's transformation from flat marshland to an innovative green city.
2, 4 — The wooden boardwalk that bisects the park diagonally floats over a water channel amid drifts of perennials designed by Piet Oudolf.
3 — A late summer herbaceous perennial border in the Light Plate features perovskia and the seed heads of echinacea.

# J Irwin Miller House and Garden

Columbus, Indiana, USA

Dan Kiley

20th century

5.3 hectares / 13 acres

US Zone 6a

Allées / Formal / Minimalist / Modern

The Miller Garden, nestled above the Flat Rock River in small-town Middle America, is celebrated as the masterpiece of the renowned American landscape architect Dan Kiley. A perfect union of mid-century home and garden, it was Kiley's first residential-landscape commission and is now a National Historic Landmark.

In keeping with post-war Modernist sensibilities, there is no excessive ornamentation in either the Eero Saarinen -designed house or the Kiley-designed landscape. Like Saarinen, Kiley embraced the relationships between spaces, juxtaposing voids with solids, such as when crab apple trees shade a chequerboard of concrete pads and various textures of groundcover.

The landscape is a study of shades of green, texture, asymmetry and geometric design punctuated with seasonal blooms, such as underplantings of tulips and daffodils or summer annuals. Like the indoor furnishings and window locations, plants are placed to hone views. An allée of honey locust trees defines an emerald lawn, terraced from the west side of the house to the floodplain. Apple trees, shaped to about 2 metres (6 feet) tall, stand as sentries at the entry to the home. Offset blocks of yew add mystery and depth to borders.

The J Irwin Miller House and Garden was built on former farmland in a suburban neighbourhood on the outskirts of Columbus, home of Cummins Inc., the Miller family business. The leadership of Miller, a noted philanthropist, was responsible for bringing notable modern architecture to Columbus, crafting the city into the Athens of the Prairie, with more than seventy buildings by outstanding architects, including Richard Meier, I M Pei, César Pelli, Robert Venturi and Eliel Saarinen.

When J Irwin and Xenia Miller died, their children donated the house with its original furnishings and the garden to the Indianapolis Museum of Art, which now manages the property.

1 — The evening sun casts shadows along an allée of honey locust trees (*Gleditsia triacanthos*) lining a gravel avenue with simple concrete benches set along the side of the lawn.
2 — The honey locust allée terminates at the north side of the house; the West Lawn beyond is hazy with mist.
3 — Panels of ivy and yew provide groundcover at the south side of the house.
4 — The landscape architect Jack Curtis revised Kiley's chequerboard landscape in 1986 after the redbuds originally planted there were replaced. A grid of crab apple (*Malus* spp.) trees now grows above an asymmetric pattern of concrete slabs with groundcover of periwinkle (*Vinca minor*) and busy Lizzie (*Impatiens walleriana*).

1

2

# Hollister House

Washington, Connecticut, USA

George Schoellkopf, Gerard Incandela

20th century

0.8 hectares / 2 acres

US Zones 6a–6b

Arts & Crafts / Cottage / Formal /
Rooms / Vistas

Entering the garden at Hollister House is like stepping thousands of kilometres across the Atlantic, because it has the style of an English Arts and Crafts garden. Its creator, George Schoellkopf, drew inspiration from Sissinghurst (see page 174) in the way he divided the garden into 'rooms'; he also created abundantly planted borders that spill over on to the walkways. The garden has a romantic atmosphere, too, in the way it anchors the timber-clad house – the oldest part of which predates the American Revolution – to the wooded New England landscape.

From the paved terrace there are fine views across the garden to the other side of the small valley and the landscape beyond. Visitors step down from the terrace on to the Upper Lawn with its Long Border, where the colour scheme is based on shades of yellow highlighted with brushes of blue and dashes of maroon-red. Across the Main Lawn below is a large pond, from where a view back reveals the house in its setting of terraces, hedges and plants.

The heart of the garden lies south of the house in a series of garden rooms defined by yew 'walls' and paved with stone. One room contains a dark reflecting pool with a fine vista through a narrow opening in the yew hedge to the landscape beyond. Gerald's Parterre, named after Schoellkopf's partner, is a small, intimate room near the house with circular cobble paving: its focal point is a plant-filled laundry copper. The box-edged Gray Garden – a formal parterre with brick-paved paths – is set at an angle and bounded on the south side by the informal Brook Walk. Here, the contrast is striking: a gravel path meanders along the small stream, twisting around large boulders. Plants are allowed to self-seed cottage-garden style: ox-eye daisies drift through *Silene armeria* and daylilies, and a colourful mix of herbaceous planting takes over as summer progresses. Like the rest of the garden, this is a cultivated gem that, although a designed space, still fits perfectly into its natural surroundings.

1—Schoellkopf's planting enhances the idyllic New England scene of the house nestled into the hillside above a dammed brook.
2—Spring sunrise illuminates quince trees framing the parterres of the Gray Garden.
3—An arch in a brick wall looks back to the house; the planting orchestrates a constant succession of flowers from spring to late summer.
4—Yellow *Iris pseudacorus* flowers along the stream, while an enormous sugar maple, *Acer saccharum*, looms above the farmhouse.
5—*Taxus* x *media* 'Hicksii,' clipped into a hedge, divides the dark reflecting pool from its backdrop of woodlands and rolling fields.
6—Hostas and ferns line a path looking out toward the nearby hill.

3

4

5

6

# Naumkeag

Stockbridge, Massachusetts, USA

| Nathan Barrett, Fletcher Steele, Mabel Choate |
| --- |
| 19th & 20th centuries |
| 3.2 hectares / 8 acres |
| US Zone 5b |
| Historic / Landscape / Water |

Naumkeag is the Native American name for Salem, the birthplace of Joseph Choate, who purchased the land in 1884. He commissioned Stanford White to design the shingle-style summer 'cottage', but for the garden he rejected a design by Frederick Law Olmsted, creator of Central Park in New York. The landscaping contract went instead to Nathan Barrett, who implemented a contrasting design: a formal flower garden with evergreen walks at the top near the house; and grassy terraces working down the slope to an orchard and the family cemetery at the bottom.

Choate's daughter Mabel inherited Naumkeag in 1929. A few years earlier she had met Fletcher Steele, considered by many to be America's first modern landscape architect. Now, she asked Steele to make her a Modernist garden with rooms, similar to gardens she had recently seen in California.

Choate and Steele worked together to develop the garden for the next thirty years, creating a unique fusion of Modern and Art Deco, with a splash of Arts and Crafts and history for good measure. What became the Afternoon Garden was Mabel's 'joy and delight'. Here seventeen Venetian 'gondola' poles define the boundaries without interrupting the sweeping mountain views, while pots of hybrid fuchsias surround the intricate, low-clipped hedge parterre and Moorish-inspired scalloped bowls and fountains.

In the 1930s Steele took full advantage of the sloping site to install landforms with abstract curves that echoed the shape of the distant hills. The iconic Blue Steps were designed in 1938, in response to Mabel's wish for an easier route through the garden. They comprise a series of fountain pools set among white birches, flanked by flights of steps with sweeping white handrails. The Chinese Temple Garden was also created in the 1930s.

The Rose Garden was added in 1953, with Art Deco mechanical curving paths cut into a lawn studded with floribunda roses. When the Moon Gate was installed in the wall of the Chinese Temple Garden in 1955, Choate and Steele considered their work complete.

1—The iconic Blue Steps rising among silver birches combine Renaissance form with an Art Deco design.
2—The shape of a circular fountain pool is echoed by a curving path and a border of small conifers in the formal Stroll Garden.
3—The sweeping edge of the South Lawn was a deliberate echo of the shape of Bear Mountain beyond.
4—'Gondola' poles salvaged from Boston harbour support the pergola of the parterre in the Afternoon Garden.
5—Wavy gravel paths snake through the Rose Garden, designed to be viewed from above.

# Fairsted

Brookline, Massachusetts, USA

| |
|---|
| Frederick Law Olmsted |
| 19th century |
| 2.8 hectares / 7 acres |
| US Zone 6a |
| Historic / Naturalistic / Rooms |

For anyone interested in the history of landscape architecture, Fairsted is a place of unique importance. This was for twenty years the home and office of the father of American landscape design, Frederick Law Olmsted, co-designer of Central Park, creator of Boston's 'Emerald Necklace' of parks, and pioneer of the preservation of wilderness for the benefit of the population. Although not as famous nor as historically significant as, say, Central Park, Olmsted's own home expresses on a more intimate scale the fundamentals of his lasting belief in the power of gardens and green spacesto enhance the individual spirit and improve urban life.

Olmsted's thinking first becomes clear at the entrance – an unusual arch made from dozens of wooden slats. The view of the house is obscured by an island of planting in the middle of a circular carriageway, and the nearby Hollow – created by filling in the original drive and front garden – is another deliberate attempt to separate the house and garden from the busy life of the city. This sunken grotto, where the path snakes among low-level green shrubs and local Roxbury puddingstone boulders, uses changes in level to create a distinctive outdoor room with a calm, meditative feeling.

In the Rock Garden, Olmsted created an area with more of a wilderness feel, where the path meanders through more boulders and seemingly unplanned, natural planting that is, in fact, a carefully organized buffer layer intended to shelter the house from the street. Beyond the Rock Garden, a vista opens to the South Lawn immediately beside the house, an expansive space that invites the visitor to relax or to play. The planting throughout the garden is naturalistic, and echoes Olmsted's deep affection for the natural American landscape. Yet, as in many of his projects, this naturalistic appearance is in fact highly contrived. Paths lead from the lawn to small, unexpected garden rooms, and stone paths, steps and arches add a picturesque feel, introducing a theme of human intervention in the landscape but also underlining its transience.

1 — This view from the South Lawn shows the house in a sea of shrubs and trees. Olmsted more than tripled the size of the 1810 farmhouse to create space for his landscape architecture practice. The house was painted red and green, rather than the original white, at the suggestion of Olmsted's daughter, Marion.
2 — A stone-edged path loops through the Hollow, the sunken garden room Olmsted created with low-level planting.

# Cloister Gardens

Fort Tryon Park,
New York City, USA

| | |
|---|---|
| George Grey Barnard, John D Rockefeller, Jnr, James Ruramor | |
| 20th century | |
| 1.6 hectares / 4 acres | |
| US Zones 6b–7a | |
| Courtyard / Edible / Historic | |

The Cloisters – part of the Metropolitan Museum of Art – lies on a hill in Upper Manhattan overlooking the Hudson River. This peaceful haven incorporates parts of five medieval abbeys brought from Europe, and contains about 5,000 works of art from the twelfth to the fifteenth century. In keeping with the buildings, the gardens are designed according to information in medieval manuscripts, and they focus particularly on the cloistered herb gardens associated with medieval monasteries.

The main garden, the Bonnefont Cloister, contains more than 250 species grown in a historically accurate amalgam of a number of monastic gardens. It contains a central well; fences made from woven saplings; pots of tender plants such as lemon, bay, aloe and pomegranate, which can be brought inside to protect them from the winter cold; and fruit trees planted against a south wall for shelter.

The plants are grouped according to their uses and are a reminder of the central role of the garden in medieval life, far beyond the kitchen. They contain household plants such as Fuller's teasel (*Dipsacus fullonum*), a natural comb for raising the nap on cloth; wormwood (*Artemisia absinthium*), a distillation of which is the highly alcoholic spirit absinthe; and hops (*Humulus*), used to treat anxiety and insomnia. Medicinal plants were important, too, and the collection here includes birthwort (*Aristolochia clematitis*), feverfew (*Tanacetum parthenium*), comfrey (*Symphytum*) and St Johns wort (*Hypericum*). Aromatic plants include meadowsweet (*Filipendula ulmaria*), lemon balm (*Melissa officinalis*) and vervain (*Verbena*), the last of which was said to promote happiness. Chaste tree (*Vitex agnus-castus*) was taken by monks to help them remain celibate, heartsease (*Viola tricolor*) was added to love potions, and chervil (*Anthriscus cerefolium*) was used to stop nightmares.

The other gardens at the Cloisters include the Cuxa Cloister, which holds a lawn divided by flower beds and paths. The Trie Cloister is a careful re-creation of a historic garden based on the plants that appear on the old tapestries displayed inside the museum. A fourth cloister has been enclosed with a skylight to create an indoor space in which a fountain plays over pebbles.

1 — The Bonnefont Cloister comes from a monastery built in the Pyrenees in the late thirteenth or early fourteenth century. Its beds contain more than 250 species planted according to their use: culinary, medicinal or magical.
2 — The Cuxa Cloister – a twelfth-century structure from the Pyrenees – is planted with lawns and ornamental borders, divided by paths.

# Wave Hill Gardens

The Bronx,
New York City, USA

William H Appleton, George Perkins,
Albert Millard, Marco Polo Stufano,
John Nally

19th–21st century

11.3 hectares / 28 acres

US Zone 6

Artistic / Conservatory / Landscape /
Plantsman / Rooms

The garden at Wave Hill is largely a creation of the last fifty years, but the house dates back to 1843, when it was built to take advantage of a prominent position overlooking the Hudson River and the dramatic cliffs of the New Jersey Palisades opposite. Late in the nineteenth century a new owner, William H Appleton, added greenhouses – which no longer survive – and gardens, and from 1915 George Perkins and his gardener, Albert Millard, carried out further landscaping. They laid out a Rock Garden, put in place paths that snaked throughout the property, and installed a gazebo and secluded viewpoints over the river.

In 1960 Wave Hill was gifted to the City of New York, and in 1965 it became a public garden. By the time Marco Polo Stufano arrived as head gardener two years later, it was in a state of neglect. But over the next thirty-five years – as head gardener and later as director of horticulture – Stufano orchestrated the garden's seasonal displays and took Wave Hill from a ruin to horticultural excellence. Assisted for some twenty years by John Nally, who came to Wave Hill in 1969, Stufano was given free rein to create a new garden that not only referenced the sense of a private estate but also offered small, intimate areas that might influence home gardeners.

Stufano and Nally travelled together to collect plants and find inspiration, which, with their painterly skills and horticultural expertise, they used to brilliant effect. Their sensitive touch allowed plants to self-seed and grow naturally, yet still kept control with deft pruning and thinning. They created seasonal scenes and intricate plantings that attracted visitors to Wave Hill from around the world. The plain names of the garden areas – Flower Garden, Pergola, Herb and Dry Gardens, Shade Border – are no preparation for the structure and beauty that awaits the visitor. Today, Wave Hill's artist-gardeners continue in the same spirit, using plants to blend colour, shape and texture in order to showcase detailed cameos as well as longer vistas.

1 — The Hudson River makes a dramatic backdrop to the Kate French Terrace, one of the garden's many small-scale areas.
2 — A formal pergola, softened by hardy Kiwi vine (*Actinidia arguta*), focuses the view towards the Palisades across the river.
3 — The Conservatory comprises three main sections, the Palm House, the Cactus and Succulent House and the Tropical House.
4 — In the Aquatic Garden *Miscanthus sinensis* frames a pond where water lilies grow with mosaic plant (*Ludwigia sedioides*).
5 — The Herb and Dry Gardens were created using the foundations of an old greenhouse.

# Battery Park Roof Garden

Manhattan,
New York City, USA

| |
|---|
| Mark K Morrison |
| 21st century |
| 0.02 hectares / 0.05 acres |
| US Zone 7b |
| Edible / Roof / Sustainable / Urban |

When international law expert Frederic C Rich wanted to combine a private garden, a vegetable and fruit garden and an environmentally beneficial 'green roof' on his condominium terrace, the plan seemed outlandish. But a team of landscape architects, horticulturists, engineers and industrial designers realized Rich's vision thirty-five storeys above Lower Manhattan. The garden they created confirms that Rich, a dedicated gardener and environmentalist, was right to believe that a wide variety of fruit and vegetables could be productively grown in a roof garden.

The result is a private space so spectacular that it even detracts from the breathtaking panoramic views of New York Harbour and the Statue of Liberty. From Rich's living room, the visitor walks under a steel-and-glass pergola softened by grapevines and climbing roses out into an entertainment area covered in blue paving stones that are interplanted with sun-loving groundcover – sedum, a green-roof necessity. Comfortable seating invites guests to linger and enjoy the plantings – there are at least 160 species – of evergreens such as white pine, shrubs such as beauty berry (*Callicarpa*) and flowering plants such as iris and dwarf lilies. An alpine garden that thrives in windy, dry conditions adds interest to an exposed corner.

From this area, the visitor passes through a small herb garden, with blue-glass fountains on either side of its paved path, into an orchard of eight fruit trees (apple, peach, nectarine and plum), and raspberry, cranberry and blueberry patches. On the other side of the deck is a vegetable garden with six raised beds that provide an almost constant supply of different vegetables.

The garden uses vertical as well as horizontal lines. The wall dividing Rich's terrace from that of his neighbour supports climbing strawberry plants; runner beans grown on vertical screens along the vegetable beds; and six varieties of pear are trained on copper espaliers. With food for the soul in its beauty, and food for the body in its produce, the Battery Park Roof Garden is a perfect model for the adventurous roof gardener.

1, 2—Eve Vaterlaus created the twin *Double Helix* fountains in the centre of the garden, with views north across the seating area and south towards a paved terrace.
3—The pergola that connects the apartment to the garden is softened by grapevines and climbing roses.
4—Among the fruit trees of the orchard, the berry frame is used to grow blackberries, strawberries and raspberries.
5—The six raised beds of the vegetable garden are used to grow green beans, asparagus, chard, peas, broccoli, celery and rhubarb.

# New York Botanical Garden

The Bronx, New York City, USA

Nathaniel Lord Britton, Elizabeth Britton, Beatrix Farrand, Penelope Hobhouse, Oehme van Sweden

19th & 20th century

101.2 hectares / 250 acres

US Zones 6b–7a

Botanical / Conservatory / Natives

A great city needs a great backyard. New York Botanical Garden is that, and more: a place to see plants displayed, an educational resource and a leading research institution. Its attractions include 16 hectares (40 acres) of the only surviving native forest in New York City; an iconic conservatory with eleven computer-controlled climates, ranging from humid rainforest to arid desert; a beautiful rose garden; and an adventure garden for children.

The garden was inspired by a visit to the Royal Botanic Gardens, Kew (see page 168) by Dr Nathaniel Lord Britton and his wife, Elizabeth, in 1888. The couple – both trained botanists – were spurred into raising funds for a similar garden in New York City, which subsequently opened in 1891.

Visitors enter the garden through the rainforest and desert habitats of the restored conservatory. Further into the site, there are striking perennial borders with textural contrasts of foliage enhanced with colourful floral displays. Designed by Penelope Hobhouse, the traditional Herb Garden is a more intimate space to soak up aromatic foliage and scented flowers set against brick-paved paths. The Rose Garden was designed by Beatrix Farrand in 1916, but only built in 1988. Its triangular shape echoes a French *roseraie*, and its roses bloom from late spring to mid-autumn. The Native Plant Garden, designed by Oehme van Sweden, has more than 100,000 plants from 454 native taxa. Throughout the park, flowering cherries, ornamental conifers, magnolias and maples accentuate different seasons.

This garden is a place to see the plants of the world, and also to examine archived native plants: the herbarium is one of the largest in the world. Specimens from the Lewis and Clark expedition of 1805 across North America to the Pacific are a highlight. The Botanical Garden is the place to discover another side of New York, too. At the heart of the garden, the Bronx River runs past ancient native trees that appear in an entirely natural setting, but whose continued existence is a result of careful management and active protection. It is like going back in time in this forward-looking city.

1, 2—The Conservatory is a Victorian-style glasshouse with a display named 'A World of Plants'. In front of it is the Perennial Garden, which is full of colour in spring and summer.
3—Some 80 varieties of crabapple tree erupt with masses of blossom on Daffodil Hill every May and bear fruit in autumn.
4—An evergreen box parterre is the formal centrepiece of the Herb Garden.
5—The Peggy Rockefeller Rose Garden is home to more than 4,000 plants, with roses in bloom for six months of the year.

# High Line

Manhattan, New York City, USA

James Corner, Diller Scofidio & Renfro, Piet Oudolf

21st century

2.3 kilometres / 1.5 miles (length)

US Zones 6b–7a

Meadow / Naturalistic / Park / Urban

At the foot of the stairs up to the High Line it feels as if one is on the way to catch some form of urban transit train, but, on ascending, the walls become clad with ochre-coloured Cor-Ten steel rather than graffiti and one sees tree branches rather than overhead power cables. Suddenly one emerges on to one of the most talked about, ingenious and surprising urban green spaces: unexpected because it is elevated and linear; unexpected because one is walking on an old railway line; and unexpected because of the views it gives of the city and the Hudson River.

Located on Manhattan's West Side, the High Line was created on a former spur of the New York Central Railway that closed in 1980 and for nearly twenty years was gently reclaimed by nature. Since then, activists, residents and the City of New York have created this iconic green space, which runs from Gansevoort Street to 30th Street and incorporates the Rail Yards. It is enjoyed by New Yorkers and visitors alike.

The exposed aggregate concrete path swings from side to side like a railway carriage between the seating zones and flower beds, which are covered with stone chips and feature rail tracks as a reminder of the park's former incarnation. The planting design – both the style and plant selection – was inspired by the years of abandonment during which tough, drought-tolerant perennials, grasses, shrubs and trees colonized the ballast below the rusting tracks. The focus is practical and aesthetic, combining hardiness and sustainability, textural and colour variation, with an emphasis on native species. Copses of trees add extra height, variety and dappled shade, while their leaves move as they are blown in the wind. Walking along the High Line and admiring the plantings, one has the feeling of being lifted out of the city and into a verdant garden, but one has only to raise one's head to see what a striking contrast this verdant stripe is with the surrounding concrete jungle.

1 — The Gansevoort Woodland is a wooded area at the southern end of the park. The planting is a mix of rugged meadow species, including clump-forming grasses that soften the linearity of the park's architecture.
2 — Birches provide dappled shade next to one of the fourteen staircases that provide access to the High Line.
3 — In the Chelsea Grasslands, grasses emerge through cracks that gradually open between the concrete slabs of the walkway.
4 — Grasses and self-seeding flowers are among the 300 taxa that grow along the High Line.
5 — *Stachys officinalis* 'Hummelo' blooming among rail tracks in July reflects Piet Oudolf's involvement (see page 220). More than one-third of the original tracks have been incorporated into the park's design.

2

3

4

5

# Donald M Kendall Sculpture Gardens

PepsiCo Headquarters,
Purchase, New York, USA

| | |
|---|---|
| Edward D Stone, Jnr, Russell Page, François Goffnet | |
| 20th century | |
| 68 hectares (168 acres) | |
| US Zone 6b | |
| Formal / Landscape / Modern / Sculpture / Vistas | |

The gardens at PepsiCo's headquarters are like a vast outdoor art gallery. Yet they are also an art form themselves, in their faithful contemporary re-creation of the spirit of the great eighteenth-century English landscape gardens.

The gardens were the vision of former chairman and CEO Donald M Kendall. After Edward D Stone designed the new PepsiCo headquarters in 1970, in seven blocks that rise like upturned ziggurats, Kendall asked his son, Edward D Stone, Jnr, to design a master plan for the landscape. Kendall's aim was to create 'an environment that encourages creativity and reflects essential qualities of corporate success', built around his sculpture collection. The collection eventually expanded to include works by major twentieth-century sculptors – Giacometti, Hepworth, Miró, Moore, Rodin – in various materials.

In 1980 Kendall commissioned Russell Page to extend the gardens, reshape the landscape and position the sculptures to best effect. Page stressed the relationships between woods, fields, water, rocks, trees and plants or groups of plants. Simplicity of line was another important factor. He spent a year studying patterns of light and shade, the volume of space created by buildings and tree groups, and the way sculptures would work against a seasonally changing backdrop of planting.

Page created three courtyard gardens among the buildings, grouped around a central fountain where *Girl with a Dolphin* by David Wynne frolics in the spray. These gardens are formal, with clipped hedges, trained trees and fountains creating a classical entrance. This cool, contemporary approach is repeated on the open sides of the building, where gardens have an intimate atmosphere.

Away from the buildings, Page designed the Golden Path, which meanders through expansive lawns, shady woodland and cool groves and around a large lake. Like a great ribbon, it links the sculptures and ties together different areas of the garden, ensuring that visitors are presented with a series of vistas along with the artworks. The company welcomes the public to explore its fine sculpture collection.

1—Robert Davidson's *Totems* dominates a view to the Golden Path and the lake.
2—Art Price's *Birds of Welcome* is sited beneath a group of willows near the lake.
3—The Golden Path leads past *Grizzly Bear* by David Wynne (right) and *Hats Off* by Alexander Calder.
4—Yew topiary animals on the lawn by the water-lily ponds add intimacy and humour to the garden.
5—The geometric water-lily ponds create a foreground for a pavilion inspired by a Humphry Repton design.

3

4

5

# Madoo Conservancy

Sagaponack, Long Island,
New York, USA

| |
|---|
| Robert Dash |
| 20th–21st century |
| 0.8 hectares / 2 acres |
| US Zones 6b–7a |
| Artistic / Modern / Sculpture / Topiary |

Madoo has mystery in abundance, just as its creator intended. Bob Dash (who died in 2013) was an artist and writer, and his garden reflected his preoccupations – it was to be, he said, 'bold, alluring, full of surprises'. Although he rejected the idea that he brought a painterly eye to the garden, Dash used a palette of vibrant colours to create effects for all seasons. Fences, gates and timber seats were painted in bold shades, sometimes in the opposite of the colour of flowers close by.

One of the defining qualities of the garden – which fits well into the surrounding landscape of Long Island – is its celebration of the art of pruning. Large specimen trees are trimmed to keep them to the required scale. In some areas, tree trunks are kept clear, so they are vertical highlights. In other places, clipped topiary stands out as solid shapes against a green backdrop created by contrasting textures of mixed herbaceous planting.

Madoo reveals itself slowly. As visitors move around, they are guided into 'reading' the garden as Dash wished, with a series of focal points that lead the eye, just as a circuit of paths directs the feet. Madoo is not a grand garden. There are plenty of simple ideas to be taken away: a path made of sawn log rounds set in gravel; well-placed empty pots that draw the eye and highlight the space in which they sit; and attractive seats of all shapes and colours from which to enjoy the different garden rooms or areas.

There are references to design ideas of the past updated with a twist: a faux stumpery of textured granite 'trunks'; and an inscribed pot at the centre of a circle of stone paving. Of particular note is a long brick path spanned by a series of rose hoops, which creates a false perspective as it narrows towards the end. The rill down the centre of the path appears to rise up through its reflection in a mirror on a brick wall, which makes a full stop at the end of the path. Climbing roses cover the hoops, and different forms of *Rosa rugosa* are planted alongside the path. Elsewhere, a fine specimen of *Rosa* 'Paul's Himalayan Musk' adds a cloud of colour in the canopy of trees.

1 — The rill, which references the Alhambra in Spain (see page 276), narrows to make it appear longer. The tough *Rosa rugosa*, with its large hips, reflects the garden's coastal setting.
2 — A gilded bust of Beethoven stares out from behind pots of evergreens, colourful exotic Caladiums and the nodding dried flowerheads of Alliums.
3 — Dash painted his summerhouse in response to an observation by the painter Manet: 'The very colour of the air is mauve.'
4 — A yellow-painted gate and arch reflect the importance of accents of vibrant colour in Dash's vision of the garden.

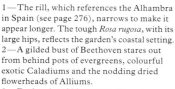

# LongHouse Reserve

East Hampton, Long Island,
New York, USA

Jack Lenor Larsen

20th century

6.5 hectares / 16 acres

US Zones 6b–7a

Artistic / Rooms / Sculpture

When Jack Lenor Larsen bought a patch of land near the south coast of Long Island in the 1980s, his main aim was to prevent developers encroaching on his existing home. But Larsen – textile designer, weaver and Japanophile – soon cleared 6,000 trees and began cultivating the property. After seven years, Larsen opened the new garden to the public as an example of how to live with art: it houses temporary exhibits and permanent pieces from such artists as Isamu Noguchi, Willem de Kooning and Sol LeWitt.

The LongHouse experience begins with the cryptomeria-lined drive, which opens into a multitude of garden experiences, including lawns and allées, dunes and forest, and the 'non-garden', a grass-covered amphitheatre reminiscent of ancient landforms. Smaller subgardens feature the themes of tropical, grasses and red.

Larsen ended up building himself a new home here. It is loosely based on a seventh-century Japanese Shinto shrine and is raised on stilts to enhance its exposure to light and air. Its foundation plantings exemplify Larsen's unusual approach. For example, he uses flowering wisteria as a prostrate hedge. Elsewhere he took a rock-garden staple – blue bird's-nest spruce – and had it grafted on to poles in order to create a mini allée. To maximize multi-season interest, Larsen's plant palette is a curated blend sourced from local nurseries as well as from Japan, Norway, Siberia and the Netherlands.

The self-taught Larsen designs fully realized landscapes, so the gardeners often move plants and trees that have outgrown their original composition. His eye for the big picture also translates to perfect siting for the pieces of art. The blown-glass spears of Dale Chihuly's *White Beluga* erupt from dunes covered in *Microbiota decussata* beneath weeping Norway spruces.

Larsen describes his art park as 'an alternative to the usual suburban backyard'. It is also an idiosyncratic expression of personal vision, an evolving fabric that exploits the dynamics of seasonality, sun and wind as well as the interplay between nature's artistry and artificial sculpture.

1—A stone and gravel path modelled on a dry riverbed runs across the lawn past dramatically scaled boulders.
2—A tropical garden was installed in 2012 by Landcraft Environments alongside the water rill.
3—Larsen's *Study in Heightened Perspective* in the red garden uses painted wooden posts to line an allée.
4—The Amphitheatre was created using the soil excavated from the new lily pond.
5—The reeds around Peter's Pond form an atmospheric setting for *Blue Spears*, a blown-glass sculpture by Dale Chihuly.

# Innisfree

Millbrook, New York, USA

| |
|---|
| Marion Beck, Walter Beck, Lester Collins |
| 20th century |
| 76 hectares / 189 acres |
| US Zones 5b–6a |
| Eastern / Landscape / Rock / Vistas / Water |

This garden had several names before being named after W B Yeats's poem 'The Lake Isle of Innisfree', a fitting label for a garden created around a large lake. Its lyrical landscape reinterprets Eastern design traditions for the West. To enter the landscape is to become an active participant strolling through an unrolling Chinese painting.

Walter and Marion Beck originally planned an English landscape garden to go with their Queen Anne-style house, but Walter instead sought inspiration from China and Japan, particularly the eighth-century poet, painter and garden-maker Wang Wei.

In the informal landscape Beck created what he described as a series of 'cup gardens', small areas where the viewer's attention is drawn to special rocks, plants or water. The inwardly focused vignettes were unified by the landscape architect Lester Collins, who was employed by the Becks from the late 1930s. Collins introduced the sequential journey that draws the visitor around the lake. One of his outstanding additions is the *yarimizu* (a Japanese-inspired oxbow in the meadow stream), which appears almost as a calligraphic element in the lawn.

The 'cup gardens' can be as simple as a rock waterfall shrouded in mist backlit by the sun, a rock colonized by wild columbine (*Aquilegia*), mosses and ferns, or a rock arch surrounded by Japanese primulas (*Primula japonica*). Strong group plantings of species such as smoke bushes (*Cotinus*) make frothy mounds, while pruned pear trees echo the shape of the landscape feature known as the Dumpling Knoll. Groves of trees formed by cultivars such as sentry sugar maple (*Acer saccharum* subsp. *nigrum* 'Monumentale') contrast with the spreading lawn. The lake's surface is broken in summer by colonies of sacred lotus (*Nelumbo nucifera*). Collins uses water effectively to catch the eye, with dramatic jets often repeating the vertical columns of tree forms.

This is a garden not of flower beds but of successful cultural borrowing that results in a great American garden imbued with Eastern principles that delight the senses and the mind.

1—Carefully placed boulders and a maple give an Eastern feel to the Terrace Gardens, planted with perennials and evergreens.
2—The Point provides a view across the lily-strewn lake to the Channel Crossing.
3—Lester Collins diverted the stream to form this *yarimizu*, or oxbow.
4—Primulas and ferns grow along the Mill Stream where it flows past a rock arch which frames the landscape beyond.

# Bartram's Garden

Philadelphia,
Pennsylvania, USA

John Bartram

18th century

19 hectares / 46 acres

US Zone 6b

Botanical / Edible / Formal / Historic

Bartram's is an accidental botanical garden – and the first botanical garden in the United States. Its creation predates the country itself. It was begun in 1728 on the banks of the Schuylkill River, in what was then New Sweden, by John Bartram, a third-generation Pennsylvania Quaker from farming stock. Bartram purchased a 41-hectare (102-acre) property on which he built a house – largely as seen today, but with additions including the greenhouse of 1760 – as well as a garden.

Aided by his natural curiosity and sharp scientific mind, Bartram began systematically to fill his garden with native North American plants, many of which he discovered himself. From 1738, and later accompanied by his son William, he made plant-hunting expeditions through Delaware, Maryland and Virginia, then Lake Ontario, the Carolinas, New Jersey and the Appalachians. In 1763 he went as far south as Florida. In total, father and son introduced more than 200 native species into cultivation.

The Bartram nursery supplied specimens to George Washington at Mount Vernon (see page 422) and Thomas Jefferson at Monticello (see page 424), as well as to gardeners in Britain, who were sent a specially designed 'Bartram Box' containing seeds of a hundred or so species. In 1765 Bartram was appointed a Royal Botanist by King George III in recognition of his contributions to natural science.

The garden around the house is a series of formal beds divided by paths. The Upper Kitchen Garden grows herbs and other edibles in raised beds; the Common Flower Garden is filled with herbaceous plants and bulbs; while the New Flower Garden was home to the plants Bartram collected on his trips or received from friends. The botanical highlight is the large Franklin tree (*Franklinia alatamaha*), which produces beautiful, scented, camellia-like white flowers with orange stamens. Found by John and William Bartram near the Altamaha River in Georgia in 1765, the tree became extinct in the wild as early as 1803 and only survives thanks to Bartram's cultivation of it.

1 — The Upper Kitchen Garden is immediately outside the house, itself a National Historic Landmark.
2 — The Franklin tree in the Common Flower Garden is one of the highlights of the botanical collection.
3 — Pipevine (*Aristolochia macrophylla*) and trumpet honeysuckle (*Lonicera sempervirens*) grow on the terrace wall.
4 — A yellowwood tree (*Cladrastis kentukea*, right) blooms behind the Common Flower Garden; it is one of the garden's oldest trees, having been found in Tennessee in 1796.

# Longwood Gardens

Kennett Square,
Pennsylvania, USA

Pierre S du Pont and others

20th century

425 hectares / 1,050 acres

US Zones 6b–7a

Conservatory / Display / Formal /
Rooms / Water

Longwood is one of America's greatest gardens. When it was bought in 1906 by Pierre S du Pont – an industrialist from a family of eager garden-makers – its arboretum, begun in 1798, was already one of America's finest. Longwood now comprises meadows and woodland and forty 'show gardens'. Such a phrase might suggest that Longwood is more akin to a garden festival than a garden, but that is not the case. Instead, taken collectively, the twenty outdoor and twenty indoor gardens (housed within 1.6 hectares/4 acres of glasshouse) offer the visitor a varied experience and a rich source of inspiration.

Du Pont's travels informed the aesthetic approach to the gardens. He had visited gardens in England, France and Italy and had become fascinated by tropical plants on trips to South America, the Caribbean, Florida, California and Hawaii. Du Pont was also a technophile, and Longwood benefited from the latest technology.

The most imposing building in the garden is the vast conservatory. Facing it is the Fountain Garden, now used for *son et lumière* shows. Water is a uniting theme, both in the greenhouses and in the wider landscape, where it is used formally in the Italian Water Garden and informally in the towering Rock Garden.

After du Pont's death, a Landscape Committee was formed in 1970. It included the renowned Californian landscape architect Thomas Church, who designed the Theatre Garden (1975), Wisteria Garden (1976) and Peony Garden (1976). In 1977 Church was succeeded by the British landscape architect Peter Shepheard, who redesigned the water-lily pools (1989). Inside the conservatory, Roberto Burle Marx and Conrad Hamerman created the tropical Cascade Garden (1992), while outside, local landscape architects have designed the Idea Garden, devoted to testing annuals, perennials and other plants. Other additions are Isabelle Greene's Silver Garden (1989) and Ron Lutsko's Mediterranean Garden (1993). Longwood remains a diversity of experiences – and most definitely not a garden show.

1 — The Main Fountain Garden was based on fountains du Pont had seen at the World Columbian Exposition at Chicago in 1893.
2 — The Italian Water Garden (1927) was inspired by that at Villa Gamberaia in Italy (see page 296).
3 — A path weaves between borders of low-growing alpines towards the Chimes Tower and the artificial Waterfall.
4 — Near the Large Lake, ashes, maples, oaks and tulip trees shade a classical temple.
5 — In the Caryopteris Allée in late summer, white *Hydrangea paniculata* standards bloom in a border of *Caryopteris clandonensis* 'Longwood Blue'.

1

2

3

4

5

6, 7—The East Conservatory was opened in 1973, but after problems with ventilation its roof was replaced in 2006 with a ridge-and-furrow design to match other buildings on the site.

8, 9—The Silver Garden was designed by Isabelle Greene in 1989 in an indoor echo of the famous White Garden at Sissinghurst in Kent (see page 174).

10—Australian purple coral-pea vine (*Hardenbergia violaceae* 'Happy Wanderer') grows on arches in the Mediterranean Garden.

11—Bromeliads and ferns grow in crevices in the rock in the Cascade Garden, designed by the renowned Brazilian landscape architect Roberto Burle Marx and Conrad Hamerman in the early 1990s.

6

7

8

9

10

11

# Chanticleer

Wayne, Pennsylvania, USA

| | |
|---|---|
| Adolph Rosengarten | |
| 20th century | |
| 14.2 hectares / 35 acres | |
| US Zones 6b–7a | |
| Botanical / Landscape / Naturalistic / Rooms / Terraces / Woodland | |

Chanticleer is a garden of contrasts and theatre where a face stares up from the bottom of a pool and a library has books of stone. The creative force behind the garden for much of the twentieth century was the Rosengarten family, owners of a pharmaceutical company, who took over the property in 1913.

The entrance courtyard is formed by the Teacup Garden, where an Italian-inspired fountain is surrounded by tender species selected for their foliage and flowers. Wall-mounted vases are planted with different, but similar-looking, plants. In the Tennis Court Garden, the five beds are planted with hardy herbaceous perennials that present flower and foliage colour from spring to autumn. Nearby are the Cut-Flower and Vegetable gardens, the latter with a potager.

The house is screened by pink ornamental cherries underplanted with hydrangea and native *phlox*, and in front of the porch is a border of sun-loving plants, including bear's breeches (*Acanthus mollis*) and various lavenders. Beyond are expanses of lawn dotted with specimen trees and cloaked with drifts of naturalized bulbs in spring.

A clockwise route through the wider gardens brings the visitor to the Serpentine, where beds of wheat and barley are backed by a sinuous avenue of juniper and a semicircle of *Ginkgo biloba*. Further on, the garden becomes wilder as it passes through the Asian Woods, an American woodland garden underplanted with oriental species, including *Arisaema sikokianum*, *Asarum splendens* and primulas. In the Pond Garden, pools mirror the surrounding trees. Lawns planted with blue *Camassia quamash* flank the stone-lined Bell's Run Creek, while Bell's Woodland is planted with species from the eastern North American forests, including azaleas, foam flowers (*Tiarella*) and ferns.

At the heart of Chanticleer is the Ruin Garden, the shell of an old house. This folly comprises three 'rooms'. The Great Hall contains a sarcophagus-shaped fountain standing on a 'rug' of stone, the Library is home to stone books, and in the Pool Room marble faces line the bottom of a fountain.

1—In the Teacup Garden *Brugmansia arborea* standards tower over gingers, pineapple, lilies and canna, and tropical plants in containers help to attract hummingbirds.
2—Climbing plants echo the golden theme of a border in the Terrace Garden.
3—*Valeriana officinalis* blooms in May.
4—The bog garden in the Asian Woods includes species such as *Polygonatum humile*, *Primula japonica* and *Primula pulverulenta*, hostas and *Acorus gramineus* 'Ogon'.
5—The Ruin Garden was created in 2000 on the site of a former house in the grounds.

3

4

5

# Dumbarton Oaks

Washington, DC, USA

| |
|---|
| Beatrix Farrand |
| 20th century |
| 4 hectares / 10 acres |
| US Zone 7a |
| Arts & Crafts / Naturalistic / Plantsman / Rooms / Terraces |

On the sloping site of Dumbarton Oaks, the garden designer Beatrix Farrand created a series of contrasting garden rooms joined by steps. The garden's poetic dimension comes from the sense of proportion in the use of plants, structures and materials. The planting uses texture and structure without relying on flowering species, although there are seasonal highlights with beautifully pruned wisteria, slopes covered in *Forsythia* x *intermedia* 'Spectabilis', billowing herbaceous borders and a Rose Garden.

Having bought the Georgian house and estate in 1920, Robert and Mildred Bliss commissioned Farrand to create a garden. The upper terraces reflect the formality of the house, with restrained planting, and balustraded terraces descend to the Rose Garden, dubbed the grand ballroom of the garden. The nearby Arbor Terrace is renowned for its pergola. The curving roof is smothered in the purple flowers of wisteria in late spring, while in summer the upright supports are clothed in white-flowered clematis.

Beyond the formal terraces, brick paths wind through walks of silver-leaved maples (*Acer saccharum*) underplanted with spring-flowering bulbs – crocus, scilla, narcissus and creeping lily-of-the-valley (*Convallaria majalis*). The informal areas show bold plantings of single species of cherry, crab apple and forsythia. At their heart is the formal Ellipse Garden, one of the most serene places in the garden. Originally just a fountain set in a lawn and surrounded by a box hedge, it now has a stunning hedge of pleached American hornbeam (*Carpinus caroliniana*).

Nearer the house is the now-dry water feature known as the Pebble Garden, which contains a large pebble mosaic of wheatsheaves that represent the Bliss family motto: 'As you sow, so shall you reap' – and the visitor will find much to harvest from this garden.

1—An overview shows a series of Farrand's rooms: the Orchard, the Kitchen Garden and the Herbaceous Border.
2—The Rose Garden is home to roses that bloom repeatedly from spring to autumn.
3—The Fountain Terrace is the one flower garden on the terraces near the house.
4—On the Arbor Terrace hydrangeas and evergreen shrubs enjoy the shade beneath a pergola that is swathed in wisteria in spring.
5—The Ellipse Garden is now surrounded by pleached American hornbeam.
6—The wheatsheaf mosaic of the now-dry Pebble Garden was designed to be seen beneath a shallow sheen of water.
7—An allée of flowering plums (*Prunus* x *blireana*) leads between the Herbaceous Borders and Cherry Hill.
8—The Lilac Circle in the northeast corner of the garden is planted with a Korean lilac.

6

7

8

# Colonial Williamsburg

Williamsburg, Virginia, USA

| | |
|---|---|
| Various | |
| 18th century | |
| 71 hectares / 175 acres | |
| US Zone 7a | |
| Cottage / Edible / Formal / Historic | |

In the eighteenth century, Virginia was the largest and wealthiest of the British colonies in America, and Williamsburg was its capital and cultural centre. An integral part of the settlement was its gardens, each demarcated as specified in a law of 1705 by a white fence, but each expressing the personality – and the means – of its owner.

Even within the similar lots, there is no blueprint for a Williamsburg garden. Then, as now, gardens were as varied as the people who created them. The gardens of ordinary colonists tended to be small and placed behind the house. They usually comprised an orchard or vegetable garden, or both, ornamented with shrubs and colourful flowers. In contrast, the Governor's Palace garden – created by Lieutenant Governor Alexander Spotswood from 1710 – was much larger and in the fashionable style imported from Britain: a formal Anglo-Dutch design, with beds picked out in low-clipped hedges of box filled with a mixture of North American plants and familiar British favourites. Ornament was provided by elaborate gates, decorative vases, steps, seats, garden houses and enclosing walls. There was also a rare water feature in the form of a canal and fish pond. Spotswood's garden was emulated by those settlers with the means, and, although not as grand as contemporary European gardens, marked the start of the American Colonial style.

Today's gardens at Williamsburg are re-creations. The capital of Virginia moved in the American Revolution to Richmond, and Williamsburg became a backwater. In 1926 restoration began with the aim of returning it to its heyday: the re-creations seen today are based on its appearace from 1699 to 1780. From the outset the gardens were integral to the programme, and to enable their authentic re-creation a huge research project gleaned information from historical sources supplemented by archaeological evidence.

Some observers criticize Colonial Williamsburg as being too manicured to be authentic, but it does provide a fascinating insight into the gardens of colonial America. The restoration of the gardens also had a significant impact on the twentieth-century American Colonial Revival garden.

1—Tulips bloom in the Governor's Palace Garden, which resembles an English country estate during the reign of William and Mary in the late seventeenth century.
2, 5—The Taliaferro Cole House was home to Thomas Crease, whose garden had three rectangular areas enclosed by fences, each planted for a different purpose.
3, 4—John Blair was an eager gardener. His kitchen dooryard has been re-created with parterres of fragrant herbs, similar to a seventeenth-century 'physic' garden.

3

4

5

# Mount Vernon

Mount Vernon, Virginia, USA

George Washington

18th century

20.2 hectares / 50 acres (garden);
202 hectares / 500 acres (estate)

US Zone 7a

Edible / Historic / Landscape /
Naturalistic / Walled

George Washington's garden at Mount Vernon is entwined with the history of the USA. He designed the garden as it has been renovated today in the 1780s, between defeating Britain in the Revolutionary War and becoming the first US president. The garden has axial lines that echo both Baroque ideas and the influence of the early English landscape garden. In essence Mount Vernon was a *ferme ornée* (ornamented farm) – a productive rural idyll.

The garden is bounded on one side by the Potomac River and on the others by ha-has, thus including the borrowed landscape in the visual experience of the garden. West of the house a walk meanders around the bowling green, or lawn. It is flanked by local tree varieties, including crab apples, honey locusts, maples and sassafras. Beyond, opening to the north and south, are twin shield-shaped walled gardens.

To the north, the Upper Garden has been re-created with gravel paths and two box parterres. The English box hedges enclosing the beds are original – a gift to Washington from Henry Lee III, the governor of Virginia. Planting today uses period-correct species (based on letters to Washington from the head gardener) including cardinal flowers, crown imperials, foxgloves, jasmine and larkspurs. Here too is Washington's greenhouse, the Orangerie, where he grew citrus and tender flowers. Behind the spinning house is what he called his Botanic Garden, where he tested new plants.

Washington was a lover of trees – a few of his plantings survive, including a tulip tree (*Liriodendron tulipifera*) – and he used trees widely. North of the house he planted a grove of honey locust (*Gleditsia triacanthos*) and to the south a shrubbery of evergreens, flowering dogwoods and red bud maples.

In the walled Lower Garden, or kitchen garden, the grass paths and formal layout have been re-created. The view of the Potomac River was framed by a wood covering the downhill slope. Washington also planted orchards and grew at least four apple cultivars, two of which – 'Newtown Pippin' and 'Nonpareil' – are still in cultivation.

1—The Lower Garden has been re-created based on plans in gardening books Washington is known to have owned.
2, 4—Traditional cottage-garden flowers –foxgloves, salvia, echinacea and eupatorium – bloom in the walled Upper Garden.
3—An espaliered fruit tree grows against the brick wall of the Upper Garden, which was originally planted almost entirely with productive fruit and nut trees.
5—These splendid cabbages grow inside a border of yellow santolina, just coming into bloom.

1

2

3

4

5

# Monticello

Charlottesville, Virginia, USA

| | |
|---|---|
| Thomas Jefferson | |
| 18th–19th century | |
| 16.5 hectares / 40 acres | |
| US Zone 7a | |
| Edible / Historic / Landscape / Naturalistic | |

History remembers Thomas Jefferson as the author of the Declaration of Independence and third president of the USA, but he was also a scholar, a founder of the University of Virginia and a talented gardener. The garden at Monticello occupied him from the time he inherited the estate in 1769, aged only twenty-six, until his death in 1826. Jefferson approached his gardening in a scientific way, keeping detailed records in his *Garden Book*. In the century following his death the garden fell into decay, but in 1939 the Garden Club of Virginia used Jefferson's own records to begin a two-year programme to restore the original gardens.

The main ornamental gardens are next to the Palladian-inspired house. In 1807 Jefferson sketched a plan for twenty oval flower beds in the four angles of the house. A year later he added the Winding Walk and its flower border to flank the large, oval-shaped lawn on the west side of the house. In 1812 he redesigned the border to bring more order to the planting, dividing it into 3-metre (10-foot) sections, each planted with a different plant type.

The display in the flower garden changes up to three times a year. The spring show is of bulbs, especially tulips, which fill the area with colour. Summer is the time of hardy annuals (sweet peas, poppies, stocks), roses, biennials and perennials. Jefferson's records indicate that he grew about 105 types of perennial, including old-fashioned favourites such as calendula, Canterbury bells, foxgloves, larkspurs and sweet William. From late summer into autumn the show is of tender plants grown as annuals, including ageratum, heliotrope, French and African marigolds, pelargoniums and zinnias.

Re-created in the 1980s following a two-year archaeological investigation, the Vegetable Garden to the southeast occupies a 305-metre (1,000-foot) terrace. The rectangular beds are today planted with heritage varieties. On the stone terrace wall is the elegant Vegetable Garden Pavilion and below it lies the South Orchard, part of the larger fruit garden in which Jefferson grew 170 varieties.

1 — The Palladian house is set on top of a hill, surrounded by trees threaded by paths. The oval West Lawn, edged with flower beds, was a favourite playground for Jefferson's children.
2 — The Vegetable Garden would have been planted far more densely in Jefferson's time than it is today.
3 — In the vineyard, Jefferson alternated between growing European vines (*Vinifera*) and well-adapted New World alternatives, such as *Vitis labrusca* and *V. rotundifolia*.

1

2

3

# Winterthur

Wilmington, Delaware, USA

Henry Francis du Pont

19th–20th century

24 hectares / 60 acres (garden); 397 hectares / 982 acres (estate)

US Zone 6b

Naturalistic / Wild / Woodland

In terms of its size, Winterthur is a shadow of what it was when Henry Francis du Pont became the third generation of the gunpowder and chemical dynasty to garden at the family's estate. What remains today is one of the last examples of an original Wild Garden, part of a design movement from the early twentieth century that enlisted the concepts of Gertrude Jekyll and the Irish gardener William Robinson. Robinson's endorsement of sweeps of plants made sense for the broad-scale compositions large landowners had the space to support. The drifts were made up mostly of naturalized exotics, designed to look as if they had appeared spontaneously, their boundaries following the contours of the land.

Even as du Pont sought to create an aesthetic seemingly untouched by the hand of man, he worked assiduously to orchestrate colour combinations, from harmonious to near-discordant, and to consider flowering times so that his lyrical combinations would extend from midwinter to late autumn.

Although Winterthur has something to offer year round, its outstanding season is spring. In its earliest flush, the March Bank hillside is awash with the white of snowdrops and spring snowflake (*Leucojum vernum*); the blues of squill, Virginia bluebell (*Mertensia pulmonarioides*) and glory-of-the-snow; and a host of yellows, including *Adonis amurensis*, bellwort and winter aconite (*Eranthis hyemalis*). Later in the season, the Sundial Garden features pinks, whites and reds with flowering quince, cherries and crab apples, as well as spiraea, viburnum and lilac. Still more colour combinations come out in the Peony Garden (a showcase of herbaceous and tree peonies) and the Azalea Woods, where du Pont planted hundreds of rhododendrons and azaleas beneath a canopy of oak, tulip trees and beech.

Other highlights of the garden are the Pinetum, a collection of conifers established by du Pont's father in 1914, the Enchanted Woods (a children's garden) and Sycamore Hill, on which drifts of yellow and white daffodils pave the way for the lavenders, reds and pinks of the blooming redbuds (*Cercis*), mountain laurel and deutzia.

1—Near the house, a peaceful pond is surrounded by small-scale shrubs and grasses.
2—Drifts of daffodils grow on a bank below clouds of pink blossom.
3, 4, 5—Azaleas and white dogwood flower along a nature trail through the extensive Azalea Woods, where du Pont planted hundreds of flowering trees and shrubs above groundcover including abundant Spanish bluebells (*Hyacinthoides hispanica*).

# Ferry Cove

Sherwood, Maryland, USA

James van Sweden, Oehme van Sweden, Raymond Kaskey

21st century

0.6 hectares / 1.5 acres (approx)

US Zones 7–8

Grasses / Landscape / Meadow / Naturalistic / Sculpture

What garden designers do with their own gardens is always fascinating. Ferry Cove, the weekend home of the late landscape architect James van Sweden, is no exception. Spare and minimalistic, the garden matches the house. The planting looks natural, so successful is its 'invisible' design.

'My fantasy has always been to have a house that floated over a meadow,' van Sweden said, and the garden at Ferry Cove is all about the meadow – there are no lawns here. The meadow connects the house with the landscape and looks as if it has always been there. Breezes rippling through it echo the shifting currents of Chesapeake Bay beyond.

With the plantsman Wolfgang Oehme, his long-standing business partner, van Sweden developed the garden in phases through experimentation and ongoing editing. Great arcs defined what he called 'the designed garden', separated from the meadow by a 3-metre-wide (10-foot) path that prevents it encroaching. But the term 'designed' is used in the loosest of ways. Trees were planted for privacy, to add layers to planting and to frame views rather than block them. Oehme recommended hackberry trees (*Celtis occidentalis*) as feature plants – they are not usually seen as garden-worthy. The placement of large plants encourages movement around the garden; grass paths mown through the meadow lead to Chesapeake Bay and a driftwood folly that doubles as sheltered seating.

In the meadow, van Sweden did not want to use irrigation or pesticides, or to do more than one mow per year. Bold groups of flowering perennials are interspersed with native wetland sedges and grasses. At first the planting looked more like a patchwork, but interplanting transformed it with plants that appear to have spread and self-seeded. On the land side, a pond hosts aquatics and marginals that do not grow in the bay. A simple rectangular swimming pool was added later on the seaward side. Ferry Cove is living proof that great gardens do not have to have lawns.

1—Sunrise lights up the front of the house, where mountain mint (*Pycnanthemum muticum*) borders bluestone paving and a spherical sculpture by Grace Knowlton.
2—A bronze snake sculpture by Raymond Kaskey doubles as a handrail to the minimalist swimming pool, added in 2000.
3—The view from the back deck looks out across the meadow to Chesapeake Bay. In the foreground is oak-leaved hydrangea, *H. quercifolia*.
4—Boardwalks allowed van Sweden to explore the garden in his wheelchair. Tall, yellow-flowered cup plant (*Silphium perfoliatum*; right) can be invasive in European climates, so is best planted in wilder reaches of a garden.

3

4

# Montrose

Hillsborough,
North Carolina, USA

Governor and Mrs William Alexander
Graham, Craufurd and Nancy Goodwin

19th & 20th centuries

24.7 hectares / 61 acres

US Zones 7–8

Perennials / Plantsman / Rock /
Woodland

Montrose is a gardener's garden.
It is particularly lovely in winter, when
its woodlands are alive with bulbs
and low-growing plants: snowdrops,
primroses and hardy cyclamen have
all naturalized under the oaks and dawn
redwoods (*Metasequoia glyptostroboides*).
Owner Nancy Goodwin encourages
visitors to get down on their knees
to study the garden's small gems.

The current house dates from 1898,
but the gardens were first laid out and
specimen trees planted by Governor
William Alexander Graham in 1842.
A major change came during the 1930s,
when the sloping site was terraced to
control erosion under a public-works
project to provide employment during
the Great Depression.

It was only when Craufurd and Nancy
Goodwin bought Montrose in 1977 that
the modern development of the garden
began. Nancy Goodwin worked within
the original nineteenth-century layout
and retained the mature trees as 'bones'
for the new garden, but enhanced them
with her planting skill and creativity.
Her belief that 'Dissonance is key to
any art form' adds unique depth to the
planting interest.

What was once a vegetable garden
has been transformed into a Perennial
Garden, with bright colours and bold
plant shapes. The Rock Garden has
been replanted, while a tropical area
includes bananas, yuccas and tender
perennials. The Dianthus Walk is a
masterpiece of silvers, greys and blues
towered over by heavily scented white
formosa lilies (*Lilium formosanum*).
Rohdeas, with their wide strap-shaped
leaves, and hardy palms edge the
woodland planting. A lath house is
a shady place for visitors and plants
alike: ferns, hostas, pulmonaria and
polygonatum all flourish there.

Goodwin has introduced a number
of plants, including the richly coloured
*Heuchera* 'Montrose Ruby'. In 1984 she
opened a successful nursery, but she
closed it nearly ten years later in order
to spend more time on the garden. The
Garden Conservancy has designated
Montrose as a Preservation Project,
which guarantees that it will continue
to be open to the public.

1—A sorghum pot forms a central feature
in the Blue and Yellow Garden, where
California poppies (*Eschscholzia californica*)
flower in the path, with yellow irises and
blue larkspur.
2—Salvia and bright red *Dahlia* 'Bishop
of Llandaff' flower in a perennial border.
3—Blue *Phlox divaricata* flowers in the
woodland in late spring.
4—Poppies (*Papaver*) make a bold show of
colour against a backdrop of climbing roses.

# Pearl Fryar
# Topiary Garden

Bishopville, South Carolina, USA

| Pearl Fryar |
| 20th century |
| 1.2 hectares / 3 acres |
| US Zone 8b |
| Artistic / Sculpture / Shrubs / Topiary |

Pearl Fryar, son of a sharecropper, does not shrink from a challenge. He's a man who believes in the power of positive thinking, hard work and determination. When confronted in the 1980s with the plantless expanse of a former cornfield surrounding his newly built house, Fryar visited a local nursery to buy some shrubs and trees. There he encountered his first topiary (a pom-pom juniper) and liked what he saw. The nursery owner, sensing that Fryar was new to gardening, warned him that the plants were high-maintenance. Undeterred, Fryar asked a few questions, and the nursery owner gave him a brief demonstration. Fryar, armed with his own electric hedge clipper, has never looked back.

Some thirty years later, Fryar's 150-plus topiaries are not just the usual animals or geometric shapes – although there are some of each – but are also astounding, free-flowing, abstract, sometimes whimsical artistic creations. Fryar's inner artist was awakened as he transformed camellia, juniper, holly and cypress from thought into form year after year. In addition to working twelve-hour shifts at a factory, he trimmed late into the night, under a spotlight. One creation, named the Fishbone Tree, took seven years of trimming to achieve Fryar's design.

Many of the trees and shrubs Fryar has shaped were originally rescued from a nursery compost heap. He does not use chemicals and does not water the garden, instead mulching with pine needles to retain soil moisture. Now retired and in his seventies, Fryar enjoys leading visitors and school groups around the garden, planning new living sculptures, lecturing and counselling at-risk youth – and constantly trimming.

The garden is the physical embodiment of a self-taught artist's beliefs. And in case visitors miss his main message, he has carved it into his large side lawn and picked out the 2.4 metre-tall (8-foot) letters with flaming red begonias: Love Peace + Goodwill.

1—The Fishbone Tree, the centrepiece of one section of the garden, took Fryar more than seven years to trim into shape.
2, 5—Fryar's self-taught skill expresses itself in complex and irregular designs far removed from the blocks and shapes employed in most topiary.
3—Fryar's remarkable topiary is complemented by his 'junk art' sculptures placed throughout the garden.
4—Few of the garden's more than 300 individual plants are spared some kind of trimming.

# Middleton Place

Charleston, South Carolina, USA

| | |
|---|---|
| Henry Middleton, John Julius Pringle Smith | |
| 18th & 19th centuries | |
| 26.3 hectares / 65 acres | |
| US Zone 8b | |
| Formal / Historic / Landscape Water / Woodland | |

Middleton Place is America's oldest landscape garden and was the birthplace of Arthur Middleton, a signatory to the Declaration of Independence. Middleton's father, Henry, created the gardens in 1741 (using slave labour), marrying French landscape design – precise geometry, axial symmetry, a sense of order and control – with curving grass terraces and serpentine woodland paths that reflect the English landscape tradition. After the Civil War, the gardens declined for sixty years until Middleton descendant John Julius Pringle Smith began a fifteen-year restoration project in 1925.

Henry Middleton would still recognize the structure of the garden, but his descendants have introduced more colour and plant variety. The central axis aligned perfectly with the hall of the original house, and continues to highlight a superb river view; its gravel path becomes a wider green sward as it steps down the curving grass terraces. Perfect symmetry about the central axis means that the grass path divides the lake into two Butterfly Lakes, so called because of their winglike shape. Two rectangular pools delineate the garden from the woodlands around it: the Reflection Pool, which retains its strong edges, and the Azalea Pool, which has developed a softer, more organic shape over the years.

Allées of trimmed trees and shrubs separate different areas. Spanish moss (*Tillandsia usneoides*) relishes the humid atmosphere; its silvery strands add an ethereal quality to trees, including the live oak (*Quercus virginiana*). Since restoration, planting ensures year-round flowers. Some of the winter-flowering camellias are more than a hundred years old. Swathes of azaleas set the hillside ablaze in spring. Summer highlights include flowering kalmia, magnolias, crepe myrtles and roses. Herbaceous planting includes hellebores and American columbine (*Aquilegia canadensis*); there are also irises, lilies and abundant daffodils.

One of the outstanding gardens of the Thirteen Colonies, Middleton Place combines the classical landscape-design principles of the Old World with a singular palette and an overwhelming sense of place characteristic of the New World.

1, 3—The main axis of the garden runs down a terraced bank and between two butterfly-wing lakes to a view out over the river beyond.
2—The Azalea Pool was artificially created but has softened over time, with vegetation colonizing and softening its banks.
4—Silver strands of Spanish moss (*Tillandsia*) add an ethereal quality to the trees above the lawn and banks of colourful azaleas.

1

2

# Longue Vue

New Orleans, Louisana, USA

Ellen Biddle Shipman, Edith Stern, William Platt, Geoffrey Platt

20th century

3.2 hectares / 8 acres

US Zone 9

Formal / Rooms / Walled

Longue Vue bewitches and confuses. The classical revival house and its avenue of live oaks (*Quercus virginiana*) gives the appearance of an antebellum plantation, but the whole estate is a twentieth-century creation. William and Geoffrey Platt built the house between 1939 and 1942 to replace one that Ellen Biddle Shipman, the dean of American landscape architects, felt no longer suited the garden she was designing.

The house and garden were intended to be viewed together. Near the house are three main areas: the Portico, Pan and Yellow gardens. The Portico Garden's formal terrace is central to the design. It is quartered with formal parterres and features a collection of camellias. A central axis leads from the house across a lawn Shipman called the Spanish Court. Destroyed by a hurricane in 1965, it was redesigned by the house's architect William Platt and its owner, Edith Stern, inspired by the Generalife at the Alhambra in Spain (see page 276). Defined by the ivy-clad, low walls that feature throughout the site, the main axis of the Portico Garden reappears as a narrow canal with water jets arcing across it from both sides.

The Pan Garden is an intimate viewing garden with a statue of the god as a focal point. On the other side of the house lies the more open Yellow Garden, with a leaping dolphin fountain. Together with the Walled Garden farther from the house, these areas demonstrate Shipman's signature style: a formal, well-scaled layout combined with geometric axes to create garden rooms, overlaid with fulsome planting. Shipman designed many wild gardens, but the example at Longue Vue is the sole survivor. It hosts a woodland of live oaks, magnolias and sweet olives.

After Hurricane Katrina in 2005 Long Vue was flooded for two weeks, killing sixty per cent of the plants. Restoration was completed remarkably quickly to restore the romantic atmosphere to the lush garden rooms.

1—In the Portico Garden, Shipman divided the space with four formal box-edged parterres. The lawn makes a green pathway from the house to the Spanish Court.
2—The Spanish Court has fountains and intricate brick paving inspired by the Generalife in Spain.
3—Along the drive, Shipman trained the limbs of the live oaks to form a grand cathedral arch.
4—The mellow tones of old brick pavers and a gentle central fountain make this courtyard a quiet, relaxing place. Golden thryallis (*Galphimia glauca*), native to South America, puts on a showy display to the left of the path.
5—Around the statue of the god from which it takes its name, the Pan Garden is planted with azaleas, Japanese magnolias, sweet olives and amaryllis.

1

2

# Fairchild Tropical Botanic Garden

Coral Gables, Florida, USA

David Fairchild, Robert H Montgomery, Marjory Stoneman Douglas, Charles Crandon, William Lyman Phillips

20th century

34 hectares / 83 acres

US Zone 10b

Botanical / Conservatory / Plant Collection / Tropical

Fairchild is one of the great tropical botanical gardens in the world. It was founded in 1938 by Colonel Robert H Montgomery, who named it after the botanist Dr David Fairchild, and soon became renowned for its collection of palms. Among the specimens, for example, is the highly attractive petticoat palm (*Copernicia macroglossa*), which is native to Cuba. The leaves are not shed as with most other palms but remain on the stem, creating a kind of rough, grey petticoat.

This is just one among more than 1,500 palm accessions planted in the Fairchild Tropical Botanical Garden, with 193 genera and more than 500 identified species represented. The garden has the largest collection of highly threatened palms in the world. This alone is reason enough to visit, but there are also huge collections of cycads and flowering vines, one of the largest tropical fruit collections in the world, a Madagascan Spiny Forest – one of the most endangered plant habitats on the planet – tons of orchids, heliconias, anthuriums, a 0.8-hectare (2-acre) rainforest, a conservatory with thousands of butterflies and, as the cliché goes, much, much more.

Not only is Fairchild a major scientific institution that carries out research projects in Madagascar, the African mainland, the Caribbean and Latin America and programmes that are crucial to the conservation of tropical plants, but it also lies in a beautiful and flowing landscape, with waterways and canals, open spaces and forests. There is a farmers' market, education programmes, plant sales, a Florida Keys Coastal habitat and Yoko Ono's wishing grove, an installation by the famous Japanese artist.

In a way this might sound as if it is all too much – but, as Fairchild shows, when it comes to gardens there is no such thing as too much.

1—An aerial view of the gardens shows the extensive lakes, some of which have been left in their natural shape, others of which have been carefully landscaped and edged.
2—The Garden House Lawn, outside the garden's main building, is ringed by palms and benches where visitors can admire extensive vistas.
3—The natural cascade and water hole in the Sunken Garden form one of the six water gardens at Fairchild.
4—The Palmetum is at the heart of Fairchild's collection of more than 500 species of palm, from the common to the very rare.
5—The Bailey Palm Glade is a carefully proportioned, flower-bordered allée that leads visitors from a small pool to a vista over lakes and islands.

# Vizcaya Gardens

## Miami, Florida, USA

| |
|---|
| Diégo Suarez |
| 20th century |
| 4 hectares / 10 acres |
| US Zone 10b |
| Coastal / Formal / Italianate / Subtropical |

Vizcaya is like no other garden. Its combination of eighteenth-century Italianate villa, Floridian excess and subtropical flora is unique. It is a mixture that can vary from the elegant to the absurd, and often has elements of both at the same time.

The winter residence of industrialist James Deering was built between 1914 and 1922 on the shores of Biscayne Bay. Perhaps its most iconic – and most absurd – feature is the large stone barge sculpted by Alexander Stirling Calder, which stands in the water immediately in front of the Main House. The barge is carved with mythical Caribbean creatures, which set the tone for the fantasy nature of the estate. For inspiration, Deering and his co-creators looked to Florence and Rome, the Everglades, North Africa and parts of Asia. The broad range of influences is reflected in various small buildings, statuary, grottoes and urns.

The garden has a central fan-shaped axis and – appropriately for its coastal location – many water features, including a fountain basin in the shape of a sarcophagus and a water staircase. Floristically, the garden and its surroundings are highly diverse. Deering preserved some of the mango groves that were once prolific in the region, as well as remnants of the once-dense subtropical Floridian forest, called rockland hammock. The forest is now home to endangered plants, such as redberry stopper (*Eugenia confusa*), Florida bitterbush (*Picramnia pentandra*) and brittle maidenhair fern (*Adiantum tenerum*). The forest is also home to eight known national champion trees (the largest of their kind in the United States).

The hallucinatory aspect of Vizcaya's formal gardens is only heightened by the heat and humidity. Parterres are set out in head-spinning geometrical arrangements. Orchids abound – more than 2,000 grow in the trees and in the rebuilt David A Klein Orchidarium. There are also many unusual plants, such as peach palm (*Bactris mexicana*), giant elephant's ear plant (*Alocasia* 'Borneo Giant') and the marvellously named *Crinum* 'Regina's Disco Lounge'.

1—A view north over the house shows the large stone barge 'anchored' in the inlet.
2—The walled Secret Garden is home to rectangular beds, borders, pot plants and rows of hemispherical planters on the wall.
3—The central area of the garden is dominated by parterres with geometric arabesques of wax jasmine (*Jasminum simplicifolium*), which Deering used instead of the more usual box.
4—At the end of a view across a formal pool rises the artificial Garden Mound, which was created to limit and vary views from and of the house.

# Las Pozas

Xilitla, San Luis Potosí, Mexico

Edward James, Plutarco Gastelum, Ivan Hicks

20th century

8 hectares / 20 acres

Humid Subtropical

Artistic / Rainforest / Sculpture

Las Pozas, in the Mexican subtropical forest of Xilitla, is filled with staircases to the heavens, perpetually blooming giant concrete flowers and what were once aviaries filled with exotic birds. The unique blend of sculpture, architecture and planting was the creation of the wealthy Englishman Edward James, a patron of the Surrealist art movement. As an escape from an unhappy divorce and his subsequent ostracization from English society, James travelled the world. In 1944 he reached Mexico. Here in the mountains of the Sierra Madre Oriental 400 kilometres (250 miles) north of Mexico City, he discovered a valley of pools and waterfalls at Las Pozas (The Place of the Ponds). It was to provide the major outlet for his creativity and a balm for the hurts he had experienced earlier in his life.

Initially James developed a collection of some 18,000 orchid plants, but in 1962 they were destroyed by unexpected frost. In response he turned to his interest in Surrealism and designed a garden that was resistant to such potential threats. Helped by his local workforce, he constructed concrete alien flower forms and garden pavilions that 'grew' among the tall forest trees. In James's hands concrete became a plastic, organic medium used to create the quirky, dreamlike features of a lush forest garden. The visitor wanders in this strange world below the tree canopy with the ground covered by the bold foliage of *Monstera deliciosa*, ferns and other species growing in the shade. Such plants also spread to inhabit the sculptural installation, giving the feeling of discovering a lost civilization.

James' sense of humour is evident throughout the garden: near the entrance are sculptures of an enlarged right hand modelled from Plutarco Gastelum, his 'right-hand man' in the creation of Las Pozas. His Surrealist inspiration can be seen into the unnecessary pillars carved in the rock of the waterfall over one of the natural bathing pools. Such details fill Las Pozas, making it truly unlike any other garden – a unique creation that rewards a long and unhurried visit.

1 — The Bamboo Palace was one of the thirty-six Surrealist-inspired concrete structures James built amid the natural tropical forest.
2 — The concrete details of Las Pozas are gradually gaining a glossy patina of moss as the tropical vegetation slowly claims back James' garden.
3 — James carefully channelled the water that fed the ponds after which Las Pozas is named to form basins from which he could water his huge collection of orchids (before they were wiped out by frost).

# Parque Ecológico de Xochimilco

Xochimilco, Mexico City, Mexico

Mario Schjetnan

20th century

300 hectares / 125 acres (park);
3,000 hectares / 1,250 acres (landscape)

Temperate Subtropical Highland

Modern / Park / Sustainable / Water

A 'twenty-four hour a day machine – not a fountain,' says the Mexican designer Mario Schjetnan of the series of water chutes entering the lake he designed at the heart of the Parque Ecológico de Xochimilco (Xochimilco Ecological Park). The park is a microcosm of the wider artificial landscape of the canals and agricultural *chinampas* (floating gardens) in which it sits, originally created by the Aztec on the edge of their capital, Tenochtitlán, now Mexico City.

The site of Mexico City, originally a marshy lake, was settled when the Aztec created artificial islands. In 1987 the area was declared a World Heritage site, and Schjetnan's educational and recreational park acknowledged the area's heritage and working landscape and restored the ecosystem, with strong design and informal planting of trees and grassland. The storm water entering the lake has been treated to remove pollutants and is used to regulate the level of the canal systems.

Beyond the entrance, the dramatic blue walls of the circular visitor centre – topped with aloes – entice the visitor into a magical landscape where even the grasses in the joints between the paving seem appropriate for the ecological mission. From the roof of the visitor centre there are spectacular views across the designed landscape to distant snow-covered volcanoes. The entrance plaza is given a strong geometry by a grid of paving and turf, but soon visitors find themselves in a more informal landscape. A 400-metre (1,310-foot) pergola takes the visitor past beds of hollyhocks, marigolds and many other flowers growing on the *chinampas* – Xochimilco means 'the place where flowers are grown'. Plants and flowers are sold in a vast adjacent market with more than 1,800 stalls.

To explore the wider and older landscape, visitors have to take a boat. Most are punted around the *chinampas* and never escape from the main waterway into the network of canals. The peace of their journey is frequently shattered by floating mariachi bands pulling up alongside. For the more adventurous visitor, the backwaters winding between the islands are quiet and still, as trees, flowers and cows seem to float by reflected in the water.

1—From the grid of paving and turf in the entry plaza the long pergola leads visitors out into the *chinampas*. Height in the landscape comes from copses of trees including pine and eucalyptus.
2—A spiral water tower dominates the plaza at the entrance to the park.
3, 4—Key to the park's water management are a series of protruding spouts that feed recycled water into the lakes. The edges of the water are planted with reeds.

# Casa Luis Barragán

Tacubaya, Mexico City, Mexico

| | |
|---|---|
| Luis Barragán | |
| 20th century | |
| 0.05 hectares / 0.02 acres | |
| Temperate Subtropical Highland | |
| Artistic / Naturalistic / Urban | |

This small gem in a residential area of Mexico City is the home of the architect and property developer Luis Barragán. It well deserves its status as a UNESCO World Heritage site. To step from the street through the modest doorway is to embark on a journey through Barragán's design philosophy. He created his buildings from the inside out, being less concerned with striking facades than with the experience of inhabiting an internal space, and his gardens reflect a feeling of comfortable scale and of being secure within the boundaries of plants and walls.

The house has examples of Barragán's characteristic coloured walls, which are so often included in his garden spaces. Although they seem dramatic, such walls were inspired by the traditional painted houses of rural Mexico. Barragán uses them to reflect light on to the 'canvas' of white walls. From the living room, the garden is revealed through a wall of floor-to-ceiling glass. The naturalistic appearance of the plants outside contrasts with the geometric precision of the architecture. This was Barragán's favoured garden style: a sea of green plants in the city, and a wild sanctuary of trees and climbers.

Ivy (*Hedera helix*) hangs in festoons from the leaning trees to create a feeling of mystery. Through a narrow opening in a garden wall is the Patio de las Ollas, a small courtyard where a corner is filled with terracotta vessels, grouped on a floor paved with lava tiles, and a small pool overflows to produce interesting patterns of water on the paving, a typical Barragán touch.

From the upper floor of the house, the garden is visible from the bedroom windows, although the foliage of climbing plants surges against the glass. A flight of stairs – glowing golden from the light flitering through a yellow glass door – leads to a surprise: the roof terrace. With white walls and one of bright pink, this space is concealed from the surrounding city. The tops of trees in the garden can be seen, and the sky provides a blue ceiling for this outdoor room. As elsewhere, Barragán's design creates a strong relationship between the garden and the internal spaces, creating a powerful experience even in a small space.

1—A glass wall in the living room gives a view of the garden, with overhanging trees festooned with long trails of ivy.
2—Barragán selected the bright colours for the walls of his roof terrace to echo the traditional colours of Mexican homes.
3—In the corner of the Patio de las Ollas, terracotta vessels are arranged on tiles of dark lava.

# Jardín Etnobotánico de Oaxaca

Oaxaca, Mexico

Francisco Toledo, Luis Zárate, Alejandro de Ávila

20th century

2.3 hectares / 5.7 acres

Tropical Savannah

Botanical / Cactus / Drought Tolerant / Modern / Palms

For those tempted to believe that botanic gardens are fusty places, Jardín Etnobotánico de Oaxaca will be an epiphany. Its fusion of contemporary art and an array of native plants from the Mexican state of Oaxaca would convert even the most disaffected visitor.

Against the dramatic backdrop of the Santo Domingo Cultural Centre, rows of cacti and succulents march across the broad entrance plaza, beckoning visitors inside the high walls and towers of this World Heritage site. The former monastery of Santo Domingo now houses a regional museum whose collections include cultural articles, gold jewellery and artefacts from the Mixtec period.

The Mexican army used the old walled orchards and gardens behind the complex as parade grounds until 1994, when renowned Oaxacan artist Francisco Toledo led a petition for the area to be conserved as part of the nation's heritage. Alejandro de Avila, who later became the garden's director, joined Toledo in a groundbreaking initiative to create a botanical garden to showcase both the state's huge floral diversity and its relationship with local traditions. Clearing decades' worth of debris took several years.

Today, imposing Hispanic-period architecture forms the backdrop of a garden in the Modernist tradition of Mexican design. The garden's layout and ground patterns derive from ancient indigenous Zapotec hieroglyphic motifs and geometric designs. Ornamental rills zigzag beside and through cleanly defined paths of blue gravel. Tall cacti resembling green organ pipes make an unusual hedge or avenue either side of a die-straight path, and are reflected at one end in a clear rectangular pool. Remnants of the monastery buildings define areas to stop and contemplate, sometimes with a water feature providing cooling sounds.

The planting style allows space to celebrate the distinctive form of many subjects. The soil in most planted areas is covered with stones of varying sizes that offset the architectural shapes of the plants, particularly cacti and agaves. This garden manages to educate, inspire and stimulate while enveloping visitors with a great sense of calm.

1—A mirror pool reflects organ pipe cactus (*Pachycereus marginatus*), traditionally used in Mexico to create boundaries and fences.
2—Zigzag paths throughout the garden echo the geometric designs of the indigenous Zapotec; plants grow among a few monochromatic rock beds and repetitive plantings of agave.
3—One of the paths passes an ornamental rill flanked by *Agave macroacantha* on the left and *Fouquieria* on the right.

440

1

# Garden in Malinalco

Malinalco, Mexico

| | |
|---|---|
| Mario Schjetnan | |
| 21st century | |
| 0.66 hectares / 1.6 acres | |
| Temperate Subtropical Highland | |
| Exotic / Modern / Tropical / Water | |

This Malinalco garden is a spectacular example of the Mexican landscape architect Mario Schjetnan's approach to design, which links architecture with topography, climate and culture. Schjetnan fused the colonial-style house with a series of striking new buildings in a garden landscape that also references the rich cultural history of the area.

Set at the southern end of Mexico's Malinalco Valley, the area is one of old fruit orchards where the Aztecs built *apantles* (irrigation channels). These ancient features remain, updated in the urban regeneration of Malinalco. The design brief for the garden was that it should have a real sense of place, and be full of tropical plants and flowers.

The only trees on the site were fruit trees growing on a mound of lava rock, the highest point of the sloping site. As a link to the past, Schjetnan incorporated both trees and rocks as the backdrop for the cascade that feeds the new lake. The garden is very much of the region: native stone forms low, rustic walls and paved terraces. Their texture contrasts with the luxuriant foliage and exotic flowers. Each area has a different ambience and is linked to other spaces by curved paths, many of which have *apantles* running alongside – flowing water makes a soothing soundtrack throughout the garden. Richly diverse planting adds to the contemplative atmosphere.

The design is an abstract mix of the clean lines of buildings and the organic curves of the lake, paths, water channels and planted areas. A guest house and terrace overhang the lake. Their simplicity recalls both Japanese teahouses and the Modernism of Mies van der Rohe. Glass walls give on to a deck shaded by the wide roof. These rectangular shapes contrast with the bold swathes of tropical plants, which recall the planting of the Brazilian Roberto Burle Marx. A curving margin of *Equisetum hyemale* edges the lake. Rocks and the dramatic century plant (*Agave americana*) rise from low-growing plants under wide-canopied trees such as the candelabra-shaped *Plumeria rubra*.

This is an exotic, exciting garden, with many different facets. Separate areas provide a diversity of experience, always with a great sense of place.

1—Traditional irrigation channels, or *apantles*, used in the coffee plantations and fruit orchards of the region are given a contemporary treatment in the garden.
2, 5—Water lilies and lotuses thrive in the lake in front of the guest house and deck.
3—The garden design blends beautiful planting with functional areas, including a paved patio for outdoor living and a tennis court.
4—Beside the guest house, sculptural *Agave americana* rises out of massed *Lantana camara*, with the taller *Plumeria rubra* and *Bauhinia monandra* providing an upper canopy.

442

# Andromeda
# Botanic Gardens

Bathsheba,
St Joseph Parish, Barbados

| |
|---|
| Iris Bannochie |
| 20th century |
| 2.4 hectares / 6 acres |
| Tropical Monsoon |
| Botanical / Plantsman / Tropical |

Andromeda Gardens is one of the treasures of Barbados, bathed in sunshine, cooled by the east coast winds and full of birdsong and the fragrance of the flowering frangipani trees. Originally begun as a hobby by Iris Bannochie on land her family had owned since the 1740s, these sprawling landscaped gardens became a consuming passion. Many of the 600 species now on display were collected by Bannochie and her husband, John, on their travels or were donated by gardening friends or botanical gardens.

The garden, which is now run by the Barbados National Trust, has twelve different areas that the visitor explores by following the Iris Walk (a gentle ramble) or John's Path (a steeper, longer walk). Both have paths made with concrete stones imprinted with deeply veined leaves from the gardens. The gardens are built around huge, pitted coral-stone boulders, some of which serve as planters (small plants are grown in the natural holes). Others divide the space into natural areas, where different plant types are accommodated, from humidity lovers, to epiphytes, to xerophytes.

The gardens contain tropical plants from around the world: hibiscus, palms, bougainvillea, begonia, crotons and breadfruit trees. The range of lobster claw plants (*Heliconia*) is remarkable, thanks to Bannochie's collecting, breeding and popularization of these odd-looking, bright orange and yellow, waxy flowers. Memorable sights include yellow-flowered mandevilla vines smothering a pergola, the pleasing contrast of pink-flowering *Ixora coccinea* underplanted with ferns and bromeliads, the use of dark purple-leaved red flame ivy (*Hemigraphis alternata*) as spectacular groundcover, and a grove of vanda orchids with their long stems supported by wire cylinders.

Above the gardens soar palm trees, such as the 27-metre-tall (90-foot) talipot palm with its 6-metre (20-foot) leaves. The palm grove has a shaded gazebo that looks out over the garden to the surf of the Atlantic Ocean beyond, while green-throated carib hummingbirds dart from flower to flower by the water-lily pond and green herons wade among the lilies.

1 — The deep blue waters of Tent Bay form a backdrop to Andromeda's lawns and tropical blooms.
2 — A spectacular bearded fig tree (*Ficus citrifolia*) looms over John's Path, paved with brick and stone.
3 — Characteristically lush vegetation surrounds a pool covered in water lilies.
4 — A pathway leads the visitor past a spectacular display of Bannochie's mixed plantings.

443

# Golden Rock Inn

Nevis, West Indies

Brice Marden, Helen Marden,
Raymond Jungles

21st century

1.2 hectares / 3 acres

Tropical Monsoon

Exotic / Naturalistic / Tropical / Palms

The apparently wild landscape of the Golden Rock Inn, on the Caribbean island of Nevis, is in fact a carefully planned, multilayered and highly personal garden. Set in an old sugar plantation of bold stone structures 305 metres (1,000 feet) above sea level on the side of Mount Nevis, with views across the sea to Monserrat and Antigua, the garden is rich with indigenous and introduced plants. It boasts more than 150 genera chosen by Miami-based landscape architect Raymond Jungles and the garden owners – Helen and Brice Marden, both artists – to reflect the natural landscape and to combine a strong colour palette with a modern touch.

Terraced walls, water features and meandering paths all fit into the mood. Large boulders dislodged during construction were arranged by Brice Marden, becoming a signature feature of the garden. An ancient, carefully sculpted fig tree anchors the main part of the garden, while offering shade and a breezy place from which to look out over the descending hillside, planted with a woven textile of vegetation.

The garden has more than twenty species of palm, such as Cuban petticoat palm (*Copernicia macroglossa*) and ruffle palm (*Aiphanes aculeata*). A wide range of trees, from baobab to red silk cotton tree (*Bombax ceiba*), powder-puff tree (*Calliandra*) and the aptly named sausage tree (*Kigelia*), grow together, while orchids and other epiphytes cling to the branches. Bold-coloured aechmea and cycads punctuate the design, drifts of low-growing, silver-leaved donkey ears (*Kalanchoe gastonis-bonnieri*) and grasses add softness, while bougainvillea and *Epipremnum aureum* cascade over rocks.

The designers' eye for the unexpected is clear from plant choices such as rare old man's palm (*Coccothrinax crinita*). Even the garden's tomato-red woodwork is a refreshing change from the ubiquitous pastels of the Caribbean. A modern water feature (incorporating an old wall and rill) and a pavilion with reflective rectangular lily ponds (designed by architect Edward Tuttle) may at first seem out of place, but in fact help to balance the dense plantings surrounding them.

1—Banana trees and elephant ears (*Colocasia esculenta*) are among dense planting lining a path; a gate picks up the reds of bougainvillea.
2—The garden incorporates shaded seating areas among its exuberant planting.
3—Stone steps introduce structure to a landscape of boulders and mixed plants.
4—Cosmos adds a splash of golden colour to a predominantly green scene.
5—Water tumbles from a rill that brought water to the cistern on the old plantation.

## South America

# Sítio Roberto Burle Marx

Barra de Guaratiba,
Rio de Janeiro, Brazil

| | |
|---|---|
| Roberto Burle Marx | |
| 20th century | |
| 40.5 hectares / 100 acres | |
| Tropical Savannah | |
| Artistic / Exotic / Modern / Plantsman | |

Plant-hunter, jewellery designer, singer, sculptor and painter: the Brazilian Roberto Burle Marx bought his home in 1949 and lived there until his death in 1994. The view from the veranda provides a stunning contrast between the formal pool in the foreground, with its abstract granite sculptures and exotic architectural planting, and the distant, natural mangrove swamps.

Such a juxtaposition is characteristic of the work of Burle Marx, one of the twentieth century's most influential garden designers. He both introduced the modern garden to South America and, through his innovative style, influenced designers throughout North America and Europe. For Burle Marx, gardening was essentially a recomposition of nature inspired by his two great loves – native plants and art, in particular Cubism and Abstractionism.

Burle Marx created gardens that complement their buildings and make the visitor feel subconsciously at ease. This garden is a work of art, a botanical laboratory and a place in which to relax, but Burle Marx was very aware that the site had once been Atlantic rainforest, so the garden also echoes the land's former state and is more naturalistic than many of his designs for clients.

Behind the house to the south is a 'green room' – an outdoor space covered by a pergola smothered in climbing plants. Flower beds, a waterfall and pools, as well as a lack of walls, blur the boundary between 'inside' and 'outside'. As the visitor climbs the rocky hillside, the feeling of being in a rainforest intensifies. Yet the bold blocks of colour created by drifts of native plants and artfully positioned architectural specimens leave no doubt that this place is a work of art – or, more accurately, of a careful balance between art and nature.

The planting reflects Burle Marx's passions as a botanist – all the plants have their ideal conditions – and as a plant collector. The garden contains more than 3,500 different plant types, including a number discovered by and named for him. So important is the plant collection that the garden was listed as a Brazilian National Monument in 1985.

1—The pool in front of the house is home to the blue water lily (*Nymphaea caerulea*), while succulents and bromeliads grow nearby.
2—The Abstract Wall was made from recycled blocks of granite from demolished buildings in Rio de Janeiro.
3—A view over the garden from the top of the rocky slope shows how Burle Marx's naturalistic planting blends into the wider landscape of the rainforest beyond.
4—*Bismarckia nobilis* from Madagascar, with its fan-shaped leaves, flourishes beside a grassy footpath.
5, 6—There are reminders everywhere that the garden is an artifice: an iron-and-panel frame supports succulents, and slender trees crowd a tiny, circular island in the pond.

3

4

5

6

# Inhotim

Brumadinho,
Minas Gerais, Brazil

Luiz Carlos Orsini

20th century

97 hectares / 240 acres (garden);
600 hectares / 1,483 acres (park)

Temperate Humid Subtropical

Artistic / Botanical / Landscape /
Modern / Palms / Sculpture

Inhotim is not merely a garden; this wide tropical landscape is also home to a sculpture park and nine modern art galleries, and the plants contribute to the dramatic effect as strongly as the artworks. The influence of the Brazilian designer Roberto Burle Marx is clear in the dramatic landscaping, especially in the sweeping beds planted with a single species, and design features such as long, curving benches. He gave advice during the site's early development, but it was Luiz Carlos Orsini who faced the challenge of integrating the galleries and sculpture into the landscape.

The gardens hold a wide botanical collection, with further diversity being provided by four large lakes, and have the space for tropical plants to display their strong forms. The visitor rapidly becomes aware that the dramatic statements made by plants can be as arresting as the artworks themselves. Hundreds of ponytail palms (*Beaucarnea recurvata*), with their bulbous-based stems and tufts of leaves, line the paths and form groups, as if a sculptor were working out variations on a theme.

Textural foliage abounds, with bromeliads and agaves offering whorls of spiky leaves, while splashes of colour in the tropical sunshine are provided by massed plantings of cultivars of Joseph's coat (*Codiaeum variegatum*) and the dramatic flowers of birds of paradise (*Strelitzia*). To heighten the drama, the large fronds of Japanese sago palms (*Cycas revoluta*) and Burmese fishtail palms (*Caryota mitis*) rise above the groundcover in the borders. Much larger palms are used as statements in the turf, especially by the lakes, where they provide strong vertical elements and their trunks are reflected in the water. The visitor is encouraged to sit and ponder the artworks and the planting on seating carved from tree trunks by Hugo França.

A wider ecological park of 600 hectares (1,483 acres) wraps around the Inhotim garden with the aim of preserving remnants of the Atlantic forest and the Cerrado (Brazilian savanna). It forms a stunning background to a garden of breathtaking ambition on a grand scale.

1, 5—Inhotim boasts the world's largest collection of palm trees, with more than 1,500 species.
2—Galeria Adriana Varejão hovers above a stone platform set in a dark turquoise reflecting pool.
3—The park's representative species include palms and octopus agaves (*Agave vilmoriniana*).
4—The sculpture *Narcissus Garden* was created by Yayoi Kusama.

3

4

5

# Baroneza

São Paulo, Brazil

| | |
|---|---|
| Alex Hanazaki | |
| 21st century | |
| 0.9 hectares / 2 acres | |
| Temperate Humid Subtropical | |
| Grasses / Modern / Terraces | |

The visitor to Baroneza is struck by the contrast between the monumental villa and the swathes of ornamental grasses. The airy flower heads of pennisetum make a sea of vegetation that ripples in the breeze, punctuated by trees that break up the facade of the house. Two timber pergolas jut into the space in front of the building, while closely mown lawn and grass paths are a textural counterpoint to the adjacent meadow.

Alex Hanazaki is one of a generation of Brazilian landscape architects who aim to meld nature into works of art whose perfection could only be contrived. His garden at Baroneza integrates architecture and landscape: the villa with the garden around it and the garden with the wider landscape beyond. A mown-grass entrance is reinforced with rows of pavers. A long stone wall houses the fountainhead of a water feature that pours down into a simple pool below. Behind the house, glass doors open to an entertaining space and a terrace with a rectangular pool, whose infinity edge highlights views down the sloping garden as well as the vistas beyond. There is a pleasing juxtaposition between the geometric formality of the garden and the wooded, hilly landscape. The design works primarily because the garden elements are simple: water, stone, timber, trees and grass. A sleek deck provides an apt surface on the long side of the pool, while the adjacent boundary planting is bamboo growing through a mulch of dark pebbles. Such planting adds privacy and also filters the wind.

To take advantage of the expansive views, Hanazaki designed an intricate system of terraces, steps and sunken gardens. Within this space, strong ground shapes appear to be based on a giant grid. In some places lawn and path edges delineate crisp lines; in others, blocks or rows of plants define a partial grid of topiary trees, clipped shrubs and tall ornamental grass. Two cantilevered belvederes give a contemporary twist to an idea many centuries old.

At night, an LED lighting system adds another dimension, delineating ground shapes, while uplighters cast beams through foliage. Thus the unusual Baroneza garden assumes an even more intriguing appearance.

1—Slender Brazilian ironwood trees and swathes of ornamental grasses soften the architectural mass of the house; the movement of the grass in the wind makes the house appear to float.
2—Three major terraces make up the garden. The cantilevered belvedere provides a great view of the football pitch below and the landscape beyond.
3—The Middle Terrace is shaped into a series of plateaus, sunken areas and bridges, given geometric precision by steel edges but softened by grasses and topiary.

452

# Odette Monteiro Residence

Corrêas, Rio de Janeiro, Brazil

| |
|---|
| Roberto Burle Marx |
| 20th century |
| 5 hectares / 12 acres |
| Tropical Savannah |
| Landscape / Tropical / Water |

This exuberant garden looks and feels like a hallucinogenic version of a grand, eighteenth-century, English-designed landscape. The neo-colonial house of Odette Monteiro, a friend of the Brazilian garden designer Roberto Burle Marx, lies within a spectacular valley of the distinctive Serra dos Órgãos mountains, the granite peaks of which are the major focal point and borrowed landscape of the garden.

The challenge for Burle Marx was to give the garden sufficient scale to have a presence, while not competing with the natural scenery. He achieved this by using water from the river on the edge of the site to create a lake around which the garden unfolds in a series of organically shaped beds filled with swathes of tropical plants selected for colour and texture. Burle Marx painted the landscape with sweeping beds of yellow-foliaged coleus, purple-leaved *Tradescantia pallida* and strongly textured, steely blue, spiky agaves. Single-species groves of flowering trees add height and hide the course of paths, conjuring a sense of mystery for the visitor, while further texture is provided by clumps of bold-leaved philodendron. Near the house, silk cotton trees (*Pseudobombax ellipticum*) produce pink flowers and coppery new leaves, which echo the colours of the architecture.

Winding paths guide the visitor on to fresh discoveries, with smaller paths and steps following the edge of a woodland, where rocks are contrasted with vertical groupings of mother-in-law's tongue (*Sansevieria*). A stream cascades down the hillside into the lake.

Because Burle Marx hid the edges of the garden, the scale of the borrowed mountains makes it impossible to judge distance. The peaks seem to rise from an ocean of trees, as Burle Marx was eager not only to obscure where the garden ended but also to regenerate the degraded agricultural landscapes that surrounded many of his clients' homes. He was an advocate of using the native flora of Brazil – breaking free of the European-dominated style of garden design – and in doing so creating a nationalistic landscape architecture and planting style. In defence of his bold plantings, he once claimed: 'Indiscriminate planting makes a salad'.

1—The mountains of the Serra dos Órgãos rise behind the lake, where the planting includes *Tibouchina granulosa*, *Canna × generalis* and *Hemerocallis*.
2—A terraced concrete waterfall feeds a pool whose clean concrete edges contrast with its organic curves.
3—The borders beside the lake are planted with beds of *Hemerocallis flava*, *Iresine herbstii*, *Solenostemon* (*Coleus*) and *Tibouchina granulosa* in Burle Marx's characteristic massing of contrasting textures.

453

# La Pasionaria

José Ignacio, Maldonado, Uruguay

| | |
|---|---|
| Amalia Robredo | |
| 21st century | |
| 5 hectares / 12 acres | |
| Temperate Oceanic | |
| Meadow / Natives / Naturalistic | |

Amalia Robredo's house at La Pasionaria says much about the owners' respect for the landscape. Unlike houses that impose themselves, La Pasionaria is almost hidden –but because the house just peeps above thick woodland, its windows provide fantastic views over nearby marshland and a lagoon. The woodland is local *monte*, patches of which are surrounded by extensive grassland. Although there is some ornamental planting, much of it using native species, the bulk of the garden at La Pasionaria is best described as managed nature. Indigenous plants are emphasized, and the central concept is to create a visually rich landscape while at the same time doing as little damage as possible to local ecosystems.

*Monte* is a kind of dwarf woodland, much sculpted by wind and almost impenetrable. It includes relatively few woody species and the occasional cactus, as well as ferns and other perennials at ground level. Amalia Robredo sculpts the *monte* in such a way as to minimize damage from the wind. Where paths need to enter it, Robredo cuts 'mouse holes' through the dense mesh of branches. The gaps are angled to reduce the impact of the wind.

The surviving *monte* is set among a grassland of native species, many closely related to more familiar North American species. Grassland is managed through different mowing regimes. *Prado* gets cut short through the summer but is allowed to grow through the (virtually frost-free) winter to flower in spring. The result is a meadow-like grassland with a rich variety of grasses and forbs, mostly members of the daisy family. Such areas tend to discourage snakes and are used near the house and for wide paths. *Pradera*, however, is cut only once a year, or even less. The reduced cutting allows grasses to build up some thick tussocks, and the plant community that results includes late-flowering perennials. Between these two extremes, other grassland communities show off more of the native flora.

The lower part of the property is given over to a coarse wetland community, with much pampas grass. Here wildlife lives undisturbed. The garden at La Pasionaria is a pioneering example of landscape management that remains very novel in South America.

1—From the lagoon, the house just shows above the thick woodland on its low hill.
2—Perennial borders around the house.
3—The base of the garden is the local *monte*, a unique association of trees and shrubs that has evolved since the sandy soil of the Uruguayan coast was first colonized by grasses.

# Casa Soplo

Manquehue, Santiago, Chile

| | |
|---|---|
| Teresa Moller | |
| 21st century | |
| 0.3 hectares / 0.7 acres | |
| Temperate Mediterranean | |
| Natives / Roof / Sculpture / Terraces / Water | |

How do you bring a country garden to the heart of the city? That was the challenge faced by the renowned Chilean landscape designer Teresa Moller when drawing up this horticultural creation at Casa Soplo. This family house and garden in the suburbs of the Chilean capital, Santiago, has more than a hint of the country about it – *soplo* being Spanish for 'blow' or 'puff'.

Not that the house itself is any country cottage. Designed by the highly respected Chilean architect Cazú Zegers, the building's undulating, bare form was inspired by the American artist Richard Serra's huge, winding sculpture *The Matter of Time* (2005). The house is long, thin and starkly modern, with a 25-metre (82-foot) outdoor pool at the northern edge of the plot and meandering garden walls to the south. Yet Zegers also prides herself on designing buildings that respond to and tread lightly on the Chilean landscape. Both the house and garden, with its series of curved, stepped, interlocking terraces, fit easily into the local terrain, at the foot of the Manquehue mountain on the northeast side of the city.

Moller shares Zeger's sympathies, and prides herself on creating gardens that, while being highly cultured, work with rather than against the local geography and flora. She therefore planted the terraces with native flowers (such as oenothera and cosmos) as well as European imports (such as lobularia). However, there are also wild grasses and agricultural species, such as fruit and almond trees, that recall rural Chile. The roof garden at Casa Soplo helps to insulate the house and also encourages self-sowing, as the plants cultivated on it – mainly meadow species – scatter their seeds.

Moller kept the designs for Casa Soplo deliberately loose in order to mirror the natural clumping and self-sowing that occurs among plants in the wild. The garden was planted only in 2012, and so the fruit and nut trees have yet to mature. Once they have, Moller's vision will be fully realized: urban dwellers will be able to sit beneath an almond tree, watch its blossom being caught by the wind and feel that the country air has truly reached the city.

1 — Seeds from the wild grasses planted on the roof garden above take root on the terraces below.
2 — Teresa Moller selected fruit and nut trees in part for their blossoms; they have yet to mature.
3 — The winding, Richard Serra-inspired walls also guide Casa Soplo's planting and flower beds.
4 — Oenothera and lobularia varieties bloom in Casa Soplo's country-inspired garden.

455

# Jardín Los Vilos

Coquimbo, Chile

Juan Grimm

20th–21st century

0.5 hectares / 1 acre

Temperate Mediterranean

Coastal / Landscape / Modern / Naturalistic / Terraces

Although the garden on the cliffs high above the Pacific Ocean at Los Vilos dates from 1996, the renowned Chilean architect and landscape designer Juan Grimm has been developing the flora there constantly. He built this beautifully modern clifftop house as his home, and his garden became his place of relaxation.

Throughout his career, Grimm has prided himself on working closely with nature, and at Los Vilos he was eager for both house and garden to be in harmony with the surrounding landscape, bringing out the best in the natural and the cultivated world. While his stark, angular house cuts into Chile's rocky shore at roughly the point where the treeline breaks away and the bare rocks begin, Grimm manages to conjure a remarkably harmonious, fertile landscape from this otherwise marginal site.

He planted Monterey cypress (*Cupressus macrocarpa*) to screen the site from its neighbours, while creeping fig placed along the walls of the house gives its abrupt form a more natural aspect. The stepped garden does not benefit from a modern irrigation system, as would be common these days in a plot of this size and at this position. Instead Grimm has chosen to feel his way around the garden, planting species that are both beautiful and naturally able to thrive in these challenging conditions.

The rocky terraces at Los Vilos lead from the house down to a circular pool more or less at the sea's edge. On the way down visitors pass orchids, alstroemeria, cacti, baccharis and other succulent plants. Yet no bed here is rigorously assigned, nor is any choice of planting pushed beyond its natural limits. Instead the designer prides himself on a slower, more impressionistic approach, where the spaces in the garden are only gradually defined. This is an approach all amateur horticulturalists can appreciate and echo, even if the results aren't quite as impressive as Grimm's.

1—Grimm's house rises like an integral part of the hill, its garden helping to soften the link between the landscape and the hard-edged architecture.
2—The garden surrounds the house on the land side in undulations that echo the surface of the sea on the cliff side of the house.
3—A massive stone arch extends from the house to frame views out over the tumbling cliff to the sea.
4—Grimm waters the plants through the dry Chilean summer, which helps bromeliads, cacti and astrolerias to thrive and flower among the bare rocks.

456

3

4

**Allée**
A formal, straight walk or path that is bordered by trees or by clipped hedges.

**Alpines**
A plant that is native to mountain regions and alpine climates; alpines are often small and hardy.

**Annuals**
In gardens annuals are usually brightly coloured flowers that go through their whole life cycle in a year: their seeds are sown in spring, they are planted out to flower in summer and die in the autumn. Tender annuals are often used for bedding.

**Arabesque**
An ornamental design of intertwined, flowing lines, sometimes used in parterres.

**Arboretum**
A collection of trees and shrubs that often has botanical value, as a display of native or introduced species.

**Architectural Plant**
A term that refers to large, woody, perennial or evergreen plants – often with a distinctive form or shape – that give structure or definition in a garden.

**Arts and Crafts**
A garden style perfected by the work of Gertrude Jekyll and Edwin Lutyens in the first decades of the twentieth century, using garden 'rooms' and close integration of built structures. Arts and Crafts was the dominant approach in garden design throughout much of the twentieth century.

**Azulejo**
A type of glazed or painted ceramic tile often used in Portuguese, Spanish and neocolonial Spanish gardens – and usually in blues but also in yellows.

**Baroque**
A highly ornate style of art and architecture popular in seventeenth- and eighteenth-century Europe; Baroque gardens are formal, and include features such as richly carved fountains, grottoes and elaborate statuary.

**Bedding**
Planting out dense arrangement of bulbs in spring and tender annuals in summer in order to create massed patterns of colour. A very labour-intensive method of gardening popular in Victorian times.

**Belvedere**
A pavilion or other purely decorative structure built on a raised area as a viewpoint over the surroundings.

**Bonsai**
A Japanese term that describes the art of raising artificially dwarfed trees and shrubs.

**Botanic**
A botanic garden is dedicated to the collection and display of a wide range of plants with their botanical names, often with specialist groupings.

**Borrowed Landscape**
The landscape beyond a garden when it is deliberately included in the garden design, such as by the use of views and vistas and the ha-ha.

**Bosco**
Italian for 'wood', referring to an artificial or natural grove of trees included in the design of a more formal Italian Renaissance garden.

**Bosquet**
A small group of trees planted to form a decorative glade enclosed by a hedge or fence, often as part of a seventeenth- or eighteenth-century French formal landscape garden.

**Border**
A strip of ground at the edge of a garden or walk used for ornamental planting.

**Bulbs**
A general word for plants that grow from an underground source, such as a corm, tuber or rhizome.

**Canopy**
A layer of foliage created by the leaves of trees.

**Cascade**
A general word for any dramatic fall of water.

**Chadar**
A Persian word that describes stepped or decorative chutes used to carry water between terraces in Islamic gardens; the surface of the chadar may be uneven, breaking up the water to make it sparkle.

**Chahar Bagh**
A Persian or Turkic term that means 'four-part garden'; it commonly describes a walled Islamic garden divided into four parts by water channels. This quadripartite layout is found throughout the Muslim world.

**Chinoiserie**
A quasi-Chinese style of decoration adopted by European designers in the seventeenth and eighteenth centuries, based more on travellers' descriptions of East Asia than on any familiarity with Chinese models.

**Conservatory**
A greenhouse in which plants are displayed.

**Cottage Garden**
An informal garden that is usually planted with a mixture of colourful flowering plants and edible crops.

**Cultivar**
A variety of plant that has been created artificially through cultivation and breeding.

**Dry**
A garden based on plants that thrive in hot conditions with little available water.

**English Landscape Style**
A style of large-scale naturalistic garden design that began on English country estates in the early eighteenth century, when gardens were designed with complex symbolic or political messages, expressed as buildings and landscape features. A purely visual version – setting out to evoke an idealized pastoral landscape – spread throughout Europe in the eighteenth and nineteenth centuries.

**Epiphyte**
A plant that grows on another plant.

**Espalier**
To train a fruit tree or ornamental shrub to grow flat against a wall, usually to take advantage of the sun and to make the fruit easy to see and pick.

**Eye-Catcher**
A feature – such as a tower or a 'ruin' – deliberately placed in the landscape to create a focal point for a broad vista.

**Event**
A term that refers to the central focus of an area of a garden, such as a viewpoint, a particular arrangement of plants, a sculpture, a water feature or any combination of such elements.

**Exotics**
Plants that do not naturally occur in a particular region.

**Folly**
A building or other structure intended to be decorative rather than useful; follies often resemble historic, ruined or fantastical structures.

**Gazebo**
A small roofed building with open sides, usually offering extensive views.

**Giardino Segreto**
Italian for 'secret garden', the phrase describes a private area in an Italian Renaissance garden that was often concealed or partly concealed from the rest of the garden and used privately by the family.

**Gravel Garden**
A garden in which a layer of gravel is spread over the ground; gravel gardens suit low-maintenance, drought-tolerant plants.

**Groundcover**
Low-growing, spreading plants that are used partly to stop weeds growing.

**Ha-ha**
A dry ditch with a vertical wall on one side, used as a sunken 'fence' to keep livestock out of landscape gardens without interrupting the view with any kind of visible barrier.

**Herbaceous Border**
A border planted mainly with perennials.

**Herbarium**
A collection of dried plants arranged to be studied.

**Hortus Conclusus**
Latin for 'enclosed garden', the term describes an enclosed medieval garden with low hedges, flowers and herbs.

**Islamic**
A garden style based on traditional Islamic styles in which gardens were walled reminders of paradise, with quadripartite layouts, an ample use of water, and the planting of symbolic flowers and trees.

**Italianate**
A nineteenth-century garden style devised by Sir Charles Barry that amalgamated Italian, French, British and Dutch Renaissance and Baroque ideas and features.

**Knot Garden**
A type of enclosed garden, originally from Tudor England, in which an intricate and symmetrical pattern is created by low evergreen hedges – often box, yew or thyme – and sometimes filled in with brightly coloured flowers or gravel.

**Meadow Style**
A nature-inspired garden planted with traditional grasses, annuals and perennials.

**Mediterranean Style**
A style of garden that evolved in Mediterranean climates, planted primarily with plants that grow in a similar climate all over the world.

**Modernism**
A functional and minimalist architectural style that originated in the 1920s, often using modern materials such as concrete. In garden design, Modernism was a similar approach, often of simple shapes, flat textures and limited blocks of colour.

**Mughal Garden**
A style of garden associated with the Islamic Mughal dynasties that ruled northern India, Pakistan and Afghanistan from the sixteenth to the nineteenth centuries. Mughal gardens were based on the Islamic tradition, with symmetrical and axial layouts, quadripartite *chahar bagh*, stone terracing, water chutes and channels, and open-air pavilions.

**Mulch**
Material that is spread around a plant to enrich or insulate the soil, suppress weeds or retain moisture; mulches can be decaying leaves, tree bark or moss, but can also be inanimate, such as gravel or larger pebbles.

**Natives / Native Plants**
Plants that naturally occur in the wild in a particular area.

**Naturalize**
To introduce a non-native plant so that it grows wild in a particular area.

**New Perennial**
A gardening movement in northwestern Europe in the 1970s and 1980s that evolved from an approach pioneered in Germany in the 1930s. It emphasized mass plantings of perennials and ornamental grasses and used seed heads and dead grasses as a pleasing display in autumn and winter.

**Orangery**
A stone or brick structure with large windows that is used for growing oranges and other tender ornamentals.

**Ornamental Grasses**
Annual or perennial grasses that are grown for their colour or texture.

**Palissade**
A clipped hedge, often hornbeam, that forms a green wall along an allée.

**Parterre**
An ornamental flower garden in which the beds and paths are arranged to create a pattern.

**Parterre Anglaise**
French for 'English parterre', used to describe a form of parterre in which spaces edged with box are filled mainly with lawn.

**Parterre de Broderie**
French for 'embroidered parterre', refers to particularly intricate flowing designs made of box against a background of grass, gravel or turf and planted with colourful flowers.

**Pavilion**
A light, roofed structure that can be ornamental and that is often used for entertaining.

**Penzai**
The Chinese form of bonsai.

**Perennials**
Plants that die back to an underground root every year after flowering; they regrow the following spring.

**Piano Nobile**
Italian for 'noble floor'; describes the principal floor of a large house used by the owners, usually the first floor or a raised floor above a basement.

**Picturesque**
An eighteenth-century English landscape style based on an artistic and literary movement that celebrated the power of untamed nature.

**Pinetum**
A collection of conifers.

**Pleach**
To entwine or interlace the branches of trees to form a hedge or provide continuous cover.

**Potager**
A type of decorative kitchen garden that emerged in formal French gardens in the seventeenth and eighteenth centuries; potagers use box or other hedging to define beds and often contain vegetables grown partly for their appearance, such as the famed purple cabbages of Villandry in France.

**Prairie**
A garden style that is the American version of the New Perennial movement, based on natural prairie or grassland, characterized by stands of tall, often mixed, grasses that are usually left unmown.

**Qanat**
An underwater irrigation canal in ancient Persia.

**Rill**
A rill is a narrow, shallow artificial stream or rivulet running between areas of a garden; rills can be either straight – as in the Persian gardens where they originated – or serpentine. They are usually lined with stone.

**Rock Garden**
A garden that is laid out among a naturally or artificially rocky area with spaces for plants such as alpines.

**Romantic Style**
The Romantic style of landscape design was based on sweeping lawns, groves of trees, ponds and follies. It evolved from the English Landscape movement, inspired by the late eighteenth-century literary and philosophical romantic movement, and spread throughout Europe in the nineteenth century, often at the expense of older formal gardens.

**Serpentine Paths**
Curving or twisting paths running through areas of shrub and tree planting.

**Shrub**
A small plant with a number of woody stems that separate at or just above ground level.

**Species**
A group of living organisms consisting of similar individuals that can naturally reproduce with one another.

**Stroll Garden**
A popular style of Japanese garden that is designed to be viewed while walking along a path – often around a lake – that reveals the garden gradually in a series of carefully constructed views.

**Succulent**
A drought-tolerant plant with thick, fleshy leaves or stems that it uses to store water.

**Tapis Vert**
French for 'green carpet', used to describe a close-cropped expanse of grass, especially as part of a formal scheme.

**Terminus**
A feature – such as a building, rock or specific plant – that is placed at the end of a vista.

**Terrace**
An external, raised, open and flat area, usually on the side of a hill or slope.

**Topiary**
The art of clipping evergreen plants, such as box and yew, into abstract or figurative shapes.

**Trompe-l'Oeil**
From the French for 'deceive the eye'. An effect designed to alter normal perception, often used in gardens to increase distances and change perspectives. It can take the form of out-of-scale plantings, trellises, mirrors or even painted surfaces.

**View**
An attractive prospect across a natural or designed landscape.

**Viewing Garden**
A Japanese term that describes a garden that is intended to be looked at from particular points rather than walked in or explored.

**Vista**
A long, narrow view that is often defined by trees or buildings.

**Water Feature**
Any kind of pond, fountain or rill used in a garden.

**Water Garden**
A garden, or part of a garden, the main purpose of which is to grow and display water plants in pools, canals or streams.

**Water Staircase**
An elaborate, large-scale garden feature in which water is carried down a slope by means of a series of steps.

**Wilderness**
An enclosed but informal area in a landscape garden, planted with trees and shrubs and featuring serpentine walks.

**Winter Garden**
An alpine or rock garden, or an indoor heated conservatory for the display of exotic plants.

**Xeriscape**
A garden or feature created in hot, dry climates and planted with species tolerant of arid conditions.

**Zen Garden**
A garden constructed to reflect the principles of Zen Buddhism by using symbolic arrangements of rocks, gravel and plants, typically as an aid to quiet meditation.

## Garden Festivals and Shows

Garden festivals and flower shows are increasingly common around the world. This selection includes the most important, but by its very nature it is not exhaustive. The festivals and shows are held annually unless otherwise stated.

### Bloom, Ireland
Held in early summer in Phoenix Park, Dublin, Bloom is the Republic of Ireland's largest gardening event and focuses on Irish designers and horticulturalists, who may draw inspiration from elsewhere. Show gardens are a key feature, ranging in scope from large wetland designs to a small edible woodland garden.
www.bloominthepark.com

### Chelsea Flower Show, UK
This world-famous garden show is held every May in the grounds of the Royal Hospital Chelsea in London. Visitors from around the world come to see the nursery and anniversary displays in the Great Pavilion; inspiring show gardens and small gardens; and the latest horticultural trends. There are numerous prizes for themed gardens, vegetables and new varieties, with a coveted special award for the most imaginative garden interpretations.
www.rhs.org.uk/shows-events/
rhs-chelsea-flower-show

### China International Garden Expo, China
This major show takes place every two years. The 2015 Expo in Wuhan will cover ecological landscaping, with 81 cities showing their gardens and 96 exhibition parks.
en.expo2013.net/en_index.html

### Cornerstone, North America
The 3.5-hectare (9-acre) Cornerstone Gardens in Sonoma, California, are a series of ever-changing, walkthrough gardens, showcasing new and innovative designs from the world's finest landscape architects and designers. The gallery-style approach is a first in the United States, both an inspiration and resource for people interested in gardens, garden design and art (see page 365).
www.cornerstonegardens.com

### Festival of Flowers, New Zealand
Since 1989, New Zealand's Festival of Flowers has been held in February in the 'Garden City' of Christchurch. The 23-metre (75-foot) Floral Carpet and Decorations laid out in Christchurch Cathedral was the traditional centrepiece, but has been changed to a River of Flowers ceremony to commemorate the 2011 earthquake. Other highlights include Floral Bungalows, designs by children and seniors, a Chinese Cultural Day and bird topiary.
www.festivalofflowers.co.nz

### Floriade, Netherlands
Cities in the Netherlands compete to host this world horticultural expo that takes place every ten years. Almere, the venue for 2022, will envision the theme of Growing Green Cities by creating a permanent green city district, the Almere Floriade. The aim is to combine a cultural, recreational and nature park that is strong on recycling and ecology.
www.floriade.almere.nl

### Florissimo, France
Every three to five years the French city of Dijon stages the exotic floral event Florissimo. Other French and European cities, botanical gardens, gardeners and florists participate with glamorous displays and settings of tropical flora, such as orchids, porcelain roses and bromeliads, enhanced by lighting and water effects.
www.florissimo.fr

### Garden Fest, North America
In late spring, the Smithsonian Institution in Washington, DC, hosts a one-day event in the Enid A Haupt Garden in order to highlight each of the Smithsonian gardens and connect people to plants through demonstrations and hands-on activities. Topics include floriculture, landscape and container design, greenhouse production, garden history and conservation.
www.gardens.si.edu/whats-happening/garden-fest

### Hampton Court Flower Show, UK
The largest flower show in the world is held in early July in the park of Hampton Court Palace in Surrey, near London (see page 172). With three main themes – Grow, Inspire and Escape – the agenda covers show and concept gardens, floral and rose marquees, talks and demonstrations. With a different character from the other major UK national show – the Chelsea Flower Show – it focuses more on environmental issues, growing your own food, and vegetables and cookery.
www.rhs.org.uk/Shows-Events/
RHS-Hampton-Court-Palace-Flower-Show

### International Garden Festival, France
Established in 1992, this festival takes place from April to October in the grounds of the Domaine de Chaumont-sur-Loire in the Loire Valley (see page 264), home of an idyllic Renaissance château. Most of the site is used for display gardens, which are conceptually designed on an annually changing theme.
www.domaine-chaumont.fr/en_festival_festival

### International Garden Festival and Reford Gardens, Canada
The International Garden Festival in Québec is held from May to September in Les Jardins de Métis on the banks of the St Lawrence River, adjacent to the historic gardens created by Elsie Reford (see page 350). More than seventy architects, landscape architects and designers from various disciplines participate each year, presenting gardens created on a wide variety of conceptual themes.
www.refordgardens.com/english/festival/

### Melbourne International Flower and Garden Show, Australia
The largest horticultural event in the Southern Hemisphere features the best in Australian landscape and floral talent over a few days in March. Staged within the World-Heritage listed Royal Exhibition Building and Carlton Gardens, it showcases award-winning displays in landscaping, outdoor entertainment and garden and floral design.
www.melbflowershow.com.au/Home

### Singapore Garden Festival, Singapore
In the splendid location of the Meadow at Gardens by the Bay (see page 90), the festival draws together dozens of world-class garden and floral designers in a tropical setting. Among the attractions are landscape and fantasy gardens; balcony gardens for high-rise living; an orchid extravaganza; and artistic cut-flower displays.
www.singaporegardenfestival.com

## Garden, Horticultural and Plant Societies

Many of the societies listed below have international branches. Those marked with an asterisk (*) are intended for professional horticulturalists rather than amateur gardeners.

Garden Forum gives a global and comprehensive alphabetical catalogue of Plant, Gardening and Horticultural societies on its website.
www.gardenforumhorticulture.co.uk/
links/societies.htm

### Argentina
Sociedad Argentina de Horticultura
(Horticultural Society of Argentina)
www.horticulturargentina.org

### Australia
Australian Garden History Society
www.gardenhistorysociety.org.au

Australian Institute of Horticulture*
www.aih.org.au

Australian National Botanic Gardens
www.anbg.gov.au

The International Tropical Foliage
& Garden Society Inc.
www.itfgs.org

The Royal Agricultural & Horticultural Society
Australia (accessed through the RHS website)
www.rhs.org.uk

### Brazil
Sociedade Botânica do Brasil
(Botanical Society of Brazil)
www.botanica.org.br

### Canada
Alberta Horticultural Association
www.icangarden.com/clubs/AHA

British Columbia Council of Garden Clubs
www.bcgardenclubs.com

Canadian Society for Horticultural Science*
www.cshs.ca

Manitoba Horticultural Association
www.icangarden.com/clubs/mha

Newfoundland Horticultural Society
nfldhort.dhs.org

Nova Scotia Association of Garden Clubs
www.nsagc.com

Ontario Horticultural Association
www.gardenontario.org

Quebec Gardens' Association
associationdesjardinsduquebec.com/wp/en

Saskatoon Horticultural Society
www.saskatoonhortsociety.ca

### Denmark
Kongelige Danske Haveselskab
(Royal Danish Garden Society)
haveselskabet.dk

### France
French Gardens
www.french-gardens.com

Parks and Gardens of France (in French)
www.parcsetjardins.fr

Société Nationale d'Horticulture de France
(National Horticultural Society of France)
www.snhf.org

**Germany**
Deutsche Botanische Gesellschaft
(German Botanical Society)
*www.deutsche-botanische-gesellschaft.de*

German Gardens
*www.germany.travel/en/towns-cities-culture/palaces-parks-gardens/palaces-parks-gardens.html*

Parks and Gardens of Bavaria
*www.schloesser.bayern.de/englisch/garden/index.htm*

**Greece**
The Mediterranean Garden Society
*www.mediterraneangardensociety.org*

**Ireland**
Royal Horticultural Society of Ireland
*www.rhsi.ie*

**Italy**
Grandi Giardini Italiani
(Important Italian Gardens)
*www.grandigiardini.it*

Società Ortoflorofrutticoltura Italiana*
(Italian Horticultural Society)
*www.soihs.it*

**Japan**
International Association of Japanese Gardens*
*www.japanese-gardens-assoc.org*

**Mexico**
Sociedad Botánica de México*
(Botanical Society of Mexico)
*www.socbot.org.mx*

**New Zealand**
Royal New Zealand Institute of Horticulture
*www.rnzih.org.nz*

**South Africa**
Botanical Society of South Africa
*www.botanicalsociety.org.za*

**Spain**
Sociedad Española de Ciencias Horticolas*
(Spanish Society of Horticultural Sciences)
*www.sech.info*

Mediterranean Gardens
*www.palmerasyjardines.com*

**Sweden**
Kungliga Skogs-och Lantbruksakademien*
(Royal Swedish Academy of Agriculture
and Forestry)
*www.ksla.se*

Swedish Society of Public Parks and Gardens
*www.swedishgardens.se*

**United Kingdom**
Alpine Garden Society
*www.alpinegardensociety.net*

The Association of Gardens Trusts, UK
*www.gardenstrusts.org.uk*

The British Cactus and Succulent Society
*www.bcss.org.uk*

Cadw Historic Parks and Gardens
*www.cadw.wales.gov.uk*

The Cottage Garden Society
*www.thecottagegardensociety.org.uk*

The Cyclamen Society
*www.cyclamen.org*

English Heritage
*www.english-heritage.org.uk*

The Garden History Society
*www.gardenhistorysociety.org*

The Garden History Society in Scotland
*www.gardenhistorysociety.org/?s=Scotland*

Hardy Plant Society
*www.hardy-plant.org.uk*

Japanese Garden Society, UK
*www.jgs.org.uk*

The National Gardens Scheme
*www.ngs.org.uk*

National Trust
*www.nationaltrust.co.uk*

National Trust for Scotland
*www.nts.org.uk*

The Orchid Society of Great Britain
*www.osgb.org.uk*

Plant Heritage
*www.nccpg.com*

Royal Horticultural Society
*www.rhs.org.uk*

Royal National Rose Society
*www.rnrs.org.uk*

Scottish Rhododendron Society
*www.scottishrhododendronsociety.org.uk*

**United States**
American Conifer Society
*www.conifersociety.org*

American Horticultural Society
*www.ahs.org*

American Orchid Society
*www.aos.org*

American Public Gardens Association
*www.publicgardens.org*

American Rhododendron Society
*www.rhododendron.org*

American Rose Society
*www.ars.org*

The Garden Conservancy
*www.gardenconservancy.org*

International Bulb Society
*www.bulbsociety.org*

International Society of Arboriculture*
*www.isa-arbor.com*

International Camellia Society
*www.internationalcamellia.org*

National Trust for Historic Preservation
*www.nthp.org*

North American Japanese Garden Association
*www.najga.org*

**Further Reading**

*The Garden Book* (Phaidon Press, 2000)

*The English Garden* (Phaidon Press, 2008)

*The Contemporary Garden* (Phaidon Press, 2009)

Baker, Barbara, *Dream Gardens of England: 100 Inspirational Gardens* (Merrell Publishers, 2010)

Buchan, Ursula, *The English Garden* (Frances Lincoln, 2006)

Campbell, Katie, *Icons of Twentieth-Century Landscape Design* (Frances Lincoln, 2006)

Compton, Tania, *Dream Gardens: 100 Inspirational Gardens* (Merrell Publishers, 2009)

Don, Monty, *Extraordinary Gardens of the World* (Weidenfeld & Nicolson, 2009)

Frieze, Charlotte M, *Private Paradise: Contemporary American Gardens* (Monacelli Press, 2011)

Hobhouse, Penelope, *The Story of Gardening* (Dorling Kindersley Publishers Ltd, 2002)

Hobhouse, Penelope, *In Search of Paradise: Great Gardens of the World* (Chicago Botanic Garden, 2006)

Jellicoe, Geoffrey, Susan Jellicoe, Patrick Goode and Michael Lancaster, *The Oxford Companion to Gardens* (Oxford University Press, 2001)

Jenkins, Mary Zuazua, *National Geographic Guide to America's Public Gardens* (National Geographic, 1998)

Jones, Louisa, and Dan Pearson, *Mediterranean Gardens: A Model for Good Living* (Bloomings Books, 2013)

Kawaguchi, Yoko, *Japanese Zen Gardens* (Frances Lincoln, 2014)

Keswick, Maggie, *The Chinese Garden* (Frances Lincoln, 2003)

Mehta, Geeta K., and Kimie Tada, *Japanese Gardens: Tranquility, Simplicity, Harmony* (Tuttle Publishing, 2008)

Musgrave, Toby, *The Head Gardeners: Forgotton Heroes of Horticulture* (Aurum Press, 2009)

Richardson, Tim, *The New English Garden* (Frances Lincoln, 2013)

Ruggles, D Fairchild, *Islamic Gardens and Landscapes* (University of Pennsylvania Press, 2007)

Schinz, Marina, *Visions of Paradise: Themes and Variations on the Garden* (Stoddart, 1985)

Silva, Roberto, *New Brazilian Gardens: The Legacy of Burle Marx* (Thames & Hudson, 2006)

Spencer-Jones, Rae, *1001 Gardens You Must See Before You Die* (Cassell Illustrated, 2007)

Turner, Tom, *European Gardens: History, Philosophy and Design* (Routledge Chapman & Hall, 2011)

Wijaya, Made, *Modern Tropical Garden Design* (Thames & Hudson, 2007)

Wilson, Andrew, *Influential Gardeners: The designers who shaped 20th-century garden style* (Mitchell Beazley, 2005)

## Gardens Directory

Many of the gardens in this book are open to the public: opening information is available on their websites. Some private gardens are not open to the public. The following list indicates gardens with restricted opening.

### Oceania

*Mawallok* – designated weekends in Open Gardens Australia scheme

*Mawarra* – designated weekends in Open Gardens Australia scheme (and for guests)

*Olinda* – designated weekends in Open Gardens Australia scheme

*Karkalla* – designated weekends in Open Gardens Australia scheme

*Stringybark Cottage* – by appointment

*Eryldene* – 2nd weekend each month, April–September

*Barewood Garden* – by appointment; member of New Zealand Gardens Trust

*Ohinetahi* – by appointment; member of New Zealand Gardens Trust

*Blair Garden* – by appointment; member of New Zealand Gardens Trust

### Asia

*Rashtrapati Bhavan* – February and March (exact days change annually)

*Saiho-ji* – by appointment only

### Europe

*Villa Mairea* – by appointment, January–May; by pre-booked, guided tour, June–September

*Dillon Garden* – afternoons, March, July, August; Sunday afternoons, April, May, June, September

*Mount Congreve* – Thursday–Sunday and bank holidays

*Little Sparta* – Wednesday, Friday & Sunday afternoons, June–September

*Garden of Cosmic Speculation* – first Sunday afternoon in May, every year

*Veddw House Garden* – Sunday afternoons, June–August; groups by appointment on other days

*Cottesbrooke Hall* – designated afternoons, May–September

*East Ruston Old Vicarage Garden* – afternoons, Wednesday–Sunday and bank holidays, April–October

*The Laskett Gardens* – Tuesdays and Thursdays for groups of 20 or more

*Upton Wold* – by appointment, groups welcome

*Montpelier Cottage* – designated dates under the National Gardens Scheme

*Highgrove* – booked tours only

*Sezincote* – designated afternoons, January–November

*Turn End* – designated days under the National Gardens Scheme; groups by appointment

*The Barn* – open one day in May, July and September under the Garden Museum scheme

*The Gibberd Garden* – designated afternoons, April–September

*Kensington Roof Gardens* – may be visited when no function taking place; check in advance

*Munstead Wood* – by appointment for groups up to 20

*Plaz Metaxu* – by appointment for individuals and groups

*Shute House* – by appointment for groups of 20 or more

*The Peto Garden* – designated afternoons, April–October

*Gravetye Manor* – Tuesdays and Fridays

*Keukenhof* – daily, third week of March–third week of May

*Heerenhof* – weekends in June; groups by appointment

*Hummelo* – Thursday, Friday, Saturday, June and August–mid-October

*Priona Tuinen* – Thursday–Sunday, May–September

*Château de Brécy* – designated afternoons, Easter–end October; groups year-round by appointment

*Jardins de Kerdalo* – designated afternoons, April–August

*Le Vasterival* – guided tours by appointment

*Jardin de la Noria* – group tours by appointment, April–September; occasional individual tours

*Jardin des Colombières* – guided tours by appointment, 1 July–10 August

*La Louve* – selected days, April–July

*Jardim do Palácio dos Marqueses de Fronteira* – morning guided tours only

*Villa Il Roseto* – by appointment

*Villa Medici* – Monday–Friday, by appointment

*Castello Ruspoli* – Sundays and public holidays, April–September; groups year-round by appointment

*Giardino di Ninfa* – designated days, April–November, guided tours only

*Giardini La Mortella* – Tuesday, Thursday, Saturday, Sunday, April–November

### Africa

*Vergelegen* – daily guided tours only by appointment

### Americas

*Les Quatre Vents* – pre-booked, guided tours on four Saturdays, June–August

*Lawa'i Kai* – pre-booked tours only (daily)

*Pool Garden at El Novillero* – occasional tours only

*Casa del Herrero* – pre-booked tours only

*Lotusland* – pre-booked tours only, February–November

*Peckerwood Garden* – designated weekends only; private tours by appointment

*J Irwin Miller House and Garden* – pre-booked tours only, designated days year-round

*Hollister House* – Saturdays, May–September; groups by appointment

*Madoo Conservancy* – Friday & Saturday, mid-May–mid-September; other visits by appointment

*LongHouse Reserve* – designated afternoons, April–October; other days by appointment only

*Longwood Gardens* – pre-booked, timed tickets only

*Montrose* – by appointment, September–May

*Casa Luis Barragán* – guided tours by appointment

*Jardín Etnobotánico de Oaxaca* – guided tours only; book in advance for English- or French-speaking guides

*Sítio Roberto Burle Marx* – pre-booked, guided tours, Tuesday–Sunday

### Useful Websites

'Garden Finder' on GardenVisit.com gives a global overview of gardens to visit by country. *www.gardenvisit.com*

'What's On' on The Gardening Website gives a global overview of gardens to visit by country. *www.thegardeningwebsite.co.uk*

The European Garden Heritage Network lists more than 150 parks and gardens in ten countries, with suggested themed and regional tours. *cmsen.eghn.org*

UNESCO World Heritage Sites has a webpage for each WHS garden, as listed below. *whc.unesco.org*

Alhambra & Generalife, Spain
Bagh-e Fin, Iran
Bagh-e Shahzadeh, Iran
Bahá'í Haifa, Israel
Bergpark Wilhelmshöhe, Germany
Blenheim Palace, UK
Château du Riveau, France
Château de Versailles, France
Chehel Sotun, Iran
Goa Gajah Temple Garden, Indonesia
Jardines del Real Alcázar, Spain
Karl-Foerster-Garten, Germany
Liu Yuan (The Lingering Garden), China
Parque Ecológico de Xochimilco, Mexico
Royal Botanic Gardens, Kew, UK
Ryoan-ji, Japan
Schloss Sanssouci, Germany
Schloss Schönbrunn, Austria
Shalimar Bagh, India
Shalimar Bagh, Pakistan
Taj Mahal, India
UNESCO Garden of Peace, France
Villa d'Este, Italy
Villa Medici, Fiesole, Italy
Wang Shi Yuan
   (The Master-of-the Fishing-Nets Garden), China
Yi-He-Yuan
   (Garden of Preservation of Harmony), China
Zhuo Zheng Yuan
   (The Humble Administrator's Garden), China

## Picture Credits

471

## Acknowledgements

Combining an authoritative reference source, a visitor's guide and a resource for those seeking inspiration on garden design and planting is a wide-reaching task. Selected by an international panel of experts and global in scope, over 250 of the world's most outstanding gardens are contained within the pages of this book, ranging from the oldest extant gardens to exciting contemporary developments. Collectively, the gardens represent half a millennium of work by leading garden designers, horticulturalists and landscape architects drawing on Western, East Asian, Islamic, New World and other traditions. All types of garden are featured, such as tropical, alpine, formal, cottage, drought-tolerant, Mediterranean, topiary, cacti, botanical, New Perennial and landscape.

A project of this scale requires the commitment, advice and expertise of a great number of people. We are particularly indebted to consultant editor Toby Musgrave and garden designer Madison Cox for their vital contributions to the book; and to the members of our international advisory panel for their knowledge, passion and sound judgement: Richard Aitken, Ravindra Bhan, Tania Compton, Patrick Goode, Brian John Huntley, Bill Noble, Dan Pearson, Christine Reid, Marc Treib, Tom Turner and Made Wijaya.

We are grateful to the following contributors: Richard Aitken (pp. 16, 18, 117, 284); Edwinna van Baeyer (pp. 166, 223, 349, 402, 429, 443); Ravindra Bhan (pp. 49, 51, 54, 55); Katie Campbell (pp. 60, 162, 200, 256, 295, 296, 298, 331, 354, 364); Ruth Chivers (pp. 98, 101, 109, 131, 152, 158, 167, 186, 197, 210, 265, 266, 279, 348, 350, 360, 367, 368, 370, 371, 384, 385, 386, 388, 389, 390, 392, 396, 403, 406, 408, 426, 428, 430, 432, 440, 442, 452); Tim Cooke (pp. 30, 41, 38, 58, 71, 92, 93, 178, 208, 218, 238, 244, 286, 316, 399); Caroline Harbouri (p. 312); Jan Hendrych (p. 321); Judith Hitching (p. 145); Tom Jackson (pp. 89, 272, 288); Louisa Jones (pp. 270, 280); Noel Kingsbury (pp. 108, 123, 126, 144, 182, 220, 221, 224, 225, 228, 230, 454); Arnaud Maurières (pp. 267, 268); Toby Musgrave (pp. 42, 43, 44, 46, 48, 50, 52, 56, 59, 66, 68, 69, 72, 74, 80, 81, 82, 84, 96, 97, 100, 102, 103, 104, 106, 107, 110, 111, 112, 114, 116, 118, 122, 124, 129, 130, 132, 134, 135, 136, 142, 148, 153, 154, 156, 160, 163, 168, 170, 172, 174, 179, 180, 184, 187, 188, 192, 193, 194, 196, 198, 202, 209, 211, 212, 214, 216, 222, 227, 229, 232, 240, 246, 250, 252, 260, 264, 252, 273, 276, 278, 285, 292, 294, 299, 300, 301, 302, 304, 306, 308, 318, 332, 334, 336, 342, 359, 365, 374, 382, 398, 404, 411, 412, 416, 420, 422, 424, 448); Jill Raggett (pp. 65, 78, 79, 86, 146, 150, 164, 236, 356, 358, 410, 418, 437, 438, 439, 450, 453); Alex Rayner (pp. 40, 64, 70, 83, 88, 226, 237, 251, 254, 282, 313, 320, 340, 344, 455, 456); Christine Reid (pp. 10, 11, 12, 14, 15, 17, 22, 24, 26, 27, 32, 33); Barbara Segall (pp. 90, 257, 258, 274, 283, 322, 326, 330, 338, 401); Jo Ellen Myers Sharp (p. 394); Lindsey Taylor (pp. 28, 362, 444); Rose Thodey (pp. 31, 34); Anne Wareham (p. 128); Chris Woods (pp. 138, 363, 372, 378, 380, 391, 400, 434, 436).

Special thanks are also due to: Tim Cooke for helping to bring the project to fruition; Hatty Thorowgood for her tenacious assistance; Jenny Faithfull, Emmanuelle Peri and Louise Thomas for their exhaustive picture research; Daniel Chehade, Laura Clarke, Julia Hasting and Hans Stofregen for design and layout; Jane Ace, Rosanna Lewis and Alice Peebles for their invaluable contributions in the latter stages; and Steve Bryant and Adela Cory for production and their attention to detail.

And finally, I would like to thank all the garden owners, designers and gardeners who have given us permission to include their gardens.

Victoria Clarke, Commissioning Editor

## Editorial Note

### Arrangement
The gardens in the book are arranged geographically, by country within continents. The order of gardens within each country is broadly arranged by state, county or other regional division, beginning in the northwest and ending in the southeast. Where necessary for convenience in allocating pages to gardens, however, the order may vary slightly.

### Climate Zones
This book uses two systems to classify the climate zones of the individual gardens. For North America, it uses the North American climate zone system, which is based on plant hardiness. For the rest of the world, it uses an adaptation of the Köppen climate classification system, which divides the globe into broadly similar zones based on average precipitation and temperature. This is an inexact science, however, so the climate zones provided are for guidance only.

### Size
Garden sizes are provided when known. Some gardens change over time, however, and sources sometimes vary or accurate figures may be unavailable. In such cases, we have used the most commonly accepted figure.

Phaidon Press Ltd
Regent's Wharf
All Saints Street
London
N1 9PA

Phaidon Press Inc
65 Bleecker Street
New York
NY 10012

www.phaidon.com

First published in 2014
© 2014 Phaidon Press Limited

ISBN 978 0 7148 6747 2

A CIP catalogue record for this book is available from the British Library.

Cover design by Julia Hasting
Interior design by Hans Stofregen
Layout by Studio Chehade

Printed in China